Empire by Collaboration

EARLY AMERICAN STUDIES

Series editors:
Daniel K. Richter, Kathleen M. Brown,
Max Cavitch, and David Waldstreicher

Exploring neglected aspects of our colonial,
revolutionary, and early national history and
culture, Early American Studies reinterprets
familiar themes and events in fresh ways.
Interdisciplinary in character, and with a special
emphasis on the period from about 1600 to 1850,
the series is published in partnership with the
McNeil Center for Early American Studies.

Empire by Collaboration

*Indians, Colonists, and Governments
in Colonial Illinois Country*

Robert Michael Morrissey

PENN

UNIVERSITY OF PENNSYLVANIA PRESS

PHILADELPHIA

Published by
University of Pennsylvania Press
Philadelphia, Pennsylvania 19104-4112
www.upenn.edu/pennpress

Printed in the United States of America on acid-free paper
1 3 5 7 9 10 8 6 4 2

Library of Congress Cataloging-in-Publication Data
Morrissey, Robert Michael.
  Empire by collaboration : Indians, colonists, and
governments in colonial Illinois country / Robert Michael
Morrissey. — 1st ed.
      p. cm. — (Early American studies)
  ISBN 978-0-8122-4699-5 (hardcover : alk. paper)
  1. Illinois—Colonization—History. 2. France—
Colonies—Administration. 3. Great Britain—Colonies—
Administration. 4. Illinois—Civilization—History—17th
century. 5. Illinois—Civilization—History—18th century.
6. Indians of North America—Illinois—History—17th
century. 7. Indians of North America—Illinois—History—
18th century. 8. Jesuits—Missions—Illinois. I. Title. II. Series:
Early American studies.
F544.M875 2015
977.3'01—dc23
                                          2014032473

For my parents, Mike and Flavia

Contents

Illustrations

Figures

Map

Tables

Introduction

An Earnest Invitation

In 1772, a pamphlet came off the presses in Philadelphia. Like many pamphlets of this era, it was a political manifesto, a rallying cry. Written by a subject of the British empire in North America, it painted an almost utopian vision of the future. Addressing fellow colonists, the author urged them to "strive to improve our situation." He confidently predicted a coming age of economic prosperity, telling his readers to expect "the perfection of their settlements." He counseled his audience to abandon outdated tradition and move forward into a brave new world of self-reliance and self-improvement. The author called for action, encouraging his audience to work for their own interests, in solidarity, as a wholly unified community. In many ways, like other pamphlets printed in the radical ferment of 1770s Philadelphia, this one was calling for change, for a kind of revolution.[1]

This pamphlet was not John Dickinson's famous *Letters from a Farmer in Pennsylvania.* Nor was it Thomas Jefferson's *Rights of the British Colonies Asserted and Proved.* Instead it was an anonymous tract, surely obscure in its day, and almost totally forgotten now, titled *Invitation sérieuse aux habitants des Illinois [An Earnest Invitation to the Inhabitants of Illinois].*[2] Written by an unknown author who identified himself only as "un habitant des Kaskaskia," it represents the voice of an obscure American colonial community.

Kaskaskia was the largest of five French villages located along the Mississippi River in the Illinois Country, recently taken over by the British government at the end of the Seven Years' War. Founded as a mission and fur trade outpost at the end of the seventeenth century, here colonists had intermarried with Indians and settled agricultural villages. These colonies, together with the Indian alliances based around them, were an important part of the former

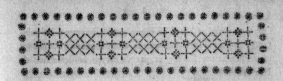

INVITATION

SERIEUSE aux HABITANTS

DES

ILLINOIS.

MES FRERES,

"LES connoiſſances ſont de peu d'uſage, lorſ-
qu'elles ſont reſtrainte à la ſimple ſpecula-
tion; mais lorſque des verités ſpeculatives
ſont reduit à la pratique, lorſque des theories, fondés ſur l'experience ſont appliqué
aux uſages de la vie, et lorſque par ces
" moyens l'agriculture eſt perfectionnée, le commerce etendu,
" les facilités de la vie rendus plus aiſé et plus agreable, &
" conſequemment, l'accroiſſement et le bonheur du genre hu-
" main augmenté, alors les connoiſſances ſant avantageuſes."

Tous les membres d'une ſocieté qui en ont la capacité et
le pouvoir, ſont ſans doute obligé de contribuer, au progrés de
ces connoiſſances. Ceux qui ne le preuvent par la communication des leurs, et de leur experiences, doivent ſoigneuſe-
ment écouter les inſtructions de ceux qui le peuvent, et qui le
font

Figure 1. Invitation sérieuse aux habitants des Illinois. Published in 1772 in Philadelphia and authored by an anonymous "habitant de Kaskaskia," this pamphlet voiced an appeal for economic development and stable government in the Illinois settlements.

French colonial empire, the midway point of a Creole Crescent stretching from Louisiana to Quebec. On the edge of empire, Kaskaskia was home to French, Indian, African, and mixed-race peoples. The *Invitation* gives us a window into this forgotten world.[3]

The *Invitation* reveals an ambitious colony looking forward to the future. But what is more interesting is that it is a window into a distinctive political tradition that had formed on the margins of empire. The pamphlet celebrates values like self-sufficiency, advising the inhabitants of Illinois to stand on their own feet and promote economic development, education, and legal order. But where other political pamphlets of this era took these same values and called for colonial independence, the *Invitation* called for almost the exact opposite course of action. Rather than making an argument for independence, the farmers of Illinois were appealing to the empire to send them a government. They expressed hope not that they could be autonomous but that the empire would come and give them "advantages" that they could not create themselves: "We are true and zealous subjects of his Britannic majesty and we doubt not at all that in a short time . . . the administration of civil government will be established among us. We are able at present only to desire these happy results."[4]

It's a surprising message for the 1770s in North America. Here was a group of colonists calling for the British empire to send them government officials, regulations, and laws. Their worst problem was not oppression, monarchy, or an arbitrary government, their spokesman said. It was neglect. Although they had suffered a bit under "tyranny," what had mostly hurt them was too little investment, too little support, which led to ignorance and backwardness. The answer to these problems was not independence, less government. It was *more* government. What the colonists wanted was not some abstract notion of "freedom"; it was a more specific notion of "benefits" and "advantages."

If the message is surprising, it is especially surprising to note that the inhabitants of Illinois were mostly French and mixed-race peoples calling for the *British* government, of which they professed to be "true and zealous subjects," to rule them. Unlike their Creole compatriots in New Orleans, who had recently rebelled against the Spanish government when the latter tried to take over their colony at the end of the Seven Years' War, the French colonists of Illinois seemed happy to put themselves under the authority of the British.[5] As the pamphlet suggested, they were flexible and adaptable enough to want to learn to speak English and to live as Englishmen, to "experience the liberty and the wisdom of the laws of that great nation."[6]

In all sorts of ways, the *Invitation* seems unexpected. But the message was actually not new. Since 1673, the initially illegal colonists of Illinois had been striving to make a colony. Settling together around a Jesuit mission, French fur traders married Illinois Indian women and eventually began to farm. The opportunistic Illinois Indians welcomed the French as neighbors and allies, establishing their own permanent villages nearby. Together they made a thriving, enterprising, and in many ways autonomous colonial world. Like the author of the *Invitation*, they sought their self-interests and pursued their own goals.

But these people could not do it alone. French and Indian peoples of this colonial region partnered with empire and from the beginning used the support of Quebec and Louisiana to their own ends. They did this not because they were "submissive" or "dependent" as myths would later hold— far from it. Indeed, many things they did in their remote colonial zone were positively contrary to imperial logic. Yet for all their autonomy, they willingly made their lives together with government authority and relied on it. The resulting cooperation produced a distinctive form of colonialism in early America and informed a distinctive political tradition that the author of the *Invitation* expressed in 1772. Even as the British colonists were calling increasingly for independence, here were French farmers calling for what this book calls *empire by collaboration*. Indeed, this was the key to their history. The authors of the *Invitation* came out of a long and interesting history of collaboration at the frontiers of empires.

❧

This book explores the interaction of peoples and governments in the middle of the continent in seventeenth- and eighteenth-century America. Even from the very beginning, when the French at Quebec established a mostly reluctant alliance with the Illinois Indians, and Jesuits and fur traders planted defiant outposts in the Illinois River Valley beyond the Great Lakes Watershed, the Illinois was a territory in tension with imperial plans. In fact, much evidence suggests that the earliest colony in Illinois was not only unplanned but clearly opposite to the designs that French officials had for their North American colonial empire. Although the colony eventually became substantial, its relationship to the imperial governments in the Mississippi Valley and Great Lakes was frequently in question. Throughout the eighteenth century, as both Canada and Louisiana alternately claimed authority over the Illinois, and as British and Spanish authorities later tried to divide the region with a political border at the Mississippi River, there was considerable uncertainty about who *really* would control this colonial region, giving the inhabitants options as they played one government off another. Illinois became a haven for fur traders, farmers, missionaries, and Indians who sought to realize alternative visions for colonial life at the edges of these competing powers. Eventually the colonists and Indians of Illinois asserted a kind of self-determination that gave the community a unique identity within the French empire. And yet the colonists and Illinois Indians were not independent. They welcomed and partnered with empire in many ways.

Scholars have often viewed the French empire as a failure, a backward system defined by weak would-be absolutists in Versailles and truculent colonists and Natives on the ground in America.[7] And while there is some truth to that depiction, it is far better to see the French empire, and perhaps colonialism in general, in a different way. Moving beyond the question of success and failure, a better question is: what was the nature of colonialism?[8] For instance, by recognizing the French government's inability to project power, we refocus our attention to the complex ways that the "empire" built strength through alliance with Native peoples.[9] And if the government did not always control its colonists with strict legal order, understanding this fact opens up windows into how a distinctive kind of colonialism was achieved even through criminal activity and legal pluralism.[10] Economically speaking, if the government never succeeded in establishing its mercantilist priorities, this only highlights the frontier exchange economies in which intercultural communities, black markets, and even creole cuisines were born as unintentional, if no less "imperial," creations.[11] Far more interesting than the question of success and failure is understanding the nature of colonialism itself as a complicated system mutually created by diverse, entangled peoples.

These realities defined the nature of French colonialism and early modern colonialism in general. And yet the theme of "failure," or at least "dysfunction," still persists in our understanding of the early modern French empire, since so much of the nature of imperialism was so unintentional, so accidental. In most parts of the early modern French empire, there was a persistent dialectic: colonists and Indians were generally hardheaded and defiant, intent on "resistance," while imperial officials remained flustered and inflexible, intent on "order."[12] What is more, their interactions proceeded in what often looks like a comedy of errors, since they made almost all of their compromises in spite of their real intentions and sometimes without even knowing they were compromising. For instance, Indians and the French

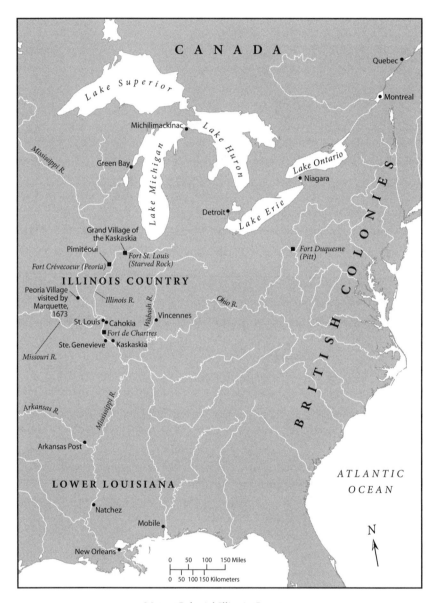

Map 1. Colonial Illinois Country.

government accommodated their differences to make imperial alliances, but they did this unintentionally and only on the basis of what one scholar calls "creative misunderstandings."[13] They never *really* saw eye to eye. And when it came to relations between French colonists and officials, compromises and accommodations were no less begrudging and tension filled. Rogues basically ran the economy in Louisiana and created a unique, contested system. But imperialists never stopped chasing after smugglers and trying to throw them in jail, and they never recognized just how much their colonies depended on black market activities.[14] In general, would-be absolutists in charge of colonial governments never stopped pursuing their unrealistic dreams of *ordre*, even fantasizing about placing symmetrical grids on an obviously resistant colonial landscape.[15] Rather than sitting down with the colonial population to "see eye to eye," so many imperialists kept up bullheaded efforts to "see like a state." For their part, rather than cooperating with government and shaping it to their ends, colonists and Indians remained resolute in practicing "the art of not being governed." The result was a frustrated, conflict-ridden, and dysfunctional kind of empire.[16]

But in this connection, Illinois presents us with an exception, one that shows a new side of the early modern French empire and a different side of early modern colonialism more generally. In Illinois, like everywhere else in the early modern French empire, Indians and colonists, slaves and officials, created an idiosyncratic order that was usually not what anybody intended. But they did this not by always clashing in a constant battle of hardheaded imperialists versus local rogues but through a rather functional and pragmatic collaboration. What is more, people in Illinois often made their collaborations *consciously* because they opportunistically saw compromise and working together as the best option for achieving goals. As a result, the "imperialism" that formed in Illinois was, in contrast to the typical themes of dysfunction and conflict, often characterized by compromise and flexibility, by diverse people purposefully acting to create a mutually acceptable order.

The result was a remarkably stable colonial culture. In Illinois, colonists, Indians, and slaves created large families and farms, featuring huge wheat fields, flour mills, and big herds of livestock. Illinois was quite prosperous, producing up to eight hundred thousand livres of flour in a year, becoming an indispensable supplier of food for Louisiana. In addition, the colony was home to one of the most durable Indian alliances in all of the French empire. On the ground, both cause and consequence of this alliance system, French colonists and Illinois Indians developed a flexible interracial order based on a huge network of kinship and fictive kinship linking together French and Native peoples. This was different from anything that imperial authorities ever wanted, but it was functional and pragmatic.

This book aims to complicate our understanding of French colonialism and empire in general by drawing new attention to the way that governments and peoples collaborated for mutual interests in frontier Illinois. It requires a reorientation of our thinking. Rather than conflict, this is a story of collaboration and compromise. As Ronald Robinson, influential historian of the British empire, observed, collaboration was always a major feature of imperial systems, across time and space.[17] Empire could not work without collaboration, and every successful imperial system required that government officials gain the assistance and cooperation of many of the people they meant to dominate.[18] Illinois is an object lesson of this principle and is only unusual because of how many people—Natives, officials, traders, farmers, missionaries, even slaves—worked together, often intentionally, to make a functional colony and culture. All of these people played active roles to make Illinois's idiosyncratic colonial order.

This is not to suggest that Illinois was some kind of utopia of cooperation.[19] As in all imperial situations, empire in Illinois was about power, and force and conflict were often involved. The most striking reminder of that power lies in the fact that almost half the people in Illinois were slaves. But in a place like Illinois, as in other borderlands situations, most people—even slaves—had options.[20] Neither the government nor people on the ground could dominate.[21] Perhaps imperialists in other places had fantasies of control, but in Illinois they could not achieve them—in many cases they could not even begin to implement them.

The would-be imperialists in Illinois admitted this basic fact and embraced it. Even at the very founding of the official colony in Illinois, when imperial officials were faced with a group of colonists and wayward former Indian allies living in the middle of the continent with no government and no laws, they wrote that they were powerless to oppose it. They could never arrest these people or stop them from pursuing their self-interests. So, contrary to stereotypes we have of absolutist French governors, they decided to make the colony an official part of the empire. "Seeing no possibility of preventing it," officials wrote, they decided to collaborate.[22]

And if they collaborated at the foundation of the colony, they continued to let the colonists shape their own colonial culture. A good example of this can be seen in the issue of intermarriage and race. In the early 1700s,

Louisiana officials complained about how intermarriage tainted the "whiteness and purity of blood" of the French colonial population.[23] But in Illinois, interracial families were a vital part of the local culture. Beginning in 1694, marriages between Frenchmen and Indian women formed the bedrock of the community, allowing the colonists and local Indians to form a strong bond through kinship. These intermarriages permitted an interracial order that rested on both integration and segregation, as Indian brides lived with French husbands, but Indian villages and the French stayed geographically separate. Serving the interests of many parties, perhaps especially the Illinois wives, this was a functional social order. As a result, arriving in Illinois, each new imperial commandant sent by Louisiana seemed to recognize the value of intermarriage and its usefulness to the colony. Time and again, officials on the ground actually condoned it and even participated, joining the interracial kinship networks that were at the heart of the colonial culture. They did this not because they "went native" but because they could see that on the ground, the system worked. It was a functional collaboration.

And if the government followed the lead of the colonists, the colonists and Indians looked to the government officials, calculating that they were better off with imperial assistance than without. For instance, take Illinois Native peoples' approach to French imperialism. Rather than resisting French colonization in their region, the Illinois collaborated, professing "French hearts." This was not because they were dependent. Rather, it was because they used the French opportunistically to pursue their goals as a powerful, almost imperialistic people in their own right.[24] Rather than resisting, they convinced local officials in Illinois to adopt their diplomatic priorities, to accept their enemies as enemies of the French. Climaxing in the near destruction of the Foxes, the Illinois-French alliance based at Fort de Chartres pursued a policy which, far from a French imperial design, was authored by the Illinois themselves.

Importantly, the French, Indians, and government officials collaborated purposefully in Illinois. A major contention of this book is that the collaboration that took place in Illinois between Indians and the French was more than simple "accommodation." As Richard White has written, Native people and Europeans on early American frontiers often got along by appealing to their faulty understandings of one another's interests and values. Rather than truly mediating their differences, they related to each other through "creative misunderstandings"—joining in diplomacy, religious ceremonies, legal traditions, and even marriages without actually knowing what each other meant by their agreements. Their accommodations solved expedient problems but were necessarily temporary and in many ways naïve.[25]

But in Illinois it was different. Interacting in permanent settlements that differed from most transient frontier environments, the diverse inhabitants of Illinois lived together, spoke the same languages, and intermarried. By the 1690s, the intercultural community in Illinois had moved far beyond the naïve accommodations of the encounter phase and had begun to understand each other and produce much more durable agreements. Far from misunderstanding each other, they got along (and sometimes did not) because they truly saw eye to eye. Indeed, the most important collaboration in Illinois took place at the level of community, where different people created a cooperative and flexible system of integration and segregation that benefited most of its participants. But nobody was naïve. This was not just accommodation; it was informed, purposeful collaboration.[26]

And if Indians and colonists formed solid collaboration, so too did imperial officials and colonists. The Illinois experienced little of the stereotypical drama of the French empire, where hardheaded imperialists tried to foster absolutism in the wilderness. Time and again, the colonists resisted imperial officials, establishing an idiosyncratic legal system, economy, and social patterns. But when colonists subordinated imperial regulations to their own priorities, imperialists came to accept it. At the same time, as they showed in their constant petitioning, as well as in many requests for government intervention, the Illinois colonists were not anarchists bent on autonomy and independence. They welcomed empire into their lives and did so willingly, not submissively. When the French empire lost control of the middle of the continent in 1763, the inhabitants even tried to partner with the British government, continuing their tradition of pragmatic collaboration.

❧

Which brings us back to the *Invitation sérieuse*, the opportunistic call for collaboration written by the anonymous Kaskaskian in 1772. While other colonists in North America were calling for independence in the 1770s, the inhabitants of Illinois wanted collaboration. Their reasons for doing so were rooted in an alternative political tradition in colonial America: a practical, pragmatic way of life at the heart of a distinctive kind of colonialism. The *Invitation* gives us a window into this lost world and, as the title suggests, is an "earnest invitation" for us to learn more.

Chapter 1

Opportunists in the Borderlands

In 1673, the French explorers Jacques Marquette and Louis Jolliet arrived at a village of the Peoria near the Des Moines River, the first Europeans to record a visit to the Illinois Country in the Mississippi Valley. Beaching their canoes at the edge of town, they shouted and made their presence known to the Indians, thereby opening the encounter between the French and these Algonquians at the margins of the Great Lakes world.[1]

The Indians gathered in the center of their village to give the Frenchmen an extraordinary and distinctive welcome. As Marquette later recounted, chief men made speeches, and villagers performed a dance featuring a calumet pipe, only the second calumet that Marquette had ever seen. After the performance and speeches, the Illinois prepared a feast including the "fattest morsels" of what to Marquette was a new delicacy, bison meat. Dressed in bison skins themselves, they then presented him with several belts, garters, and other artifacts made from the skin of bison, caribou, and elk, and they may have given him the famous hide robes that now survive in the Musée du Quai Branly. Some of these were elaborately adorned with decorative motifs, notably a bison and a large hawk or thunderbird. After singing to him, they presented him finally with a "little slave."[2]

Perhaps because it contained so many new and unfamiliar objects and symbols, Marquette considered the calumet ceremony baffling—"altogether mysterious." Read carefully from an Illinois perspective, however, the calumet and the Illinois's welcome ceremony are windows into the recent history of this place and the powerful people who lived here at the time of contact. Although Marquette did not realize it, the Illinois were newcomers, invaders who had moved to the Illinois Valley over the previous few generations and were now making one of the most significant bids for power in seventeenth-century North America. Their history had diverged from that of the larger Algonquian world with which Marquette was familiar. In their welcome ceremony, the Illinois were showing Marquette—and us—who they were: an adaptable and ambitious people seizing advantages in a special borderlands region.[3]

The dance featured many symbols of this distinctive and opportunistic history. For instance, there were the bison materials and bison meat. Bison was the product of the ecosystem—the tallgrass prairie—that the Illinois had recently occupied, and it was the basis of the new lifeway that made them much more prosperous than their Algonquian neighbors. Symbols on the Illinois's robes probably reflected conquest and assimilation of Siouan-speaking people whose territory they had conquered. The calumet ceremony itself was also a western tradition, suggesting the newcomers' creation of a "transitional culture" as they adopted the previous inhabitants of the Illinois Valley into their collective.[4] And the slave reflected the violence of their invasion and the domination that they had achieved, as well as the basis of a newly emerging economic system that the Illinois were developing in the borderlands: the slave trade. Taken together, all these aspects of the dance added up to an expression and celebration of Native power and opportunism.

Marquette did not really understand the significance of these symbols in the calumet ceremony, but we can. To do so, however, we need to look back to a *Native* colonial history of Illinois before European contact.[5] Beginning in the 1200s, climate change reshaped the Midwest, powerfully affecting the environment and human subsistence south of the Great Lakes.[6] Seizing opportunities during this period of change, the proto-Illinois moved west from the region south of Lake Erie and the Ohio Valley into the Illinois prairies and began a unique trajectory in a unique environment. While many Algonquian agriculturalists struggled during this "dark period," the proto-Illinois experienced expansion and not declension, establishing themselves on the tallgrass. When conflict broke out in the Great Lakes region in the mid-1600s with the start of the so-called Beaver Wars, the Illinois could have stayed out of it. Instead, they became aggressors, making a dangerous bid to capitalize on the violence.[7] This is a story of Native power and expansion, of risky behavior and bold intentions.

It could hardly be otherwise, given the setting. The Illinois was a borderland, a place of important divisions, natural and cultural. Ecologically it was the transition between the two major biomes of the middle of the continent,

Figure 2. Capitaine de La Nation des Illinois. Louis Nicolas depicted the Illinois chief with military accessories and smoking the calumet, a western diplomatic tradition, while wearing what is probably a painted bison robe. This evokes the Illinois's ethnogenesis as a "transitional culture."

the grasslands of the West and woodlands of the East. Socially and culturally, it lay at the division between two major cultural groupings of Native North America, Siouan-speakers of the Plains and Algonquians of the Great Lakes. And it was also the continental divide that separated the Mississippi Valley from the Great Lakes. In all of these ways, the place was a unique landscape of division, a setting for dynamic human history at the edge. Moving into this space, the proto-Illinois were taking a bold step, seeking power.[8]

The Illinois's colonization was a remarkably successful effort to take advantage of this place of division in a specific moment of change. In the transition, the Illinois found new means of subsistence, as well as sociopolitical opportunities that gave them advantages. Here, on the edge of different worlds, the Illinois seized new prospects and built a new lifeway. When the French arrived, the Illinois would only continue their innovation. The history of empire in Illinois must begin with Native efforts to exploit power in the borderlands. The story begins with Cahokia.

ↄ

Before European arrival, the region that would become Illinois Country was home to the biggest Native city-state on the continent, Cahokia. Numbering twenty thousand inhabitants at its height, Cahokia shaped the trade and culture of peoples in a huge portion of the continent. Although the story of Cahokia is well told by historians, it is often treated in isolation, disconnected from later historical events. For our purposes, we need to view it as part of a long-term set of processes that continued long after Cahokia was no more.[9] The Illinois were not descendants of the Cahokians, but the Illinois's rise in the Illinois Valley can be seen as a consequence of some of the same forces that brought Cahokia to an end.

Cahokia rose in a region at the confluence of the Missouri, Mississippi, Illinois, and Ohio rivers, the "American Bottom."[10] Based heavily on corn agriculture, the civilization spread its power throughout the Midwest, as revealed by archaeological evidence of trade and tribute coming into the metropolis from the eleventh through the thirteenth century from throughout an expansive territory.[11] Beginning as an ordinary village in the Late Woodland period, Cahokia experienced a "big bang"—a sudden and dramatic rise to power.[12] By the 1200s, the twenty thousand people in Cahokia represented the largest pre-Columbian city north of Mexico. It is not clear whether Cahokia was a truly centralized political regime, but the Cahokia Mississippians exercised wide regional influence through a hegemonic culture and trade.[13]

The middle of the continent was a likely place for the most powerful pre-contact Native society for the same reason that Chicago and St. Louis rose in the nineteenth century: the Midwest contained a tremendously rich variety of ecological resources.[14] Given the major river systems that defined the region, the landscape contained numerous alluvial environments with resources for human exploitation. These environments featured wetlands and forests, often with extensive floodplains. Above the river valleys were a mix of hardwood forests, dominated mostly by oak-ash-maple and oak-hickory forests. These forests transitioned into park-like edge habitats, probably maintained by purposeful burning and natural fire, which in turn gave way to plains and the Midwest's distinctive tallgrass prairies. A discrete biome unto itself, the tallgrass prairie was where evaporation and rainfall were roughly equal but where trees could not establish themselves because of periodic fire, dense grass roots, and other factors.[15] While 39 percent of the modern state of Illinois was forested before the advent of the steel plow, fully 55 percent of the state's landscape was covered with prairie. Much of the rest was dominated by wetlands.[16]

Despite all the diversity of the region, the Cahokians took advantage of a relatively small portion of the ecological opportunity in the middle of the continent. Because environmental conditions were so favorable for farming, their subsistence focused on a small area, near the confluence of the rivers, and was heavily concentrated in the bottomlands.[17] This proved perilous. Climate change started to affect the region in the 1100s. For 140 out of 145 years beginning in 1100, Cahokia experienced drought, probably reducing farming yields.[18] Sediment in the Missouri River owing to drought-forced erosion on the Plains may have produced a shallower channel in the Missouri and Mississippi rivers and increased spring flooding in the bottomlands, compromising agriculture.[19] Meanwhile, even as drought challenged their subsistence, it seems clear that Cahokians overexploited resources, especially wood, in their local environment, which may have led to difficulties in the city.[20] In the 1250s, a new Pacific climate event began to change conditions again, bringing cooler summers and harsher winters, and drier conditions overall.[21] With the onset of the Pacific episode, farming became even more difficult at Cahokia. As a result of this and probably other social and political changes, the entire region began to empty out, leaving the middle Mississippi Valley, the lower Illinois Valley, the lower Ohio Valley, and the entire American Bottom increasingly devoid of people. The emerging "vacant quarter" was a dramatic end to the great civilization at Cahokia.[22]

With the end of the Cahokia, smaller groups reoccupied the region of Illinois. Most likely these migrants came from the West as climate change extended the so-called prairie peninsula and made conditions on the Plains drier and colder. Seeking refuge for a mixed-subsistence lifeway in the river valleys of the Illinois, these people were the Oneota, the ancestors of later Siouan-speakers like the Winnebago, Otoes, Ioways, and others.[23] Compared to Cahokia, they lived on a smaller scale and took advantage of a much larger variety of the ecology of the region.[24] In contrast to the complexity of Cahokians, they were "simple" and regularly relocated villages to take advantage of different aspects of the local ecology.

Although we cannot be precise about details, archaeological evidence suggests that the Oneota newcomers were factionalized and organized into small social units.[25] They also lived a rather Hobbesian existence, since violence was endemic in the Illinois after Cahokia's decline. Archaeological sites from the 1300s and 1400s in the Illinois Valley reveal fortified villages and other evidence of warfare between Oneota and Middle Mississippian groups. Perhaps the most dramatic evidence of violent lifeways in this period is an Oneota village, dated to the year 1300, in the central Illinois Valley. The site contains a cemetery with 264 burials. Sixty-six percent of the people interred at the cemetery had been decapitated or scalped at death.[26] Life was hard in the wake of Cahokia.

In addition to warfare, other factors kept the population of the Oneota villagers low. Continuing the trend of the Pacific event that started in the 1200s, another climate episode began in the 1400s: the Little Ice Age. While this created well-known disturbances around the world and especially in Eurasia, it also brought about a significant shift on the North American continent.[27] By some estimates, the Little Ice Age may have reduced the average summer temperatures by 1.5 degrees Celsius in mid-America.[28] The temperature shifts may have produced as many as thirty-four fewer frost-free days in the modern state of Illinois. The continuing low human population in the vacant quarter that this and previous climate events helped occasion may be responsible for producing a rather sudden and dramatic species shift in the region. With few people in the Illinois Valley, and thus so few potential hunters, the population of wild animals may well have spiked.[29] By the 1500s, the great wild ungulates of North America, bison, had invaded the grasslands east of the Mississippi River in large herds, probably extending the prairies with their grazing as they advanced.[30] They came in great numbers, congregating by salt licks and springs, such as near Starved Rock in the Illinois Valley.[31]

There is an important reason why bison revolutionized lifeways for the Oneota occupants of the midwestern prairies. As is well-known, tallgrass prairies in the middle of the country sat atop the thickest topsoil layer anywhere in the world.[32] Yet the dense root systems under the grass made it impossible to farm these soils until the invention of steel plows in the nineteenth century. Native Americans did not have plows or metal farming tools of any kind, and so they normally did not exploit the prairies as farmland. Instead, they used hoes to farm the fertile soils of the bottomlands. Meanwhile, although game species like deer and elk could be found in the tallgrass prairies, they were most commonly located at the "edges" where grasslands and forests overlapped. Remarkable evidence of prehistoric trash pits suggests that prairie environments were largely underutilized. In one Huber phase Oneota trash pit from the 1400s, for instance, only 2.4 percent of the animals used by the residents came from the prairie, while the vast majority came from the valley floors, forests, and wetlands.[33] This was probably typical. For much of the prehistoric period, it seems clear that the prairie itself probably went relatively unused by human inhabitants of the region.[34]

This is important because prairie made up close to 55 percent of the land in the modern state of Illinois, even more in the modern state of Iowa. Since they could not easily exploit this land for farming, and since their preferred game did not usually congregate in prairies but on its edges, this meant that the Native inhabitants of these regions left prairies as a largely untapped ecosystem. Here were calories, produced by grasses, which the Oneota villages had little means to exploit. Humans, of course, could not eat the grasses, nor could they easily replace them with edible plants.

The large-scale invasion of the bison into midwestern grasslands from points west thus created a great new subsistence opportunity for people whose climate was changing, and particularly for farmers whose calorie yield was compromised by both rainfall shortages and possible flooding. Newly arriving bison of course could use the prairie grasses, eating them up to become what one historian calls "reservoirs of biomass."[35] In ecological terms, bison were able to convert the "vast energy stored in the . . . grasses for human use."[36] Deer and elk were certainly important before, but bison arrived in the region in huge herds and were relatively simple to hunt, provided one had a cooperative group to help direct the animals to a kill zone. Indeed, bison hunting produced calories on a totally different scale than deer hunting: each animal weighed 2,000 pounds, containing at least 675 pounds of useful meat. Hunts in the tallgrass prairies regularly yielded hundreds of animals at a time.[37] For Oneota people accustomed to starchy agricultural diets, the new resource created a dramatic increase in nutritional quality, fairly quickly.[38] The invasion of the bison brought tremendous change to Native life in Illinois between 1500 and 1800.

By turning the prairies from wasteland to productive, the arrival of bison vastly increased the amount of calorie-producing land in the future Illinois Country. The new animal resource was so attractive that it inspired migration among many of the inhabitants of the region. The eastern spread of bison pulled more Oneota people to the West, back out onto the prairie peninsula and closer to the plains environment, as they increasingly specialized in bison hunting.[39] This "bison revolution" confirmed the Oneota's status as a "bridging culture," connected to the two biomes and lifeways of the woodlands and the plains.[40]

To be sure, not everyone went west. The so-called Huber phase Oneota sites remained in the northern part of the Illinois River Valley. These were prosperous places, now augmented and altered by bison exploitation. Trash pits at the Fisher site in the upper Illinois Valley from this period reflect a great deal of diversity in the diet of these Oneota people, who now added bison to an extensive list of flora and fauna that they exploited on a seasonal and cyclical basis.[41] The survival and persistence of these Oneota culture groups in the wake of Cahokia set the stage for the protohistoric and historic transformations in Illinois.[42]

℘

Meanwhile in the East, Algonquians living south of Lake Erie and in the Ohio Valley were also suffering from climate change that made agriculture difficult. As in the Illinois Valley, this produced violence and warfare, even what one archaeologist calls a period of "ethnic cleansing" as proto-Algonquian groups struggled to survive.[43] Some Algonquians, concentrated in settlements just to the south of Lake Erie, interacted and shared pottery traditions with a group identified by archaeologists as the Fort Ancient people, who lived in modern-day southwestern Ohio.[44] Pottery traditions and archaeological assemblages suggest that these proto-Anglonquian groups began to trade with Oneota peoples at the Huber phase sites in the upper Illinois Valley in the 1500s. Before long, they were in close contact with these Oneota groups, carrying prestige goods back and forth across the modern state of Indiana in a flourishing trade network.[45] Interestingly, calumet pipes, the diplomatic tool of western Siouan-speakers, were some of the materials that Algonquians received from this new trade.[46]

But it was not just prestige goods and diplomatic symbols that passed back and forth between these Algonquians and their Oneota neighbors. Sometime in the 1500s, the Fort Ancient culture adopted another facet of the lifeway of their neighbors to the northwest: they started hunting bison. Limited numbers of bison had arrived in the Ohio Valley in the 1500s. There is no way to know whether the Fort Ancient hunters learned bison hunting from their Oneota trading partners, but it seems possible. Like their neighbors to the northeast, these Ohio Valley hunters experienced a bison revolution.[47]

It was probably bison that inspired the next important turning point in this story. In the late 1500s, a new pottery tradition known to archaeologists as Danner-Keating shows up in the Huber Phase sites in the upper Illinois Valley. Importantly, this Danner-Keating tradition strongly resembles pottery found in the Fort Ancient sites. Moreover, a very similar pottery tradition, which may be a root tradition for Danner, is found in sites to the south of Lake Erie.[48] Examining this pottery, scholars now speculate that the people identified with the distinctive Danner-Keating material culture and its possible Fort Meigs antecedent moved over time across the established trade networks between the Lake Erie settlements, Fort Ancient sites, and Huber phase Oneota settlements, and into the northern Illinois Valley. By the early 1600s, Danner-Keating appears in the same locations long occupied by the Huber phase, whom archaeologists believe were the historic Winnebago. Before long these Danner-Keating migrants replaced their hosts.[49] It is almost certain that the bearers of this new Danner-Keating archaeological tradition were the historic Illinois and their Miami kinsmen.[50]

Was the invasion violent? It's not clear.[51] As we have seen, many Oneota peoples—Siouan-speakers and the ancestors of the Missouria, Ioway, and other groups—had recently moved west from the Illinois Valley to exploit the bison more intensively. The proto-Winnebago moved north out of the Illinois in the early 1600s. The southern Illinois Valley remained a vacant quarter in the wake of the Oneota-Mississippian violence between 1200 and 1400, and the new bison hunters saw the opportunity to seize it. The broad history is one of "replacement" or possibly "intermixture," as the Illinois came to this region.[52] But one thing is clear: the Illinois were colonizers.

In his study of the Cheyenne in the Great Plains, historian Elliott West tells how the Cheyenne moved out of the upper Mississippi Valley onto the Plains to exploit the bison in the 1800s, reenvisioning the region and giving it "a new meaning." Committing fully to an equestrian lifestyle, they became the "called out people." Of course, the Illinois were never equestrians, but their migration west in the early 1600s may have had a similar dynamic. They were committing to a new lifestyle, a new ecological resource, while invading a rich region, much of which had long been left vacant by climate change and violence. Like the Cheyenne's migration, this was a bold, opportunistic process as they reenvisioned the tall grass and its possibilities.[53]

࿐

Over the course of the next generations, the Illinois-speakers colonized the whole region formerly occupied by the Oneota in modern-day Illinois. Moving into their new homeland, the Illinois adopted bison hunting as the basis of a radically new lifeway. Perhaps because the Illinois still spoke an Algonquian language at contact, French eyewitnesses often did not emphasize in their accounts how different the Illinois were from other Great Lakes Algonquians by that time. In fact, upon moving into the prairies, the Illinois embarked on a total transformation, becoming the only bison-based Algonquians, with many new cultural and economic practices.[54]

The Illinois newcomers perfected the seasonal lifeway previously established by the Oneota peoples. Like the Oneota, they were farmers, but evidence suggests they became more committed to hunting and abandoned less useful, less nutritious agricultural resources.[55] At the same time, they became consummate bison people. While archaeological evidence suggests that they took advantage of various animals in their yearly cycle, it is clear that bison made up a great percentage of their subsistence. One study suggests that bison constituted 57 percent of the meat at a contact-era Illinois village. Deer and elk were another 30 percent, and fish and birds together constituted no more than 4 percent of the meat.[56] Like the Oneota before them, the Illinois committed to the bison.

Bison hunting shaped the Illinois's new lifeway. Descriptions of bison hunting in the post-contact period make it clear that this was a communal, cooperative, and well-organized enterprise. Unlike hunting for deer and other species, which was solitary and required stealthy stalking in the forest edges, bison were herd animals for which different strategies were required. Nonequestrians, the Illinois hunted bison in large groups, in carefully coordinated expeditions and by employing new tools for the prairie environment, especially fire.

Contact-era evidence of this new bison lifeway comes from several important eyewitness sources.[57] For instance, Pierre-Charles de Liette, a commandant at Fort St. Louis des Illinois, an early French outpost in the Illinois

Valley in the 1690s, went hunting with the Illinois and reported their technique. As he explained, the Illinois worked together in groups to slay a large number of the animals at a single time.

> The next day we saw in a prairie a great herd of buffalos. A halt was called and two old men harangued the young men for half an hour, urging them to show their skill in shooting down all the buffalos that we saw, and to manage so as to make all those that they could not kill move toward us. After removing us to the nearest spot, they started out in two bands, running always at a trot. When they were about a quarter of a league from the animals, they all ran at full speed, and when within gunshot they fired several volleys and shot off an extraordinary number of arrows. A great number of buffalos remained on the ground, and they pursued the rest in such manner that they were driven toward us. Our old men butchered these.[58]

Explorer René-Robert Cavelier de La Salle gave another description, noting that fire was essential to the Illinois's bison-hunting technique: "When they see a herd, they assemble in great numbers and set fire to the grass all round, with the exception of a few passages which they leave open, and at which they station themselves with their bows and arrows. In attempting to escape from the fire, the cattle are thus compelled to pass by these savages, who sometimes kill as many as two hundred in a single day."[59] As eyewitness descriptions make clear, this was a cooperative, shared enterprise. Liette also described how the Illinois ensured the success of their hunts by enforcing teamwork and punishing behavior that would threaten the group's success.[60]

Other evidence from the contact period fleshes out our picture of communal bison hunts, which were at the center of the Illinois lifeway. The Illinois-language dictionary made by Jesuit Jacques Gravier in the 1690s gives the most interesting window into the Illinois's subsistence.[61] Of particular note are a number of Illinois words and phrases relating to bison hunting, which taken together help us understand the Illinois's adaptation as pedestrian bison hunters in the tallgrass prairies. Like Liette's description, Gravier's dictionary suggests that Illinois hunters worked in large groups, sometimes embarking on long-range hunting expeditions of several days' duration, echoing explorers in the 1680s who noted that the Illinois "went inland" on long journeys to hunt bison.[62] Finally, the dictionary shows their important strategy of burning the prairie to encourage game and to corral the bison toward a kill site. Myriad words detail the use of fire in Illinois's hunting.

Table 1. Bison-Hunting Vocabulary in Contact-Era Illinois Language

Aiagamire8i	Fire is drawn from the other side of the prairie	4
Caki8re8i	Fire is everywhere in the prairies	93
Caticat8nama8a	Hunt close [to the village] and return with nothing	103
Chibicai88a	Hunt for a long time	112
C8r8er8ki irenans8ki	We still discover more bison	139
Inenans8a	Bison	172
Kicacat8i	Prairie: you don't see anything but prairie	181
Kinta8aki8i; kinta8iki8i	Burned prairie	205
Ki8atere8	Fire all around	208
Kipakinegab8aki irenans8ki	Bison taken standing up	211
Nikit8enan, ainghi kit8enanga nina	Hunter who kills many beasts one by one	229
Matarichita8i	Hunt with different villages	257
Nimatchiki8e	Hunt with everybody	259
Ninatas8a	Hunt animals that I make flee by setting fire	327
Nat8nama8i8ni	Hunt for a day	329
8anapakite8i	Burned prairie	368
8araten8i	Prairie surrounded by woods	373
8e8entire8i	Fire comes from two sides and joins	381
Nipacas8aki	Hunt with fire	411
Pess8e8aki	Fire in the prairies to hunt a deer	461
Nipitat8nama8i	Hunt for one day or two	478
Nipitcheracha	Hunt for several days	478
P8kicaki8aki irenans8ki	Bison are surrounded in the daytime and flee	484
P8n8maninghigi aie8aki pintiki8aki	Bison surrounded where they are expected	488
Niressig8	Fire in the trees to make the animal come out	507
Tchecam8cakita	Hunt with others	548
Tchic8kite8i	Prairie all burned	554
Tchiram8si8aki	Fire in the prairie	559

Source: Jacques Gravier, *Kaskaskia-to-French Dictionary*, ca. 1690, manuscript held at Watkinson Library Special Collections, Trinity College, Hartford, Conn.

Unlike woodlands hunters, the Illinois had given themselves over to a resource that required organization and scale. This probably made the prairie bison hunters into a more unified and cohesive society than was typical of Algonquians and pre-bison Oneota. The new lifeway may have given rise to a more hierarchical social structure, and it certainly required larger villages, especially in the summer and winter when the Illinois came together for the bison hunt. Whereas other Algonquians broke up into small villages to chase animals like deer and bears, the Illinois could stay together in their large groups throughout the year.[63]

The bison economy also fostered another change, which was a new gendered division of labor. Contact-era evidence suggests that women processed the hides, smoked the meat, and made bison products like wool and robes.[64] Moreover, since each male-headed household in Illinois "owned" the specific meat that its male hunters killed, and since each family processed their meat separately, this created an incentive for each man to have lots of women in his household.[65] The bison economy may have helped encourage the polygamous households that were common among the Illinois at the time of contact, just like among bison hunters on the plains.[66]

Given the huge size of bison herds in the region, bison hunting made the Illinois prosperous. Herds spread across the prairies of Illinois in the 1600s and remained large through the colonial period.[67] Marquette counted herds of 400 in 1673, and others counted herds in the thousands.[68] Typical hunts produced 200 animals or more, according to the seventeenth-century sources, and the Illinois were taking at least 2,000 bison annually by the early 1700s.[69] Bison provided the largest source of meat to the Illinois and likely a good portion of their overall calories.[70] It seems likely that this made them healthier than other Algonquians of their era and better-off than pre-bison Oneota as well. At contact Marquette was impressed by the prosperity of the Illinois people. As he wrote, "They raise Indian corn, which they have in great abundance, have squashes as large as those of France, and have a great many roots and fruits. There is fine hunting there of Wild Cattle, Bears, Stags, Turkeys, Ducks, Bustards, Pigeons, and Cranes. The people quit their Village sometime in the year, to go all together to the places where the animals are killed, and better to resist the enemy who come to attack them."[71]

The bison also became central to the Illinois's material culture. Liette noted that the Illinois used skins for clothing, shelter, and other purposes. They made tools out of the animals' bones. Marquette noted that bison was the main medium for the Illinois's artistic traditions, and on several occasions

Figure 3. "Chasse Génèrale au Boeuf, mais à pied," published in Antoine-Simon Le Page du Pratz's *Histoire de Louisiane* (Paris, 1758). Le Page du Pratz's depiction of non-equestrian bison hunting resembles many of the descriptions from eyewitnesses to the Illinois in the contact period.

during his travels he remarked on belts, garters, and accessories that were given as gifts or worn by prominent people among the Illinois. These included the scarves, made from bison hair, that distinguished the "captains" of the Illinois, "made, with considerable skill, from the hair of bears and wild cattle."[72] Indeed, the new animal gave the Illinois a distinctly different material culture from that of many of their Algonquian neighbors. While Indians in the region of Illinois had poor beaver resources, Marquette noted that "Their wealth consists in the skins of wild cattle."[73]

Bison hide painting became an important artistic expression in the Illinois culture. As Marquette noted, "[Bison hair] . . . falls off in Summer, and the skin becomes as soft as Velvet. At that season, the savages use the hides for making fine Robes, which they paint in various Colors."[74] It is intriguing to speculate about how the bison became central to the Illinois culture as they migrated, perhaps even helping create a new kind of identity. But this was not simply a *new* culture but something more complex. It was a blended culture, a synthesis of Oneota and Algonquian. To the point, consider the bird motif on the hide robe that Marquette supposedly brought back from Illinois in 1673. Evidence suggests that this was a very important motif in Oneota culture, perhaps even associated with Oneota ethnogenesis centuries before the Illinois's arrival. According to one scholar, birds—and particularly hawks—were at the center of Oneota ritual tradition and identity.[75] The hawk motif on Marquette's hide robe closely resembles a similar decoration on pottery unearthed in an Oneota site in Polk County, Iowa.[76] It is also similar to the thunderbird pictogram used to represent the Winnebago—descendants of the Oneota—at the 1701 Great Peace treaty at Montreal, which ended the Beaver Wars. Of course it is impossible to be conclusive about what these similarities really suggest, if anything. But it does seem possible to read this rare pre-contact Illinois material culture as a reflection of how the Illinois newcomers assimilated and integrated the culture of the Natives in the region and incorporated it with their own identity in the seventeenth century, together with the bison material itself.[77] The Illinois had colonized the region and adopted the transitional lifeway pioneered by the Oneota.[78] They had become a cooperative, cohesive, hybrid set of colonizers.

☙

The thunderbird on the Illinois hide reflects possible social interactions and affiliations between Oneota people and the Illinois newcomers and hints at

Figure 4. Bison arrow-shaft wrench. Made from bison femur, unearthed at Guebert site, eighteenth-century Illinois village in Illinois Valley. The Illinois based much of their material culture on bison products.

Figure 5. Illinois hide robe with thunderbird. A long tradition has it that this robe was presented to Marquette when he visited the Peoria Indians on the Des Moines River in 1673. Hide robes like this are an artistic tradition the Illinois picked up from their grasslands neighbors and are not typical Algonquian art forms. They reflect the Illinois's "transitional culture."

Courtesy of SCALA Archives, Musée du Quai Branly, Paris.

how the Illinois may have integrated or assimilated outsiders as part of their colonizing history. It is impossible to know for sure how the Illinois newcomers made community and negotiated social life as they arrived in the Illinois Country. But what does seem clear is that as they colonized, the Illinois built a strong and complex network of villages, united by language and probably kinship.

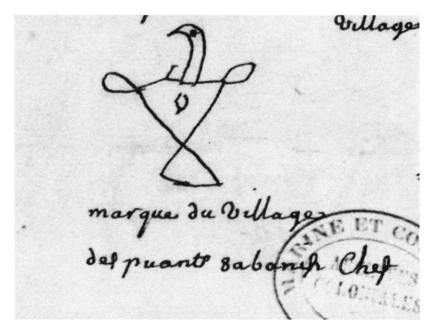

Figure 6. Winnebago pictogram on 1701 Great Peace treaty, Montreal. Note the symbol for the Winnebago, Siouan neighbors of the Illinois, is the "thunderbird." C[11a], vol. 19, fols. 41–44v, ANOM.

Courtesy of the Archives Nationales d'Outre Mer, Aix-en-Provence, France.

Although we must rely on post-contact descriptions for much of our understanding of Illinois social life, there are some things we can be reasonably confident about regarding the Illinois in the early 1600s. For one thing, as it was for all eastern North American Indians, kinship was the most important means of separating friends from foreign peoples.[79] Contrary to how European observers saw them, the Illinois did not really organize themselves primarily into a "tribe" or "nation" or even a "confederacy." Rather, they did most things in life—resided, went to war, negotiated, identified—as families. Families were the center of life. While we don't know a lot of specifics about the social organization of the Illinois-speakers in the pre-contact period, what is certain is that the Illinois created extensive lineages, possibly similar to the *doodemag* among Algonquians like the Anishinaabeg.[80] Among the Illinois-speakers were at least fourteen distinct subgroups—or *familles* as La Salle called them—at the time of contact: Peoria, Kaskaskia, Tamaroa, Coiracoentanon,

Chinko, Cahokia, Chepoussa, Amenakoa, Oouka, Acansa, Moingwena, Tapuaro, Maroa, Ispeminkias, and Metchigameas.[81] As a later French observer would say of the Illinois, these were inclusive units not necessarily based solely in biological kinship and included "degrees of kinship that [Europeans] . . . would not even call cousins."[82] In any event, these patrilineal "familles" were the primary units of identity among the Illinois. As Illinois-speakers moved into their new territory, they likely used intermarriage, as well as adoption and other kinds of fictive kinship, to build bridges, to welcome other newcomers into their familles, and to create borders. For the Illinois-speaking newcomers in the 1600s, the world was organized into "a8enti8aki"—relatives—and "ninaca8atisi"—strangers.[83] Kinship created obligations, identities, and responsibilities that helped the newcomers negotiate their immigration to the borderlands.

Extended and intermarried families were almost certainly the basis for the decentralized and autonomous villages, which were the most important social units in pre-contact Illinois.[84] One early observer said that there were fully sixty villages of Illinois-speakers in the 1640s.[85] On the first contact-era map of the Illinois, Marquette drew seven distinct villages of Illinois-speakers that he saw with his own eyes in just a month's time, which probably represented just a fraction of the total that actually existed. As Marquette's map shows, the Pe8area (Peoria) were divided into three villages, while the Moing8ena (Moingwena), Kachkaskia (Kaskaskia), Maroa, and Metchigamea all lived in distinct villages. La Salle noted that the numerous villages on early maps constituted "*only some* of the tribes composing the nation of Illinois."[86] La Salle also emphasized that the pre-contact Illinois lived in distinct villages, far away from one another, both to the east and to the west of the Mississippi.[87] The demands of bison hunting probably joined with kinship to create the bonds and relationships that united local groups into larger familles. Indeed, it is likely that bison hunting, since it required large groups, was helping to "unite" some of these villages in the pre-contact era.[88]

In addition to whatever kinship ties may have joined Illinois villages in the prehistoric period, trade certainly helped create a loosely unified identity among the Illinois-speakers and structured relationships with neighbors. Over the course of their colonization of the Illinois Country, trade clearly came to the fore of Illinois Indian life. In Native societies in the Midwest, trade was an important way of expanding power, building cohesion, and dealing with outsiders.[89] Trade connections could even produce fictive kinship bonds, as trading partners became a kind of kin.[90] Illinois-speakers also

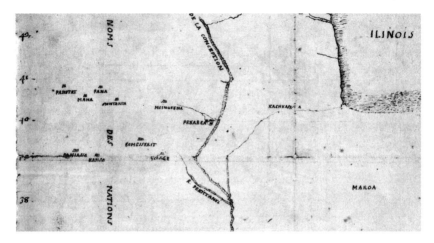

Figure 7. Marquette map of 1673. This map depicts the Kaskaskia village in the Illinois River Valley, as well as several other Illinois villages west of the Mississippi. From Sara Jones Tucker, *Indian Villages of the Illinois Country* (Springfield, Ill.: Illinois State Museum, 1942).

Courtesy of the Illinois History and Lincoln Collections, University of Illinois, Urbana-Champaign.

established trade connections beyond their local region, creating an interregional trade network that allowed them to import materials from foreign regions. Exotic goods in protohistoric Illinois archaeological sites included prestige goods like Olivella shell beads, marine shell gorgets, and other objects from the lower Mississippi Valley, as well as exotic materials from the Plains.[91] By the early 1600s, north-south trade networks were augmented by east-west trade networks, spanning the Algonquian and Siouan borderlands.[92]

The Illinois began trading for European metal as early as the 1620s and possibly earlier.[93] Archaeologists argue from this evidence that the Illinois were aggressively pursuing trade with the Wendats, far to the north in the Great Lakes, probably beginning in the early 1600s.[94] Other evidence suggests that they then carried these metals farther south and west, toward modern-day Missouri, where they traded them for profit and to make alliances among the Siouan neighbors, descendants of the Oneota. In other words, by the mid-seventeenth century the Illinois had emerged as merchants, middlemen, and go-betweens.[95] As newcomers to a region that was borderland between Siouan and Algonquians, as well as at the crossroads of cultures, the Illinois used trade to build consensus, friendships, and cohesion.

One sign of the opportunistic stance in the Illinois newcomers' human relationships is the calumet. Like bison hunting and other aspects of the Illinois's lifeway, the calumet was a recent adoption. As Algonquians among the Siouan Oneota-speakers, the Illinois probably used it frequently when they arrived in the new territory, relying on it to "speak to strangers."[96] The first and most detailed early examples of calumet ceremonialism among the Illinois reflect the fact that they used the calumet not only for peace but also to intimidate and to declare and celebrate their hegemony. The dance featured scenes of conflict, the dancer "repairing his arms, attiring himself, running, discovering the foe, raising the cry, slaying the enemy, removing his scalp, and returning home with a song of victory." Marquette noted how the whole setting for the dance was decorated with war paraphernalia, "the weapons used by the warriors of those Nations . . . namely: clubs, war-hatchets, bows, quivers, and arrows."[97] The dancers reenacted a battlefield victory, with the one dancer, near defeat, turning around in defiance and "caus[ing] his adversary to flee." The climax of the dance was a speech about conquest. As Marquette said, the dance ended with "a lofty Discourse, delivered by him who holds the Calumet . . . he recounts the battles at which he has been present, the victories that he has won, the names of the Nations, the places, and the Captives whom he has made."[98]

One way to read the calumet among the Illinois, then, is that it was an accommodation to the language of their new territory. But within this ostensible accommodation was actually a declaration of Illinois power. Through kinship and alliance, rather than Cahokia's territorialism and hierarchy, the Illinois had expanded. The Illinois at contact were probably close to fifteen thousand people.[99] They had repopulated the prairies with close to the same number of people who had once inhabited the city at Cahokia. The Illinois Country was no longer a vacant quarter but was home to an aggressive, opportunistic group of newcomers. At midcentury, their world began to feel the effects of a different colonialism in the East.

ev3

In the 1650s, powerful and unified Iroquois warriors, supplied by their Dutch allies at Albany, began to attack people of the Great Lakes in an effort to subject Algonquians, gain captives, and control fur resources in the region.[100] For several groups—the Wendats most especially—the result was near devastation.[101] Refugees fled through the Great Lakes, pushing west. Meanwhile, the French at Quebec adopted a policy of supporting the Algonquian allies of the Great Lakes against the Iroquois violence, hoping to prevent them from making peace with the Iroquois and their Dutch and English allies. With French support, the Algonquians counterattacked against the Iroquois. The previously "limited-indecisive" warfare characteristic of pre-contact Native American societies turned much more violent, now producing thousands of casualties, prisoners, and deaths.[102]

The Illinois felt some early effects of this violence, on a relatively small scale. In 1653, a "small village" of the Illinois was attacked by the Iroquois.[103] They suffered another attack a few years later.[104] But Illinois warriors bounced back from these episodes. In fact, in the 1650s at least, they counterattacked against the Iroquois and may have got the better of them.[105] More important, far from simply defensive, the Illinois became aggressive. It was as if the Iroquois violence and resulting disorder in the region combined with the Illinois's colonizing trajectory to trigger their own ambitious bid for supremacy. In the 1650s, Illinois warriors attacked the Winnebago and routed them.[106] Later they attacked an Iroquois party and took forty Iroquois "who were on their way to hunt beaver in the Illinois Country."[107] The Illinois were not militarily defeated. In the 1660s, they attacked the Sauk and Fox.[108] They attacked enemies to the south and west.[109] Soon they were at war with "seven or eight" different nations.[110] Illinois-speakers were not defensive or desperate; they were belligerent.

Moreover, if we look closely at the Illinois engagements, one important pattern emerges. Not only were the Illinois routing their enemies, they were also usually taking huge numbers of captives. Against the Winnebago, they took an entire village captive. As one French account put it, "So vigorous was their attack that they killed, wounded, or made prisoners all the Puans, except a few who escaped."[111] Describing the Winnebago after the same event, another account told how "All the people of this Nation were killed or taken captive by the Iliniouek."[112] Far from defeated, the Illinois were on a concerted campaign to capture slaves.

Like so many other things in Algonquian life, the central logic of slavery among peoples of the Great Lakes was based on kinship. Since kinship networks were fundamentally how people gained their status, identity, and power in the world, a person's lineage and family were absolutely central to his or her life. Maintaining and extending a kinship network was fundamental to a person's success in trade, warfare, political diplomacy, and marriage. Kinship was the bedrock of life.[113]

This context helps explain the phenomenon of slave raids among Algon-quians like the Illinois. As war and disease impacted Native societies during the Beaver Wars, people died by the thousands. This created great disorder among Great Lakes Indians in the seventeenth century, as many kin went missing. The fundamental logic of Indian warfare was that the deceased needed to be replaced. Captives could fill the spaces left vacant by deceased relatives in the kinship order. Adopted into the family, they could literally replace the dead.[114]

It is no accident that many of our best informants on Indian slavery were eyewitnesses to the Illinois, where captivity became such an important part of life during the contact period. As one Jesuit visitor to the Illinois Country in the seventeenth century wrote, expressing the logic of Indian captivity and slavery, "When there is any dead man to be resuscitated, that is to say, if any one of their warriors has been killed, and they think it a duty to replace him in his cabin,—they give to this cabin one of their prisoners, who takes the place of the deceased; and this is what they call 'resuscitating the dead.'"[115] Another priest in the Illinois Country, Jacques Gravier, lived with the Illinois in the 1690s. His dictionary of the Illinois language contains a virtual primer for understanding the subtleties of Indian slavery in this period. One telling term for slavery in the five-hundred-page dictionary expressed the essence of the phenomenon: *nirapakerima:* "I adopt him in place of the dead."[116]

This was the basic principle of Native warfare throughout the Algon-quian world in this period. In the wake of disease and violence, the dead needed to be replaced. But this was a complicated business, and certain requirements governed the taking of slaves. Most important, a captive could not be kin or the kin of allies.[117] As the French would learn as they began buying and receiving slaves from Indian allies, owning a slave immediately antagonized the culture and lineage to which that person belonged.[118] In the Algonquian-speaking world in the midst of the Beaver Wars, many groups had consolidated, uniting kin lines in an effort to reestablish their networks. For instance, the Anishenaabeg created a new collective identity out of pre-viously disparate local identities.[119] In this context, Algonquian-speaking cap-tives were often useless, for attempting to enslave or adopt them into a lineage would only upset neighbors in the mixed-up world of the *pays d'en haut.* Only true "strangers" would do, those who were not only not kin but also did not share kin with an ally. For this purpose, in the Algonquian Great Lakes, Siouan-speaking groups from the West made the best slaves. They had no kin—they were complete strangers. And so they could become *a8enti8aki*—relatives.[120]

Given the preference for "strangers" in the business of captive adoption, the Illinois-speakers had a hugely important strategic advantage in slaving. They lived in, and increasingly controlled, the borderlands. They could raid among the Siouan-speakers of the West, very few of whom had kinsmen among the Algonquian-speakers of the Great Lakes. The Illinois took advantage of this as they raided in the 1660s.[121] When they attacked the Winnebago, taking the whole village captive, they were enslaving a group of Siouan-speaking people who would not make them enemies among the other Algonquian-speakers in the North. The same goes for their reported raids to the south and west in the 1660s.[122] When the Jesuit Claude Allouez reported that the Illinois were engaged in wars with the Iroquois on one side and Siouans on the other, he thought it was a lamentable situation for them. It was actually the heart of the Illinois advantage.[123]

It is important to note that when they went on slave raids in the pre-contact era, the Illinois probably mostly captured women. Not only was this typical of most Algonquian slave systems, and certainly typical of the Illinois's practices in the contact era, as we will see, but the Illinois's new bison economy gave women a new significance in the 1600s—as laborers. Evidence from the contact era suggests that female slaves were welcomed into polygamous families among the Illinois as second and third wives and put under the subordination of a mistress.[124] As La Salle would write in the 1680s, by the early contact period, female slaves in Illinois were not just replacement kin but people "who they compel to labor for them."[125] It seems almost certain that the bison economy's labor demands and the traditional kinship-replacement imperatives of slavery dovetailed in Illinois in the contact era. The Illinois's location in the borderlands allowed them to replace kin and to expand the capacity of their bison-based mode of production.

By the 1660s, through slavery and adoption, the Illinois had probably begun to replace the people they had lost in early Iroquois attacks and probable epidemics, as their population figures suggest.[126] This created a fork in the road. It seems clear that the Illinois might have stayed out of further conflicts, safe from the fighting that embroiled the Algonquian world. They could have remained, heedlessly hunting bison west of the Mississippi, avoiding Iroquois aggression. Instead the ambitious Illinois continued their opportunistic trajectory. Taking advantage of a respite from Iroquois attacks beginning in the late 1660s, the Illinois resumed their trading to the north vigorously. Several French accounts from this period report the Illinois making their first visits to newly established French outposts in Green Bay, the Fox River, and Lake Superior (St. Esprit).[127] As Allouez wrote in 1669, by this time the Illinois were entrepreneurs, traveling north "from time to time in great numbers, as Merchants, to carry away hatchets and kettles, guns, and other articles that they need."[128] Allouez commented that one Illinois merchant—Chachagwessiou—had distinguished himself as a skilled trader and a tough negotiator. Commenting on the Illinois, Allouez wrote: "They act like traders and give hardly any more than do the French."[129]

But every good merchant needs a commodity for sale. For the Illinois, their prairie homeland lacked lakes and woods that made for good beaver habitat, as many French pointed out. And so it just made sense: living in the borderlands, the Illinois were in a strategic spot. They projected power both in the Algonquian world to the northeast and in the Siouan-speaking world to the south and west. They were slavers, having restored their own depleted population with a whole village of Winnebagos and probably others. They had a long tradition of acting as merchants and middlemen. Taking a bold and aggressive step, they combined the roles. The Illinois continued to capture and trade for ever more slaves in the south and west, Siouans and Caddoans like the Pawnee, Osage, and Missouri. Then, following the trade routes that they had established earlier in the protohistoric period for trade with the Huron, the Illinois now brought these slaves north. Using a market-oriented logic, they began to "traffic" in slaves, as one French observer later put it.[130] Ambitious merchants who lacked good beaver for the fur trade, the Illinois took advantage of the other commodity available to themselves: people. By 1673, when Marquette visited the Illinois, the strategy was consummate: "They are warlike, and make themselves dreaded by the Distant tribes to the south and west, whither they go to procure Slaves; these they barter, selling them at a high price to other Nations, in exchange for other Wares."[131]

Like their migration to the Illinois Valley in the late 1500s, the Illinois's embrace of slavery and slave trading was not defensive but aggressive. And as Marquette realized while traveling to the Illinois Country, the aggressive Illinois were now "feared" by groups all over the pays d'en haut. In the 1670s, the Ketchigamis saved two Illinois prisoners from death for fear of reprisals by the Illinois.[132] The Menominees told Marquette not to travel any farther south than the Fox River, on account of the Illinois—the "ferocious people"—who lived beyond.[133] The Illinois themselves told the French that they held influence over all the "remote nations" and "very distant savages" to the South of them.[134] It was likely their power as slavers that made them so feared. First exploiting bison and then slaves, the Illinois had invaded and conquered the borderlands, seizing opportunity.

ೞ

It is precisely this kind of opportunism that the Illinois used to welcome the French when they showed up in the Illinois Country during the 1670s. The Jesuits Marquette and his partner, Claude Allouez, were among the first Frenchmen to travel to the Illinois's new homelands. Arriving at Illinois villages on the Mississippi and Illinois rivers, the Frenchmen met a powerful Indian group, whose "traditions" were all about innovation, flexibility, and conquest. As they reveal in their earliest writings for the *Jesuit Relations* from Illinois, the Jesuits thought that the Illinois were very eager Christians. What is more accurate to say is that the Illinois were extraordinarily opportunistic and willing to experiment with the Jesuits' ideas just as they had done in their recent cultural, ecological, and social adaptations while moving to the prairies. They had a "tradition" of innovation, and it was the cornerstone of their history.

From Allouez's very first meeting with the Illinois at St. Esprit, he singled them out as exceptionally enthusiastic about Christianity. As he wrote in 1670, the Illinois "offer[ed] a fine field for Gospel laborers, as it is impossible to find [a group of Indians] better fitted for receiving Christian influences."[135] Unlike many other Indian groups, the Illinois were not hostile to missionaries and were open to prayer. "If they do not all pray as yet, they at least esteem prayer. They are far from having an aversion to it, or from dreading it as a dangerous thing, as all the other Savages of this New France did when we began preaching the Gospel to them."[136] Their speeches had "no savor of the Savage,"[137] and they listened attentively to the priests' lengthy sermons.[138] Not only did the Illinois at St. Esprit eagerly await Allouez's lessons, they also promised to become evangelists in their own right.[139]

The Illinois began to experiment with Christianity willingly in almost every one of the early encounters between themselves and the Jesuits. In 1673, Marquette proudly watched Indians worshiping the cross with animal skins.[140] Allouez noted that the Illinois mixed Christianity into a spiritual practice featuring dreams and thrilled at how the Illinois reported seeing Jesus in their dreams.[141] During their visit to the mission of St. Francis Xavier in 1674, Allouez observed some Illinois burning tobacco at the altar.[142] Especially interesting was the Indians' treatment of the church building itself. As

Allouez noted, Illinois chiefs began to pray *to* the church, "address[ing] their speeches to this house of God, and speak[ing] to it as to an animate being." Then they began to do something even more unusual: "When they pass by here they throw tobacco all around the church, which is a kind of devotion to their divinity." Finally, the Illinois Indians "also [came] sometimes and offer[ed] presents [to the church], to beg God to have pity upon their deceased relatives."[143] Combined with their feasts honoring Jesus and the fasts that they conducted in order to find God in their dreams, these gestures suggested an idiosyncratic, but positive, embrace of Christianity. The priests proudly boasted about the "honors they pay to our Holy Church, after their fashion."[144] The Illinois approached the priests and the other-than-human spirits they represented in typical fashion, opportunistically.

It is almost certain that Christianity became another additive to a diverse and complex Illinois spiritual worldview.[145] The Illinois practiced Christianity alongside more traditional manitou worship, itself likely newly tailored to the Illinois environment. The Illinois were flexible and adaptive, and this is what made them such good pupils. "They honor the lord among themselves in their own way," as Marquette noted.[146] Of course, it is hard to imagine them doing it any *other* way. After all, they were powerful and not desperate. Indeed, Marquette himself seemed to acknowledge the Illinois's own agency in the creation of a hybrid version of Christianity. Recognizing the Illinois's active participation in appropriating Christianity to their own needs, Marquette noted how an Illinois man on his deathbed went "to go take possession of paradise in the name of the whole nation."[147] If a "spiritual conquest" was happening here, the Illinois were the ones conquering Christianity, on their own terms.

To the Jesuits, the Illinois's openness and curiosity were encouraging, though the priests surely did not fully understand the Illinois's engagement with Christianity. For instance, Allouez and Marquette considered the Illinois to be almost monotheistic, which was not true.[148] Allouez perceived that the Illinois recognized one spirit—the "maker of all things"—above all others.[149] This was optimistic—and false. The Jesuits interpreted the Illinois custom of feasting as similar to communion.[150] And in general, the early Jesuits thought that the Illinois were nearly Christian, writing that missionizing here was a matter of exploiting close parallels between Christianity and indigenous spirituality. As Marquette wrote, "we keep a little of their usage, and take from it all that is bad."[151] However, rather than true similarities between Christian and Illinois worldviews, what the Jesuits were actually perceiving was the Illinois's willingness to experiment. Their engagement with Christianity really reflected their openness, their flexibility, and their interest in gaining an advantage. Almost certainly they were hoping to capitalize on the newcomers' power—spiritual or, if that proved useless, at least material. The Illinois were opportunistic.

ↄ

Arriving in Illinois, the Jesuits often believed that they were the most important thing happening in the Illinois's world. But in fact the Illinois had reformed almost everything about their lives over the previous several generations, making the French newcomers just one of a whole series of changes. The Illinois had moved to the borderlands, colonizing and taking advantage of new possibilities to build power based on bison hunting and slavery. Adapting themselves to the new ecological opportunities, they also adapted culturally, assimilating many aspects of the Siouan peoples whom they replaced and incorporated in these borderlands. When Marquette arrived among them, he ignored the real symbols of Illinois power and history that they presented him—the calumet ceremony, the bison skins and meat, Siouan iconography, and the slave. Focusing on the Illinois's positive reception of Christianity, he did not understand that this was part of an ongoing set of adaptations that had defined their recent ambitious history.

In any event, the Jesuits sent their optimistic reports about Illinois back to Quebec and on to Paris. They tried to drum up support for this promising new mission project in the distant Illinois Country. Reading these reports, however, imperial officials back in Quebec were mostly indifferent to the idea of colonial activity in the remote borderlands. Even with news of the Illinois's initial embrace of Christianity and the glowing descriptions of the rich Illinois Valley landscape, nobody in the administration of New France much cared about this place in 1673. To the contrary, officials mostly opposed expanding the empire to include these distant and different lands and peoples.

But in 1680 the Iroquois Wars took a sudden turn. And when they did, the Illinois were at the center of it. Suddenly, in spite of their initial indifference, officials could not ignore the Illinois—the people and the region demanded French attention. Soon, following Marquette, more explorers, with diverse imperial goals, ventured to Illinois to join the powerful Native people who had recently conquered the region. Opportunism would continue to shape the Illinois's response to empire.

Chapter 2

The Imaginary Kingdom

In 1680, an army of the Iroquois invaded the Illinois with a force of five to six hundred warriors, renewing the Beaver Wars. Chasing the Illinois from their villages in the Illinois Valley, they desecrated graves, burned buildings, and ruined fields. Catching up with their victims, they committed, according to one French account, "mutilation, by slaying, and by a thousand tortures besides."[1] After this destruction, the Iroquois aggressors left the Illinois Valley full of markers of their violence, including "the half denuded skulls of Illinois dead" and pictographic memorials commemorating the Iroquois victory.[2]

To the French in Quebec and throughout the pays d'en haut, who were only barely familiar with the region, this looked like devastation. Recounting the Iroquois attacks on the Illinois, La Salle wrote that there were seven hundred casualties and four hundred slaves taken.[3] New France intendant Jacques Duchesneau put the number even higher.[4] To the French, this episode was a major blow, if not a crushing one, for the Illinois people whom the French considered weak and "indifferently warlike."[5] According to French sources, the Illinois were "well nigh exterminated."[6] They had to "abandon their country" and "seek refuge in distant parts."[7]

In viewing the Illinois as devastated victims, the French exaggerated and misunderstood this episode of Indian warfare and underestimated Illinois power. Nevertheless, the Iroquois attack of 1680–81 marked a turning point in French diplomacy with regard to western peoples like the Illinois. Convinced that the Iroquois were poised to dominate the Great Lakes, the French faced an important choice. One alternative was to allow the Iroquois to continue their aggression against the Illinois and other Algonquians, which would put at risk the fur trade and balance of power that New France relied on. The other alternative was to support the western allies, unify them, and help them defeat the Iroquois. In fact, this was no real choice at all. Over the course of the next several years, French officials committed to becoming the mediators of the alliance, the "glue" of the Algonquian world.[8] They resolved to support the most important targets of Iroquois attacks, the Illinois.

This change produced enormous effects for the Illinois. Nowhere near as devastated by the attack in 1680 as the French thought, the Illinois continued on an opportunistic trajectory they had begun well before contact. With French support, they expanded their power to the Southwest, increasing their activity as slavers in the Siouan borderlands. Coalescing in larger groups, they united at the so-called Grand Village of the Kaskaskia, modern-day Starved Rock, which soon became the largest population center north of Mexico. Here they created a center of exploitation, basing their tremendous power on bison, slaves, and now the French alliance. Far from devastated by the attack in 1680, the Illinois moved into an even more ambitious phase of their history.

But if these changes in French diplomacy had important effects for the Illinois, they also had important effects for the French themselves. For in resolving to help build the Algonquian alliance and support the Illinois, Quebec officials were committing themselves to a whole new policy regarding the distant West. Prior to the 1680s, the only people who went to the remote country of the Illinois Valley were schemers with quixotic and even defiant plans. These included Jesuits, explorers like Robert La Salle, and, most important, fur traders. Officials in Quebec openly opposed western expansion of the empire. Now, in the mid-1680s, the imperatives of Indian diplomacy forced officials to change their views. Importantly, officials had to look to the schemers on the ground in Illinois as the agents of their new Indian policy. For their part, visionaries like La Salle had to look to the government as essential partners in their projects.

This was the beginning of a unique, halting, and uncertain colonial experiment on New France's periphery. To support the Indian allies, New France officials relied on an "infrastructure" of disloyal explorers, priests, and fur traders whose activities they previously discouraged.[9] Fur traders pursued their self-interest, but they gained imperial support and military assistance. Priests and fur traders disagreed about priorities, but they came together and cooperated to solidify their fledgling presence among the Illinois. The necessities of Indian affairs forced the French—with all their competing priorities and different interests—to find a common ground. It was the beginning of empire by collaboration.

Meanwhile, of course, the real winners were the Illinois. This period marked the height of their power. Far from devastated, they launched an aggressive phase, uniting at the Grand Village of the Kaskaskia. Here, exploiting bison and the slave trade, they made one of the most important bids for power in all of seventeenth-century America. Together, Indians, French schemers, and Quebec officials collaborated to realize disparate goals.

☙

The period from the 1670s through the 1680s witnessed the first explorations of the Illinois Country by Frenchmen. Even before Marquette's famous exploration in 1673, Jesuit priest Claude Allouez made initial contact with Illinois Indians on Lake Superior in the 1660s. In 1671, Simon-François Daumont de Saint-Lusson explored the westernmost edge of the Great Lakes and interacted with Illinois Indians.[10] In 1673, Jacques Marquette and Louis Jolliet made their famous voyage into the Mississippi Valley watershed, exploring the Wisconsin, Mississippi, and Illinois rivers. Robert La Salle and Louis Hennepin entered the Mississippi Valley several times beginning in 1680, and in 1682 La Salle voyaged from Illinois almost to the mouth of the Mississippi River. In several of these early explorations, French travelers passed through the Illinois River Valley and first laid eyes on the territory that later would be known as the Illinois Country. Crossing the watershed that separated the Great Lakes from the Mississippi Valley, they entered into "strange lands."[11]

What they found impressed them. Explorers reported how "you could not find any land better [suited] for the production of wheat, and for vines, and for other fruits as well."[12] The land featured bison and game that were "innumerable"[13] and soil in the bottomlands that "looks as if it had been already manured."[14] They found the Illinois Indians affable, "of good birth," and eager for trade and religious instruction.[15] The rumors concerning the presence of hostile Indians here in the Mississippi Valley proved false, and explorers quickly found ways to win friends among Indians in the region.[16] One explorer was especially direct in his praise of Illinois: "It may be said to contain the finest lands ever seen."[17] Jesuits found Illinois to be a "fine field for Gospel laborers."[18] Taken together, these discoveries inspired explorers with visions of empire.[19]

But officials were more than skeptical. In 1663, the royal government had taken over New France after years of company management. The French government reorganized the colony and embarked on an era of centralized planning.[20] New royal officials, led by Minister of the Marine Jean-Baptiste

Colbert, brought new priorities. As they saw it, fur trade was important, but trade should not dominate or overshadow other potentially profitable activities in the colony. Nor could it be allowed to tempt would-be farmers into the woods.[21] The stability of the colony relied on settling Frenchmen in the St. Lawrence Valley and employing them in productive industry there. Without outposts in the West, Colbert believed, "the settlers would be obliged to engage in fishing, prospecting, and manufacturing, which would yield them far greater benefits."[22]

Practical realities added to the official bias against western expansion. Iroquois attacks had destroyed western outposts of New France in the 1640s, and Iroquois power had reached its zenith in 1651. The missions and fur trade outposts in the West had been pulled back, and trade dried up through much of the 1650s and 1660s.[23] Reestablishing these posts would be expensive and risky. In 1666, Colbert announced the major principle of his imperial vision when he called for a tightly focused colonization in New France: "It would be worth much more to restrain [the colonies] to a space of land in which the colony would be able to sustain itself, rather than to embrace too great a quantity of land which one day we might have to abandon with some diminution of the reputation of His Majesty and the crown."[24]

Ignoring this opposition, Jolliet was the first Frenchman to seriously propose an outpost of an expanded French empire in the Illinois Country in 1673.[25] Of all the lands he saw in the new Mississippi Valley, Jolliet praised the Illinois Country, just beyond the Great Lakes watershed, and south of Lake Michigan, as "the most beautiful and the easiest for inhabiting."[26] The weather was mild. Unlike in the valley of the St. Lawrence, "A *habitant* here would not have to work some ten years to knock down the trees and burn them; the same day he arrives, he could put the plow in the field."[27] It was a land of plenty: there were prairies that stretched out for twenty miles and Indians who were "honest . . . and obliging."[28] To realize his plan, Jolliet proposed a harbor at the southern end of Lake Michigan, by which his colony would maintain easy communication with Michilimackinac. Further, if the continental divide meant that the rivers here flowed south, and away from New France, Jolliet envisioned conquering this inconvenient geographical circumstance. A canal joining the Chicago and the Illinois rivers, he asserted, would connect this Mississippi River Valley to the Great Lakes, integrating the newly discovered territory into New France in the north.

Jolliet proposed building his canal in the area where he and Marquette had recently found the Kaskaskia, a prosperous village of Illinois-speakers.

Jolliet did not mention them as part of his plan, but clearly he singled out their homeland as the prime place for French colonization. Containing a growing population of Indians eager for trade, this was the village to which Marquette had promised to return the following year to establish a permanent mission. It could become the heart of a new French colonial region.

But when Jolliet made his proposal for a colony in Illinois, the official answer was, simply, no: "His Majesty does not want to give to Sieur Jolliet the permission which he has asked to establish himself with 20 men in the Country of Illinois. It is necessary to multiply the habitants of Canada before thinking of other lands, and [the governor of New France] should hold this as your maxim in regard to new discoveries which are made."[29]

Meanwhile, however, Marquette did not even wait for permission. Returning to the precise area that Jolliet described at the top of the Illinois Valley, in 1674 he established the mission of the Immaculate Conception in the village of the Kaskaskia. Having shared a number of interactions with the Illinois at various mission outposts in the Great Lakes in the 1660s, Marquette and his partner, Claude Allouez, now would have a home base right in the center of Illinois Country. This is where Marquette intended to create a flourishing mission among these Indians whom he already knew to be enthusiastic about and receptive to Christianity. However, having disapproved Jolliet's plan for a colony in Illinois, New France officials opposed the Jesuits' earliest efforts in Illinois as well.

დ

A specific logic underlay official opposition to Jesuit activity in the West. In addition to centralized settlement, Colbert's reforms in the 1660s also included an idealistic goal of assimilating Indians into the French colonial population. As Colbert saw it, the role of religious missionaries was to work to settle Indians in the St. Lawrence and integrate them, adding them to the productive and military strength of the colony. Formalizing a policy known as Frenchification, Colbert wrote to intendant Jean Talon: "To increase the colony . . . the most useful way to achieve it would be to try to civilize the Algonquins, the Hurons, and the other Savages . . . and to persuade them to come to settle in a commune with the French, to live with them, and educate their children in our mores and our customs."[30] A key component of this assimilation program clearly rested on *proximity*: Indians had to be settled in what were known as "reserves" or "réductions" near the French population centers where they could gradually acquire the habits of Frenchmen.

Over several generations of missionary work in New France, the Jesuits had developed a strategy almost completely opposite to these principles.[31] In the 1630s, they had begun going with the Indians into their villages and translating Christianity to a Native context. This was in keeping with Loyola's charge to teach and live "in a way that is accommodated to those people, [and their] understanding."[32] In their famous *Relations*, Jesuits narrated their heroic efforts in "following [the Indians] into the deep forest" and "reducing the principles of their own language."[33] The point was not to teach Indians to live as Frenchmen but rather for the priests to adapt themselves to Indian ways of living. As one Jesuit in this early period wrote, "A great step is gained when one has learned to know those with whom he has to deal; has penetrated their thoughts; has adapted himself to their language, their customs, and their manner of living; and, when necessary, has been a Barbarian with them, in order to win them over to Jesus Christ."[34] Far from Frenchifying Indians, Jesuits actually aimed to keep Indians *apart* from Frenchmen, whom they thought only corrupted the Natives. As one Jesuit summed it up in later years, "The best mode of Christianizing them was to avoid Frenchifying them."[35]

Although many of the Jesuits' early "flying missions" in the Great Lakes were destroyed in the 1640s by Iroquois attacks, peace between the Iroquois and New France beginning in 1667 had allowed for new activity.[36] Over the next ten years, the Jesuits extended their missions to ever more remote sites, weeks away from Quebec. In 1666, Allouez traveled to Chequamegon Bay, where he established the mission of St. Esprit. In 1668, Marquette left Trois-Rivières to found a mission at Sault-Ste. Marie. After Claude Dablon joined Allouez and Marquette in the West in 1669, the priests pushed even farther into the interior. While Marquette took over St. Esprit, Allouez went to establish the mission of St. Francis Xavier in Green Bay in December 1669. Two years later, Allouez pressed on to a Mascouten village on the Fox River.[37] These were the places where the Jesuits first encountered the Illinois Indians.

Throughout this period, Colbert disapproved. He wrote to condemn the Jesuits' new distant missions and their method of "keeping the converted Indians' ordinary lifestyle [rather than] bringing them among the French." From his perspective, he wrote, "it is only too obvious how such a course is harmful both to Religion and to the State."[38] The king himself urged the Jesuits to change their ways, to "attract [the Indians] into a civil society and to quit their form of living, with which they will never be able to become good Christians."[39] In 1672, the new governor Frontenac criticized the Jesuits' distant missions as "pure mockeries." As he told the minister, "I don't think that [the Jesuits] should be permitted to extend them any further than they already have until we see in one of these places a church of Indians better formed."[40]

But the Jesuits remained convinced that distant missions were the best way to convert Indians. Indeed, when Marquette founded the Immaculate Conception mission in 1674 it was not merely another distant mission, it was *the most distant* mission the Jesuits had ever established.[41] Deep in the West, totally outside the priorities of the French empire and remote from the influence of French colonists, here the Jesuits could foster among the Natives an ideal "primitive Christianity," "just like the First Christians."[42] Far from making the Indians live as Frenchmen, Marquette, setting out for the Illinois Country in the 1670s, predicted that he would soon be living on *their* terms: "After the fashion of the Savages, the Illinois wish for us in order that we may share their miseries with them, and suffer every imaginable hardship of barbarism. They are lost sheep, that must be sought for among the thickets and woods, since for the most part they cry so loudly that one hastens to rescue them from the jaws of the Wolf."[43]

All this helps us understand why the Jesuits were so thrilled to report how Illinois Indians practiced a kind of idiosyncratic Christianity in their earliest encounters, "honor[ing] our Lord among themselves in this own way."[44] As Jesuits saw it, the Illinois had spiritual traditions that echoed Christianity, which was why Marquette could boast that "we keep a little of the usage, and take from it all that is bad."[45] Here was the realization of the Jesuit ideal. Isolated from the French colonial project, they made a new indigenous Christianity, "in their own fashion."

In some ways, the Jesuits must have been glad when the administration rejected Jolliet's plan. They viewed Illinois as an opportunity to conduct a religious mission separate from other French colonial activity, and Jolliet's project—canal and all—would only have attracted Frenchmen to corrupt the infant church. But of course the French government did not reject Jolliet in order to preserve the Jesuits' isolated mission. French officials opposed the Jesuits, too. Taken together, the earliest Frenchmen in Illinois had incompatible visions and no support from the government. If this made prospects for empire in the region look dim, Robert La Salle only added to the discord when he arrived in the region.

❧

Just as Jolliet received news of the king's rejection of his plan in 1677, La Salle was visiting the Illinois for the first time and devising a new vision of empire. Having heard about the discovery of the Mississippi River in the 1670s, La

Salle began to imagine a future colonial project centered at the Gulf of Mexico and oriented to the South, where a port could remain open all year round. From here, free of the cold-weather challenges faced by Quebec, La Salle anticipated a more profitable fur trade and better agricultural possibilities.

New France officials, interested in protecting their fur trade at Montreal, were naturally skeptical of this new project. But La Salle gained an ally in Governor Frontenac, who was himself opposed to the Montreal fur traders. With his help, La Salle began creating a new trade route beginning in 1672 that extended south of the Great Lakes. After establishing a fort on Lake Ontario, La Salle won permission to create an outpost in Illinois, the first settlement in his future imperial scheme.[46] He established a fort in Illinois in 1680 near the Kaskaskia village, where he settled several men under his command in what would become the base camp for his ambitious enterprises.

It was in 1682 that La Salle finally reached the Gulf of Mexico after descending the Mississippi River. Here he made clear his intention that the little colony in Illinois would now belong to a whole new imperial system, outside of New France. Planting a cross and a flag at the bottom of the Mississippi, La Salle conducted a brief but elaborate ceremony in front of a small audience of Indians, signaling the official start of this new colonial project. Shouting "vive le Roi" and "chanting the *Te Deum, the Exaudiat, the Domine salvum fa Regum*," La Salle took possession of the entire Mississippi Valley, which he promptly renamed "this country of Louisiana." He then placed in the ground a lead plate, inscribed with a short description of his historic journey from the Illinois down the Mississippi, nearly the entire extent of his possession. As part of the legal proceedings, he made a note of the fact that various Indians present had consented to this possession and allied themselves to this future government in Louisiana. Within this list of Indians were the Illinois, among "the most considerable nations dwelling therein."[47]

La Salle's ceremony was the mirror image, in many ways, of a similar ceremony conducted by the explorer Simon-François Daumont de Saint-Lusson in 1671. Standing on the edge of Lake Superior, Saint-Lusson had claimed the entire western Great Lakes for France, also in front of an audience of local Indians. Like La Salle, he had made a note of the various Indian groups whose territory he meant his claim to include. And like La Salle, he singled out the Illinois among these. So while Saint-Lusson had claimed the Illinois as part of an empire oriented to the north and centered in Quebec, La Salle now *reversed* this orientation and reimagined their territory in a landscape oriented *south*. When La Salle claimed Louisiana, he included the marginal Illinois Country as an important part of his claim, providing a vision that located the territory within a new empire separate from New France. When he created his new outpost in the Illinois Country in 1681, he called it Fort Saint Louis de Louisiane, reflecting its inclusion in this alternative plan.

Officials in New France strongly opposed La Salle's vision for a Mississippi Valley empire, as well as his specific activities in Illinois. As they knew, La Salle intended to siphon away fur trade from the northern route and from Montreal. Even before the actual creation of the Illinois outpost, New France authorities worried about competition from the new project and forced La Salle to promise never to interfere with the northern trade.[48] During the initial stages, La Salle's project was frequently under suspicion of such illegal trading activity.[49] In 1680, Intendant Duchesneau complained to the king that La Salle was not just an explorer but an illegal fur trader and empire builder: "La Salle, under the pretext of [making] a discovery sent two traders and himself traded in the Outaoases [Ottawa] nations which are not part of his [Illinois] concession. And he gave licenses to several individuals and *habitants* who he does not at all use for discoveries, to go and trade [in the north]. . . . All this is very bad for the colony [of New France]."[50] The fledgling colony in Illinois was a threat to New France interests, especially as long as Frontenac was governor. The rivalry between the Illinois proprietors—La Salle and his partner, Henri de Tonty—and New France officials over the fur trade would only grow over the course of the 1680s.[51]

But if La Salle caused frustration for New France officials, on the ground he had his own frustrations, owing most of all to insubordination among his men. The problems started with La Salle's earliest settlement in Illinois, when nearly every one of his men deserted either en route or shortly after arriving in the region.[52] Altogether, La Salle lost at least thirty men and spent most of his time during these early expeditions chasing after deserters.[53] After building a small fort on the Illinois River in November 1679, La Salle returned to Fort Frontenac for more supplies. Arriving back in Illinois in July 1680, he found that his remaining men had abandoned him and destroyed his fort.[54] As the priest Louis Hennepin wrote, even the very name of this first fort in Illinois, called Fort Crevecoeur, or broken heart, was a testament to the frustration the leaders felt toward their disloyal men: "We named it the Fort of Crevecoeur, because the desertion of our Men, and the other Difficulties we labour'd under, had almost broke our Hearts."[55] Having fled Fort Crevecoeur in the spring of 1680, a member of the deserting party turned and scrawled a message in a wood block hanging on the remains of the looted fort: "Nous sommes Tous Sauvages" ("We are all savages").[56]

Much to La Salle's frustration, these defiant deserters pursued their own interests. A good example is a man called Michel Accault, a fur trader who accompanied La Salle to the interior. As one priest later wrote, he was "famous in this Illinois country for all his debaucheries."[57] In 1680, Accault almost certainly participated in several attempts to mutiny against La Salle's leadership. Assigned to help Father Louis Hennepin explore the Mississippi in 1680, Accault abandoned the priest and stole the goods that had been entrusted to him as gifts to the Indians.[58] This left Hennepin alone with a single guide to travel through an unknown country.[59] Hennepin later found Accault returning from a fruitful hunting season, "descending the River of Bulls with [a] Fleet of Canow's well stor'd with Provisions."[60] He was "reproached for a Base Fellow, who had refus'd to accompany us for fear of being famished by the way."[61] But he survived, and he profited.

Indeed, men like Accault were opportunistic and self-interested. On one occasion, Hennepin recalled a conversation he had with Accault, one of the very rare moments in which the words of a fur trader are captured in the record. Standing at a fork in the road, disagreeing about which way to turn, Hennepin and Accault began debating about responsibility and authority in the middle of the Illinois woods in 1680. When Hennepin insisted on Accault's obligations to the government in New France, as well as to La Salle, Accault and some others rejected this notion: "My men would never consent, telling me that they had no Business there, and they were oblig'd to make all the haste they could towards the North, to exchange their Commodities for furs. I told them, that the Public Good was to be preferr'd to the Private Interest; but I could not persuade them to any such thing."[62] Accault felt no allegiance to larger imperial goals or to La Salle's project, and he did not quibble with Hennepin's view that he was pursuing only his *private interest*. In fact, he embraced this description, emphasizing the lack of political allegiance he felt to the government or to local authorities like Hennepin. As Hennepin recalled, "[Accault] told me that every one ought to be free." Accault then led the canoe up the river, to where he wanted to go.[63]

Men like Accault were successful, profiting greatly in the Illinois. For their part, Illinois Indians welcomed these men. But in spite of successes like Accault's, or indeed perhaps because of them, the whole colony frustrated Quebec officials. In 1683, the new governor-general of the colony of New

France, Joseph-Antoine Le Febvre de La Barre, wrote a memorial to the king, informing him about La Salle's activity in Illinois. "You will please tell me what you want me to do," he wrote, for "Sieur de La Salle by his arrogance has turned his head." La Barre especially complained about La Salle's efforts to effect "his plan, which is to attract *habitants*" to what amounted to an outlaw plantation, full of men like Accault. The governor worried that he would soon "debauch all the lazy and idle men of this country [New France]" by recruiting them to his illicit settlement. As La Barre told it, La Salle aimed to make his own independent colony or, in the words of the frustrated governor, "to try to make an *imaginary kingdom*."[64]

Of course, given La Salle's struggles to control his men, La Barre's description was apt. Although he had grand imperial visions, La Salle could not realize them. Nor could the Jesuits, whose hopes of keeping the Illinois separate from the French were now dashed by the arrival of La Salle. Meanwhile, the government in New France opposed colonial activity in the region altogether. It was hard to see what kind of empire would possibly come of these competing agendas, chaotic beginnings, and quixotic visions. None of them was likely to be realized. In the early 1680s, Illinois was an imaginary kingdom, indeed. But this was when Indian affairs suddenly and radically changed the situation.

಄

When the Iroquois attacked the Illinois in 1680, it appeared to the French like the Illinois were too weak to defend themselves. As the Iroquois descended the Illinois Valley, Illinois men pathetically ran away and did not even defend the women and children of their villages. Poignantly, most of the several hundred victims of the attacks were women.[65] Moreover, French audiences familiar with descriptions of the Illinois in the *Jesuit Relations* and other colonial correspondence might have remembered a previous episode in which the Illinois men similarly abandoned women and children to Iroquois violence.[66] Shocked by this apparent cowardice, the French concluded that the Illinois were just devastated. La Salle, who gave the most graphic account of the attack and its aftermath, said they were "incapable of resistance."[67]

As the Iroquois attacks on the Illinois were followed by more attacks on other Algonquians, the French realized that they had few options. Over the course of the Beaver Wars, the French had supported several Algonquian groups in an effort to prevent the Iroquois from dominating the Great Lakes. The future of the fur trade and the very existence of New France seemed to hinge on making sure Algonquians remained motivated to resist the Iroquois and, most important, never to ally with them.[68] When English traders began moving into the Illinois Country in the 1680s, attempting to coax the Illinois into an alliance against French-allied tribes in the Great Lakes, pressure on the French increased.[69] The attack on the Illinois in 1680 was a dramatic beginning to a change in policy. As the French now saw it, failure to support the Illinois would be perceived by the latter as "abandonment," raising the possibility that the tribe would align against Quebec.[70] Meanwhile, French explorations in the Illinois region in the 1670s and 1680s had made it clear that the Illinois were a key population in the West. They were, one priest wrote, "the Iroquois of this Country here who will make war with all the other nations."[71] Summing up the new attitude toward the Illinois alliance, the king himself wrote in 1686, "There is nothing more important than sustaining the Illinois and the other allied nations against . . . those that the Iroquois send in war. It would be better to engage them than to let [the Iroquois] destroy these nations when all of them can be sustained by commerce."[72] Despite reservations, and despite how remote the territory was from Quebec, the French policy became to "hold the hand of the Illinois."[73]

The decisions to support the Illinois and to extend commercial routes into their territory represented major changes for a government still reluctant to send traders into the interior, let alone into such a distant zone. The French government now began to send gifts and ammunition regularly into the interior. For the most part the new policy was a program to supply the Illinois with trade goods, arms, and military assistance. In 1686, the government of New France supplied 400 rifles to the Illinois living around Fort St. Louis des Illinois. Another load of supplies that year included 150 firelocks and 300 muskets. In exchange for supplies, according to the proprietors of Fort St. Louis, the Illinois chiefs "promised to do their duty to fight the Iroquois."[74]

In addition to providing ammunition, the French also supported the Illinois through military organization. In 1683, La Barre raised troops and planned a joint French-Algonquian attack on the Iroquois. When it failed at the last minute, the Illinois felt betrayed. In the wake of this debacle, the king recalled governor La Barre.[75] His replacement, Jacques-René de Brisay Denonville, quickly summoned all the Algonquians to support the Illinois in a major counterattack against the Iroquois in 1687, which was successful.

But gifts and military supplies, while important, were not enough to secure the Illinois to the alliance, especially in a period when French support seemed to waver. As Duchesneau put it, the French must mediate the rivalries among the Algonquians and "keep these people united" under the leadership of Onontio, the French governor.[76] And yet if the French hoped to have the Illinois and all their Algonquian neighbors follow the commands of Onontio, they had to learn "to take cognizance of all their differences, however trifling these may be."[77] This was not a simple matter. The Illinois, like most Algonquians, dealt with outsiders only after they had been turned from strangers into relatives. Algonquian diplomacy relied on personal relationships and face-to-face negotiations. Thus the alliance could not be achieved remotely from Quebec by a figurehead like Onontio. Instead it had to be achieved by actual people who had established personal relations with the Illinois.

Fortunately for the officials, there were people who had done just that. Since the 1660s, the Illinois had welcomed French newcomers into their world, especially at Kaskaskia. Examples abound. An Illinois chief named Oumahouha adopted the Recollect priest Zenobé Membré in 1680, welcoming him and telling him that "he loved him like a son."[78] A French trader named Villeneuve was assimilated into an Illinois lineage, his identity so thoroughly transformed that he wore the distinctive tattoos of an Illinois warrior all over his torso.[79] French fur traders married into Illinois families. Priests were treated to calumet ceremonies. These were the kinds of relationships that turned French strangers into Illinois kinsmen.

These relationships could be instrumental for mediating the alliance. Consider the example of La Salle himself, who used personal connections and status in Kaskaskia to mediate an alliance between the Illinois and Miami in the early 1680s.[80] As a fur trader observed, longstanding enmity had poisoned the relationship between the Miami and the Illinois, who "hate each other reciprocally."[81] In the early 1680s, this mutual antagonism threatened the whole French strategy, as the Miami and Iroquois colluded to attack the Illinois.[82] Since this would have started a major war for which the French were clearly not prepared, the diplomacy became complicated.[83] The French needed to make the Miami stand down.

It was La Salle who achieved this, and he did so through on-the-ground relationships that were clearly impossible for French administrators to establish back in Quebec. Together, the Illinois, Miami, and La Salle worked out an arrangement whereby La Salle became a trusted kinsman, helping to seal the alliance. To do this, La Salle adopted the identity of Ouabicolcata, a deceased Miami chief. He *became* Ouabicolcata, reincarnated. Delivering a speech to the Miami, he promised them that his identity had transformed:

"Think him not dead; I have his mind and soul in my own body; I am going to revive his name and be another Ouabicolcata; I shall take the same care of his family that he took in his lifetime. . . . My name is Ouabicolcata; he is not dead; he lives still, and his family shall want for nothing, since his soul is entered into the body of a Frenchman, who can provide his kinsmen abundantly with all things needful."[84] With this speech, La Salle appealed to the Natives in language that, as he said himself, was "perfectly adapted to their sensibilities." He promised to become, like Ouabicolcata had been, a provider, bringing goods and "all things needful." In so doing, La Salle was welcomed among the opportunistic Miami. Through him, a kinsman, they allied themselves to the Illinois.[85]

This kind of mediation was impossible for the French to achieve just by sending weapons and goods. It was agents like La Salle and the Jesuits who could provide the important "infrastructure" of the alliance.[86] The nascent colony at Fort St. Louis and the mission of the Immaculate Conception were the necessary infrastructure of French policy and alliance among all these crucial Indian groups of the West. Ironically, La Salle's installation in Illinois, envisioned as a separate colonial project and formerly opposed by New France officials and merchants, was now indispensable to New France as officials sought to prosecute the war. Collaborating, officials and colonial schemers worked together for mutual goals. Now the Illinois outpost was becoming an unplanned, even unintentional, part of the empire. But an even more unintentional reality was this: the French were supporting an Indian world on the rise.

သ

As they came to support the Illinois, the French misunderstood the Illinois's power. For instance, as Indians gathered around the Grand Village of the Kaskaskia, La Salle boasted that they were there to be with the French and that they were "dependent" on him.[87] In fact, Illinois motives in this period went well beyond what the French understood. Rather than meekly seeking protection, the Illinois were continuing a decades-old rise to power and following a course that was aggressive, not defensive. Even moments that the French perceived as signs of weakness—such as the attack they suffered in 1680—can actually be read as a sign of the Illinois's power and ambition in this period. The Illinois were building strength, and French support only added to an ongoing bid for power.

Although La Salle thought that the Illinois's arrival at the Grand Village was a response to his presence, the Illinois were actually coming together well

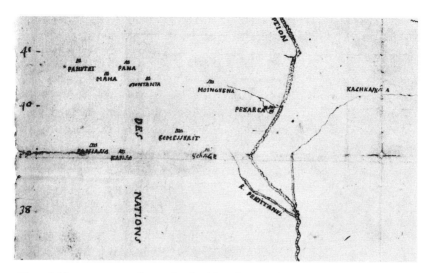

Figure 8. Marquette map of 1673, detail. Although most Illinois villages were located to the west of the Mississippi River in the 1670s, they moved east in the 1680s to unite at the top of the Illinois River Valley.

Courtesy of the Illinois History and Lincoln Collections, University of Illinois, Urbana-Champaign.

before the French arrived in Illinois. Frenchmen often badly misinterpreted what was happening as Illinois migrants moved to the Grand Village in a massive consolidation that had begun years earlier. Father Claude Allouez is a good example. As he wrote in 1666, "[The Illinois] used to be a populous nation, divided into ten large Villages; but now they are reduced to two."[88] Allouez said "reduced," but the villages he visited at the top of the Illinois Valley were much larger than previous Illinois settlements. Moreover, additional Illinois-speakers were arriving here from the West all the time. As Allouez himself confirmed in the 1670s, Kaskaskia had grown huge. "I found this Village largely increased," he wrote of Kaskaskia, as the village increased from seventy-five to about three hundred cabins in 1675.[89] After the attack by the Iroquois in 1680, the Illinois-speakers immediately gathered even more people together at Kaskaskia, right in the center of the violence. They simply continued a consolidation that was already underway. In some respects, they were not weakened but strengthened.

It is important to note that when the Iroquois attacks began, many of the Illinois were located to west of the Mississippi River, where they had built power on bison and slaving. Surely when violence began in the Illinois Valley, they could have stayed to the west, out of the way and aloof from the Iroquois Wars. Instead they began to move east, back to the Algonquian world, to the top of the Illinois River Valley, and into the heart of the violence. As Allouez said, they were collecting at Great Kaskaskia in a huge melting pot: "Formerly, it was Composed of but one nation, that of the Kachkachkia; at the present time, there are 8 tribes in it, the first having summoned the others, who inhabited the neighborhood of the river Mississippi."[90] Allouez acknowledged that the Illinois were moving *eastward* in this violent time. By 1681, as La Salle reported, the Grand Village was even more mixed up, containing "some of the tribes composing the nation of the Illinois [including] the Peoria, Kaskaskia, Tamaroa, Coiracoentanon, Chinko, Cahokia, Chepoussa, Amonokoa, Cahokia, Quapaw, and many others." Together they "form[ed] the village of the Illinois made up of about 400 huts."[91] Three years later, the village included the same lineup, including now the Tapouero and Maroa as well.[92] In the concept of historian Michael Witgen, the Illinois were "shapeshifting," adopting the unified identity of "Illinois" even as they preserved their "microlevel" identities as members of what La Salle called their "familles" or, perhaps, doodemag.[93] Significantly, it was kinship, the common ancestry dating back before the contact era began, that helped make this shapeshifting possible. La Salle made the point that "all of these nations are comprised beneath the name Illinois because they are related and because there are a few families of each within the village of Kaskaskia."[94]

In addition to shapeshifting, this consolidation was facilitated by an inclusivist political strategy.[95] In the Grand Village, outsiders were welcomed. Chickasaw and Shawnees, who spoke a totally foreign language, were welcomed to the area of the Grand Village in the 1680s, as were Miami after 1681.[96] A short distance away, other groups settled as well, adding to the population center with possibly five to ten thousand more people.[97] And of course the Illinois welcomed Frenchmen like La Salle. The Illinois incorporated these "strangers" into their community and built strength. By 1683, they were in the largest population center on the continent north of Mexico—twenty thousand people within walking distance of one another.

The massive size of the Grand Village gave the Illinois safety, allowing them to redouble their efforts in slaving. Throughout the 1680s, La Salle and Hennepin frequently noted how the Illinois brought slaves up the Illinois River after their raids in the West.[98] Many of these captives were probably assimilated into the patrilineal households of the Illinois as second and third wives. Put to work as farmers and especially as meat and hide processors in

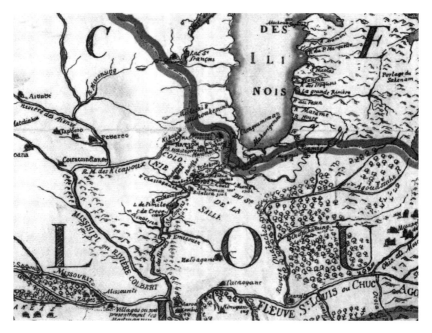

Figure 9. Detail of Franquelin's map of 1684, with the Grand Village of the Kaskaskia. Many of the groups in this massive settlement at the top of the Illinois Valley were Illinois-speakers who had moved from the West, making the Grand Village and surrounding settlements North America's largest population center in the 1680s.

Courtesy of the Library of Congress, Geography and Map Division.

the bison economy, they became slaves "who they force to labor for them," according to La Salle. Many others were traded to other Algonquian groups in the Great Lakes who were in need of replacement kin. These were, again in the words of La Salle, the "slaves which they are accustomed to traffic."[99] In the context of continued Iroquois violence, the captives became a key to Illinois strength.

As they consolidated, the Illinois continued their violent trajectory from the pre-contact era. Each year, the annual cycle would feature agriculture, a winter hunt, and sometimes a summer or a fall expedition. Frequently in the 1680s, they would go to the east, supported by the French, and make war on the Iroquois, as they did in 1687.[100] But their more typical annual routine was to go west for slaves. In 1689, the Illinois brought back 130 captives from a raid on the Osage.[101] In the 1690s, they organized an expedition with 1,200 warriors against the Osage and Arkansas.[102] Indeed, by the 1690s, French observers noted that "almost all the village marches, and even many women accompany them."[103] The results were impressive. In one march, they "carried away captive [all] the people of a village."[104] And this wasn't an isolated incident. The general reputation of the Illinois in this period was that "they carry off entire villages."[105] In 1690, slaves brought through the Illinois Country included Siouans and Caddoans from the distant West, like the Kadohadacho, as well as Pawnee, Osage, and Missouria.[106]

As the Illinois expanded their reach into the Southwest, Siouan-speakers treated the Illinois as regional hegemons. The Illinois were so powerful that Indians like the Osage appeared each year at the Grand Village, as Liette noted, "to recognize some of their people [the Illinois] as chiefs."[107] New France intendant and Indian expert Antoine Denis Raudot echoed Liette: "This honor that they receive makes them believe that all the ground should tremble under them."[108] These were the wages of a hundred years of expansion in the borderlands.

French support helped the Illinois build power, both militarily and economically. With French alliance, the Illinois continued their business as merchants, trading both slaves and bison hides to the French and Algonquian allies.[109] In turn, they took French goods to allied groups in the Southwest. The demand for goods there was high, and the Illinois took advantage: "These [western] people not being warlike like themselves and having need of their trade to get axes, knives, awls, and other objects, the Illinois buy these things from us to resell to them."[110] They also likely benefited from the mediation of the French, who helped them make alliances with Algonquians like the Ottawa and Miami, former enemies whom they now were able to provide with slaves.

The Illinois's culture became quite militaristic in the Grand Village. As mentioned, their yearly cycle included a season of warfare. Liette noted, "It is ordinarily in February that they prepare to go to war." At this time of year, chiefs hosted feasts, collecting dozens of warriors together to convince them that "the time is approaching to go in search of men."[111] The war tradition in Illinois was animated by patrilineal kinship lines, traced through fathers and brothers.[112] Male relatives organized raiding parties to replace their lost brothers, uncles, and fathers. Demonstrating the imperative for patrilineal kinship replacement, one Illinois chief rallied male relatives together for an expedition: "I have not laughed since the time that my brother, father, or uncle died. He was your relative as well as mine, since we are all comrades.

If my strength and my courage equalled yours, I believe that I would go to avenge a relative as brave and as good as he was, but being as feeble as I am, I cannot do better than address myself to you. It is from your arms, brothers, that I expect vengeance for our brother."[113]

Although Liette noted the rituals involved as the Illinois prepared "to go in search of men," the more usual situation was that they went in search of women, as noted. This was probably owing in part to the logistics of warfare, since women and children captives were easier to subdue and control. More-over, the bison economy, as we have seen, created a demand for female labor-ers in Illinois. Perhaps most important, the preference for women captives may have had to do with the patrilineal kinship systems common to Algon-quian peoples of the Great Lakes that made women better candidates for assimilation than men.[114] In any event, commenting on the Illinois warriors in battle during the 1660s, French commissary and early historian Claude-Charles Bacqueville de La Potherie noted how they had "the generosity to spare the lives of many women and children, part of whom remained among them."[115] Marquette noted the same practice among the Illinois in the 1670s: "The Illinois kill the men and scalp them and take [prisoner] only the women and children, whom they grant life."[116] At the Grand Village in the 1690s, the tradition continued: "They always spare the lives of women and children unless they have lost many of their own people," Liette noted.[117]

The massive introduction of female slaves shaped life at the Grand Village. As La Salle said, there were "many more women than men" in Kaskaskia.[118] Relatedly, all eyewitnesses noted the polygamy practiced by the Illinois. La Salle wrote that most Illinois men had multiple wives in this period, as many as ten or twelve.[119] What the French often did not realize was that many of these wives were likely slaves.[120] A specific logic underlay these slave-based polygamous marriages. In the Illinois's patrilineal society, children took the identity of their fathers, regardless of whether their mothers were native Illinois or outsiders married in, or even slaves. Thus marriages with multiple slaves strengthened the Illinois's numbers, since all children would be raised as Illinois.[121] This mode of reproduction combined with the bison-based mode of production to encourage female slavery among the Illi-nois in this period.

Indeed, the large number of female slaves among the Illinois in the contact-era forces us to rethink the supposedly devastating attack on the Illinois by Iroquois in 1680. In many French accounts, this was a decisive blow, as the Illinois lost 700–1,200 of their people.[122] As Iroquois warriors invaded, Illinois men ran away, leaving women and children behind undefended. To the French, it was a sign that the Illinois were insufficiently warlike, passive victims, and utterly desperate for French support. But what the French did not realize was that the Kaskaskia village in 1680 was likely full of slaves, almost all of them women. The fact that the men gave up this number of women might not be a sign of Illinois weakness or timidity. It is probably better understood as a sign of how many slaves the Illinois had or how many they had access to. In fact, a likely reason the attack was so successful is because "more than half" of the Kaskaskia men were themselves away on a slaving mission.[123] The slave economy dominated the Illinois's life at Great Kaskaskia.

Meanwhile, they underwrote all of this slave-based power by taking advantage of the other unique resource of their borderlands environment: bison. Many descriptions of the Illinois by French observers noted the huge scale of bison exploitation that the Illinois undertook in this period. Hennepin recalled hunting with the Illinois from the Grand Village and observed their capture of four hundred animals. La Salle did likewise. But the most important eyewitness was Pierre-Charles de Liette, the commandant at Fort St. Louis des Illinois in the 1690s.[124] On one single summer hunt that Liettes accompanied, the Illinois pursued a "great herd" and killed a "great number of buffalos" after shooting off "an extraordinary number of arrows." The bottom line? One single hunt that Liette witnessed in the Illinois Valley yielded 1,200 animals.[125] Since a typical bison yielded 675 pounds of food, the Illinois utterly maximized their bison advantage at the Grand Village to support their massive population.

The Illinois used their strength to take revenge on the Iroquois. Frequent reports arrived back in Quebec detailing the gruesome rewards of the crucial alliance with the Illinois. In 1688: "96 Iroquois were killed [by the Illinois], the scalps of which victims were brought to fort Saint-Louis."[126] In 1689: "Our Illinois have brought us 25 [Iroquois] slaves. We have caused them to be burned. I did not count those that were killed on the spot."[127] Year after year, the tally grew; in 1694 the governor of New France estimated that the Illinois had taken a total of 400–500 Iroquois casualties.[128] The Illinois revenged themselves for their previous losses against the Iroquois.[129]

The French certainly contributed to the Illinois's power. They helped mediate disputes with the Ottawa and especially the Miami. But Illinois power was largely independent of the French, and the real logic of Great

Kaskaskia was opportunism, not desperation or dependency. Although they could have stayed out of it, they united at the Grand Village during a moment of violence, becoming the masters of the slave trade and the borderlands. Indeed, while the French flattered themselves by thinking that the Illinois were dependent, in fact the Illinois probably came to this place because doing so enabled them to combine their various advantages—bison and slaves—with the new opportunities of the French material support and Algonquian alliance.

❧

As New France supported La Salle's colony and the Jesuit outposts, this created an unusual colonial situation. For the officials, the imperatives of Indian diplomacy meant tolerating and even supporting a nascent colony that had placed itself apart, outside of the normal rules of French government. Because the administration in New France was dependent on the agency of La Salle and the Jesuits for the alliance, administrators could not easily dictate how the colony ought to operate. Things happened here that would not have been allowed in other parts of the empire.

One example is the fur trade. In 1681, Colbert reformed the fur trade, instituting a license system that limited the number of traders allowed into the West. But Illinois remained outside of the new rules, and La Salle and Tonty had authority to issue their own trade permits.[130] La Forest, who became Tonty's partner in the mid-1680s, explained the logic: the Illinois colony was on its own, financially. If the king wanted the Illinois alliance, he would have to permit Illinois colonists to trade for their own profit.[131] As a result, the king did grant exclusive trade rights to the proprietors in 1686 "in order to give them the means of meeting the expense of maintaining the fort."[132] Indeed, by 1686, the officials in New France had to recognize that the Illinois Country was the exclusive trade property of La Salle's partners. Denonville complained that Tonty and La Forest excluded licensed New France traders from the Illinois trade.[133] But nothing was done to stop this, even after Tonty and La Forest confiscated the goods of licensed Canadian traders in the Illinois.[134] No other part of the Great Lakes interior operated like this, with its own rules. Even as Colbert had tried to systematize the fur trade, Illinois was outside the system.

Another example is land. La Barre was frustrated that La Salle issued grants to habitants. For instance, in his 1683 grant to a voyageur called Jacques Bourdon, La Salle gave seigneurial rights, as though the colony was its own entity free of restrictions from New France.[135] This practice continued through the 1680s, and administrators often wondered whether this was even licit. As La Barre complained, the colony was attracting habitants and "debauch[ing] all the lazy men of [New France]."[136] To the New France authorities, the whole settlement flew in the face of efforts to keep farmers in the St. Lawrence Valley. Governor Denonville wrote in 1687, "M. de la Salle has made grants at Fort St. Louis to several Frenchmen who have been living there for several years without caring to return. This has occasioned a host of disorders and abominations." Elaborating this view, Denonville complained: "These people to whom M. de la Salle has made grants are all youths who have done nothing toward cultivating the land. . . . These people set themselves up as independent and masters on their grants."[137] In other areas of the West, illegal settlers were recalled and arrested. In Illinois, New France did not shut them down but rather allowed these "independent" colonists to be their own "masters."

Another problem with the Illinois colony from an imperial standpoint was the question of authority itself. New France officials realized that La Salle considered his new colony to be autonomous. "I have been advised," wrote Governor Denonville, "that Monsieur de la Salle claimed that the commandant of his fort in the Illinois was not under my orders."[138] The government of New France became increasingly upset about the state of the Illinois colony in the late 1680s. In 1688, for example, the governor persuaded the king to revoke the charters in Illinois. The fact that this legal action had no effect on the actual goings on at Fort St. Louis reflects the very weak control that New France possessed over the outpost. Still, it is notable: "In regard to the concessions made by Sieur de La Salle in the area of Fort Saint-Louis, since these cause disorders similar to those which have been noted, His Majesty permits that they be revoked."[139] Probably owing to the continued necessity of the Illinois alliance in the war against the Iroquois, the concessions were all renewed in 1690 when the king transferred the official charter of the colony from La Salle, who had died in 1684, to Tonty and La Forest. Not only did the king reconfirm the old concessions, but he granted to Tonty and La Forest the right to make new ones and charged them to "maintain and grow" the outpost.[140]

If all this suggests that Illinois was in a special position in the empire, perhaps the most dramatic demonstration of its distinctiveness occurred in 1693. It was in that year that Michel Accault, the former *engagé* and fur trader, signed a contract and paid six thousand livres' worth of beaver in exchange for a surprising new status—*landlord* of Illinois. Along with just one other man, Accault now officially controlled the small outpost in the Illinois Country.[141] This was the same Michel Accault whom Hennepin once called "a Base Fellow," "famous in this Illinois country for all his debaucheries." In the 1680s, he had deserted, disputed, and rebelled. Now he was the landlord, half owner of an official concession.

It is easy to see why Accault was in control in Illinois. Accault was extremely able and powerful in the colony. For one thing, according to La Salle himself, he was expert in dealing with the local Illinois-speaking Indians. He was "tolerably versed in their languages and manners." Moreover, he "knew all their customs and was esteemed by several of these nations [in Illinois Country]." In the often difficult task of winning the trust and affection of Indian groups, Accault "succeeded completely." And his character was impressive. Summing up Accault's qualities, La Salle wrote that the trader was "prudent, brave and cool."[142]

That a man like this took control of Illinois Country in 1693 tells us something important about Illinois's earliest history and its relationship to the French empire. Many early visions for colonial activity in Illinois had failed. New France had failed to keep its empire restricted to the St. Lawrence. Jesuits had failed to keep Illinois an isolated, primitive church. La Salle, now dead, had not created his alternative empire—it remained just an "imaginary kingdom." And yet Accault had succeeded. He became an important figure amid a powerful Indian population center, a place now reluctantly included in the French colonial empire. Accault's authority represented compromise and collaboration—among Indians, Frenchmen, and imperialists. To realize their goals, officials would have to collaborate with a man like Accault.

↝

In the 1680s, Indian affairs created a unique situation in Illinois. After the Iroquois attacks, the French became the "glue" that held together a fragmented social world of Algonquians in the pays d'en haut.[143] In Illinois, however, the exigencies of Indian policy also had another effect, which was to hold together diverse French people with competing visions of the French empire. While in most of the pays d'en haut it was *French glue* bonding *Indian fragments*, here in Illinois there was *Indian glue* uniting people with diverse schemes for empire. The imperatives of the Beaver Wars forced collaboration among Jesuits, fur traders, schemers, Indians, and officials.

But this collaboration seemed to be only as durable as the need for alliance against the Iroquois. Like so many relationships and experiments on the early American frontier, these accommodations were surely temporary and expedient. But meanwhile, on the ground, affairs at the Grand Village were entering a new phase. In the Grand Village, Jesuits, fur traders, and Indians were coming to understand each other, to forge relationships that went beyond the short-term imperatives of the fur trade or the Iroquois Wars. In 1694, an event was about to take place that would change the history of Illinois forever. Moving far beyond the hasty accommodations of the early years, this would be the beginning of a much more serious collaboration and the foundation of an idiosyncratic colonial community.

Chapter 3

Collaboration and Community

At the dawn of the 1690s, the French empire included an unintentional colonial outpost in the Illinois Country. Containing Jesuits, fur traders, Indians, and the defiant inheritors of La Salle's early Louisiana concession, it was a far cry from what anybody—whether in the government of New France or on the ground in Illinois—might have hoped it to be. Only the strategic imperative of Indian affairs, the all-important alliance against the Iroquois, kept imperial officials and the people in and around Fort Saint Louis collaborating. But while the resulting collaboration followed nobody's ideal design, there were measured successes. The Jesuits baptized hundreds of Indians during brief sojourns at their small mission. La Salle's concession contained a bustling fur trade center. Fur traders like Michel Accault profited. And the government had "infrastructure" to secure its important alliance with the Illinois.

Of course, the real success story of this period belonged to the Illinois themselves. In part owing to French support, the opportunistic Illinois at the Grand Village had reached the climax of their power, built on slaves, bison, and French merchandise. Having reached its maximum strength at twenty thousand persons in the early 1680s, the Grand Village complex still contained an enormous population, so many people that they were forced to relocate to Lake Peoria for more fuel in the early 1690s. From here, the new village known as Pimitéoui, or "fat lake," the Illinois continued to dominate the Illinois Valley corridor, funneling slaves from Siouan- and Caddoan-speaking communities in the West to Great Lakes Algonquians in need of captives to replace their war dead.[1] Exploiting their unique opportunities in the borderlands, the Illinois were some of the most powerful people in North

America. But pressures inside the village, pulling at the very fabric of Illinois society, were about to change everything.

Inside the village, tensions went along with the great power of the Illinois. Since their arrival in the prairie borderlands, Illinois-speakers had built power by assimilating outsiders. Much of this assimilation rested on violence and slave trading. In the melting pot of Kaskaskia, this produced resentment among certain individuals who did not feel fully integrated into the dominant culture. The most important tension at the Grand Village and Pimitéoui was clearly related to gender. The Illinois had survived and expanded by creating a mode of reproduction based on slavery and polygamy. But in this context, many women resented their treatment. In a violent culture, they were victimized at home, abandoned in battles, and oppressed as slaves. Under the surface, Illinois society simmered with conflict between the sexes.

In the 1690s, disempowered women among the Illinois found one place they could turn. Jesuits had been in Illinois since the 1670s trying to establish an Illinois church. Frustrated by the presence of fur traders, they probably considered abandoning the mission and mostly neglected the Immaculate Conception project after Marquette's death in 1674. But in 1689, a new group of priests, led by Jacques Gravier, reestablished the mission. This second generation of Jesuit priests in Illinois soon had a thriving presence. Unlike most others in the transitory Illinois frontier, they committed themselves to staying in Illinois for a long time and began to build intimate relationships with their hosts. One index of their intimate relations was their expertise in communication. As one observer in this period said, "the reverend Jesuit fathers speak the Illinois language perfectly."[2]

They spoke it most perfectly with Illinois women, who found in Christianity lessons that were useful for them. Working together with Gravier and other Jesuits in the 1690s, Illinois women created spiritual principles that helped them combat unfavorable polygamous marriages and the oppressions they experienced in the slavery-dominated social world of Great Kaskaskia. Their society had been shaped by slavery, and Christianity gave them a perfect way to resist.

It is not surprising that this produced conflict and threatened the accommodations that had allowed people to get along in the Illinois to begin with. Gravier criticized Illinois men and French fur traders and helped his female students refuse their abuses. No longer convinced like Marquette that most of the Illinois were "near Christians," Gravier confronted Illinois shamans and disrupted their ceremonies. Illinois men, for their part, rejected the priests and Christianity, subjecting their daughters to punishments when they attended mass. Meanwhile, disturbed by the tension that Gravier created, fur traders and the officials in La Salle's tiny fort in Kaskaskia refused to support the Jesuits and even openly opposed them. It was an uneasy situation, dividing the outpost and destroying early intercultural harmonies.

But then, on the verge of a crisis in the community, several of the competing interests in Illinois found a sudden and surprising way to get along: marriage. In 1694, the Jesuit priest Gravier solemnized a wedding between the fur trader Michel Accault and Marie Rouensa, daughter of the chief of the Kaskaskia. This marriage, which represented a complex compromise among many different interests, was the beginning of a new era in the colony, when pragmatic compromise brought people together. Importantly, unlike the early transitory collaborations in Illinois, this marriage was not just a temporary or expedient accommodation. Accault, Marie, Gravier, and the Rouensas came together without any of the "creative misunderstandings" that characterized early frontier relations. To the contrary, thanks to their sophisticated intercultural communication, these people knew and understood each other quite well. Their compromise was the beginning of a real community, a genuine collaboration.[3]

This would shape the rest of Illinois Country history in unique ways. Totally unplanned and contrary to the agenda of most people in the colony, let alone the government, the new community was an improvisation. With the marriage of Accault and Rouensa, Illinois was no longer just a bunch of defiant fur traders, opportunistic Indians, and schemers. The marriage created the kernel of an interracial Christian community, around which an idiosyncratic colonial culture would soon develop. Even as the consolidated Kaskaskia village at Pimitéoui was coming apart, this community would persist.

It is Gravier who gives us a window into this set of events. Not a totally reliable narrator, he probably exaggerated many things in the long letters he wrote to his Jesuit superiors. But Gravier's accounts of intercultural collaboration cannot be dismissed as mere propaganda, nor as the consequence of naïve misunderstanding, delusions of grandeur, or the failure to try to see the Native perspective.[4] Like other Jesuits of his generation in the Grand Village, he deeply understood the Illinois, had close alliances with them, and thus was probably one of the most sensitive observers of the Illinois's culture, ever.[5] His dictionary and writings are the best sources to understand this period of transformation, and together they reveal a depth of knowledge

about the Illinois.[6] And if Gravier's accounts were based on real understanding, so too were those of other eyewitnesses, such as Pierre-Charles de Liette,
Tonty's nephew and a military officer who arrived in the Illinois Country as
commandant in 1687. Like Gravier and the other Jesuits, Liette studied the
Illinois and deeply understood them, producing a 195-page manuscript, perhaps the most sensitive quasi-ethnographic description of any Algonquian
people in the seventeenth century.[7] Through sources like these, we can wit-
ness so much about the beginnings of this idiosyncratic, pragmatic colonial
community. Moving beyond transitory frontier relations, the inhabitants of
Illinois began a new era of real intercultural understanding.

༄

Jesuits and Illinois Indians made early and opportunistic accommodations at
the mission of the Immaculate Conception in the 1670s. But for various reasons, the earliest Jesuits did not spend much time in their new mission after
1675. Indeed, the initial conversions and baptisms, all the optimistic descriptions of the early mission in the *Jesuit Relations*, rested on surprisingly little
contact between the Illinois and the priests. Marquette was only able to spend
about three months in Illinois villages before his death in 1675. His partner,
Claude Allouez, spent most of his time traveling and moving throughout the
Great Lakes region from 1666 through 1689.[8] He thus spent no more than a
few months with the Illinois prior to 1676 and only a short time with them
during the 1680s.[9] When Allouez and Marquette wrote their reports of harmonious accommodation in Illinois, they were really describing a highly itinerant
and impermanent frontier in which they themselves were sojourners.

    When Jacques Gravier arrived to reestablish the neglected mission proj-
ect of Illinois in 1689, he ushered in a whole new phase of the missionary
frontier. In many ways, he brought the same goal that had motivated the
early Jesuits: an idiosyncratic Christianity on Illinois terms. But although he
had the same hopes, he and his fellow second-generation missionaries in
Illinois had a very different experience. The biggest difference was permanence. Because they lived in Illinois for such a long period of time, Gravier
and his partners among the second generation came to truly know the
Illinois.

    The differences between the first and second generations of Jesuits in
Illinois are many, but the most important place to begin is with numbers.
Before 1676, Marquette and Allouez spent no more than a few months
in Illinois villages, *in total*. By contrast, the second generation—including

Gravier, Gabriel Marest, Jean Mermet, Jean Baptiste Le Boullenger, Sébastien Rasles, Jacques Largillier, and Pierre-François Pinet—began a period of truly remarkable stability for Jesuits in the mission. By the end of his life, Gravier had spent fifteen years in Illinois. Marest spent sixteen, Pinet spent close to four years, and Mermet was an eighteen-year veteran of the mission by the time of his death. Le Boullenger, who arrived in Illinois in 1702, would spend fully thirty-seven years in Illinois. And Jacques Largillier would also spend more than thirty years of his life there.[10] Meanwhile, a number of other non-Jesuits also became particularly rooted in the colony. Most important, Pierre-Charles de Liette would spend many years in the colony through the early eighteenth century.

Because they lived there on a permanent basis, the French in Illinois, and particularly the Jesuits, were able to establish much better channels of intercultural communication with the Illinois in the 1690s. Allouez and Marquette had been able to achieve a basic competency in the Illinois language, which they viewed as "somewhat like the Algonquian."[11] Using an Illinois prayer book and assistance from a slave Marquette had received from Ottawa allies at St. Esprit, the early priests were able to communicate with the Illinois sufficiently to, as Allouez put it, "make myself understood."[12] By contrast, the men of the second generation expended heroic efforts to develop true fluency in the Illinois language. Indeed, the second generation of Illinois priests included five of the most exceptional linguists in the history of New France—Marest, Pinet, Gravier, Le Boullenger, and Rasles.[13] Jacques Largillier, a lay brother who lived in the Illinois Country from 1676 to 1714 and who copied Gravier's dictionary into the final form that survives today, was also an impressive linguist.[14] Together this group of priests achieved mastery of the language, as surviving sources demonstrate.[15]

How they mastered the Illinois language matters for our story. Like other Jesuits throughout North America, Gravier and his partners practiced, by necessity, a kind of "total immersion" language acquisition program in Illinois.[16] One aspect of their method consisted of constant practice and a great deal of solitary study.[17] Upon his arrival in the Illinois colony in the late 1690s, Gabriel Marest demonstrated the typical dedication to language learning: as one of his fellow Jesuits described it, Marest threw himself into the task.[18] In addition to working "excessively during the day," he reportedly sat "up at night to improve himself in the language."[19] Sébastien Rasles worked hard to master pronunciation, noting the various phonetic sounds in Illinois that were difficult for French-speakers.[20] Other Jesuits worked tirelessly to master the *mechanics* of the language, to comprehend rules of grammar, and to master the operation of verbs.[21]

But independent study and practice were not enough. As Rasles wrote, learning Indian languages like that of the Illinois was "very difficult; for it is not sufficient to study its terms and their signification, and to acquire a supply of words and phrases—it is further necessary to know the turn and arrangement that the Savages give them, which can hardly ever be caught except by familiar and frequent intercourse."[22] They simply had to go and live with the Indians, since "there are no books to teach these languages, and even though we had them, they would be quite useless; practice is the only master that is able to teach us."[23]

The second generation of Jesuits lived and traveled with the Illinois throughout their yearly cycle. This had always been Allouez's plan, to "live among them in the beginning . . . after their own mode."[24] But while Allouez seems to have spent just one winter traveling with Illinois hunters,[25] Gravier and his partners pursued the Illinois wherever they went, all year long, for years on end. As Marest wrote, the winter bison hunt was a major challenge. "It is then that we wish that we could multiply ourselves, so as not to lose sight of them. All that we can do is to go in succession through the various camps in which they are, in order to keep piety alive in them, and administer to them the Sacraments."[26] But if this was "all they could do," it was a lot. Following the Illinois, the Jesuits traveled through the country in order to maintain constant relations: "During the winter we separate, going to various places where the savages pass that season."[27] Rather than hanging back at the fort at the Grand Village or returning to Michilimackinac, Gravier and Marest followed the Indians through the prairies nearly every year, sometimes splitting time between two different camps. As Gravier recalled of the Kaskaskias, "One of our missionaries will visit them every 2nd day through-out the winter and do the same for the Kaoukia, who have taken up their winter quarters 4 leagues above the village."[28] Marest once traveled thirty leagues (seventy-five miles) to the winter quarters of some of his neophytes.[29] With tasks like these he was thankful that he was "fitted to travel over the snow, to work the paddle in a canoe," and that he had, "thanks to God, the necessary strength to withstand like toils." But it was all in the life of the Illinois missionary: "I range the forests with the rest of our Savages, of whom the greater number spend part of the winter in hunting."[30] As Marest concluded, "These journeys which we are compelled to take from time to time . . . are extremely difficult."[31]

In addition to travel, the Jesuits adopted many other aspects of Indians' lifestyle. For example, the Jesuits embraced the Indian diet and used meal-times as an opportunity to converse with the Illinois. As Rasles wrote, an exotic diet was the price they paid to remain close to the Illinois. Rasles related how a chief urged him to stay for a meal: "I answered that I was not accustomed to eat meat in this manner, without adding to it a little bread." But Rasles learned that he would have to adapt. "Thou must conquer thyself, they replied; is that a very difficult thing for a Patriarch who thoroughly understands how to pray? We ourselves overcome much, in order to believe that which we do not see." Rasles realized that he had to accommodate some of the Indians' lifeways if he wanted them to accommodate Christianity: "We must indeed conform to their manners and customs, so as to deserve their confidence and win them to Jesus Christ."[32]

The Jesuits were extremely enthusiastic about this collaborative project. After all, the ideal of Jesuit missionary activity was to live with the Indians in order to make a version of Christianity that was, as Loyola put it, "accommo-dated to those people."[33] Perhaps the most visible and important part of this project was language. The Jesuits had to translate their ideas into terms that made sense to the Indians. Surviving Jesuit dictionaries from the Illinois mis-sion reveal the important intercultural cooperation that enabled them to learn and to translate as they lived together with the Indians. Le Boullenger's dic-tionary, for example, suggests a happy collaboration between the priests and the Natives: "I help him to think, to speak."[34] Gravier's dictionary reflects the assistance he received from Native instructors: "I try to speak; examine what I say."[35]

Through such collaboration, Jesuits cultivated the ability to thoroughly *converse* in the Illinois vernacular. Not content just to read translations and preach to the assembled Indians—simply to "make myself understood," as Allouez had put it—the Jesuits' goal now was to both "understand *and* be understood."[36] Sébastien Rasles spoke of the challenges of understanding Indian speech, which required, in effect, becoming a student of the Illinois: "I spent part of the day in their cabins, hearing them talk. I was obliged to give the utmost attention, in order to connect what they said, and to conjec-ture its meaning; sometimes I caught it exactly, but more often I was deceived, because, not being accustomed to the trick of their guttural sounds, I repeated only half the word, and thereby gave them cause for laughter."[37]

Gabriel Marest, arriving in his first mission assignment in 1695, em-phasized the importance of being able to comprehend what the Indians themselves said about their religious experience. This was an extra challenge: "I have still more difficulty in understanding the Savage tongue than in speaking it, [even though] I already know the greater number of the words."[38] To help himself, Marest created a dictionary of the language: "I have made a Dictionary of all these words according to our alphabet, and I believe that, considering the short time that I could spend among the Savages, I had begun to speak their language easily and to understand it."[39]

It is worth considering the form of the dictionary Marest made. Although it did not survive, his description of it implies it was similar in form to Gravier's dictionary that is extant. Significantly, this was an "Illinois-to-French dictionary," not a "French-to-Illinois dictionary." Such a dictionary would likely have been useless for a Frenchman who was trying to *speak* Illinois, or translate concepts from French *into* the Illinois language. Instead, its more appropriate use would be to *listen* and *understand* what the Indians were saying in their own language. This reflects the idea that, for these Jesuits, learning language was not simply about introducing new ideas into the Illinois culture but fundamentally being able to understand the language in all its complexity. The form of the Gravier dictionary (and presumably Marest's as well) thus signals that the Jesuit often was a passive listener, struggling to understand. Such language tools differed fundamentally from prayer books such as the one carried by Marquette and Allouez and reveal the much greater comprehension that the second generation of Jesuits was able to attain in their mission over the course of time. Gravier's dictionary is a 590-page testament to the increased sophistication of his abilities *as a listener.*

By the early 1700s, one observer noted that the Illinois priests "speak [the Illinois] language perfectly."[40] With this ability, the Jesuits were no longer clumsy observers of Illinois lifeways and culture, misunderstanding all they witnessed. Instead they became, over time, almost like modern-day anthropologists—participant observers in the foreign culture that they increasingly came to understand on its own terms.

The results of improved communication were ambiguous, however. Better able to understand the Illinois, the Jesuits now learned that they were not as universally enthusiastic about Christianity as Marquette and Allouez had said. As his dictionary makes clear, Gravier had a much more sophisticated understanding of the spiritual worldview of Natives. "Manitou" was not an equivalent concept to the Christian God, "feasting" was not the same as communion, and "traditionalism" was still strong.[41] One word in Gravier's dictionary meant "I still have my old superstitions."[42] Jugglery, or what the

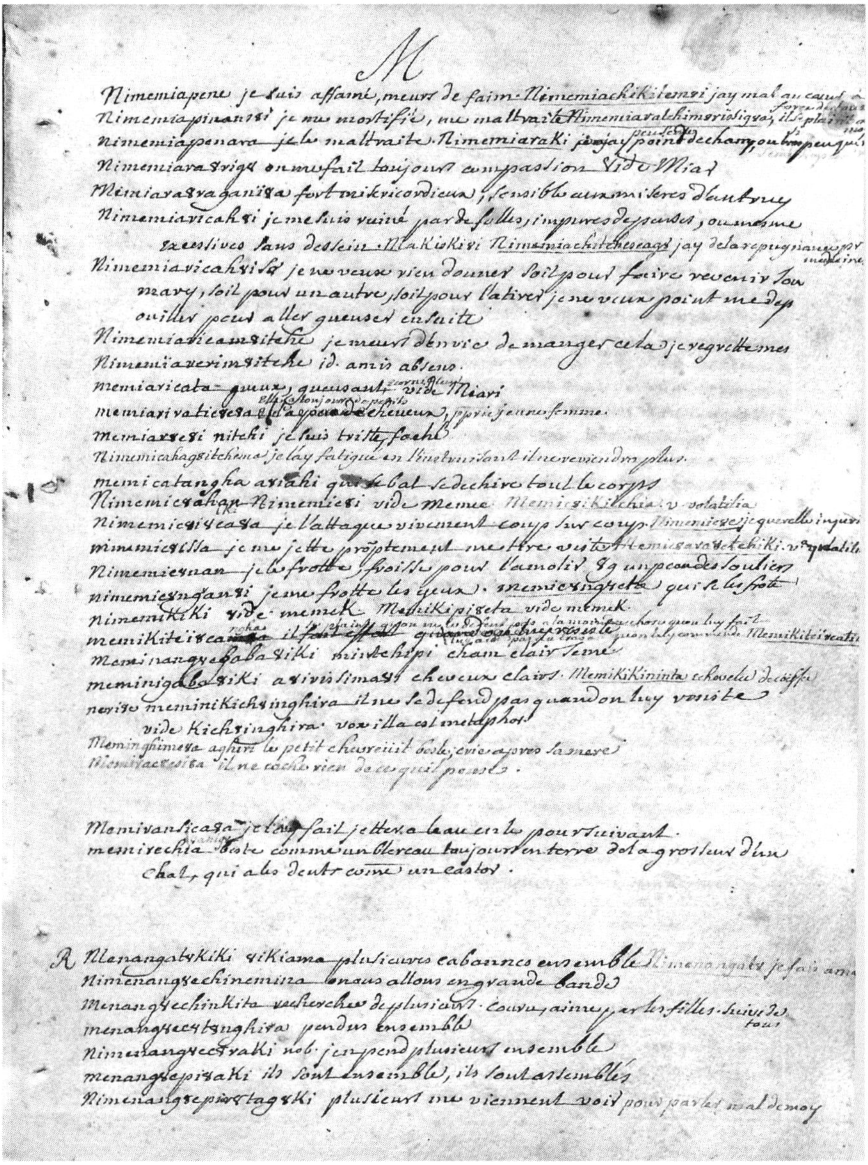

M

Nimemiapene je suis affamé, meurs de faim. Nimemiachikiitemsi jay mal au cœur

Nimemiapinanssi je me mortifie, me maltraite. Nimemiaratchimsiriiga

nimemiapenara je le maltraite. Nimemiaraki je ... point de champ

Nimemiarasriga on me fait toujours compassion. Vide Miar

Memiarasraganiisa fort misericordieux, sensible aux misères d'autruy

Nimemiaricahsi je me suis ruiné par de folles, impures despenses, ou mesme excessives sans dessein. Makiskisi Nimemiachitchesragi jay de la repugnance pr medecine.

Nimemiaricahsisa je ne veux rien donner soit pour faire revenir son mary, soit pour un autre, soit pour l'attirer je ne veux point me despouiller peut aller gueuser ensuite

Nimemiarieamsitchi je meurs d'envie de manger cela je regrette mes

Nimemiaverimsitche id. amis absens.

memiaricata gueux, gueusant vide Miari

memiarivaticisa ... cheveux, ppie jeune femme.

memiarsesi nitchi je suis triste, fasché

Nimemicahagsitchima je lay fatigué en l'instruisant il ne reviendra plus.

memicatangha ariahi qui se bat se dechire tout le corps

Nimemicsahan Nimemiesi vide memec Memicsikitchia v. volatilia

nimemicsiseasa je l'attaque vivement coup sur coup. Nimemicsesi je querelle injuri

mimemicsisa je me jette promptement mettre vite ... v. volatil.

Nimemiesnan je le frotte, froisse pour l'amolir &g un peu de soulier

nimemiesnganti je me frotte les yeux. memiesngreta qui se les frotte

nimemikiki vide memek Memikipigeta vide memek

memikiteiseama il fait effort

meminangsebabasiki minkehpi cham clair teme

meminigabasiki a rivissimass cheveux clairs. Memikikininta echevelé decoiffé

nerise meminikichsinghira il ne se defend pas quand on luy veut

vide Kichsinghira vox illa est metaphor.

Meminghimesa aghiri le petit chevreuil ... apres sa mere

Memisaccesita il ne cache rien de ce qu'il pense.

Memivansicasa je luy fait jetter a l'eau en le poursuivant.

memirechia beste comme un blereau toujours en terre de la grosseur d'un chat, qui a les dents come un castor.

R Menangatskiki sikiama plusieurs cabannes ensemble. Nimenangats je fais am

Nimenangsechinemina nous allons en grande bande

Menangsechinkita recherchée de plusieurs. Courus, aimée, ... les filles. suivie de tous

menangsecstsnghita pendus ensemble

Nimenangsecsraki nob. j'en pends plusieurs ensemble

menangsepisaki ils sont ensemble, ils sont assemblés

Nimenasgsepirstagski plusieurs me viennent voir pour parler mal de moy

Figure 10. Illinois-to-French dictionary by Jacques Gravier, 1690s. Like Liette's 190-page ethnography, Gravier's dictionary was a 590-page monument to his sophisticated understanding of the Illinois.

Courtesy of the Watkinson Library Special Collections, Trinity College, Hartford, Conn.

Jesuits identified as Indian traditionalism, was still widespread among the
Illinois, and Gravier knew it. As he wrote in a *Relation* of 1694, there were
many non-Christians in the villages, and he spent much more time now
"disabus[ing] them of the senseless confidence they have in their manitous."[43]
His dictionary showed a much more sophisticated understanding of Illinois
spirituality. In many ways, better understanding destroyed old naïve
accommodations.

This might have produced pessimism as the Jesuits realized that the Illinois were far from Christianity and that Native spirituality remained strong.
And yet there was another consequence of improved communication. As they
learned more about the Illinois, they became expert observers of a culture in
the process of transformation. Even as they learned about the persistence of
Illinois's non-Christian spirituality, the Jesuits could tell that the lifeway of
the Illinois was full of tension and contradictions. And they especially understood the costs of these tensions for one group of people in Great Kaskaskia:
women.

℘

The Grand Village of the Kaskaskia, and now Pimitéoui, had been built
on bison and slaves and exploitation. In Iroquois attacks and other warfare
throughout the second half of the seventeenth century, the Illinois had lost
lots of people and had used slavery and adoption as a means of replacing lost
kinsmen with outsiders. As we have seen, this strategy allowed the Illinois to
experience strength during a period when many Algonquians were reeling.
Arriving right at the height of the Illinois's power, Gravier became a kind of
sociologist observing this community's strategy and its result: the might and
dominance of the Illinois in the borderlands. And yet Gravier and his partners could also see something else: the way that this system of exploitation
produced tension. Gravier and his partners realized how slavery and adoption
failed to create a fully integrated society.

As a social strategy, the Grand Village was based on certain assumptions
and ideas. Most important, it was premised on a borderlands faith in the
flexibility of identity and in the potential for assimilation of outsiders.
Illinois-speakers at the Grand Village welcomed outsiders as they had always
done throughout their protohistoric migration into the Illinois prairies: by
adopting and assimilating them into patrilineal kinship lines. This is what it
meant when Oumahouha adopted Father Membré or La Salle "became"
Ouabicolcata. Behind this practice was an ideal: fictive kinship and adoption
would allow for complete identification and assimilation of newcomers and

captives within Illinois familles. But if this was an old strategy, in the 1680s and 1690s, the Illinois-speakers did it on a much greater scale.

Gravier and other second-generation Frenchmen in Illinois understood the logic of assimilating outsiders. Gravier's dictionary contained many terms that express these ideals of assimilation. "Relatives who I hardly remember are not my real relatives" was the sentiment expressed by a word for "relative" in the Illinois language.[44] Liette described how the expansive Illinois kinship system was designed for solidarity and inclusion: "It should be stated that they almost all call each other relatives."[45] All of the Illinois were supposed to feel connected to powerful men, identifying as "sons and relatives of chiefs."[46] Adoption was meant to incorporate newcomers and strangers fully as kin.

But if the Illinois hoped to make strangers into kin in the mixed-up world at Grand Village, there were people in this society who were not so well integrated. As words in Gravier's dictionary make clear, not everybody felt assimilated. Examples include words that meant "I don't love him like a real brother" or "I don't regard him as a relative." There were kinsmen who were totally powerless: "They don't notice me. I am not the master of it being a stranger." Another Illinois term could express alienation from a family lineage: "I am regarded in my family like a stranger. The others are more beloved." Gravier's list of such expressions was extensive: "Here I am like a stranger. I am not the master of anything."[47] And finally: "I am out of my country, of my village." "You don't treat me as a relative."[48] As these "definitions" suggest, in the mixed-up, slavery-dominated world at the Grand Village, there were many divisions. Although adoption and shapeshifting were supposed to turn strangers into family, some kinsmen continued to feel as "strangers" or simply as second-class kinsmen. Furthermore, fictive kin lines, and even real kin lines, did not always produce such strong bonds. As Liette said, "I have got men to agree a hundred times that their fathers, their brothers, and their children were worse than dogs."[49]

As Gravier and other Frenchmen learned, some men felt alienated from their kin lines. But if this produced a level of anomie for certain men of the Illinois society, it was nothing compared to the alienation experienced by many women. By the 1690s, Frenchmen like Gravier had a fuller understanding of how slavery affected women in Illinois society, especially through the polygamous and violent relationships that were part of the slave system.

Polygamous households among the Illinois seem frequently to have contained great tension. For instance, according to terms in Gravier's dictionary, one wife in a polygamous household was "the best loved wife" and one was "the wife who is the master of all the others."[50] One word in the dictionary, "onsam8eta," referred to "jealousy" and alluded to conflict, such as "she prevents him from going to her rival, to his second wife."[51] It seems clear that some Illinois women resisted marriage to a man already married, suggesting that the practice had clearly recognized downsides. Later in the contact period, a Frenchman noted that "The husband has full power and authority over his wives, whom he looks upon as his slaves, and with whom he does not eat."[52]

In addition to polygamy, Frenchmen understood that some Illinois women endured oppression and even violence in their relationships in the 1690s. Whether slaves or free, many women in Illinois had very little control over their own bodies.[53] According to Liette, brothers at the Grand Village made marriage arrangements on their sisters' behalf, forcing them to marry into families that they did not want.[54] Father Julien Binneteau put it this way: "According to their customs, [Illinois women] are the slaves of their brothers, who compel them to marry whomsoever they choose, even men already married to another wife."[55] Perhaps worse, as Hennepin noted, parents frequently pressured their daughters (possibly slaves) to use their sexuality for material gain.[56] Brothers even used their sisters to cover wagers "after having lost all they had of personal property."[57] Liette also noted how Illinois women were seduced and abused by powerful medicine men, "who they dare not refuse."[58] This produced strong alienation on the part of Illinois women.

If women could not choose their mates or avoid unfavorable polygamous marriages, these were not the only downsides of the Illinois gender order in the Grand Village. For women also endured a double standard when it came to fidelity. Several French eyewitnesses by the 1690s noted that Illinois husbands were free to have sex with other women but that women were expected to remain faithful and chaste. Some Illinois husbands abandoned their wives, and several terms in Jesuit dictionaries reflect the pain of a scorned wife.[59] For instance, Gravier listed words to express "I believe that he loves another; [said by] a wife who suspects him of loving a woman other than his wife." Another term meant "I believe that he wants to leave me. I believe that he loves another woman."[60] To be sure, these descriptions and terms contain the biases of Europeans for whom monogamy was the norm. However, while we cannot be sure philandering husbands were such an oppression for Illinois wives, violence is a different story.

In the 1690s, Frenchmen witnessed how women in Illinois experienced violence at the hands of their husbands and in their relationships. Frenchmen in this period took note of mutilation, including the cutting off of noses and ears, inflicted by "jealous" husbands on their wives.[61] In the most dramatic account, Liette described a gang rape of an Illinois woman who was caught in an extramarital relationship.[62] This was clearly a bad situation for many women. Living in Illinois households, whether as the direct subject of violence or even as the "best loved wife," was likely unpleasant. And while much of the harsh treatment was probably directed most importantly toward slave women, there is evidence that even some native Illinois women experienced a degraded status.[63] This may explain why, as Liette said more than once, it "rarely" happened that there was true affection in an Illinois marriage.[64] As another French observer wrote in this period, these patterns of violence and oppression made the Illinois distinctive: "Perhaps no nation in the world scorns women as much as these savages usually do."[65] Almost all of this was likely a consequence of the slave mode of reproduction in Illinois, which led to female oppression.

Meanwhile, in addition to violence, women in Illinois simply had hard lives. In traditional Algonquian communities, a division of labor separated the female agricultural and domestic labor and the male hunting and military work. But the bison economy in Illinois had skewed this balance in the 1600s. By the 1690s, according to Sébastien Rasles, the Illinois were killing two thousand bison each year.[66] Since hide processing and meat preservation were both gendered female, women had tremendous work burdens in the bison-based culture.[67] And while it was fairly standard for contact-era Europeans to remark on the disparity of work between genders in Native cultures, the Jesuits understood that the bison economy in Illinois actually did create an exceptional burden for Illinois women, adding to their agricultural duties.[68] As one Jesuit remarked, the women in Illinois were "humbled by work."[69]

The upshot was that Illinois culture was defined by great tension in its gender relations. Women looked for an escape, a way to resist. Gravier could perceive this. He began to work with them, in particular, building a Christianity catered to their needs. The initial goal of the Jesuits, as Gravier said, had been to convert the "whole nation" in Illinois. But if the divisions he now perceived made that less likely, they also created the opportunity to divide and conquer, to use the tensions within the society to make Christianity attractive to a portion of the whole. By the 1690s, many Illinois men "still had their old superstitions," so the Jesuits began focusing on the women. Together the Jesuits and young women made an Illinois Christianity based on a mutual understanding of each other's values and needs.

❧

Right from the start of the mission, Illinois women were among the most faithful attendees at church. As one Jesuit commented, "The women are . . . more disposed to accept the truths of the Gospel."[70] While men stayed home, the women and children went to mass regularly.[71] Even among the Peoria, more resistant than other Illinois-speakers to Catholicism, many women and children went to mass.[72] In Gravier's words, "The young women here greatly contribute to bring prayer into favor, through the instructions and lectures that I hold for them."[73] In the first few years, the Illinois Jesuits thus experienced exceptional success in baptizing women: "The women and girls . . . are very well disposed to receive baptism; they are very constant and firm, when once they have received it; they are fervent in prayer, and ask only to be instructed; they frequently approach the sacraments; and, finally, are capable of the highest sanctity."[74]

Gravier noted the remarkable ways in which the Illinois women approached the sacrament of confession. Importantly, this intimate, one-on-one interaction was only possible because the Jesuits had made tremendous strides in their linguistic skills. As Gravier wrote, "most of the older girls confess themselves very well, and some have made general confessions to me of their whole lives, with astonishing accuracy."[75] One girl, Gravier wrote, "has bared the depths of her soul to me, with much ingenuousness, I am convinced that she has a horror of everything that may be contrary to purity."[76] But she was not alone in making confession a popular sacrament in the Illinois church: "There are many who confess frequently and very well; and two young girls from 13 to 14 years of age began by making a general confession of their whole lives."[77] Confession was a site where Indian women and Jesuits established an intimate bond.

Illinois women were active agents in the creation of their version of the Christian faith. According to Gravier, they were especially skilled as translators, helping transform the Jesuits' sometimes broken Illinois speech into more eloquent and rich language. To the Jesuits, this assistance in expressing Christian ideas "in their manner" was invaluable. On one occasion, for example, Gravier relied on a woman to help him explain the Old Testament to an assembled crowd. "She explains each [Bible story] singly," he wrote, "without trouble and without confusion, as well as I could do—and even more intelligibly, in their manner."[78] When it came to the catechism, Gravier deferred to a young woman who showed a knack for creating effective translations. She "taught it as well as I . . . to the children."[79] In fact, Gravier admitted that because the women themselves were such good instructors, and held their own prayer meetings alongside those of the priests, the attendance at his own catechism lessons declined. This was no problem, Gravier wrote, since Illinois women were just as capable of giving Christian instructions as he was.[80] In any event, Illinois women were key participants in the construction of Illinois Christianity.

As the Jesuits no doubt understood, Christianity gave young Illinois women a value system and authority by which to resist the oppression that many experienced from their male relatives. While Gravier and his partners were not feminists, they nevertheless realized that lessons about Christian marriage and female piety were particularly interesting to women who they thought could "profit from [our] teaching."[81] Clearly the most important themes of Illinois women's Catholicism were chastity and piety. Gravier's dictionary shows how he helped cultivate a spiritual language against the common Illinois marriage and sex practices. For example, he most likely glorified ideas of chastity, such as "*ac8api8a avare*: A girl who is difficult to have in marriage, or to corrupt [sexually]."[82] He also probably emphasized monogamous values: "She prohibits her husband from going to a rival, a second wife."[83] Gravier almost certainly lamented the fate of prostitutes, as in "all the young boys abuse that prostitute."[84] He chastised practices that allowed for "debauched girls and daughters." Through all of these, and many more terms, the Jesuits and Illinois women constructed a Christianity for resisting the Illinois gender order.

Jesuit accounts from the Illinois mission in this period are filled with anecdotes about how women used Christianity to resist arranged marriages and polygamy and to preserve autonomy and chastity. In one case, for example, an Illinois woman, skeptical about the man her brother had chosen for her to marry, announced her intention never to marry but to remain celibate. Her reasons were rooted in the authority and meanings of Christianity: "Despite the threats that her family gave her" and the "persecutions that they continually forced her to undergo in her family," this woman insisted that no one would "change the resolution that [she had] made." As she concluded: "No, my Father, I will never have any other spouse than Jesus Christ."[85]

Other women used Christian-based arguments to resist polygamous marriages. One girl, for example, made her father promise never to marry her in a polygamous union. As she reasoned to him, "God forbids those who marry to espouse a man who already has a wife."[86] More dramatically, another girl first refused to consummate her marriage to the man her parents had chosen and then refused to marry that man's brother when the first died. It was Christianity that provided her with reasons to reject the Illinois practice of marriage whole cloth. As she explained to a priest, "The resolution that she had taken to live always alone—that is, never to marry—was due to the aversion that she felt for all that she heard and saw done by the married people of her country."[87] Thus did Illinois women resist the slave-based polygamy that now dominated their culture.

And if women used Christianity to resist polygamy and unwanted marriages, they also adopted Christian models of femininity and Christian wifehood as templates for their lives. Gravier's conversations with the Illinois women featured discussions about important female saints like St. Cunegonde, who reluctantly married St. Henry and then convinced him to take a vow of chastity. Gravier encouraged his neophyte women to model their marital behavior after Cunegonde and other "Christian Ladies who have sanctified themselves in the state of matrimony—namely, St. Paula, St. Frances, St. Margaret, St. Elizabeth, and St. Bridget." In a culture like that at Kaskaskia—violent and frequently oppressive to women—the role models of these pious saints were a means for women to resist.[88]

Soon there was a whole female subculture in Illinois that was built around Christianity. As Gravier observed, "most of the older girls confess themselves very well."[89] Binneteau wrote that "the women and girls have strong inclinations to virtue."[90] Thanks to Christianity, "the number of nubile girls and of newly-married women who retain their innocence is much greater" than among other groups, according to Gravier.[91] Soon the Jesuits could generalize that Christianity was a means for the Illinois women to resist the gender expectations of their own people: "There are some among them who constantly resist, and who prefer to expose themselves to ill treatment rather than do anything contrary to the precepts of Christianity regarding marriage."[92]

Given how Jesuits and Illinois women were using Christianity to resist polygamous marriages, it is not surprising that men would come to resent the Jesuits and to reject their teachings.[93] But Gravier made this resentment worse by enlisting the women to goad the men. He created an out-and-out battle of the sexes in Illinois. As Liette summed it up in the 1690s, "Although this nation is much given to debauchery, especially the men, the reverend Jesuit fathers, who speak their language perfectly, manage (if one may say so) to impose some check on this by instructing a number of girls in Christianity, who often profit by their teaching, and mock at the superstitions of their nation. This often greatly incenses the old men and daily exposes these fathers to ill-treatment, and even to being killed."[94]

Emboldened by his success among the women, Gravier redoubled his opposition to "jugglers." Gravier tried to stop them from performing their ceremonies.[95] He confronted those who "scoffed at all my solicitations to win them to Jesus Christ." No longer oblivious to competing meanings within Illinois spirituality, he understood the antipathy that many harbored toward his message and actively tried to "prevent evil conversations that take place in most of the cabins at night."[96]

This produced open conflicts and division. In particular, some of the chiefs, especially among the Peoria, came to oppose Gravier, the other Jesuits, and the women. As Gravier wrote, "The chief of the *Peouareoua* and of all the jugglers, with some of his relatives—of the same party, and among the most notable persons of the village—omitted nothing to embitter [people] against the Neophytes and against the Missionary." At one point, the Peoria men "had resolved to prevent the people from coming to the chapel to listen to me, because I inveighed against their customs and their juggleries."[97]

By the 1690s, many men in Illinois were opposed to the Jesuits. As Binneteau wrote, "the young men are no less opposed to the progress of Christianity than are the jugglers. Among them are monsters of impurity, who abandon themselves without shame to the most infamous actions; this is the reason why we find hardly a single young man upon whom we can rely for the exercises of religion."[98] The resistance was clearly widespread.[99] For Gravier, this all led to a pessimistic conclusion: "The inconstancy of all these savages and the corruption among all these southern tribes are so great that there is more to fear for the *Illinois* than St. Francis Xavier had to dread in the case of the Indians of the East."[100]

Resentment against the Jesuits was especially strong among the Peoria as they became aware of what the Jesuits truly expected. When an epidemic disease struck Kaskaskia in 1694, the first serious outbreak in the records, this exacerbated the tension as many among the Peoria blamed the priests. One Peoria chief in particular declared that prayer was "worthless." The Peoria men even came to articulate a new consciousness of themselves as non-Christians, opposed to the Jesuits' teachings. As Gravier explained it, "One of the oldest among the elders—full of zeal for the ancient customs of the country . . . went through the village, calling out: 'All ye who have hitherto hearkened to what the black gown has said to you, come into my cabin. I shall likewise teach you what I learned from my grandfather, and what we should believe. Leave their myths to the people who come from afar, and let us cling to our own traditions.' "[101] The Illinois Jesuit Thierry Beschefer had a similar experience a few years later: "They inveigh against our religion and against the missionaries. 'Where is the God,' they say, 'of whom the black gowns tell us? What does he give us to induce us to hear them? Where are the feasts they give us?' "[102]

These Peoria were articulating a new understanding of difference. The world was divided between Christians and non-Christians, and this difference was "innate."[103] This new understanding added to the breakdown in solidarity among the Illinois at Great Kaskaskia and Pimitéoui. Meanwhile, some of the tensions between men and women over Christianity produced even larger divisions in society, particularly between the *familles* of the Kaskaskia and the Peoria, who began coming apart dramatically in the 1690s. Echoing these divisions, one word in Gravier's dictionary suggested open rivalries: "he hates the Kaskaskia for love of the Peoria."[104] The Peoria and Kaskaskia were increasingly dividing themselves into *us and them*.

☙

As we have seen, language skills and an improved channel of communication helped the Jesuits both create a community of faith among Illinois women and simultaneously see how most Illinois men were opposed to them. This tension called for a resolution; it was unsustainable, obviously, to create an all-female church separate from the Illinois men or to go on encouraging the young girls to "mock the superstitions of their elders," even as the latter maintained their traditional practices and opposed Christianity.[105] Meanwhile, French fur traders came to Illinois in greater numbers, threatening not only to strengthen the Illinois men's opposition to the Jesuits but also to "debauch" the women in Illinois. In an unexpected way, Gravier found the resolution to this dilemma in 1694 in an event that transformed Jesuit strategy, and Illinois Country life in general, forever.

In 1694, the chief of the Kaskaskia, Rouensa, arranged a marriage between his daughter and the fur trader Michel Accault and excitedly announced that "he was about to be allied to a Frenchman."[106] Such an alliance could be valuable to both men, since it promised Rouensa better access to the fur trade and presents of the French and gave Accault the kinship connections that could facilitate a privileged position among the Illinois. However, it happened that Rouensa's daughter Marie was one of Gravier's best students, and she immediately refused the marriage. Like other women who had converted to Christianity, Marie insisted that "She had already given all her heart to God, and did not want to share it." In fact, she declared, "she had consecrated her virginity to God." Gravier gloated over this news, insisting that "these were her own words" and that he had not encouraged her refusal.[107] Of course, because Accault was well-known as a libertine and was "famous for his debaucheries," Gravier was staunchly opposed to the marriage and happily refused to perform it.

But the Illinois men struck back. In retaliation, chief Rouensa gathered all the chiefs of the village together, who quickly prohibited their daughters from attending mass. The chiefs sent a man armed with a club to chase off all the girls at the church and to desecrate the altar. Chief Rouensa himself punished Marie and expelled her, naked, from his home.[108] Meanwhile, the commandant Liette and the fur traders sided against the Jesuits; Liette warned Gravier that he would perform the marriage himself if the priests would not.[109] The situation was dire; Gravier now faced nearly all of the men in Illinois—both French and Native—united against him and the few women and girls who still dared to declare themselves Christians.

Gravier and Marie Rouensa began to realize that the entire fate of the mission was on the line. "All the threats against me trouble me not," Marie said, "and my heart is content. But I fear for God's word."[110] Marie Rouensa realized that her continued refusal would probably mean the end of the Jesuit mission. Thus she pragmatically changed her mind. Days after the crisis began, Marie proposed a new course; she would marry Accault on the condition that he join her and Gravier in trying to develop the church. Accault would give up his "debauchery." More important, a second condition of the marriage was that the Rouensas—Marie's parents and relatives—would renew their lapsed conversions and become firm Christians.

The solution had several advantages and turned the Jesuits' mission in Illinois on a new course. First, the marriage attracted the first family of Kaskaskia to the Christian project. Chief Rouensa, no stranger to pragmatism, took back all he had said against the Jesuits. As a condition of the marriage, in fact, Gravier forced Rouensa to become his ally in spreading the gospel: "But, before concluding it entirely, I wished the father [Rouensa] to gather all the chiefs of the villages in his cabin, and retract all that he had said, because it was all untrue; to express his regret for having forbidden them to pray to God; and to tender some satisfaction, at which I wished to be present."[111]

A second advantage of marrying Marie to a Frenchman was the effect it had on Accault himself. For when Accault and Rouensa married, Accault the

Frenchman became a newly dedicated Christian. "The First conquest she made for God [after the marriage] was to win her husband," wrote Gravier, "who was famous for all his debaucheries."[112] As Gravier said, through the instrument of the marriage, Accault became a new man, repenting for his "past life": "I have such a horror of my past life, he said, that I hope, with the assistance of God's Grace, that no one will ever be able to make me abandon the resolution I have undertaken to lead a good life in the future."[113] After his marriage to Marie Rouensa was formalized, Accault soon became committed—along with his wife and Gravier—to building the Christian community in Illinois. "Accault is now as zealous for the conversion of the Illinois as he was formerly opposed to it," Gravier wrote. He "renders good service to the mission."[114] Later another priest at Cahokia would praise Accault for performing "every service in his power" to help the missionary priests in their work.[115]

The marriage marked a clear change in strategy for the Jesuits. Long opposed to intermarriage, Gravier had always "prevented the French from forming alliances [with Indians]."[116] Furthermore, the Jesuits had originally imagined Illinois as a mission isolated from the polluting influences of fur traders like Accault. But Gravier was confident that this marriage was taking place according to Christian expectations. Marie understood and desired the life of a Christian wife; she prayed especially to St. Cunegonde and other female saints. Now the Jesuits began to consider that intermarriage might be not just a necessary evil but even a positive good. Indeed, in 1707, Gravier himself would write to the authorities in Rome to get their permission to continue "the contracting of marriages between a Christian and an infidel," which he viewed as "of the greatest importance for the strengthening of Christianity."[117] Meanwhile, Marie Rouensa would continue to strengthen the Christian community that the Jesuits and Illinois women had begun in Kaskaskia.[118]

But if Gravier, the Kaskaskia women, Accault, and the Rouensas created an authentic language of Catholicism and the beginnings of a Catholic community, others moved even further away. In fact, resistance within the divided village, especially among the Peoria, grew intensely after Rouensa's conversion. As the Kaskaskia women and now chief Rouensa grew closer to Christianity, one Peoria dramatically reflected on the divisions this exposed: "Let the *Kaskaskia* Pray to God if they wish and let them obey him who has instructed them. Are we *Kaskaskia*? And why shouldst thou obey him, thou who art a *Peouareoua*? Since he has vexed thee, thou must declare publicly that thou abandonest Prayer; that it is worthless."[119]

As this Peoria's words suggest, the optimistic early phase of easy accommodations in Illinois, the early intercultural dialogue helped along by "creative misunderstandings," was over. No longer misunderstanding each other, the Peoria declared themselves to be non-Christians and the Jesuits agreed. After the events surrounding the wedding, Gravier knew that his "flock" was now "divided." Binneteau in 1699 noted how the Peoria "inveigh against our religion and against the missionaries."[120] The final straw in the Peoria's rejection of Christianity would come a few years later when a Peoria man tried to murder Gravier.[121] The Peoria did not want him around at all.

But others did. Indeed, the Illinois women and their Kaskaskia families did want the Jesuits. And just as the Peoria and Jesuits were no longer living in a world of "creative misunderstanding," these people who *did* collaborate were not misunderstanding each other either. These new collaborations were something different than the early accommodations of the encounter period. Gravier and the Jesuits and the Illinois women did not get along because of naïve misunderstanding, the inability to see what each other really meant and expected. Instead, they knew full well what each other needed, expected, and gained from their collaboration, and on that pragmatic basis, they proceeded. Far more significant than a transitory frontier, this was now a real intercultural community. It would shape the rest of the colonial history of this place. All empire, all Indian diplomacy, everything, would happen through the infrastructure of an intercultural community that was taking shape without any government support at all and contrary to nearly every plan that people initially brought to the Illinois Country. It would be the anchor of an empire by collaboration.

☙

There is no evidence that the French government knew anything about this. In the 1690s, even as the drama of the Rouensa-Accault marriage was unfolding, New France began to contemplate shutting down the Illinois outposts. Soon the Beaver Wars would end, rendering the Illinois outpost more and more superfluous to the Quebec government's goals. Even as a new community had formed in Illinois, the outpost might no longer be necessary to the French empire.

Meanwhile, people began to disperse from Pimitéoui. As a military strategy, the consolidation that the Illinois had achieved at the Grand Village and Pimitéoui was no longer advantageous. Indeed, epidemics in the large population center during the previous several years had begun to reduce the population, adding to intramural conflicts in the village and motivating many to consider abandoning the massive settlement. At the same time, slave-trading expeditions in the 1690s were taking the Illinois-speakers more and more to the Southwest, where they encountered new economic opportunities separate from New France. Perhaps most important, the bison population upon which the settlement relied may have been diminished by years of overexploitation.[122] The large population center in the upper Illinois Valley was coming apart.

In this context, the new colonial community of Jesuits, fur traders, and Illinois might not have lasted long. But then, in 1698, La Salle's long-dreamed-of colony in the lower Louisiana valley was finally established. This changed the situation for the fledgling community, creating new opportunities for them as well as for people throughout the Great Lakes/Mississippi Valley borderlands. Learning about the new colony, the Kaskaskia abandoned the Peoria and moved down the Illinois Valley to the Mississippi River in 1700. The Jesuits followed. Marie Rouensa and Michel Accault and their children went, too. And so did several other Frenchmen who had married Illinois women in the succeeding years. And if the empire hardly even knew about these people, and knew little about the collaboration that they had established in 1694, officials would soon have to pay attention. The autonomous community—Illinois, Jesuits, and illegal fur traders—were about to make a colony where they would force government to collaborate on a significant scale.

Chapter 4

A Dangerous Settlement

In 1715, imperial officials in Quebec were surprised to receive a report about a settlement that had "secretly" formed near the junction of the Illinois and Mississippi rivers in Illinois Country: "About 100 Frenchmen, who secretly went up to Michilimakinak two years ago, after consuming the wares of the merchants who had equipped them, went to the Tamaroa on the Mississippi River, where 47 were already established."[1]

Although Canadian officials had grown accustomed to frustrating reports concerning independent-minded Jesuit missions, La Salle's defiant "imaginary kingdom," and rampant illegal trade in the Illinois region, the news about this settlement was especially disturbing. Totally unplanned and without government sanction, it sounded far more substantial and permanent than anything that previous *concessionaires* and missionaries had been able to achieve. If previous Illinois outposts were bustling stopovers for mostly transient populations, this was different: "He reports that [the illegal settlers] are living there at their ease; as grain thrives in that region they have built a mill, and have a great many cattle. They get as many savage slaves as they wish, on the river of the Missouris, whom they use to cultivate their lands."[2]

The high degree of development in this settlement was a shock to the colonial officials, as were some of the activities that these settlers were undertaking. In addition to robbing Canadian merchants, this report alleged, these renegade colonists, many of them married to Indian women, were also trading Indian slaves with the English in Carolina. As colonial officials complained elsewhere, the three leaders of this slave-trading operation were "leading lives which were not only scandalous but also criminal in many ways."[3] For the Canadian officials, none of this was good news: "This settlement is a dangerous one, serving as a retreat for the lawless men both of this Colony [i.e., Canada] and of Louisiana."[4] The colony was thriving and it was growing, all out of the control of the colonial government.

For historians, as for Canadian officials, this report from 1715 affords the first clear picture of an unplanned, self-directed colony on the margins of the French empire and outside government authority. While reports of illegal traders were not uncommon in the colonial correspondence relating to the pays d'en haut in this period, this development in the Illinois was something quite different. Here illegal colonists had clearly dug in for the long term, establishing families and creating farms and houses and windmills, all of which implied not mere sojourning but real community building. The size of the colony—150 Frenchmen, a third of whom had been there for longer than two years—also set this settlement apart from the typical tiny and transient fur trade outpost. The affluence of the colony suggested the seriousness of the enterprise as well, as colonists had obviously done well for themselves. As another report remarked, the Illinois colonists were "very industrious. . . . They help each other and possess about a hundred head of cattle and about fifty horses."[5] The news from Illinois, then, gives a view into a remarkable colony created wholly on local initiative—an independent settlement directed by colonists themselves, along with missionaries and Indians, at the margins of the empire.

But if the news from Illinois in 1715 was surprising for these reasons, what may be more significant from a historian's standpoint was the government's response. Since the 1690s, Canada had pursued a rigid policy of restricting trade and travel in the West, particularly in Illinois Country where illegal trade flourished. The official response to illegal colonists like these in the Illinois Country usually involved arrest warrants and orders to return to the St. Lawrence settlements. Judging from past experience, then, one would have expected French authorities to try to shut down this colony in 1715. But what administrators did instead was something totally different and thus significant. Acknowledging the failure of recent policy on the frontier, administrators admitted they had become impotent to restrain the will of illegal traders and the Jesuits whom they saw as supporting them. In the case of this new Illinois Country settlement, where colonists obviously had invested so much labor, the governor in Quebec knew he faced an especially great challenge. "We see no possibility of preventing it," he wrote. The best officials could hope for, the governor admitted, was to try to *work with* the colonists. Rather than arresting them and shutting them down, the French officials resolved to embrace the settlement, to channel the agency of the colonists toward a mutually acceptable order on the frontier. The idea was to create a kind of collaboration between local agency and imperial goals: "But as we see no possibility of preventing [the settlement], we believe, Sir, that we might render it useful for the service of the King and of the Colony by sending there a dozen Soldiers, Commanded by an officer, who could build a fort there, and gradually establish order among those Frenchmen."[6]

Here was a novel approach to governance on the French frontier of North America: not top-down, rigid planning directed from Versailles but acquiescence to and purposeful collaboration with the colonists themselves. In 1717, the French government officially moved Illinois out from Canadian jurisdiction to that of the permissive Louisiana colony. No arrests were made, and no attempts to shut down the illegal colony were seriously considered. Louisiana sent its first provincial commandant to Illinois in 1719, whose efforts to "establish order" mostly ordained and legitimated what the colonists themselves had already done on their own. Appointing the first provincial officials, the new commandant, Pierre Dugué de Boisbriant, chose local men in Illinois who only recently had been considered criminals by the government. Despite the fact that Louisiana had moved to ban intermarriage between Indians and Frenchmen in 1715, the practice was endorsed and continued in Illinois. No top-down imposition of strict regulations, this new governing style defined Illinois as an official colony but one that was conspicuously shaped by local agency. A distinctive imperial style was taking shape on the frontier of the French empire in Illinois: empire by collaboration.

એ

In the 1690s, Illinois was home to men like Michel Accault, men who lived for their own opportunistic interests. Accault, the former *engagé*, had become an official proprietor of La Salle's concession in 1693, and he married Marie Rouensa, the daughter of the Illinois chief, a year later. He, like other Frenchmen in this nascent community, had benefited from the ambiguous and disordered imperial politics of the late seventeenth century. In the eyes of the government, however, men like Accault were still outlaws, as a report from the governor of New France made clear: "[The Frenchmen] have been living [in Illinois] for several years without caring to return. This has occasioned a host of disorders and abominations. These people to whom M. de la Salle has made grants are all youths who have done nothing toward cultivating the land. They keep marrying, after the manner of the savages of the country,

Indian squaws whom they buy from the parents with merchandise. These people set themselves up as independent and masters on their grants."[7]

Men like Accault had succeeded in setting up an autonomous settlement with Indians in Illinois, but their lifeway was coming under considerable threat. During the Iroquois Wars, imperial administrators in New France had reason to tolerate and even support the illegal Illinois settlers. But by the turn of the century, two things happened. First, a glut of beavers meant that furs from Illinois—which were viewed as inferior in any case—were not wanted anymore by merchants in Montreal. Second, and more important, the Beaver Wars wound down and officially ended in 1701. New France's alliance with groups like the Illinois Indians, so important during the war against the Iroquois, was now a lower priority. Officials in Quebec drew up a new plan under which Indian alliances in the pays d'en haut could now effectively be managed at two major outposts—Detroit and Michilimackinac—while the rest of the French outposts in the West could be considerably reduced, if not completely abandoned.[8] In 1697, New France intendant Jean Bochart de Champigny proposed abandoning the western posts among the Illinois and Miami altogether.[9]

But imperial advocates of western expansion had already found a new justification for their projects. Writing in 1694, Tonty observed the mounting dangers posed by the English incursions into the West via the Ohio River. In 1688, he himself had intercepted Englishmen on their way through Illinois to the Mississippi, an event that had prompted the king to order a repossession of the Illinois Country and surrounding areas after it had been temporarily abandoned that year.[10] As he argued, the English threat now had replaced the Iroquois threat as the new imperative for continuing Mississippi Valley settlement. Even Canadian officials agreed that "[the English] are our most dangerous enemies from whom we have the most to fear."[11] By the 1690s, Canada received reports that English had infiltrated the Ohio and Wabash rivers.[12] One deserter from La Salle's party, Jean Couture, traveled to Maryland and later to Carolina, where he allegedly assisted English traders in penetrating the Ohio River Valley. As Tonty wrote, the English of Carolina were already "well established on an arm of the river which falls into the Ohio, which falls into the Mississippi."[13] If the English succeeded in their designs of continuing west, "they would not fail to submit all the nations of the upper country and by consequence, they would master the trade of our allies the Miamis, Illinois, and Ottawa, without whom this country [Canada] cannot subsist."[14] The king was convinced; in 1698 he called on Pierre Le

Moyne d'Iberville, who departed for the Gulf in 1699 to establish the colony of Louisiana once and for all.

The creation of the Louisiana colony had several immediate consequences for the Illinois Country. First, it introduced new commercial projects in the Illinois, in particular the fur outpost and tannery established in 1700 by Charles Juchereau de Saint-Denys on the lower Wabash River. This was the very kind of project that likely would not have happened under Canadian authority in this period.[15] Second, Louisiana created a refuge for the illegal traders from Canada, who found a permissive government in Louisiana claiming jurisdiction over all of the Mississippi River. Having finally dedicated the resources to create the colony, the king now hoped to populate the Mississippi Valley with Frenchmen and French-allied Indians, a goal that trumped the desire to arrest illegal coureurs de bois from Canada, who roamed Louisiana's new jurisdiction with impunity. Further encouraging these fur traders, Louisiana opened a new market for furs that Canada would no longer purchase except according to a strictly regulated license system.

Intra-imperial rivalry and competition between Louisiana and New France shaped the Illinois Country from this moment forward. The commission Iberville received from the king for the new colony drew the limit of the Louisiana jurisdiction at the Illinois River. Arriving in the Gulf in 1700, Iberville began making alliances with groups previously considered to be within the Canadian sphere of influence, including the Illinois.[16] But if Louisiana's plans for commerce and Indian affairs clashed with Canadian interests, it was the Louisiana colony's permissive stance toward Canadian coureurs de bois that really angered Governor Callière and Intendant Champigny. As soon as the Louisiana colony was established, men flooded to the Illinois and beyond, escaping the new restrictions of Canadian fur trade. By 1700, Callière and Champigny wrote to complain that all of their efforts to make the coureurs de bois return to the St. Lawrence settlements were undermined by the news of the Louisiana colony. "Only 20 have returned. . . . We are in difficulty making [others] return on account of the establishment of Mississippi, where we have learned the majority has gone."[17] In 1701, they similarly complained of continuing lawlessness in the West, perpetuated by the coureurs de bois thanks to the "welcome they will meet with on the Mississippi also, where they will take their furs." As Canadian officials worried, "this will induce many other unruly men here to do the same."[18] For men like Accault, here was the new lifeline.[19]

The development of Louisiana radically changed the Illinois colony's prospects. If the Canadian authorities looked to crack down on the illegal trade in the West, Louisiana soon opened up new opportunity for the continuation, and growth, of the Illinois colony. Just as the Illinois outpost was losing steam and Canada was instituting a neo-Colbertian policy, Louisiana became a reality. Indians and Frenchmen moved into the Mississippi Valley where they thrived in the new borderland between Louisiana and Canada.

The Indians were the first to move. New opportunities drew the Illinois toward what historian Stephen Aron calls the "American Confluence" of the Missouri, Mississippi, and Ohio rivers. Here the Illinois had for years built power and alliances among Siouan-speaking neighbors outside of the Algonquian world. With the end of the Iroquois wars, opportunities to sell Siouan and Caddoan slaves to Algonquians declined. But the foundation of Carolina in 1670 had created a new market for Indian slaves at Charleston.[20] Traveling via the Ohio and the Tennessee rivers, the Illinois could now bring slaves to Carolina. A 1709 memorandum from Louisiana shows that the English had established a slave-trading alliance with "neutral" Indians on the Mississippi, likely Illinois.[21] Probably in response to these opportunities, the Tamaroa moved back down the river, uniting in 1699 in a village with the Cahokia and possibly the Metchigamea.[22] When one French traveler passed through this village in 1699, he counted three hundred cabins, which was a huge population.[23]

Louisiana only added to these attractions. In 1700, the Kaskaskia, still the largest group of Illinois-speakers, left Pimitéoui for a new village location on the Mississippi near modern-day St. Louis. Getting ready to relocate to the new village, Rouensa himself said that he was being "called" by the governor of Louisiana, who evidently sent emissaries to the Illinois encouraging their move. Soon the Kaskaskia chief boasted that he was in a special alliance with the French in the South. As one priest put it, Rouensa "makes large promises and gets himself believed when he says that he is called by the great chief of the French [in Louisiana], as Father Maretz [Marest] has told him."[24]

By the early 1700s, all the Illinois-speakers except the Peoria had abandoned Pimitéoui and opportunistically settled several villages along the Mississippi. The Kaskaskia village, initially located at the Des Peres River, was the biggest settlement, led by Rouensa. His village, like Great Kaskaskia before it, became a multiethnic and inclusive population center containing many familles, including the Metchigamea, some Tamaroa, and Kaskaskia. In 1703,

this entire group abandoned the Des Peres site and migrated to its new location on the Kaskaskia River, the site of an older Metchigamea village, where
it would mostly remain for the rest of the colonial period.[25] Meanwhile, fifty
miles to the north, the remaining Tamaroa settled along with the Cahokia in
another sizable village.[26] When the settlements suffered a bad epidemic in
1714, many Indians renewed an old strategy of assimilation in these new
villages, "adopting" outsiders.[27]

Priests joined these new villages, relocating their missions and welcoming
the opportunity to abandon the French fur traders at the outpost at Pimitéoui.
In 1700, Gravier and Binneteau moved the Immaculate Conception mission
to the Kaskaskias' new village on the Mississippi River. Meanwhile, priests of
the Foreign Missions in Quebec, a competing religious order whose members
were known as Seminarians, arrived in the late 1690s in Illinois, ready to
form a mission. After a brief dispute, the Jesuits and Seminarians divided up
the territory of Illinois. The Seminarians settled a permanent mission with
the Cahokia, while the Jesuits settled the Immaculate Conception with the
Kaskaskia.[28]

If the priests hoped to keep the relocated missions isolated from fur
traders, they were quickly disappointed. For one thing, Juchereau's tannery,
established at the Wabash, was a major operation that drew a lot of traders
to the region. Here French and Indians traded in the bounteous bison hides
and meat—especially the *plats côté* or dried "flat ribs" of bison—which
became a significant food supply for Louisiana.[29] The new location in the
confluence area gave the Illinois hunters access to the two important bison-
hunting territories of the prairies: the Illinois Valley and the Wabash Valley.
In just a few seasons, the Illinois processed no fewer than fifteen thousand
hides at the tannery before an epidemic ended Juchereau's life and the project.[30] But the Juchereau venture reflects the tremendous scale of the Mississippi trade that began almost instantly after the establishment of Louisiana.
By September 1704, Iberville estimated that there were about 110 Frenchmen
roaming the various villages in the Illinois and on the Missouri.[31] In 1706, 50
traders came down to Mobile from Illinois. According to the official report
for that year, "These 50 men have every design of establishing themselves [at
the Illinois]."[32] Two years later, Louisiana officials estimated that "More than
60 errant Canadians [are] in the Indian villages situated along the Mississippi
River without the permission of any governor. By their bad, libertine life with
the Indian women they destroy everything that the Foreign Missionaries, and
others teach the Indians regarding the Christian Religion."[33]

The economic opportunities for this mostly transient population expanded in Illinois after 1700, as connections were established between the Illinois and the Louisiana jurisdiction via the Mississippi River. In addition to Juchereau's tannery, there was a significant beaver trade. Tonty brought nineteen traders with him to Mobile in 1701, all of whom carried beaver furs, the beginning of what would become a steady fur trade down the Mississippi.[34] In 1704, Louisiana invited fur traders from Illinois to bring down their loads of beaver and bison for the first time. As one official put it, "Many Canadians and voyageurs, who are at the Illinois and at the Sioux country . . . have beaver and . . . are supposed to descend to the bottom of the Mississippi in August 1704."[35]

Not all the Illinois trade went to Louisiana, however. Illegal trade with the English was another component of the economic activity that brought increasing numbers of coureurs to the Illinois Country in this period. The trade between Carolina and Illinois began sometime before 1701. In that year, Canadian officials noted of inhabitants in Illinois, "Some of these bandits have been to the English colonies at Carolina to draw commerce with them. They have been very well received."[36] Englishmen made ventures into the Illinois Country in 1702, trying to engage the Miami into a trade network on the Ohio River.[37] Although officials in Canada were likely disturbed by this news, in Illinois it was received gladly by opportunistic traders. Frenchmen reciprocated, traveling up the Ohio and Tennessee rivers to trade.[38] In 1702, they diverted enough of the fur from the pays d'en haut to boost the fur intake at Carolina by 100 percent.[39] Historian Marcel Giraud claims that thirty to forty traders in Illinois in 1701 had declared themselves independent and were trading illegally with the English.[40] In 1709 officials in Louisiana complained of persistent English plots to infiltrate the Mississippi. "This makes us think that [the English] desire to make themselves masters of the Mississippi and to dispossess us," wrote François Philippe de Mandeville in a memoir on Louisiana. "This has been confirmed to us by some neutral Indians to whom they told it. They even proposed to go to the Illinois in order to attract them to themselves and to make an alliance by promising them [to supply] their needs, and to enter in to trade with the Frenchmen who are married and established in that country, which seems to us certain unless we cause them some obstacle."[41]

In 1714, Frenchmen in Illinois continued trading with the English and even tried to recruit the Illinois and Ottawa to join the illegal trade between Carolina and the Illinois Country. As Canadian officials worried, "If we let them carry out their projects, it is to be feared that they may draw away from the Illinois a part of the other Ottawa nations into the interests of the English of Carolina, for both commerce and war."[42] By this time, a whole ring of illegal traders was operating independently out of Illinois. Canadian officials wrote of their discovery that several traders aimed "to introduce the English of Carolina to the Illinois."[43]

In addition to trading in beaver furs and especially bison hides, illegal French traders in Illinois joined the Illinois in their other main economic and social activity, the slave trade. In 1708, Louisiana received its first report from the Illinois that "Some French-Canadians living among the Caskaskias Illinois were inciting the savage nations in the environs of this settlement to make war upon one another." As the report continued, the purpose of these wars was to procure slaves: "The French-Canadians themselves were participating in order to get slaves that they afterward sold to the English."[44] Of course, the report had it wrong; the Illinois needed no "inciting" to make war for captives—this had been the heart of their social and economic lives for some time. The Frenchmen merely joined in this activity, bringing an ever-stronger commercial motive to an Indian activity traditionally motivated by kinship replacement. Additional reports of Illinois traders engaging in slave trade arrived in Canada in 1715 and in Louisiana in 1711 and 1720.[45] As a typical report on this subject elaborated: "[Traders in the Illinois Country] try to sow division among the savages and encourage them to make war in order to procure slaves which they sell. This is not only contrary to the ordinances of his Majesty, but also very prejudicial to the good of the Commerce of the company."[46]

And so the slave trade and fur trade attracted increasing numbers of Frenchmen to the Illinois outposts in the early eighteenth century. All the while, these transients created in Illinois the typical disorders of the pays d'en haut. One minister complained that the "lawlessness of the *coureurs de bois* is so great that it is absolutely necessary to make an example of some of them, in order to restrain them and to enforce upon them obedience to the officers in the upper posts."[47] In addition to drunkenness and activities such as slaving, the settlers engaged in illicit sexual liaisons with Indian women. Officials complained about how the Frenchmen were "Debauching the daughters and wives of the Illinois, and dissuading them from being converted to our religious faith."[48] In Cahokia, one priest wrote, there were "some libertines who do not love the Missionary's presence, because they wish to continue their evil conduct."[49] In 1711, Marest wrote to Louisiana for help restraining the

coureurs de bois from their promiscuous activities near the Jesuit mission at
Kaskaskia. Marest even asked Louisiana to send an officer and some soldiers
to break up the chaotic settlement.[50] That expedition arrived in 1711 and
chased away a number of illegal fur traders who were then in Kaskaskia.[51]

As far as Louisiana officials were concerned, this disordered settlement
was a useless colony. The inhabitants were "corrupt." Immoral and opportunistic, they were "not ready to make establishments nor to attach themselves
to agriculture because the majority have abandoned themselves to libertin-
age."[52] But even as officials complained, Illinois was changing. On the few
occasions when Louisiana officials sent travelers up the Illinois River after
1710, they witnessed something truly different from the image of a chaotic
frontier. A group of Frenchmen had begun putting roots in the Illinois
Country around the Jesuits' mission in Kaskaskia.

ↄ

It is simply not clear why Frenchmen started farming intensively in the Illinois Country. They certainly were not following any imperial directive. It
seems as though they did it spontaneously, without design. Explorers had
always noted that the soils of Illinois, and particularly in the bottomlands,
were well suited for agriculture. Having moved down to the Mississippi Valley, perhaps fur traders in Illinois anticipated the future development of a
market for crops and meat in the lower Mississippi Valley and began farming
opportunistically. Or perhaps they saw agriculture as a way to live independently. Whatever their logic, by the 1720s, there was a cluster of farms and
families in Illinois. By the time traveler André Pénicaut arrived in 1711, the
colony was transforming: "Wheat grows there as fine as any in France, and
all kinds of vegetables, roots and grasses."[53] They also raised livestock: "Here
they graze horses which they buy from the Caddo [a western tribe on the
Missouri River]. They have a great deal of livestock, such as bullocks, cows,
etc."[54] The fledgling population of Frenchmen and Indians had embarked
full scale on agriculture. "They have three mills to grind their grains," Pénicaut wrote, "namely one windmill, belonging to the Jesuit fathers, and 2
others belonging to the inhabitants."[55] In 1715, according to two travelers
who passed by the colony, settlers in Kaskaskia were "living at their ease; as
grain thrives in that region they have built a mill, and have a great many
cattle."[56] By the early 1720s, the colony was "composed entirely of farmers,"
and "[e]veryone here is devoted to agriculture."[57]

Accompanying the shift to agriculture was another change: permanence. French fur traders and Indians settled down in Illinois. In 1706, reporting on the status of the coureurs de bois in the Mississippi Valley, Louisiana governor Bienville wrote that all of them had returned to Canada or Louisiana except certain numbers who were "settling" in the Illinois.[58] These latter, he suggested, were digging in for the long term. In a 1718 report of the French settlements in the Mississippi Valley, a Louisiana official referred to the village of Rouensac (Kaskaskia), "where the fathers are settled and where some Frenchmen live."[59]

It was the mission at Kaskaskia, among the Christianized Indians, which was the center of this new agricultural activity and permanent settlement. Although they resisted the libertines, Jesuits began to welcome the presence of farmers, considering them "conducive to the progress of the Gospel."[60] In 1712, Marest wrote with great satisfaction that the Christianization of the Illinois had begun to attract Frenchmen to settle, explaining how "All these advantages are extremely favorable to the plan that some Frenchmen have of settling in our village."[61] As the Jesuits saw it, here was a win-win. The Frenchmen taught the Illinois Indians how to farm with a plow and raise livestock, which promoted the conversion of the Indians. As Marest said, "Many raise chickens and pigs, in imitation of the Frenchmen who have settled here."[62] Meanwhile, if Frenchmen were helping convert the Illinois to Christian lifeways, pious Illinois women were having a similar effect on libertine Frenchmen.

The marriage between Accault and Marie Rouensa had established an important precedent. As noted, when Accault and Rouensa married, Accault—the Frenchman—converted from his wayward life as a coureur and settled down. Looking back on his life, Accault acknowledged the powerful effect that his Indian bride had had in altering his conduct.[63] As Gravier reported, "He has admitted to me that he no longer recognizes himself, and can attribute his conversion solely to his wife's prayers and exhortations, and to the example that she gives him." Having lived for years as a "libertine," Accault was now a strong advocate for Christianity. He and Marie soon had a family, raising their children as Christians. Father St. Cosme in 1698 even sent their son to Canada, in the hopes that he could be trained as priest in the Seminary College. Michel and Marie continued to work for the church and performed every service, Marie teaching the catechism and Michel in other ways helping develop the mission.

We obviously must read Gravier's description of Accault's supposed conversion with a grain of salt, given the propagandistic purpose of the *Jesuit Relations*. But the conversion of Accault the "libertine" was apparently not an isolated event. Indeed, between 1695 and 1718, the Jesuits married twenty-three more Frenchmen to twenty-five Indian women (two widows remarried), reflecting their continued confidence in the initially experimental strategy of performing these marriages.[64] By many accounts, these were successful and stable relationships, helping to root the transient fur traders and the "inconstant" Illinois women in a stable community. Before entering into marriage, according to the Jesuits, the Illinois women sought promises from their husbands that they would live as good Christians. Like Accault, one "libertine" in 1712 promised to live as a Christian in order to convince an Illinois woman to marry him.[65] And even after marriage, the Jesuits wrote, Indian women continued to exercise a pious influence: "They exhort their husbands to be virtuous; they ask them at night whether they have said their prayers, they urge them to approach the Sacraments frequently."[66] As the traveler Monsieur Lallement wrote after visiting Kaskaskia and Cahokia in this period, the results of all of this were impressive: "There are many French inhabitants who are married to Indian women, even the most important ones, and they live very well together."[67] Rather than a disordered frontier of libertines, the Illinois was becoming an ordered settlement of family farmers.

☙

Louisiana officials knew only a little bit about the colony in Illinois, but what they did know gave them cause for worry. First, of course, they worried about the illegal activity perpetrated by criminal slave and fur traders. They worried about the infiltration of the region by English traders. But the most important thing they worried about in the 1710s were the relationships between Frenchmen and Indian women in Illinois. To officials' eyes, Illinois was a colony that was dangerously blurring boundaries between Indian and French social worlds. In addition to violating concepts of order, it disrupted emerging racial identities in the Mississippi Valley.[68]

To be sure, Louisiana officials had started off optimistic about intermarriage between Indians and Frenchmen.[69] But by the early 1700s, officials had lost their confidence in the policy.[70] As in New France, many Louisiana officials now doubted the possibility of assimilating Indian women into the colonial population—or "Frenchifying" them—through marriage.[71] In 1709, the governor of New France, Philippe de Rigaud, Marquis de Vaudreuil, wrote what was to be the first in a long line of objections to the intermarriage between Frenchmen and Indian women. The whole policy of Frenchification had been a pipe dream, he wrote, since "Bad should never be mixed with good."[72] He also said, "Our experience in this country ought to prevent us from permitting marriages of this kind [between Indians and Frenchmen], for all the French men who have married savage women have been licentious, lazy and have become intolerably independent; and the children they have had are even lazier than the savages themselves. Such marriages should thus be prohibited."[73]

Here Vaudreuil expressed an increasingly common view on intermarriage among French officials. Far from a tool for assimilation and *increasing* the colony, these marriages had become a means for Frenchmen to *go native*. The Frenchmen who married Indian girls tended to remain in the Indian villages instead of establishing farms. Further, the marriages were not stable, as Indian women often left husbands on a whim.[74] Meanwhile an even greater concern lay in the children of such marriages, as Vaudreuil's words suggest. As some officials observed, these children were "worse than the Indians themselves" because they were viewed as lazy and independent.[75] Furthermore, officials worried about the effects these children might have on the long-term economic growth of the colony. Since the Coutume de Paris, the French customary legal code, provided for the inheritance of a deceased man to pass half to his widow and half to his children, imperialists realized that intermarriage could result in large portions of the developing colonial land and capital winding up in the hands of Indians and mixed-blood children.[76]

Thus in the 1710s, viewing the practice of intermarriage as an increasingly problematic way to increase the colony's families, officials began to look in another direction: women from France.[77] "The most sure [way]," wrote one official, "is to send women there [from France] for with difficulty will one check the course of concubinage among the backwoodsmen and the soldiers."[78] Antoine Laumet, dit Lamothe Cadillac, the ambitious colonial official who had founded Detroit in the early 1700s, had formerly been a strong proponent of intermarriage and Frenchification. Now the governor of Louisiana, Cadillac recognized in 1713 that the plan of intermarriage had been unrealistic in Louisiana.[79] It simply wasn't working.

In this context, Louisiana officials viewed all they heard about the Illinois Country and its interracial community with great skepticism. Commissary of Louisiana Jean-Baptiste Dubois Duclos wrote a short study in 1715 in which he articulated the accumulated wisdom on the subject of intermarriage and why it should be banned once and for all. The Illinois was his case in point. "The Indian wives of French settlers," wrote Duclos, "especially in the Illinois, have changed nothing or at the very least very little in their manner of living."[80] Second, the marriages were unstable, as "Indian women very often leave their [French] husbands," which "even the Jesuit missionaries to the Illinois cannot remedy."[81] Like Vaudreuil, Duclos concluded that intermarriages only served to attract Frenchmen toward an Indian lifestyle: "And although there are several examples of Indian women who have contracted such marriages especially at the Illinois it is not because they have become Frenchified, if one may use that term, but it is because those who have married them have themselves become almost Indians, residing among them and living in their manner."[82] Duclos wanted to ban the practice. He persuaded the navy to recommend prohibition in 1716.[83]

There are several reasons why this new policy decree was significant. First of all, the French officials' indictment of Illinois Jesuits' intermarriage policy reflected an important change of positions. After all, when the Jesuits came to Illinois in the 1670s, they were consciously rejecting Colbert's réductions and "Frenchification" project in favor of a distant mission where Indians would not experience corrupting French influence of any kind. For the Jesuits, intermarriage was never supposed to be part of the program in a mission selected precisely for its isolation and remoteness from French civilization. It was only through the Rouensa-Accault marriage that Gravier and his partners began to change their minds about the role of intermarriage in their strategy. Meanwhile, imperial officials had usually *favored* intermarriage, often criticizing the Jesuits' Illinois outpost and other "distant missions" precisely because there would never be enough Frenchmen present for their favored programs of Frenchification and intermarriage to actually work. The 1716 decree reflected how thoroughly these positions had reversed: officials now opposed intermarriage while Illinois Jesuits were the ones embracing it. Observers must have been struck by the great irony of imperial officials complaining about the Jesuits' new "Frenchification" attempts in Illinois.

A second reason why the 1716 debate was significant, however, has to do with the *rationale* behind Louisiana officials' changing stance on intermarriage. It is important to note that the logic of this imperial decree in 1716 was racial, one of the very early racial discourses in American history.[84] Officials worried about the effect of intermarriages on the French *race*, articulating objections to intermarriage on the basis that it ruined the "purity" of French blood. Mixed-race marriages like those taking place in Illinois were to be feared because of "the adulteration that such marriages will cause in the whiteness and purity of the blood in the children." These relationships were going to result in a colony that was racially other: "The colony would become a colony of halfbreeds who are naturally idlers, libertines and even more rascals as those of Peru, Mexico and the other Spanish colonies."[85] As the Navy Council argued, colonists should not be allowed to mix "good blood with bad," which would produce "only children of a hard and idle character."[86] Intermarriages, these officials reasoned, should be prohibited.

But on the ground in Illinois, Jesuits like Father Marest disagreed with this logic, and Jesuits kept performing the marriages. Indeed, the curate of Louisiana, Henri Roulleaux de La Vente, wrote to defend the practice of intermarriage in Illinois, arguing that the Illinois were an exception.[87] Encouraged by the many success stories he heard from Jesuits in the Illinois Country, La Vente proposed "to permit marriages between Frenchmen and Catholic Indian women and to prefer those of the North who are the . . . Kaskaskias, Tamaroas, Illinois, and all those of the Missouri."[88] In Kaskaskia, intermarriage was different than in the South; it was actually creating a Frenchified community.

Why was La Vente so confident about the relationships between Illinois women and Frenchmen? As he put it, the Illinois women were special: "The women of these nations are Whiter, more laborious, cleverer, neater in the household work and more docile than those of the South."[89] This defense basically accepted the racial logic of Duclos's prohibition but simply moved to define the Illinois women as acceptably—and exceptionally—"white." La Vente's argument thus singled out the Illinois colony as a unique situation and Illinois women as uniquely able and willing to assimilate based on their distinctive racial identity.

As strong as this argument might have seemed to his intended audience in eighteenth-century Louisiana, La Vente certainly could have made a different argument about what made the Illinois women different and more amenable to Frenchification. For whatever their supposed skin color or talents at household labor, there were several things that truly did set them apart from Native women in lower Louisiana. For one thing, perhaps unlike their southeastern counterparts, they were motivated to marry out. As we have seen, Illinois women's negative experiences within the polygamous gender system in Illinois clearly led to tension and anomie and had already inspired many women to seek refuge in Christianity. Violence against women, both slave and free, continued in the early 1700s and may well have played a role in some Illinois women finding Christian marriage to a Frenchman attractive. Even the skewing of the traditional division of labor occasioned by bison processing might have played a role in attracting Illinois women to monogamous and agrarian French families, particularly in the early 1700s when Juchereau's tannery must have radically intensified the labor burden of Illinois women, and may have fed into the further commodification and degradation of women that many priests and observers noted.[90] There were many reasons why certain Illinois women may have viewed marriage to a Frenchman as an attractive prospect.[91]

Second, and perhaps more important for understanding why the Illinois women seemed more willing than their southern counterparts to "Frenchify," or at least to live in stable marriages with Frenchmen, they had a very different understanding of kinship. Most southeastern Indian peoples around Lower Louisiana practiced matrilocal kinship organization and matrilineal descent. That is, in cultures such as the Choctaw, among whom many French traders married in the early 1700s, it was typical for husbands to join their wives' families, not vice versa. What is more, children of these marriages normally assumed identities of the mother's family or clan.[92] So if the ideal of Frenchification was that Indian women would assimilate into French society and assume their husband's identity within a patriarchal home and culture, Indian brides in Lower Louisiana had the opposite expectation.[93] When Frenchmen married among these southeastern groups, it makes perfect sense that, as Duclos said, Frenchmen wound up "residing among them and living in their manner."[94] And it also made perfect sense that the children of these families were raised not as French but as members of Indian clans.

But Illinois families had a patrilineal, not matrilineal, kinship system.[95] The Illinois were organized into patrilineal exogamous clans that were a primary component of corporate and individual identities.[96] In this system, kinship identities passed from fathers to children, rather than from mothers to children. Wives were expected to accommodate their identities to their husband's kin groups.[97] Moreover, in addition to being patrilineal, the Illinois were also patrilocal, or possibly neolocal (meaning that newlyweds set up a new, independent household, separate from their parents). Evidence is thin, but the available sources suggest that after an initial postmarriage period in the house of the wife's family, a newlywed Illinois couple lived permanently with the husband's family or on their own.[98] Since all of these traditional Illinois practices would have predisposed intermarried Illinois wives and their children to adopt "French" identity, this gives us a better way to understand why mixed-race marriages among the Illinois worked differently than in Lower Louisiana and why Jesuits kept solemnizing them. Illinois women had motivations as well as a set of expectations that may well have predisposed them toward identifying with the fledgling "French" colonial culture in Illinois.

But the Jesuits still must have worried about the stability of these relationships and the firmness of French and Frenchified identities among their participants. After all, long precedent suggested that Frenchmen engaged in marriages with Indian women for instrumental reasons, simply as a means to establish kinship connections in Native families for purposes of fur trade.[99] The Jesuits must have feared that these marriages could easily dissolve at the whim of an opportunistic French husband, moving on to the next fur trade post. Meanwhile, things were no less fragile when it came to the Illinois brides. By marrying Frenchmen, the Illinois women, and especially their children, were exiting the patrilineal kinship world of their birth, the most important shaper of Algonquian identities. Could these marriages actually create stable families—let alone Christian identities—as the Jesuits hoped? To help firm them up, Jesuits and these married couples created an idiosyncratic but extremely important strategy for solidifying mixed-race unions, one that rested on the most important theme of Indian life: kinship. By using the rituals of godparentage, the priests and families created kinship and fictive kinship bonds to link individuals together in a dense and cohesive network. Extensive baptismal records from early Kaskaskia reveal how godparentage helped root these families in an emerging Christian, French community.[100]

The married couples on the earliest Kaskaskia baptismal records were tied together in a dense community. Following Catholic ritual, the Jesuits required that each child baptized in the Illinois colony should have both a godmother and godfather, a practice that created fictive kinship bonds linking individual families together in the frontier colony.[101] Throughout the period 1694–1718, baptismal records show that the twenty-five interracial families of Kaskaskia gave birth to at least thirty-six children and probably many more. Using the baptismal records from Kaskaskia, it is possible to analyze the way that godparenthood helped create a community among the early interracial families of Illinois.

Although we can use baptismal records to examine individuals and their discrete family trees, the importance and function of godparenthood and fictive kinship in Illinois only become clear when we stand back and look at the entire community together.[102] Social Network Analysis allows us to do this.[103] By examining every marriage and godparent relation in Kaskaskia between 1694 and 1718, we see some basic characteristics of the resulting community.[104] Figure 11 depicts the network of married couples and godparents in Kaskaskia, with each link representing either a person standing godfather or godmother to a parent's child or else a marriage.[105] The godparent arrows indicate that these relationships were *directed*; that is, the arrow represents the *action* of godparenthood and thus points to the mother or father of the baptized child, the receiver of the action of godparenthood. The network created by godparenthood and marriage in Kaskaskia through 1718 linked eighty-five men and women together, leaving just a few people outside the main, continuous network. Conspicuously, the interfamilial links created by godparenthood in Kaskaskia resulted in one large, dense, and continuous network, rather than several small, isolated networks. The fictive kinship bonds created by Christian ritual formed few obvious cliques or major divisions in the community. Further, within the network, while some individuals were connected to just one other individual, many were connected to two or more, reflecting a relatively dense social network. By standing as godparents to one another's children, Indian women and Frenchmen connected their families together into a tight and stable community.

Clearly the figure demonstrates relatively high cohesiveness in the network. But Social Network Analysis also gives us insights into who the most important people in the network were. They were not the fur traders, as in other parts of the pays d'en haut.[106] For instance, although Domitille Ch8ping8a was married to the most important trader in the colony, she had very few godparent connections to others in Illinois. Rather, the most important people in the network were farmers. For instance, Catherine 8abanakic8e, who was connected to four other women in the network, was married to Jean-Baptiste Guillemot dit Lalande, an emerging farmer in the colony. Other important women also were married to farmers, suggesting that the network functioned not for fur trade or to link Frenchmen to an Indian world but to orient the community toward an emerging agrarian community. The most highly connected individual in the early network was Marie Rouensa, Gravier's most important pupil. As Gravier wrote, "It gives her great pleasure to be chosen as Godmother."[107] She connected herself to eight other families by serving as godmother or by inviting others to stand godparent to her many children. Her high connectivity also supports the hypothesis that the function of the network was probably to orient the community toward an emerging agrarian, Catholic community. Christian families linked to other Christian families so that they did not stand alone.[108]

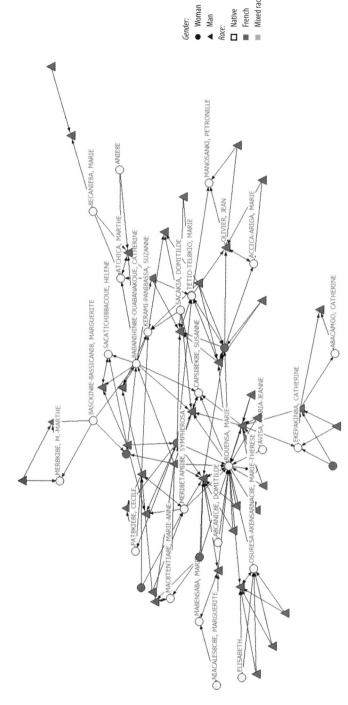

Figure 11. Godparent network in Kaskaskia, 1694–1718. The Social Network Analysis of every baptismal record in early Kaskaskia reveals a dense and cohesive network of kinship and fictive kinship that probably functioned to create community and solidarity among the mixed-race families of Illinois. The most important people in the network were Catholic members of agrarian households.

Data from *FB* and *KM*. Image created with and courtesy of Stephen P. Borgatti, *NetDraw Software for Network Visualization* (Lexington, Ky.: Analytic Technologies, 2002).

The solidarity of this kinship network and its orientation toward key Christian figures is especially important when we think about it from the perspective of the Indian women. As we have seen, Illinois women had their own reasons to join this new Christian community as wives to the Frenchmen. By marrying Frenchmen, they escaped the slave-based polygamy of Illinois culture during the early 1700s and committed themselves to a Christian life apart from their culture. But this represented a daunting transformation in their identities, as they exited the patrilineal kinship culture so important to Algonquian life. The godparentage network helped them replace the kinship connections that they lost by marrying out of the patrilineal clans of the Illinois. Godparentage thus probably played an important role in creating identity for these women, whose expectations about the importance of kinship probably made these fictive kinship bonds of godparentage especially significant. Godparenthood and Algonquian kinship expectations overlapped here, providing a means to help define the community.

In 1712, Gabriel Marest wrote to reflect on the changes that had taken place among the Indians of the Kaskaskia mission in recent years: "The Illinois are much less barbarous than other Savages; Christianity and intercourse with the French have by degrees civilized them. This is to be noticed in our Village, of which nearly all the inhabitants are Christians."[109] According to Binneteau, another Jesuit, "There are many [Illinois] women married to our Frenchmen, who would be a good example to the best regulated households in France."[110] The Jesuits were optimistic about these conversions. Although Louisiana officials worried about the interracial relationships in Illinois, the colony was operating by the old logic of Frenchification. But even more, it was operating by its own logic—kinship created the foundation for a newly emerging agrarian community that was unplanned by government officials and even stood in direct opposition to their goals.

❧

It was in 1715, just as Louisiana officials were debating intermarriage, that Quebec officials heard the alarming report that opened this chapter. Illinois had become a sizable colony. Intermarried with Indians, the illegal colonists were "living at their ease." They were trading Indian slaves. They represented a "dangerous settlement." Something had to be done. In 1717 the king officially moved Illinois out from Canadian jurisdiction to that of the Louisiana colony, finally clearing up the ambiguity that had characterized French policy for some time.[111] And in 1719, Louisiana sent an expedition to formally establish a government in the illegal colony.

Officials in Louisiana chose Pierre Dugué de Boisbriant to lead a new administration, an official provincial government. Boisbriant had grown up in Montreal, the son of a famed Canadian soldier.[112] He had risen quickly in the Canadian military during the time of the Beaver Wars and relocated to Louisiana when that colony was founded. There he became one of his cousin Bienville's most important officials, helping establish Fort Mobile and negotiating with the Choctaw.[113] His mission for Illinois was simple—to establish control: "They have reported that the Illinois Country, incorporated into [the Province of] Louisiana, is already inhabited by a great number of Frenchmen, which grows every day without it seeming there is any measure taken to exercise justice."[114]

Boisbriant's new administration was faced with the task of establishing order in the previously autonomous frontier villages of the Illinois. Documents from the period unfortunately are scarce, so we have only the barest clues about his plans and how he realized them in this connection. We do know that he came well supported to impose a new regime. Along with a hundred men, miners, and soldiers, Boisbriant brought several officers, including Lieutenant Pierre Melique and Captain Charles-Claude Dutisné.[115] To the latter went the charge to govern "the *habitants* as well as the strangers who happen to establish themselves [in the Illinois settlements]," an order that acknowledged the haphazard way in which the population was taking shape in the colony.[116] Together, the new administrators were expected to make sure that, as the new charter of the Company of the West designated, "The commandants, officers, soldiers, and *habitants* and others who are or might be at the Illinois recognize the General Commandant of Louisiana and obey and listen to him, without any contravention of any sort or manner."[117] The orders sounded strict, a plan for top-down imperial order.

Arriving in the villages in 1718, Boisbriant took stock of the situation. We have no sources to tell us what he thought. But Boisbriant must have realized that a certain order already existed in this colonial outpost. For rather than try to utterly change everything, Boisbriant simply followed along. He made no arrests, and no records suggest that he imposed any onerous regulations on the inhabitants. Indeed, he endorsed their trade. Rather than trying to restrict the activities of traders in Illinois who caused "disorders," Boisbriant issued licenses to them. To other officials in the colonial administration of Canada, this was "very wrong." It appeared as though Boisbriant was offering amnesty to "fugitives from Canada" who created the "disorder among the Savages" that he was supposed to prevent.[118]

As for the illegal French settlement at Kaskaskia, he left it where it was. Although the colonists had established the villages with no input from the government, Boisbriant confirmed legitimate titles to the lands that the squatters in Illinois had already assumed outside official channels.[119] By 1719, he legitimated the illegal colonists' landholdings and "caused to be designated to each inhabitant his respective land." What is more, as he created the seigneuries of the Jesuit mission, Cahokia, and a number of others, Boisbriant granted land *en franc alleu*, or fee simple, the most liberal terms available under French law.[120] Several petitions for land reflect that this kind of land tenure became the hope—if not the expectation—of several Illinois landholders in this period.[121] Of the aforementioned twenty-three men in the early Kaskaskia marriage network, land grants from Boisbriant survive for ten of them.[122] While presumably many of these were granted with the normal obligations of landholding *en routure*, at least three new landlords—Renault, Chassin, and the priests—were granted their lands in fee simple.[123]

Moreover, Boisbriant legitimated the unusual common fields agricultural system that the farmers had established on their own in Illinois. This system, which was distinctive to Illinois and only a few other places in French North America, required an unusual collectivist management system and likely made government slightly more complex. But Boisbriant did not dismantle or alter it. According to historian Carl Ekberg, Boisbriant "simply clarified, regularized, and affirmed a system of longlots that the habitants at Kaskaskia had already established before he took command of the region."[124]

The only major action Boisbriant did take was to support the Jesuits' request to move the Indian villages away from the French village at Kaskaskia. Indeed, the French agrarian settlement was too close to the Indian villages, and this was causing problems. In 1719, the priest de Ville had asked for Louisiana's help firming up the borders between these settlements, so that Indians and French no longer should live "pesle mesle" together. Boisbriant separated the villages almost immediately after arriving in 1719.[125] His rationale was that the Indians were killing French settlers' pigs, "under the pretext that they destroy [the Indians'] corn."[126] Over the next several years, a hallmark of Boisbriant's administration was firming up the separation of different populations in the region. By 1721, Boisbriant even further divided the Christian Indians, moving the Metchigamea mission apart from the Kaskaskia mission and relocating it nearby the new French Fort de Chartres, which Boisbriant also established. It is not clear why he did this, only that "it was thought proper to form two villages of [Christian] Savages instead of one."[127] By the time the priest and historian Pierre-François-Xavier de Charlevoix arrived for a visit to Illinois in 1721, there were several distinct villages. All of this probably reflected Boisbriant's desire to keep tensions among the distinct communities to a minimum and to support the Jesuits' efforts to create a Frenchified frontier community.[128]

But if he moved Indian and French villages apart, he did not in any way enforce Louisiana's proposed ban on intermarriage. Under his administration, intermarriage continued. In 1724 Henry Biron married an Indian woman, Marie Medan. That same year, Jacques Fouillard married a Natchitoches Indian named Anne.[129] And Louis Turpin married Dorotheé Michi8e8a.[130] Despite Louisiana's prohibitions, Boisbriant did not interfere with the social system of Illinois. Indeed, he joined right in with the intermarried social order. In 1720, Boisbriant himself stood godfather to Charles-Pierre Danis, son of Charles Danis and Dorotheé, his Native wife.

If Boisbriant's regime basically legitimated and made official what had been a self-directed colony, nowhere was this more evident than in Boisbriant's treatment of the former coureurs de bois who for years had gathered in Illinois to the frustration of Canadian authorities. He made no arrests but rather turned them into legitimate colonists. A good example of his policy comes from the way Boisbriant treated Jacques Bourdon, a fairly typical Illinois settler in 1719 when Boisbriant first arrived. Bourdon had been a denizen of the pays d'en haut since the 1690s, beginning his career as an illegal woodsman just after the king banned the fur trade in 1696. In 1703, he was a guide for the missionaries in the Illinois Valley, conducting a group from Cahokia to Detroit. By 1712 he was an accomplished and daring trader, a participant in the illegal Carolina trade now based on the Mississippi River in the Cahokia and Kaskaskia villages. As one Canadian account held, Bourdon was leading a scandalous, criminal life introducing English traders into the Illinois Country and fomenting divisions among the tribes at Pimitéoui.[131] Because he was one of the leaders of this illegal commercial ring, Bourdon was at the top of Canada's list of wanted men in the 1710s. "These Frenchmen lead reprobate lives," the report had said.[132] In 1713, Ramezay complained that Bourdon and his partners had become enemies of the state.

> Sieurs de bourmon [Bourgmont], bisaillon, and bourdon are still
> more Criminal, in the design which they have conceived of introducing the English of carolina to the illinois, which I have learned
> by the Letters of the Reverend Father deville (Jesuit missionary

among the savages of that nation) and by a letter of Sieur Deliette, who commands there. . . . As it is almost impossible to seize these men in so distant a country, Monsieur the Marquis de Vaudreuil hopes, Monseigneur, that you will be pleased to obtain orders from his Majesty to lay hands on them, whenever a favorable occasion offers, as being guilty of lese-majesté.[133]

By 1714, owing to the behavior outlined in these reports, the ministers in France issued a warrant throughout French North America for Bourdon's arrest.[134] In 1715, Ponchartrain in Louisiana issued a second warrant for Bourdon's arrest.[135] But Bourdon was never caught. Eluding authority in the wilderness of the Illinois Country, Bourdon was like so many of the fur traders of the pays d'en haut, an independent operator.

Arriving in Illinois in 1719, Boisbriant now had a chance to arrest Bourdon and bring him to justice. But Boisbriant did no such thing. Indeed, not only did Boisbriant not arrest Bourdon in 1719 for the crimes of his previous life, he appointed him militia captain. Despite Bourdon's career as a criminal for so many years, Boisbriant now made the former renegade effectively into a member of the provincial authority in Illinois, an agent of the empire. Having long served his self-interest, Bourdon now was expected to serve the interests of France in the wilderness. The transformation of Bourdon from fur trader to legitimate colonial agent mirrors the transition of Illinois from outlaw settlement to official imperial colony.[136]

℘

Digging a little deeper, it seems clear why Boisbriant did not arrest Bourdon. Like many fur traders in Illinois, Bourdon was not just some criminal. Sometime after 1715, he married a widow of a Frenchman at Kaskaskia, a Kaskaskia woman named Domitile Chopinqwata.[137] This was a clever marriage, as documents attest, because Domitile had just gained control of half of the estate of her previous husband, a wealthy fur trader named Antoine Baillarjon. Bourdon used this inheritance to create a huge farm at Kaskaskia. He befriended the Jesuits; later documents from his deathbed suggest he became a fervent Catholic.[138] By 1719, when Boisbriant arrived in Kaskaskia, Bourdon was no longer the reprobate that he had been before 1715. Wealthy and a committed farmer, he was among the most solid colonists in the newly legitimate town of Kaskaskia. In 1722, in fact, Diron D'Artaguiette singled out Bourdon as "one of the most worthy among them."[139] Bourdon had traveled an interesting and considerable distance—from outlaw fur trader to rooted colonist.

He did not make this transformation in prison or because of legal enforcement. He did this on his own. His life changed with new opportunity. Like Accault and many other Frenchmen in the Illinois, he had made a new life as a frontier farmer. Together with their wives, who themselves had their own clear motivations for joining an emerging French Christian community, they were establishing families. And while none of this was part of an imperial plan or compelled by an imperial decree, in 1719 it was useful to the empire. And so they collaborated. Such were the beginnings of the official French colony of the Illinois Country.

But this unprecedented colony would be a challenging experiment. In the 1720s, the establishment of imperial hierarchy in Illinois seemed to be going well. One visitor noted that the Jesuits had an *empire absolu* in their missions which, as one administrator noted with surprise, "they have even succeeded from time to time in extending over our Frenchmen."[140] Further, the Frenchmen seemed genuinely to appreciate the hierarchy that Boisbriant, a noble and well-born military officer, created in the Illinois. They did not seem to resent his authority but rather "adored him for his good manners."[141] Under his command, they formed orderly militia units, arming themselves to "[give an] agreeable reception" to a visiting colonial official.[142] In February 1725, Boisbriant wrote to his superiors that the post of the Illinois was filled with industrious, productive workers making incredible progress in agriculture. The population was growing. Landholdings were expanding. Illinois livestock were so numerous they were trampling over the country. As Boisbriant wrote, "One can hardly believe the work these *habitants* have done since I arrived here."[143] The Illinois inhabitants, it seemed, were now good, loyal subjects.

But were they? Some were not so sure. For in becoming good farmers, the inhabitants of Illinois were becoming independent. They had plentiful meat, and they grew extraordinary quantities of wheat and corn, which gave them a healthy subsistence and, before long, a surplus. They had even begun to grow grapes for wine, which Boisbriant contemplated as a potential export.[144] As one visitor commented, all of this raised the possibility that these distant habitants, not relying on the French government for subsistence, would reject the administration. One visitor wondered "if it is wise to permit these Jesuits and all other individuals to plant vines and make wine. If the habitants of Martinique had been able to grow wine and wheat perhaps they would no longer even be under the obedience of France."[145] Time would tell what kind of colonialism collaboration would create in Illinois.

Chapter 5

Collaborators: Indians and Empire

In 1730, a delegation of Illinois Indians traveled to New Orleans to meet with French officials. Their purpose was to offer condolences for French losses sustained during the Natchez rebellion the previous year at Fort Rosalie. As a Jesuit priest in Louisiana wrote, "They came hither to weep for the black Robes and the French, and to offer the services of their Nation to Monsieur Perrier [the Illinois commandant], to avenge their death."[1] The rebellion had resulted in 120 French killed, and now British-allied Indians such as the Chickasaw threatened further violence against the French in the Mississippi Valley, reflecting intensifying imperial rivalry in the region. In this context, the Illinois tried to reassure the French of their firm loyalty and willingness to fight to protect the similarly vulnerable settlement at Illinois. "We always place ourselves . . . before the enemies of the French," Chikagou, chief of the Metchigamea, said. "It is necessary to pass over our bodies to go to them, and to strike us to the heart before a single blow can reach them." In an elaborate diplomatic ceremony, Chikagou presented the French with two calumets to symbolize the Illinois's dedication to the alliance. As he said, "We have come from a great distance to weep with you for the death of the French, and to offer our Warriors to strike those hostile Nations whom you may wish to designate. You have but to speak."[2]

Mamantouensa, chief of the Kaskaskia, also made a speech. Adding to the gifts already presented, Mamantouensa gave "two young *Padouka* slaves, some skins, and some other trifles." As Mamantouensa said, these were not gifts designed to make the French reciprocate with presents of their own. Rather, they were the symbols of a mostly unconditional alliance: "All that I ask of you is your heart and your protection. I am much more desirous of that than of all the merchandise of the world." As Jesuit Le Petit reflected, the Illinois were "inviolably attached to the French, because they had given them daughters."[3]

To some French observers, this amazing declaration of loyalty probably suggested the Illinois's increasing submission to and dependency on the French. In 1730, the French Illinois colonies were growing, and they had become an official outpost of the empire. Visiting Kaskaskia in 1721, a traveler named Sieur Lallement theorized that the balance of power in Illinois had radically changed: "Formerly [the Illinois Indians] insulted the French because they outnumbered us, but at present it is not the same any more. Mr. de Boisbriant keeps their respect and they fear him very much. We do with them what we want today."[4]

But even a cursory review of the relationship between the Illinois and the French suggests that this was an overly simplistic reading of the situation. First of all, even after years of warfare, the epidemics of the 1690s, 1702, and 1714, the Illinois remained far stronger numerically than the French colonists, numbering at least 2,500 in 1730.[5] And while the Illinois promised in 1730 to "place themselves before the enemies of the French," in the previous twenty years the reverse scenario was actually far more common. Since the beginning of Boisbriant's regime, the Illinois had persuaded the new French government to pursue Illinois interests and had made Boisbriant abandon some of his most important plans. For instance, in 1719 it was Boisbriant who was promising—against the general objectives of French policy—to commit French forces in order to "protect you [the Illinois] against the nation of the cunning Foxes, your inveterate enemies."[6] Indeed, when it came to the central questions of Indian affairs in the Mississippi Valley—alliances and the slave trade—the new provincial government followed Illinois logics and priorities, often against the official plans of the French empire.

As at the opening of contact in 1673, these distinctive Illinois logics and priorities were symbolized in the gifts that the Illinois presented to Louisiana officials in 1730. The calumets reflected the Illinois's membership in a western alliance system and social world that the French had to decipher and respect. The skins were almost certainly bison, reflecting the Illinois's distinctive economic interests, separate from the beaver trade in the North. And the slaves—identified as Padoukes—reflected the Illinois's participation in a slave trade and alliance network that the Louisiana government had once tried to oppose but only reluctantly were coming to support. Even as they professed their loyalty in 1730, the Illinois brought reminders of their distinctive priorities and needs. Implicitly, the Indians were sending a message that the French had to run their policy in ways that followed these priorities.

Mamantouensa and Chikagou did not profess loyalty out of a sense of abject dependency. Rather, the Illinois offered support with an expectation of reciprocity. As Mamantouensa put it, the Illinois demanded of the French "your heart and protection."[7] It was an important condition. Continuing the opportunism that went back to their original migration to Illinois in search of bison, the Illinois were willing to work with the French because collaboration brought them benefits. But they made the French promise to uphold their end of the bargain, and they pushed back when their needs were not met. The French and Illinois had a surprisingly durable and close alliance in the colonial period, perhaps one of the closest and most successful alliances in the Mississippi Valley. But that is because they made an alliance that reflected Native, and not always imperial, priorities.[8] This collaboration reshaped the priorities of the French empire in the middle of the country and forced the French to abandon simplistic imperial visions for Indian affairs in the Mississippi Valley and pays d'en haut.

⁊

The show of strong alliance between the Illinois and the French at Louisiana in 1730 is surprising when we look back to the deep tensions in the Illinois's relationship to the French at the beginning of the eighteenth century. After the Iroquois Wars, the Illinois had become alienated by the policies of Onontio, the French governor at Quebec. Their particular objection had to do with New France's determination to create a pan-Algonquian alliance system in the wake of the Iroquois Wars, one that included the Foxes. For strategic reasons and also because of longstanding enmities, the Illinois wanted to keep the Foxes out of the French alliance. By the 1710s, competing visions of the postwar order opened up a huge rift between the French and the Illinois, who tried hard to throw French plans for the West into disarray.[9]

The French planned a simple, if not simplistic, Indian policy for the Great Lakes at the end of the seventeenth century and beginning of the eighteenth. Since the 1680s, when New France committed itself to becoming the "glue" of the Algonquian alliance system, officials in Quebec were convinced that the Algonquians should set aside their differences and join in a common alliance under the leadership of Onontio. During the Iroquois Wars, the French had succeeded in uniting Algonquians against the common

Iroquois enemy. As the wars wound down, the French looked to preserve their great alliance system not only because of the potential military power it represented but also because it provided some assurance against incursions by the English on the Ohio River, a growing concern.[10] The 1701 Great Peace at Montreal dramatically symbolized New France's vision for a unified pan-Algonquian world. The actual treaty document contained thirty-nine pictographs representing diverse individuals, clans, tribes, and moieties which, the French hoped, would continue to ally themselves together as children of Onontio.[11] After the Great Treaty of 1701, French policy among their Algonquian allies was "to persuade them to be reconciled and to live in peace."[12]

But this vision ignored the Indians' own longstanding politics. Great Lakes Indians did not necessarily want a single alliance at the end of the Iroquois Wars. As Perrot said, "There is not a savage tribe which does not bear ill-will to some other. The Miamis and the Illinois hate each other reciprocally . . . and it is the same with the other tribes. There is not one of those peoples that does not consider itself justified in waging war against the other."[13] All sorts of potential animosities seemed likely to interfere with the French alliance system. For instance, the Ojibwes were allied to the Sioux, while other Algonquians, such as the Ottawa, hated the Sioux. Meanwhile, the Ottawas and Miamis also felt mutual tension.[14] At the end of the Iroquois Wars, the Algonquian world broke apart into regional blocs, clusters of ethnic groups living together at five locations in the pays d'en haut: Detroit, the Ohio River, Green Bay, Michilimackinac, and, of course, Kaskaskia. While these blocs were often—though not always—internally harmonious, the relations among them often featured hostility, disputes, and tension.[15] War against the Iroquois had briefly united them, but with the threat of the Iroquois Wars gone, the Algonquians seemed poised to return to hostility and competition. New France's plans for the postwar future seemed to ignore this reality. As Perrot wrote, "We can only expect successive and inevitable wars, unless we [do something to] prevent them."[16]

The biggest division in the Algonquian world was probably the animosity felt by many Algonquians against the Foxes. Many Algonquians felt bitterness toward the Foxes, reflecting the continuation of tensions and conflicts dating back to the Iroquois Wars.[17] And although the anti-Fox feelings were shared widely, the Illinois's acrimony for the Foxes was especially fierce. Indeed, one Illinois chief expressed his feelings about the Foxes in extremely bitter terms, declaring them "devils on earth." As he explained, "[The Foxes] have nothing human but the shape. . . . One can say of them that they have

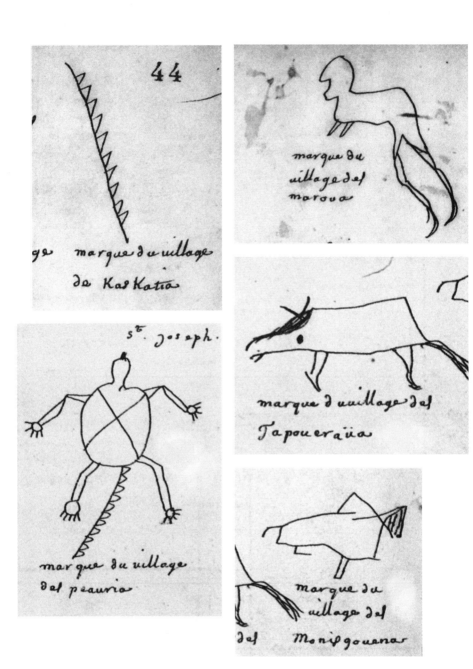

44

marque du
uillage des
maroua

ge marque d a uillage
de Kas Katia

marque d uaillage des
Tapouerauia

st. Joseph.

marque du village
des peauria

marque du
uillage des
des Monipgouenar

Figure 12. Signatures of Illinois-speaking villages on 1701 Great Treaty. The Illinois-speakers' signatures reveal that they preserved distinct identities in the 1690s and that their massive consolidation at the Grand Village did not erase divisions among themselves. From C[11a], vol. 19, fols. 41–44v, ANOM.

Courtesy of the Archives Nationales d'Outre Mer, Aix-en-Provence, France.

all the bad qualities of the other nations without having a single one of their good ones."[18]

The roots of this profound hatred were various. The animosity may have started with simple resource competition before the contact era. Both the Foxes and the Illinois, together with the Mascoutens and Kickapoos, were Algonquians who had moved into the prairies in the seventeenth century. Both were also involved in slave trading to the West and were middlemen between the Great Lakes and prairie worlds. They occupied the same liminal position in the borderlands and may have become rivals to control their particular economic niche between Siouans and Algonquians. When the contact era began, moreover, they competed for access to French traders. The Foxes had tried to prevent the French from opening a mission in the Illinois in the 1670s. Perhaps as a result, in the mid-1670s the Illinois attacked the Foxes, the first known military encounter between the two groups.[19]

In addition to these rivalries, it also seems clear that the Foxes' actions during the Iroquois Wars were particularly damaging to the Illinois and caused resentment. During the wars, the Foxes made alliances with the Senecas, the Iroquois who were the main aggressors against the Illinois in the 1680s.[20] Foxes recruited the Iroquois to attack and "destroy" an Illinois village in the 1670s.[21] When the Illinois raided the Iroquois, the Foxes ransomed the resulting captives and then sent them back to the Iroquois.[22] In 1694, Foxes even considered establishing a joint fort with the English and the Iroquois on the Wabash River, threatening the Illinois.[23]

These longstanding antagonisms help explain the Illinois's desire to keep the Foxes out of the alliance. But the Illinois wanted to exclude the Foxes for other reasons as well, and these had less to do with the Foxes themselves and more to do with the Illinois's relationship with the rest of the Algonquian world. Importantly, the Illinois's position in the Algonquian world was precarious; although they were powerful, they lived at the margin of the Algonquian world, in the borderlands, and their violent history made them prone to conflicts. They had longstanding enmities with the Miamis and had gone to war against the Ottawas in the past as well. With the end of the Iroquois Wars, the Illinois looked toward the Algonquian world with uncertainty. Particularly dangerous was the prospect of several groups aligned against them. Now that the Iroquois Wars had ended, the Illinois needed a new common enemy to help them deflect any animosities from Algonquian neighbors. The Foxes filled this role perfectly. Continued warfare against the Foxes was functional for the Illinois—it channeled the aggressions of the

Algonquians onto the Foxes and kept the Illinois happily allied with the Ottawas, Miamis, and Ojibwes.[24] But the danger was clear: if the Foxes should become allies with the rest of the Algonquians under Onontio, the Foxes might be free to attack the Illinois. Worse, the other Algonquians might also join them or exercise their own aggression toward the Illinois-speakers. For all these reasons, in addition to the Illinois's own hatred of the Foxes, the Illinois objected to the French vision for alliance. For the Illinois, division, and not a single alliance, was the key to security.

Even as the Illinois worked to keep the Foxes out of the Great Lakes alliance system, they had to guard against other dangers, too. As was well-known, the Foxes were sometimes allied with the Sioux.[25] Alienated from the Algonquian alliance, the Foxes might build their power through ever more extensive alliances in the West, such as with groups like the Osages, Missourias, or Ioways. Given their own reliance on western alliances, the Illinois had to be careful to prevent this, even as they worked to disrupt Fox membership in the French alliance. The Illinois had to keep the Foxes isolated both from the Algonquians and from Siouans like the Missouria. Fundamentally, then, the Illinois envisioned a completely different alliance system from the one the French hoped to create.

And so the Illinois actively opposed New France policy in the early 1700s. Alienation from New France's plans for alliance was probably part of the reason why the Illinois listened when they were "called" by the Louisiana governor to abandon the upper Illinois Valley in the early 1700s.[26] But if the Illinois distrusted Quebec's vision for alliance in 1700, they were even more alienated when Antoine Laumet de La Mothe, sieur de Cadillac, set up the colony of Detroit and then began to invite Algonquians to settle in the vicinity. Cadillac recruited the Ottawa and Miami to be some of the early residents of the new French outpost, and his successor, Henri de Bourgmont, looked to mediate a dispute that had broken out between them in 1706.[27] Having accomplished this mediation, Bourgmont then invited the Fox to settle at Detroit. When conflict broke out, Bourgmont tried actively to reconcile the Foxes to the Ottawa. As Brett Rushforth has observed, this was "naïve," since it ignored the Indians' own longstanding political animosities.[28] But in addition to being naïve, it was also particularly disturbing to the Illinois.

The Ottawa rejected Bourgmont's attempts at mediation. Together with their erstwhile enemies the Miami, they put the Fox under siege at their village outside Detroit, reflecting the way animosities against the Fox could unite Algonquians. Soon thereafter, the Illinois showed up at Detroit eager to stoke the conflict and ensure that efforts to reconcile the antagonists were unsuccessful. Arriving with a large army, the Illinois rejected the Foxes' peace offerings and vowed to destroy them. As the Illinois chief Makouandeby said to the Fox chief Pemoussa: "Better than [the French governor] does, we know your evil heart, and do not intend to abandon him to your mercies. Return at once to your fort; we merely await that to renew the action."[29] Denouncing the Foxes as "dogs," the Illinois prepared to exterminate them.[30] The standoff climaxed in a terrible fight: one thousand Fox were captured and killed, just one hundred men escaped.[31]

Two things are important about this moment. First, of course, the Illinois rejected Ontontio's attempts at alliance making and insisted on their own definition of friends and enemies. Second, and just as important, they did this by partnering with their own western Siouan allies. When they attacked the Fox in 1712, they did so with an "army of the nations of the south." As Charles Renaut, Sieur de Dubuisson, remembered, "Casting my eyes toward the woods, I saw the army of the nations of the south issuing from it. They were the Illinois, the Missouris, the Osages, and other nations yet more remote. They were also with them the Ottawa chief Saguina and also the Potawatomis, the Sacs, and some Menomonees. Detroit never saw such a collection of people."[32]

This was significant. By organizing these diverse groups and leading them in the fight against the Foxes, the Illinois were achieving two strategic goals at once. Even as they were keeping the Foxes isolated from the Algonquians, they were simultaneously isolating the Foxes from the western Siouans. By recruiting the Missourias and Osage to join their efforts, the Illinois drove a wedge between those groups and the Fox. Defying the simplistic categories that the French wanted to impose, the Illinois realized a different alliance system that excluded the Foxes but included western Indians like the Missourias and Osage.

It was a great coup for the Illinois, but in many ways it represented a complete rejection of the French policy. After the disaster of 1712, soon the French had to change their stance. As New France official Claude de Ramezay said, the main principle of French policy had always been "to reunite the divided nations to the end of maintaining these people in unity."[33] But after 1712, this was impossible. The collective action of the Illinois-led army of Algonquians and westerners against the Fox now meant that the empire would have to accept the Fox as enemies. As Vaudreuil wrote, "It is no longer possible to deal gently with that nation [Foxes] without incurring the contempt of all the others."[34] Now, to prove their faithfulness to the Illinois and other Algonquians, the French were forced to join conflicts among the very Indians they had been trying to reconcile. In 1716, after years of embarrassing setbacks that lessened the French credibility even further, Louis de la Porte de Louvigny organized an army to attack the Foxes and bring them to terms.[35]

But it was not yet over. In 1716, after leading an army against the Foxes, Louvigny considered that the French had done enough and could finally bring the Foxes into the alliance in a way that satisfied all the Algonquians. But when Louvigny made peace with the Foxes in 1716, the Illinois regarded this as yet another betrayal. First of all, the Illinois claimed they would have preferred to see Louvigny simply exterminate the Foxes. What was worse, the 1716 peace agreement contained clauses that once again tried to impose a French logic on the alliance. The most important element of the treaty involved major captive exchange. The Foxes promised to return their captives to the Algonquian allies such as the Illinois, and in return, the Illinois would be obliged to return theirs. Even the French promised to return their Fox slaves, the symbols of alliance that Algonquians like the Illinois had presented to the French over many years.[36] These captive exchanges, the French hoped, would remove the impetus for revenge attacks on the part of the erstwhile rivals. Meanwhile, to compensate for captives each group thus lost through the exchanges, the Foxes promised to "go to war in distant regions to get slaves, to replace all the dead who had been slain during the course of the war."[37] This was meant to appease the allies and erase the causes of ill feelings among them.

But once again, the terms of this peace clashed with the Illinois's own politics. While the treaty recognized the importance of captive taking and kin replacement in Indian warfare, the terms of the treaty were objectionable nevertheless. Of course captives were symbols of alliance, useful for defining outsiders and enemies. To Algonquians like the Illinois, the idea that the French would ransom all their Fox slaves or ask the Illinois and other allies to ransom theirs was offensive. Moreover, the plan to encourage the Foxes to seek new captives "in the distant regions" was probably equally offensive to the Illinois, since this put the Foxes in direct competition with the Illinois for mastery of the western trade. The new plan sent the Foxes to the West to trade with the very people the Illinois considered their own strong allies. Since this threatened the Illinois's position in the borderlands, the whole plan was anathema.

According to intelligence that reached Quebec after 1716, the Foxes quickly began to follow the terms of the treaty. As the governor of New France later reported, they sent slaves back to the Illinois on eight separate occasions.[38] Moreover, Foxes began to discourage their allies—the Mascoutens and Kickapoos—from making any further attacks on the Illinois. But while the Foxes were supposedly trying to uphold the terms of the treaty, the Illinois did not reciprocate. To the contrary, in "various encounters" starting in 1718, the Illinois attacked the Foxes, killing and taking captive several victims.[39] It was an inauspicious beginning to the new Algonquian peace.

All of this was happening in the period before the French had an official provincial government among the Illinois. But in 1719, Boisbriant showed up in Kaskaskia to make it an official part of Louisiana. Now French administrators finally had a person on the ground in Illinois to help guide the alliance and influence the defiant Illinois. As the governor of New France wrote, Boisbriant was supposed to "[urge] the Ilinois to respond [to the Foxes] by some Concession on their side."[40] Indeed, with Boisbriant in the colony, officials hoped that peace was just around the corner.[41]

Arriving in Illinois, however, Boisbriant did not sound like a man dedicated to an Algonquian alliance on the terms that New France envisioned. Making speeches to the Illinois in 1719, he did not urge them to conciliate with the Foxes. Rather, he seemed to stoke their aggression. He promised the Illinois that he would "protect you against the nation of the cunning Foxes, your inveterate enemies." Offering support of "arms, guns, powder and bullets," he pledged "to defend [you] against your mortal enemies, the Foxes." And then he said this: "And if they should have the temerity to defy you while I reside on your lands . . . I shall march at the head of my brave warriors, French and Illinois, with large guns, that will strike with thunder those audacious braggarts, and we shall make cannon wads of their scalps."[42]

Boisbriant's rhetoric here is surprising. New France officials in this moment were frustrated with the failure of peace, and they blamed the Illinois most of all. As the governor of New France wrote, "All would be peaceful on this continent but for the war which still continues between the Ilinois, and the Kickapous and Mascoutins, in which the Renards now find themselves involved, because the Ilinois have attacked them on various occasions since last year, killing and taking prisoners several of that nation."[43] As New France officials saw it, the Illinois were the aggressors, and the Foxes mere— and even *sympathetic*—victims. Vaudreuil even wrote that the Foxes' recent actions "seemed reasonable to me."[44] It was the Illinois who were to blame for attacking the Foxes and the Kickapoos "at a time when they themselves [the Foxes] were only desirous of living at peace with all the Nations."[45] In 1719, the consensus in New France was that all of this was on Boisbriant's shoulders: "It will prove impossible to arrange this peace, unless the officer in command among the Illinois is able to induce that Nation to make overtures to obtain it."[46] Boisbriant was meant to persuade the Illinois to accept Quebec's vision.[47]

But Boisbriant was coming to accept the Illinois's vision instead. Now on the ground in Illinois, Boisbriant had a different understanding of the causes of conflict. As he could easily perceive from his new position, New France visions of alliance fundamentally conflicted with the Illinois's strategic interests. Quebec authorities imagined erasing the divisions among the Algonquians. But this very idea—an Algonquian world without divisions—placed the Illinois in an insecure and vulnerable position. Illinois security, Boisbriant and his officials realized, rested precisely on isolating the Foxes and preserving divisions among them and the Algonquians. For it was division—animosities among the Fox and the Ottawa and the Miami and others—that prevented any one of these groups from making war on the Illinois.[48]

༄

By the mid-1720s, Vaudreuil began putting more pressure on Boisbriant to carry out the plan of reconciling the Illinois and the Foxes. Writing in May 1724, he complained, "I have been Informed that the Illinois had not yet given any satisfaction to the Renards with regard to their prisoners, although the latter had sent theirs back to the Illinois. I think you feel with me that it is important to induce that tribe to send back in good faith the prisoners of the others."[49] He wrote again later that summer, "The renards . . . claim to have Grievances against the Illinois, because the latter detain their prisoners. I am convinced that, if they were to give satisfaction to the Renards on this point, it would not be difficult to induce the latter to make peace."[50] In 1724, Constant Le Marchand de Lignery, the French military officer and commandant at Michilimackinac, wrote to pressure Boisbriant to encourage the Illinois to return their slaves. As he put it, "The Fox Are indignant because, when peace was made in 1716, they sent the Illinois back Their prisoners while The Illinois did not return Theirs, As had been Agreed upon in The treaty."[51] Now, New France proposed sending an emissary to examine whether the Illinois were in fact holding Fox slaves and to negotiate their return.[52] Meanwhile, Lignery established a peace between the Ojibwes and the Foxes in 1724, bringing the alliance closer to fruition.[53] Since the Ojibwes were one of the Foxes' most dangerous enemies, this peace was bad news for the Illinois.

In response to all of this, Boisbriant and other Illinois officials began to defend the Illinois in 1724 and to object explicitly to New France's policies. They made several arguments rejecting New France's interpretation of what was happening. First of all, contrary to Quebec's impression, the Foxes were not innocent. Illinois officials and priests detailed the attacks that the Fox had perpetrated against the Illinois, not just on Indian villages but on the French settlements as well.[54] The French sent dramatic testimony from three Illinois who wrote a litany of what the Fox had done to them since the treaty, listing thirty-nine Illinois victims by name. As the Illinois chiefs themselves put it: "The Renards cannot Ignore or dispute what is stated here, both that they have Been the aggressors, and even that they have Induced several nations to come and kill us and to kill the French, our allies."[55]

Second, Illinois officials insisted that the accusations against the Illinois were false. As Charles Claude Dutisné, Boisbriant's second in command and successor, put it most succinctly, "Our Illinois have no Slaves belonging to the Renards, and have Never acted Treacherously toward them. They [merely] defended themselves."[56] The Illinois themselves also denied possessing Fox slaves, challenging the French to come and examine their villages to see if they could find any unredeemed Fox slaves among them.[57] The story that the New France officials were telling themselves, featuring innocent Foxes and treacherous Illinois, was totally backward, Illinois officials protested.[58]

It was important for the Illinois authorities to insist that New France had the story wrong. But their defense of the Illinois wasn't simply a matter of clearing up who did what to whom. The Illinois officials made a much more fundamental argument, defending and sympathizing with the Illinois's strategic logic and rejecting French policy on that basis. In 1725, two priests in Kaskaskia, Jean Le Boullenger and Joseph François Kereben, critiqued New France's policy on behalf of the provincial government and wrote specifically about the peace that New France emissaries had recently made between the Foxes and the other Algonquians. As they wrote, while this peace reconciled the Ojibwes and the Foxes, it left the Illinois isolated: "The peace he has made between the renards and the Lake tribes is hurtful to this province, and will undoubtedly break up its Trade with three or four nations against whom the renards had to defend Themselves. They [the Foxes] will have only the illinois to Contend with, and the French, Their allies, will support Them."[59]

The missionaries' logic here was clear, if tersely stated. The new treaty between the Foxes and the "Lake tribes" meant that "three or four nations"—groups like the Ojibwe, Ottawa, and Potawatomi—would cease their conflict with the Foxes. This in turn meant that traders could safely resume their activities everywhere in the northern pays d'en haut, which was of course a good prospect for fur merchants in Montreal. But while the new peace ended hostilities among the northern groups, this freed up the Foxes to make renewed attacks on the Illinois. While the Fox formerly had to worry about their hostile neighbors among the "Lake tribes" and therefore would not venture major expeditions to the Illinois Country, the new peace eliminated this danger. Worse, some of the Algonquian "Lake tribes" against whom the Foxes "formerly had to defend themselves" now would probably participate in renewed Fox attacks against the Illinois. As Dutisné observed, "As allies of the Renards, they will join them to come and Continue Their Cruelties Upon us."[60] Keeping the Algonquians divided was better for the Illinois and therefore for the Illinois colony. According to Dutisné, "Had those Gentlemen let the tribes alone, we would have had to Fight against fewer Enemies."[61]

Dutisné's protest here was ostensibly a defense of the Illinois "province" and its trade. As the Illinois officials saw it, the treaty was a simple sellout of the colony's interest. Viewed from an Illinois perspective, the New France traders so eager to establish peace with the Foxes were just greedy, "People of [the] Kind [who] Sacrifice Their country to obtain Beaver-skins."[62] Canadian fur traders were prioritizing profits in the fur trade over the safety of the Illinois colony, and New France policy had effectively abandoned the Illinois to Fox aggression: "We Are not Spared; The Traders from your Quarter give [the Foxes] to understand that we Are other White men."[63] As the priests wrote, speaking for the Illinois colonists, the Canadians "gave account to make [the Fox] believe that we are not Frenchmen of the same nation as those of Canada."[64] Clearly the Illinois officials' discontent with the policy was partially a reaction to its effect on the French colony. As they wrote, "by Letting The Renard attack us, [New France would] prevent this Country from being settled."[65] As Dutisné summarized, "If the ruin of this colony is desired, that is the way to Succeed."[66]

But underlying this argument about the fur trade and the colony's interest was a deeper understanding of and sympathy with the Illinois's strategic interests as well. Because of the unique interests of the Illinois Indians, Bois-briant and Illinois officials developed views about Indian policy that went against the simplistic Canadian logic of pan-Algonquian alliance. By defend-ing the Illinois and articulating opposition to New France policy, Boisbriant and Dutisné opened up a rift in the Illinois's identification with New France, as the evidence presented suggests. But they also won the loyalty of the Illi-nois themselves. As they made clear in several diplomatic ceremonies in the 1720s, the Illinois viewed Boisbriant and Dutisné and the priests with real trust and affection. Addressing Boisbriant, the Illinois professed how happy they were to collaborate with the "French chief" in Illinois but not Onontio in Quebec: "We listen only to the French chief [in Illinois]. It is for him to decide on peace or war."[67] They saw how the Frenchmen in Illinois shared their suffering at the hands of common enemies, perceiving a difference between the local colonists of Illinois and the French on the "Canada side."[68] The Frenchmen in Illinois were different; they understood and followed the Illinois's priorities and were not greedy. As one Illinois chief said, "I admit that we do not kill as many Beavers as the People of the lakes; but our traders here are not Interested [in beavers], and do not supply our Enemies either with powder or with guns to kill us."[69] The rhetoric here expressed solidarity. And while the Illinois spoke of "our traders," the French reciprocated, calling their Indian allies "our Illinois." As Dutisné wrote in one dispatch, "I shall stop our Illinois from going to that country; but they shall Remain with us at their Head, to defend us on our lands."[70]

This solidarity was a reflection of collaboration in Illinois Indian policy. Rather than top-down imposition of imperial priorities, Boisbriant's adminis-tration had sympathized and cooperated with the Illinois during the Fox Wars, even when that meant going against New France's goals. The provin-cial authorities accommodated with the Illinois and made an idiosyncratic Indian policy that defied a naïve and simplistic French program of alliance sponsored by Quebec. But in neglecting to follow Quebec policy, they had succeeded in creating a strong alliance from the bottom up.[71] They did the same thing in the Missouri Valley.

の

Taking control of the Mississippi Valley and the Illinois Country in the 1720s, officials of Louisiana looked west. Since Louisiana was officially managed by the so-called Company of the Indies, a mercantilist project whose priority was profit, officials opportunistically sought ways to exploit the western territories. When Boisbriant arrived in Kaskaskia, one of his goals was to begin to establish a route up the Missouri River, from whence traders could bring back valuable furs and possibly other commodities. Equally important, officials of the company began planning a commercial route to Santa Fé, a Spanish outpost that had valuable resources but was badly supplied by Mexico. As Bienville wrote, "These Spaniards [at Santa Fé] are the middle of gold and silver, but they lack all needful things."[72] If the French could manage to establish an overland trade route, they could profit greatly. Henri de Bourgmont, a former deserter and partner-in-crime of Jacques Bourdon, was appointed by Louisiana officials to establish a fort on the Missouri River for trade and security.[73]

To realize any of their ambitions for commerce, of course, the French had to start with Native alliances. The Missouri River Valley in the early 1700s was home to diverse groups—Missouria, Osage, Wichita, Quapaw, Pawnee, Apache, and Comanche. Obviously, given French goals of establishing trade routes, warfare and conflict among these diverse peoples represented a serious obstacle. As Bienville wrote, "In this view, it would be desirable that all the nations who are between us and that kingdom should make peace."[74] Projecting a vision that seemed quite close to New France's naïve hope for a single Algonquian alliance at the end of the Iroquois Wars, the Louisiana officials planned to reconcile the westerners into a common French alliance system.

A major part of this plan concerned the slave trade. To achieve their hoped-for peace and alliance system in the West, the imperial officials planned first and foremost to shut down the slave trade among western Indians, or at least French settlers' participation in it. Imperial officials had complained about the illegal slave trade in the Mississippi Valley for years, calling it one of the great "dangers" of the settlement in Illinois in the early 1700s and worrying that it would disrupt efforts to control alliances in the Mississippi Valley.[75] As Louisiana officials saw it, Frenchmen were instigating wars among otherwise peaceful tribes in order to get slaves for their farms or for trade to the British in Carolina. In 1720, the directors of the Company of the Indies sent a directive to Bienville complaining that "French voyageurs are buying slaves from the warring tribes of Illinois, Missouri, and Arkansas" and ordering that the slave trade in Illinois be shut down.[76] Louisiana officials ordered Boisbriant to prohibit this activity altogether.[77] As they wrote, "The voyageurs who come to trade try to sow division between the savages and to bring them to make war in order to make slaves which they sell, which is not only contrary to the ordinances of his majesty but is very prejudicial to the good of commerce of the company and to the establishment which he has proposed to make in the said country."[78] Louisiana officials ordered Boisbriant to "arrest and confiscate the merchandise of voyageurs who come to trade in this place of this commandant without getting his permission and without declaring the nations with whom they are going to trade."[79]

Louisiana's logic here was simple, even simplistic. If French voyageurs stopped buying Indian slaves and instead dedicated themselves to peacemaking with the Indians, officials reasoned, the western groups might stop capturing slaves from among one another. And even if that never happened, ending the slave trade would reduce hostilities toward the French, which would open up further opportunities for trade. Creating peace and prosperity was a simple matter of stopping the French from greedily buying slaves. Following this logic at the new outpost of Fort Orleans in the 1720s, a French trader named Poudret conducted a trading expedition on the Missouri during which he tried to redeem a number of slaves to their respective nations.[80] This reflected the imperial vision of reconciling the otherwise peaceful tribes by removing the cause of resentment among them.

But as in the case of the Fox Wars, Boisbriant quickly perceived shortcomings and problems with the logic behind this policy. Although the empire saw the slave trade as perilous, Boisbriant became conversant with the western alliance system and realized the important diplomatic function of slavery in the Missouri Valley. The Illinois and Missouria had long been involved in a widespread slave trade among the western Siouans and Caddoans, from whom they captured or purchased slaves to adopt, to torture, or most commonly to trade to allies. This was, Boisbriant wrote, their "natural profession."[81] While French officials in the 1710s and 1720s blamed this slave trade on French traders who tried to "sow division" among these Indians, in fact the situation was more complex. These slaving expeditions had their own indigenous logic, and they reflected an alliance system and system of enmities that had nothing to do with the French.

In particular, like the Algonquians who united in their common hatred of the Foxes, the western Siouans were all aligned against western groups, especially the Comanche or, as Algonquians called them, Padouke. "All the nations of the Missouri," wrote Boisbriant in 1720 "have made peace with the PaniMaha [Pawnee], but they utterly refuse to make peace with the Padoka. The Otoptata and the Canzes have been at war with the latter [Padoka]. They have taken 250 slaves. . . . This news has been brought to

Sieur Boisbriant by four Frenchmen whom he had given permission to go and buy horses from the Panyouessa [Wichita]. Before the arrival of these French, that nation had also defeated a village of Padoka. It had led away 100 slaves whom it had burned without mercy."[82] As Boisbriant summed up, "All the people of the Missouri have an implacable hatred against the Padouka."[83] Boisbriant realized this was a diplomatic and cultural system with its own logic, and it was best not to resist it. As Poudret discovered, meanwhile, other enmities were equally impossible to reconcile, regardless of what the French did. When Poudret tried to encourage the Osage and the Pawnee to make peace, the Pawnee explained that his efforts were misguided: "they had eaten the Osage and would continue to eat them."[84]

In this context, Boisbriant realized that the French plan of ending the slave trade could actually be dangerous. By refusing to trade in slaves, French officials in Illinois would not be perceived as helpful mediators but as enemies. This was because, as Boisbriant knew, the slave trade for the Missouri was "the only profit they draw from the war and their unique trade [métier]."[85] After a short period of time in Illinois, during which he presumably sought to put the brakes on the slave trade, Boisbriant noted in dismay that "The Nations of the Missouri find it very strange that the French don't want to buy their slaves." By trying to end the slave trade, Boisbriant risked making the most important Indian allies—the Illinois and Missouria—angry. "It is even to fear," he wrote, "that this refusal won't have but unhappy consequences."[86]

And so Boisbriant realized that the French plan to end slave trading in Illinois foolishly jeopardized friendships with the Indians of the Missouri Valley and points southwest. But this was not all, for the misguided policy also risked pushing those groups into alliances with the Foxes. The Foxes of course were opportunistic for alliance in the West since being isolated from the Algonquian alliance system. If the French did not participate in the Missouria and Osage slave trade, then these erstwhile western allies would be, as French officials feared, enticed toward the Foxes. Without French buyers, "These people will have to bring their slaves to sell to the Renards [Foxes] and those pure enemies of the French." Once allied, the Missouria and the Foxes would become a menace to the Illinois, which, as Boisbriant knew, "could very well bring the French a bad coup."[87] Elaborating this point, Boisbriant argued, "If we continue not to buy them, they will continue to sell them to the Foxes. The alliance that this trade would form among those nations cannot but be dangerous for us. The Foxes, our irreconcilable enemies, might draw the Missouris into their sentiments, and possibly engage them to make war on us as well as the Illinois in the middle of whom we are. In that case our settlements would be insecure and thus indefensible."[88]

Boisbriant concluded that the French had been naïve to hope that they could end the slave trade. Indian affairs were more complex than the directors of the Company initially realized. "One should not flatter oneself that the wars between them can be stopped," Boisbriant wrote. In October 1720, even as Louisiana officials contemplated banning the slave trade outright, Boisbriant at Fort de Chartres in the Illinois Country adopted a new policy: actively buying Padouke slaves from the Missourias, Osages, and Otos.[89] The logic was not only economic but political.[90] Convinced of Boisbriant's argument, Bienville wrote approvingly: "However easy M. de Bourgmont may believe it is possible to make peace with the Padoucas, we should drop the idea and push our tribes toward war with them to trade in slaves for the account of the company."[91] Here was the empire endorsing the very thing that Boisbriant had been sent to prohibit among the illegal settlers in Illinois. Following the logic of the Indians' own system, Bienville wrote, "My view is to permit the purchase of slaves from the Missouri."[92]

Thus, despite his original orders, Boisbriant presided over an expansion of the slave trade in Illinois.[93] No record suggests that anybody was ever arrested for trading Indian slaves in Illinois. In 1726, just a year after the end of Boisbriant's administration, there were 68 Indian slaves owned by Frenchmen in the colony, a number that climbed to 110 by 1732. We know little about their individual stories, but it is clear from baptismal records that some were Padoucas, "Patokas," Pawnees, and Natchitoches. These were precisely the groups that Illinois and Missouria Indians defined as enemies. By owning these slaves, the French accepted them as enemies, too. The slaves were symbols of alliance with the Illinois and Missouria Indians. Just as he let the Illinois define the French policy toward the Foxes, Boisbriant allowed the Illinois and Missouria Indians to drive French policy with respect to the western alliance and the slave trade.[94]

೧

As the alliance between the Illinois and French in Illinois became stronger, a paradoxical thing was happening: the Indian and French communities on the ground in Illinois were becoming more and more distinct from one another. Although the French and Indians had lived "pesle mesle" with no division in the early years of the Kaskaskia mission, the villages had separated in 1720 or 1721. All evidence from the 1720s suggests that the separation between the villages of Indians and French in the Illinois increased over time.[95] D'Artaguiette's map from 1732 shows "Caskaskias Éstablissement Français" and "Sauvage Caskaskias" were clearly differentiated spaces, and every map from that period forward in Illinois confirms this fact. Sometime in the 1720s, the Metchigamea were resettled into another separate village outside of Chartres. Even in Cahokia there was a clear distinction between the French village and the "Land occupied by the Cahokias [Indians]."[96] In these increasingly divided villages, intercultural life in Illinois featured "intimacy from a distance."[97] Indian wives of course lived with their French husbands in the French villages. But the French and Indian villages were distinct and segregated.

Not only did French and Indians have separate villages, but there were relatively few opportunities for them to interact within these distinct spaces. While other contact zones in colonial America featured gathering places like taverns and markets for Indians and French to interact and create hybrid cultures, no evidence suggests those things existed in Illinois.[98] For instance, the churches were separate. French Kaskaskia's Immaculate Conception parish was distinct from the Kaskaskia Indian mission, and the two even conducted their rituals in different languages.[99] Indians made some appearances at the notary in Kaskaskia, but these decreased over time, suggesting that Indians had less of a presence in the everyday life of French Kaskaskia and Chartres in the 1730s.

If they did not have common spaces within Illinois, however, French and Illinois people interacted a great deal *outside* their villages.[100] Their most important interactions revolved around military affairs, hunting, and trade. In the former, French and Illinois warriors joined forces regularly, such as in expeditions against the Chickasaw in 1722 and against the Foxes in 1729. More regularly than that, French traders employed Illinois on fur trade and hunting expeditions. Evidence from the notarial records suggests that Illinois and French hunters went together to kill bison and other animals.[101] And Illinois Indians traveled outside Illinois, clearly with delegations of Frenchmen, in order to trade in places like Lower Louisiana, as they did in 1735, as evidenced by a famous watercolor painting by Alexandre de Batz.

And certainly even when Frenchmen were not physically around, the Illinois's lives were affected by their relationships with the French. Trade with the French became the primary economic focus for the Illinois. In the 1730s, in addition to furs and hides, the French requested their Illinois allies to

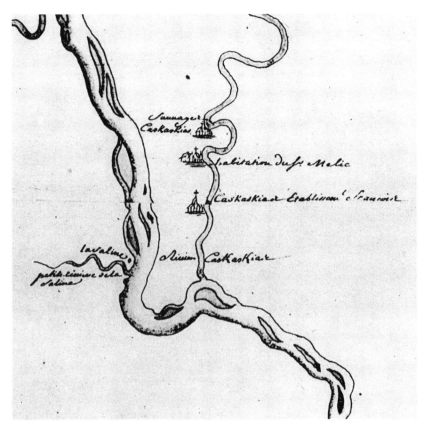

Figure 13. Map of two Kaskaskias, by Diron D'Artaguiette, 1732. This map, based on
a description by Diron D'Artaguiette, shows "Sauvage Caskaskias" and "Caskaskias
Établissement Français" as clearly distinct villages, reflecting the segregation between the
Indian and "French" colonial communities in the Illinois Country.
From Sara Jones Tucker, *Indian Villages of the Illinois Country* (Springfield, Ill.: Illinois
State Museum, 1942).

produce bear oil, tallow, and meat for the colony and for export.[102] In 1736,
one trader from Illinois furnished roughly 8,000 pounds of salted buffalo and
35 tongues to Louisiana.[103] That same year, another trader sold just over 3,000
pounds of salted bison meat, as well as 60 salted tongues.[104] Illinois women
dressed animals for trade and did "porcupine work, which is very well known
in France (where a good deal of it has been sent)."[105] And if they produced
for the market, their lives were also transformed by new technology and

goods they received in exchange for their commodities. French people sold them guns, for instance, and trade goods such as copper kettles, steel knives, axes, and other tools were embraced.[106] Although they preserved many aspects of their material culture, they also learned and embraced "the French way of dressing."[107] Moreover, as the Jesuits pointed out, the Illinois learned French farming techniques and raised livestock and horses. Of course the biggest change was Christianity. By 1730, the Kaskaskia were widely reputed to be the most Catholic Indian group in Louisiana.[108]

But for all these "French" aspects infiltrating Illinois culture, the Illinois had very few "French" people living with them when they went home at night. Their world was bordered. The Illinois Indian women who had married Frenchmen provided a strong link between the French and Native world, as did economic relationships and diplomacy. But the communities were largely segregated. Building on shared understandings developed since the 1690s, the French and Illinois knew what they shared, and what they did not.[109] The texture of contact in Illinois Country was no dense weave. Rather, Illinois's fabric was comprised of a number of distinct patches with certain threads tying them together, albeit tightly.

乙ソ

By letting the Illinois define the terms of alliance in the Illinois Country, Boisbriant and his early administration set the relationship between the French colony and its Indian neighbors on a very strong footing. Reflecting the mutual significance of this alliance system to both the French empire and the Illinois and Missouria Indians, a delegation of Illinois and Missouria Indians agreed to accompany Bourgmont to Paris in 1725, along with Father Jean Beaubois. It was a diverse crew, including the Metchigamea chief Chikagou, four other chiefs, a Missouria woman who may have been Bourgmont's mistress or daughter, and a Comanche slave from the West.[110] Among the people represented by the delegation were all the most important groups from the immediate vicinity of the French Illinois Country villages: the Illinois, including Metchigamea and Kaskaskia, and Oto, Osage, and Missouria. In addition, the Kaskaskia chief Mamantouensa, although he did not travel, sent several speeches to be presented to the French officials in France.[111]

By traveling to Europe, the Illinois and Missouria Indians became part of a select group of Native peoples who willingly put themselves on European ground in the eighteenth century.[112] Fortunately for historians, these relatively rare visits by Natives to European cities drew wide interest, and the Illinois's visit was no exception. The Illinois Indians' tour was covered extensively in the eighteenth-century French periodical the *Mercure de France*. The vivid press coverage makes up the most important archive of Illinois Indian speeches in this period, providing a view into the nature of the relationship between the French and Illinois in 1725.[113]

Like the episode in Louisiana at the beginning of the chapter, many moments in the Illinois delegation's trip to Paris can be read as manifestations of the Illinois's submission and dependency. In the face of the size, power, and opulence of Paris, the Illinois visitors were supposedly overwhelmed. Walking the streets of Paris, one Indian considered the trip the climax of his life. As the *Mercure de France* reported, "He was so pleased with what he had already seen in France that if he were to die at that instant, he would be satisfied and a thousand lives such as he had led would not be able to overcome this satisfaction."[114] The authors of the article in the *Mercure* deployed familiar tropes, noting the Indians' delighted reaction to the opera, their confusion at the size of French buildings, their astonishment at the plentitude of food in a French kitchen, and in general their bafflement at the wonders of French civilization. Given their supposedly primitive sensibilities, one of the delegation reportedly said, they did not even know "how to comprehend the diverse beauties": "Your subjects, your soldiers, your court all astonish us, Your sovereign power, the dazzling aura of your person, Your cities, gardens, palaces, spectacles, And even more the gifts with which you surpass our desires. We carry everything back with us, graven in our memories."[115] The poor Illinois were supposedly embarrassed, looking at their own meager gifts for the French king as paltry. As one member of the delegation said, "We carried with us several skins and works done by our wives, but you would not have held these in great estimation, having already an abundance of more beautiful and costly things."[116]

But even as the authors of the *Mercure de France* tried to highlight the Indians' wonder at French civilization, the Illinois's own quoted words suggest this was not the main theme of their visit. In their own words, the Illinois were soon impatient with the dazzle of Paris. As Chikagou said, he was there to see the king, not to mess around at the opera: "I have come here to see the King in the name of my Nation and its young people. When will I be able to see him? All the pretty things that I see will be meaningless if I do not see the King, our true father as well as yours, and if I do not hear his words to report to my young people."[117]

Indeed, recalling the serious business that the Illinois had come to discuss, the delegates became irritated, reminding the Duke of Bourbon that young people in Illinois "cast toward this place impatient looks" and insisting that all was not well just because the French king had fancy gardens.[118] As the chiefs remarked to all the officials they met, they had complaints, mostly concerning French neglect of their Mississippi Valley possessions. As the chief of the Missouria said, "Our lands have been yours for a long time; do not abandon them. Move Frenchmen there; protect us as your true soldiers and give us White Collars, Chiefs of Prayer, to instruct us. Have pity on us here and everywhere; we are in your hands and you have a large heart."[119] Like the Missouria, the Illinois felt neglected, too, and resented how few resources went into the development of their colonial outpost, particularly their church. As Chikagou explained: "I am so ashamed after having seen the Spanish Chapel at Pensacola, where I helped my father de Bienville in his capture of the place. Yes, my Father, I am ashamed, and it is this that makes me ask you frankly to be generous in our Houses of Prayer, in those of the Metchigamis, in those of the Kaokias and the Tamaroas, and in those of my own nation."[120]

It may have been true that the Illinois were astonished at French wealth, but part of their reaction to Paris clearly was to feel resentment. For as they saw it, wealth created obligation. A truly good father ought to provide for his children. Indeed, as Chikagou explained, the Illinois felt abandoned: "What I see of beauty among the French impresses me; however, these things also make me appear meagre in my own eyes and I despise myself for it."[121] Far from mere submission, what the Illinois delegation expressed was a sense of need and an expectation that the French ought to be good partners: "relieve me of the shame I feel. I also want for all my Nation and its various villages to feel your protection more and more."[122] The Illinois Indians called on the French to invest more in their relationship.

Meanwhile, as Mamantouensa wrote, they also reminded the French about how to be good neighbors. Specifically, the Illinois begged the king to support Boisbriant's promise to keep the French and Illinois population separated. "We have ceded to [the French] the land we formerly occupied at Kaskaskia," he wrote. "That is fine, but it is not good that they come mingle with us and put themselves in the middle of our village and our surrounding lands. I believe you who are the great chiefs, you must leave us masters of the land where we have placed our fire."[123] Speaking to the king himself, Chikagou echoed this sentiment: "I further beseech you, my Father, to confirm the promise made to me in your name by my father de Boisbriant. He promised me that no one would disturb me in my village, that no one would force me to make further moves in order to make room in it for Frenchmen, my brothers and your children, who are thus my kinsmen."[124]

Here was a serious demand. If the French were going to live among them, they had to keep their pigs out of the Indian fields, and they had to keep their population separate. Boisbriant had already made these assurances, but the Indians sought the king's own guarantee that the French would respect their boundaries.

When they finally got to see the king, after meetings with numerous officials, the Illinois continued to present demands. In front of the king himself, however, they turned to a different subject. Revealing the main priority of the Illinois delegation and suggesting the reason that they had agreed to travel to France in the first place, the Illinois focused their conversations with the king on a new topic: the Foxes. Of course, the Illinois had already succeeded in forcing Boisbriant to accept their war against the Foxes and to accept the western slave trade on their terms. But now they wanted the king and the ministers—the "great chiefs"—to pull the entire French empire around to this position. As Chikagou said: "We all love prayer; we are French at heart; and we always wish to follow your commands. Speak when you wish and we will obey. The Fox are your enemies and ours also. Well enough! Order the French to go with all the Nations to strike them down, and I, Chicagou, will myself lead the way and teach them how to cut off a scalp. That is all."[125]

This was significant. Chikagou, also known as Agapit or Anakapita, was the same man who in the previous year had sent to officials in New France a six-page litany of the suffering experienced by his people at the hands of the Foxes.[126] Counting numerous dead, he had made a plea for the French to change their policy and to exclude the Foxes from the alliance once and for all. Now here he was in front of the king himself, urging the monarch to "order the French to go with all the Nations" on a vengeful attack. Chikagou was insisting on the Illinois's own vision of alliance, the one that they had already forced the French at Illinois to accept, an alliance embracing "all the Nations" *except* the one that they defined as outsiders—the Foxes. Having for years resisted New France's attempt to reconcile a pan-Algonquian alliance, now the Illinois presented their alternative vision to the king himself and sought his support for renewed action. Rather than seek reconciliation, the king should pursue an outright war against the Foxes. The Illinois would lead the king's new army into battle.

Accompanying the Illinois Indians in their audience with the king, Father Beaubois also spoke up on behalf of the colony and their Native allies. Informing the king of Canada's misguided policy, Beaubois mocked the Canadian governor, elaborating a point of view that Illinois officials had tried to impress on their compatriots in Quebec for years. "Monsieur de Vaudreuil will amuse the Court by Writing that it is our fault if we have not peace," was Beaubois's message. "He seems to have no other desire than to allow the vein of Beaver skins to flow."[127] A better way was to accept the Illinois's proposal. Standing behind the Indian delegation, the French priest explained that the provincial government of Illinois was united in support of their Indian allies and against Canada's policies.

Now it was the king's turn to respond. He answered them with promises. As the *Mercure de France* quoted him, the king told the Illinois delegation to "Always persevere in the fine sentiments that you now have and depend on my acting in a way that will make you as content when you have returned home as you are here. I will always keep your Nation and its Chiefs in mind."[128] But he clearly went far beyond these platitudes. He spoke to the Illinois-Missouria delegation for more than an hour.[129] Together they likely discussed specifics of French policy, and although there is no record of what they actually agreed to, it seems clear from later French action that the king was persuaded. Henceforth, the French empire as a whole, and not the Illinois colony, would prosecute the war according to what were effectively Illinois priorities.

Chikagou knew that he had succeeded. Reflecting on the meeting with the king, he celebrated the triumph of Illinois diplomacy: "It is over; I am now entirely French and there are no longer any differences between the French heart and my own. Tell the Chief of Chiefs and the Father of the French on my behalf that in my mind he is the finest as well as the greatest of all Chiefs and that I will always love him and want him never to cease loving me and my Nation, which will always love prayer and the French."[130]

The meeting with the king was not a show of subjection, even though the *Mercure* highlighted that theme. It was instead an exchange of promises and demands, resulting in the king's promise to "keep your Nation and its Chiefs in mind" and the Illinois's declaration that "[we are] entirely French." When the Illinois said that they had "French hearts," they were not expressing dependency. They were negotiating as collaborators.

Over the next years, the negotiation produced results for the Illinois Indians. Even though Lignery made one more attempt to reconcile the Foxes and the Illinois in 1726, the Illinois continued their hostility against the Foxes, now confident of increased French support.[131] They made peace with the Kickapoo in 1729, removing one more pillar of the Foxes' strength.[132] By the late 1720s, the Foxes, still isolated, decided to seek protection by traveling east to Iroquois Country where they planned to make a new security alliance. While traveling through the Illinois Valley en route to the East in 1730, however, the Foxes encountered Illinois Indians of the Cahokia famille. After a brief scuffle, the Cahokias rejected Fox requests for safe passage, provoking a new confrontation. The Foxes fortified their camp south of the Kankakee River while the Cahokias sent for reinforcements. The commandant at Fort de Chartres, Robert Groston de St. Ange, quickly arrived with one hundred French colonists and troops and three hundred Indians. They put the Fox under siege.[133]

It was the climax of the Fox Wars and undoubtedly one of the most dramatic battles in colonial North American history. Quebec quickly sent support to the battlefield, marshaling resources and allies—"all the Nations," to quote Chikagou—to support the Illinois just as the king had promised. The siege lasted for a month and involved French soldiers and French-allied Indians from all over the pays d'en haut. The Foxes offered to surrender, but unlike Louvigny in 1716, St. Ange and his allies refused. When the Foxes tried to escape the siege in September, the Illinois and their allies annihilated them, taking hundreds of captives and casualties. By the time it was over, the Quebec government had invested twenty-two thousand livres in the operation. This reflected how the entire imperial policy had been bent to the goal of excluding the Foxes from alliance.

Back in Quebec, the French celebrated news of the victory and the benefits it promised to the empire: "The routes to the Mississippi, as well as to the Sioux settlement will now be open. The Green Bay country will be tranquil, and we will be able to build a good settlement there. The farmers of Lake Erie's Detroit will cultivate their gardens in complete safety . . . this is a general peace whose authors deserve to be rewarded."[134]

What officials did not acknowledge was that this outcome was nothing like what they had originally planned. At the end of the Beaver Wars, the French in Quebec had tried to reconcile the Foxes to the larger Algonquian world; they originally hoped to keep the pays d'en haut tranquil not by exterminating the Foxes but by allying with them. It was the Indians—and especially the Illinois—who insisted on a different path. In 1730, French forces participated in an attack on the Foxes that was actually the realization of the Illinois's vision of alliance, not New France's. It was precisely what Chikagou and the others had gone to France to request: collaboration.

∾

It was in that same summer of 1730 that a group of Illinois Indians went down to New Orleans on the condolence mission discussed at the beginning of the chapter. Expressing sympathy, they offered to do whatever the French asked of them. As Chikagou said, "We have come from a great distance to weep with you for the death of the French, and to offer our Warriors to strike those hostile Nations whom you may wish to designate. You have but to speak. When I went over to France, the King promised me his protection for the Prayer, and recommended me never to abandon it. I will always remember it."[135]

As Jesuit priest Le Petit put it, these Indians were not just pretending or performing. Demonstrating their Christianity, they prayed even when priests weren't looking. Showing their mastery of the catechism, they made it clear that they were more knowledgeable about Christianity than most Frenchmen were. The Illinois were sincere. They were not only all "of the prayer," but "in other ways they are inviolably attached to the French by the alliances which many of that Nation had contracted with them, in espousing their daughters."[136]

In addition to kinship, the reason for this attachment was clear. The Illinois were not desperate or dependent, and it was misleading to suggest, as Lallement did, that "[the French] do with them what we want today." With French help, the Illinois had extended their alliances in the West through slaving and secured western groups like the Missourias away from competitors like the Foxes. Exercising their strength, they then pushed the French to isolate the Foxes from the French alliance in the North, turning the entire French policy on its head. Indeed, with French support, they had not only excluded their Fox enemies but largely destroyed them. Meanwhile, they had remained masters of their territory, segregated from the colonial French population but enjoying the benefits of alliance, trade, and cultural exchange.

The French were not stubborn or absolutist in their relationship with the Native people of Illinois. Understanding the Illinois's needs, they collaborated and bent their policy to the Illinois's priorities. They saw the logic of the Indian system, sympathized with it, and adapted their agenda accordingly. Adopting a policy that was in many ways contrary to imperial plans, the French became collaborators.

Figure 14. Illinois Indians, 1735. This image, *Dessiens de Sauvages de Plusieurs Nations*, shows a delegation of the Illinois trading in New Orleans in 1735. Detail of Alexandre de Batz, 1735 watercolor.

Courtesy of the President and Fellows of Harvard College, Peabody Museum of Archaeology and Ethnology, Harvard University, PM 41-72-10/20 (digital file 60741527).

For their part, the Illinois were collaborators, too. Asserting their "French hearts," they were positioning themselves as allies to the increasingly powerful people that, like them, were trying to control the Mississippi Valley. Indeed, Chikagou's statement that he was "entirely French" is an important reminder that Indians like the Illinois were not wedded to a static "traditional" identity but were flexible and opportunistic when faced with empires in their midst.[137] No different from colonists in their ambitions to improve their conditions, they did not remain inflexibly connected

to a traditional sense of self. At the same time, when they went to Louisiana, just as when they went to Paris, the Illinois in 1730 brought presents
that reminded the French of their particular situation: calumets, buffalo
skins, and Comanche slaves.[138] Presenting these gifts, the Illinois made an
implicit statement: recognize who we are, and do not ignore our own needs.
On this basis, and not on the basis of dependency or misunderstanding,
they collaborated.

Chapter 6

Creolization and Collaboration

When Anglo observers arrived in the Illinois Country in the late 1700s, they recorded their impressions of the French creole people who lived there. Their biased descriptions, as Edward Watts has shown, constructed the French colonists as a foil against which to contrast a heroic image of enterprising Anglo settlers in the early American West.[1] Where the English-speaking and Protestant settlers were entrepreneurial, carrying values of rugged individualism and industry to the frontier, the French were the opposite. Farming lazily in the compact and humble villages of Kaskaskia and Cahokia, the French were peasants—Old World, traditional, and communal. Moreover, like slaves and Indians, the French were what Alexis de Tocqueville called *willing* peasants, in that they were too foolish or passive to see—much less pursue—their own interests in the newly emerging capitalistic order.[2] As land speculator and businessman Gilbert Imlay described them, they were "naïve" and simple, not acting on the landscape but "united with it."[3] Rather than individualistic, they were communitarian. Moreover, while liberty-loving Anglo settlers resented and ignored government authority, the French submitted to the authorities that restricted their enterprises, such as the Catholic Church and the arbitrary commandants who governed their lives. As missionary and pioneer author Timothy Flint said in a typical line on this theme, the French were "Accustomed to the prompt and despotic mandate and decision of a commandant."[4] This image of the French was a useful stereotype for Americans who considered them the antithesis of the self-interested and competitive American individual. Destined to be left behind, the Creoles of Illinois were Old World peasants trying to preserve Old World traditions in the sleepy, isolated villages of the Mississippi Valley.

Actual eighteenth-century creole colonists like Jacques Bourdon would have been surprised to hear themselves and their community described in these terms, of course. After all, Bourdon was a fur trader and farmer, and nothing if not enterprising. To farm his massive holdings in Kaskaskia in the 1720s, he exploited the labor of several slaves. At his death, his estate settlement involved 125 debtors and creditors, including nine Indian partners, reflecting his career as an opportunistic and even exploitative businessman. Socially his life was defined by multicultural adaptation, since his wife was an Indian woman. And while she and Jacques seem to have had a fondness for French culture, they were not interested in peasant stuff. They had fancy things: pewter dishes, walnut furniture, and fancy clothes of limbourg, taffeta, and Dauphiné, an expensive kind of cloth, reflecting their participation in an acquisitive and materialistic economy that extended well beyond the isolated community and across the Atlantic world.[5] Bourdon was exactly what the stereotype said that the French were not: a forward-looking and innovative entrepreneur.

What is more, many of Bourdon's neighbors in Kaskaskia were like him or wanted to be. Bourdon was connected to a lot of people in Kaskaskia by commerce. Figure 15 represents the connections between Bourdon and his business partners, based on contracts, debts, and estate settlements in the notarial archives of Kaskaskia. Reflecting his entrepreneurial activities, Bourdon's connections were to nearly everybody in town. However, many of these people were connected to one another, too. This whole town was not lazy and passive; it was instead a town on the make. It was a town of businessmen and strivers.[6]

Far from passive and traditional, the French colonists of Illinois in the eighteenth century were opportunistic and innovative.[7] Not wedded to tradition, they were flexible and adaptable. After all, two of the most noted characteristics of the culture in Illinois were interracial marriages and a heavy reliance on racial slavery, hardly signals that the tradition and timelessness of "La France Profonde" were transplanted to Illinois.[8] On the face of it, the people of Illinois were not reconstructing an old world, they were creating a new one. Scholars have coined the term "creolization" to refer to the process whereby colonial populations invented new cultures, lifeways, politics, and identities as they adapted to new conditions on the ground.[9] In the early 1720s, the inhabitants of Illinois became Creoles by creating a culture that was not conservative but pragmatic and even exploitative. Social and economic patterns in Illinois defined an idiosyncratic colonial community.

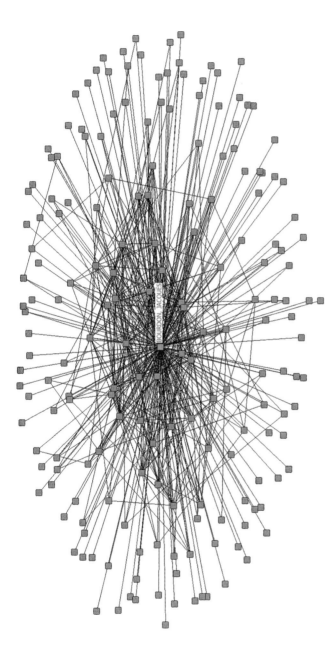

Figure 15. Jacques Bourdon's commercial connections, 1720–25. Based on a comprehensive Social Network Analysis of every notarial transaction in the Kaskaskia Manuscripts in this period, this "ego net" of Bourdon shows all of his commercial ties and connections. Not only did Bourdon have business connections with almost everybody in Kaskaskia—contracts, sales, witnessing of transactions, and so forth—but many of the people he connected himself to were also connected to one another.

Data from *KM.* Image created with and courtesy of Stephen P. Borgatti, *NetDraw Software for Network Visualization* (Lexington, Ky.: Analytic Technologies, 2002).

And if they were not timeless peasants, nor were they submissive. Their entrepreneurial way of life resulted in an often contentious relationship with imperial authorities. As we have seen, Louisiana officials tried unsuccessfully to prohibit interracial relationships in the early years of the colony. In the 1730s, the tension between imperial visions and the colonists' own priorities continued, extending into many areas of life. While French authorities had their own visions of order in this period, the colonists focused less on abstract ideas of order and more on what worked in their frontier setting. French colonists in Illinois did not try to preserve traditional identities or social boundaries. They did not try to follow French law and imperial decrees rigidly. They were flexible, self-interested, and practical. The most conspicuous thing about Illinois as it grew was that it was defined mostly by pragmatic innovation, not timeless tradition. Far from naïve peasants, the Illinois French colonies were inhabited by creole frontiersmen.

℘

A new economic activity began in Illinois in the 1730s: export. The colony had of course exported furs, meat, hides, and slaves to distant markets from its inception, and the Illinois Country settlements had sent wheat to lower Louisiana as early as 1713, inspiring officials to plan an agricultural export economy in the middle of the continent.[10] A 1735 document advertised that the "first" wheat cultivation in Illinois had happened in 1718, which may indicate when the colony first began shipping agricultural produce downriver to New Orleans in large quantities.[11] In the 1730s, however, records in Louisiana illustrate that a new era in Illinois history had arrived. In 1730, New Orleans received 100,000 livres' worth of flour from Illinois.[12] In 1732, the yield was 200,000 livres of flour, carried on 30 pirogues, the distinctive flat-bottomed boat that the Illinois used to navigate the river.[13] The same year, Louisiana received salted beef and bacon, cured hams, bear oil, and tallow. A blight or parasite in 1736 reduced the harvest to only 40,000 livres of flour.[14] But production again picked up in 1737, and the colony exported 100,000 livres once more.[15] By 1738, New Orleans received 300,000 livres of flour. And by 1748, reflecting a sharply upward trend, the Illinois colony exported 800,000 livres of flour.[16]

As agricultural produce went down the river, Illinois merchants stopped off at Natchez and Pointe Coupée, confirming Illinois's position as a supplier to numerous French settlements in North America.[17] Voyageurs traveled to virtually every French colony from Illinois, but none more so than New

Orleans, to which they carried produce and brought back merchandise in increasing quantities.[18] In return for their agricultural bounty, the Illinois farmers imported all sorts of goods—manufactures, textiles, clothing, and even things like billiards tables. Meanwhile, people took these goods and brought them farther into the interior. Fur trade contracts registered at the Kaskaskia notary rose from 16 in the 1730s to 103 in the 1740s, reflecting the increasing availability of trade merchandise and the overall expanding economy. Diron D'Artaguiette described the Illinois economy as he saw it in the 1720s:

> The trade of the inhabitants of the Illinois, who are Canadians, French or discharged soldiers, consists in selling their wheat and other products to the company for the subsistence of the [Louisiana] troops, in exchange for merchandise (which they are obliged to fetch from New Orleans) which they trade to the Indians for quarters of buffalo, bear oil and other meats, which serve them for food or which they sell [in Louisiana] in exchange for merchandise. They also trade in skins, such as beaver, buck and deer, buffalo and bear skins, and other peltries, which they get very cheap from the Indians, and which they sell at a very high price to the traders who come down from Canada every spring and autumn, and who give them merchandise in exchange.[19]

It was a complicated system of enterprise, and D'Artaguiette described it well. What his account from 1722 does not capture, however, is the sheer growth and expansion of this system. As the export economy took off, the entire colony transformed. If the Illinois colony had ever been sleepy and isolated, it was no longer. Illinois became dominated by commodity production, growth, slavery, and striving.

Several detailed censuses from Illinois show the major economic transformation of the colony in the 1720s and 1730s, as agrarian production defined life in the Illinois Country.[20] The period witnessed a massive expansion in land under cultivation between 1726 and 1732, from 2,243 arpents in cultivation to 3,359, an increase of just under 50 percent in six years. Of course, the Illinois inhabitants had a huge advantage relative to colonists in other regions when it came to farming, for it was relatively easy to clear land in the rich bottomlands around Kaskaskia, Prairie du Rocher, Ste. Philippe, and Cahokia. In Canada, clearing two arpents was a summer's work for a single man.[21] In Illinois, Boisbriant observed, "the clearing of the land is easy. . . . The prairie sod is taken up with a mattock [pioche], after which the land is easy to work. Several habitants plow it with one horse."[22] Meanwhile, their farms were populated also with livestock, the numbers of which grew radically. Between 1726 and 1732, the number of cattle grew from 366 to 840, a 130 percent spike. The number of horses increased to 217. A final reflection of the transition to agrarian economy was in the number of mills in the colony, which increased from three or four in 1715 to nineteen in 1732.[23]

Accompanying the shift to agrarian production was a large increase in population. In the 1720s, increasing numbers of migrants began to flock to the Illinois Country.[24] We know that *at least* 226 distinct French individuals migrated to Illinois between 1715 and 1730.[25] Some of these newcomers came with permission, others simply arrived.[26] Of the 87 migrants in this period whose origins are known, the majority (64 percent) were from Canada, although a considerable percentage came directly from France.[27] Certainly rumors of the richness of the Illinois were widespread, and there is evidence that missionaries and proprietors made efforts to attract farmers to the region.[28] In 1723, when D'Artaguiette ordered the first census of the colony, there were 334 free inhabitants in Illinois. The official count from Illinois decreased slightly in 1726, falling to 317, before climbing back up to 379 on the 1732 census.

Single men arrived as they always had, as *engagés*.[29] But another important share of the population growth was composed of Canadians who uprooted their families from St. Lawrence settlements in order to transplant them to the Illinois Country. This brought a new group to the area: Frenchwomen. When Madame Le Sueur visited the outposts of the Illinois in the early 1700s, the presence of a Frenchwoman was so unusual that she was treated as a curiosity by the Kaskaskia Indians.[30] Frenchwomen became less of an oddity in Illinois in the 1720s, as at least forty-two joined the great migration to the area. Most came with husbands, but a few might have arrived in Illinois as part of a government program to provide wives to Louisiana settlers.[31] However, even as many Frenchwomen arrived, there were still lots of interracial couples. It seems clear that more than half of the brides in the French villages of the Illinois Country were Indian in these early generations. By 1730, at least sixty-five Frenchmen had married Indian women since the start of the colony, and at least fifty-one different Indian women had married Frenchmen in Illinois.[32]

By the 1730s, then, families dominated social and economic life in the villages. On D'Artaguiette's census of the Illinois Country for 1723, there were 66 wives numbered in the French villages and 70 by 1732, meaning that 60.9 percent of the habitants had wives. The free population in the village of Chartres in 1732 was dominated by families, since fully 30 out of 43 men, or 70 percent, were married with their wives present. In Kaskaskia, the proportion of men with wives was even higher, since 37 out of 52 were married. Furthermore, these households had lots of children. By 1732, there were 194 children in the colony, accounting for over half the population in the French villages.[33] Perhaps this gives some credence to the Illinois boosters of the eighteenth century who bragged of the colony's agricultural and reproductive fertility: "The earth is very fertile," one wrote, "the climate salubrious, and the women fecund."[34] In any event, by 1732, of the 379 free people in Illinois Country, 302, or 80 percent, could be counted as a member of a family unit present in the colony, whether as a father, mother, or child. These families were a reflection of the agrarian economy, as families obviously constituted the most important unit of labor on the growing farms of the colony.

But it was not just families that did the labor on these new and growing farms. Another feature increasingly characterized the Illinois colonies in this period: slavery. The 1726 census shows 198 total slaves; six years later that number climbed to 275. This meant that the slave population of the Illinois villages made up 42 percent of the total inhabitants. To be sure, Indian slavery had always been a part of Illinois life. But this expansion of the slave population was a rather stunning development, as the export-oriented economy became defined by slave labor.

The population of slaves was made up of both Indians and Africans. Like the immigration of Frenchmen to Illinois, the means by which most of the slave population came to Illinois are obscure. As for the Indian slaves, evidence suggests that they mostly came out of the Missouri Valley Indian slave trade; some entries of slaves in the parish registers refer to the Indians as "Padouca," "Patoka," or "Panis," reflecting the origins of the slaves among Caddoans and other groups in the Great Plains.[35] Illinois inhabitants continued this trade in the 1720s, now with the blessing of the government, and it is likely that the increase in slaves in this period in Illinois came mostly from this channel.[36] At the same time, captives from the ongoing Fox Wars might have provided some additional Indian slaves to Illinois, though the inhabitants constantly denied this.[37] Additionally, some were taken as captives during wars against the Chickasaw in the Southeast.[38] And a surprising number of "Outa8ois" slaves appear in the records as well.[39] The 110 Indian slaves in Illinois constituted 40 percent of the total Indian slaves in the villages. A majority of the Indian slaves, about 60 percent, were women, reflecting the typical pattern of Indian slavery among the Illinois and their western Siouan and Caddoan trade partners.[40]

Roughly 60 percent of the slave population in Illinois was African, and evidence suggests blacks were a major component of the workforce in the new export economy. Indeed, when Boisbriant bragged about the progress of farming in Illinois, he specified that "the clearing of the land is easy with Negroes."[41] A small number of blacks arrived in the Illinois Country before 1720, as wills and estates indicate.[42] These first blacks in Illinois probably arrived with Jesuits in the 1710s. But the great majority were imported in large groups early in the new Louisiana-sponsored administration. Before coming to Illinois in the 1720s, Philip Renault purchased 200 slaves in Santo Domingo, some of whom he brought to Illinois. We know almost nothing about their origins, save for clues we glean from certain individuals' names— "Senegalle," or "Baptiste Banbara," or "Diamant" (i.e., Martinique)—for instance.[43] As soon as the first slaves arrived there was a tremendous demand for more; a 1726 waiting list of slave buyers in Louisiana listed 110 Illinois settlers ready to purchase even though they already possessed 128 slaves.[44]

As the waiting list suggests, slavery was widespread among the households of Illinois. Out of 103 landholders on the 1732 census, more than half owned slaves. The most typical situation was a household with two or three slaves, and 46.6 percent of households had between one and ten in 1732. Only a small number of households were plantation-style operations. These households, like that of Antoine Carrière, had hundreds of arpents under cultivation and more than 20 slaves. Interestingly, while households possessing more than 10 slaves represented only 4.9 percent of households in Illinois, they accounted for around a third of the total population of enslaved people. In other words, owning more than 10 slaves made a French master an atypical planter. But *being owned by* a master with more than 10 slaves was not so unusual for a slave. What is more, over the course of time, these plantation-style farms came to control a slightly larger percentage of total slaves, around 40 percent of enslaved people by 1752. Still, 60 percent of the enslaved population remained on farms with fewer than 10 slaves throughout the French period, and 33.8 percent lived in households with five or fewer.

With its labor system rooted in families and slavery, Illinois witnessed an impressive expansion of farms. Of the 116 households on the 1726 census, 61 of them would find a place on the 1732 census, making it possible to track their progress over six years. In many cases, the households of these "stayers"

Table 2. Distribution of Slaves in Illinois Households, 1732, Aggregated

Number of slaves	0	1–5	6–10	11–15	16–20	21–25
Number of households	50	37	11	4	0	1
Percent of households	48.5%	35.9%	10.7%	3.9%	0.0%	1.0%
Total slaves in category	0	81	85	49	0	22
Percent of total slaves		34.2%	35.9%	20.7%	0.0%	9.3%

Table 3. Illinois Households with Fewer than 10 Slaves, 1732

Number of slaves	0	1	2	3	4	5	6	7	8	9	10
Number of households	50	15	11	3	5	3	3	3	1	2	2

experienced growth in wealth, children, and slaves over the interval. Counting only the householders with cleared land, the size of farms averaged 25.4 arpents in 1726 and grew stunningly to 41.9 in 1732.[45] Even though Illinois was relatively young, this average farmstead was on par with those in Canada.[46] What is more, between 1726 and 1732, the middle 50 percent of landholders in the colony tripled the size of their farms on average to 18.5 arpents of cleared land. The colony was a boomtown.

Yet if 61 out of 116 habitants stuck around and prospered in Illinois between 1726 and 1732, suggesting impressive continuity, what about the other colonists in the 1726 census? What happened to the 55 other heads of households who did not remain in Illinois to be counted in the 1732 enumeration? Of course, some of these men died, and because we lack the vital records required to firmly establish what became of them, our understanding is necessarily speculative. But it does seem clear that a sizable portion of those who did not appear on the 1732 census simply *left* the colony. And meanwhile, whatever the explanation for why these individuals disappeared, *new* people kept arriving. On the 1732 census were 57 men and 37 women who had not been there six years previously, a considerable influx of new people. Indeed, if you add the 57 new households to the 55 householders who were in Illinois in 1726 but were now gone, this adds up to 112 "mover" householders either on their way in or on their way out. That's far more than the 61 who stayed put through the period. And this must have made the place feel just like what it was: an enterprising colony full of opportunistic and competitive strivers. It was a boomtown, not a permanent settlement of timeless peasants. Like most other places in the Atlantic world, it was a world in motion.[47]

And if these patterns of demographics and social life suggest the myth of Illinois as a colony of timeless peasants doesn't quite fit, Illinois also was not a place where people were, as Imlay said, "naïve," lacking initiative, or submissive to government. Having begun without the assistance or design of any imperial authorities, the Illinois colonies evolved in many ways out of step with empire, creating an idiosyncratic and distinctive order. Much of the colonists' distinctiveness evolved from their unique circumstances as a remote colony in the borderlands. The abstract logic of empire often did not work with the particular and pragmatic culture of the frontier.

❧

With the official announcement of Louisiana's supremacy in 1717, the Illinois Country became one of nine districts under the control of the Louisiana Superior Council. Like each of the nine districts, Illinois was controlled by a Provincial Council, which was both a court and a minor policymaking body. The first Provincial Council in Illinois was appointed and established in 1721 by an order titled "The establishment a Provincial Council at Illinois to exercise Justice in the First Instance, both Civil and Criminal, and to Guide the Affairs of the Company of the Indies in this Place of her Dependence."[48] The council was composed of four officials. The commandant, originally Boisbriant, was the chief and first judge. The role of the first councillor went to the principal commissioner of the company in Illinois, the primary nonmilitary officer in the provincial government. The so-called *garde magasin*, in charge of the military and civil provisions in the colony, was second councillor in the Provincial Council. Finally, the Greffier, clerk, or notary was the third councillor and the secretary of the council.[49] These justices together were in charge of civil cases up to a certain degree of severity and criminal cases to an even higher degree. Above them, of course, was the Louisiana Superior Council, to which certain cases could be appealed and to which other cases by necessity had to be referred.

Two major codes of law theoretically governed life in the colony. Dating back to the original 1712 charter of the colony of Louisiana, the Coutume de Paris was adopted as the main civil law code for the colony of Louisiana at large. Legally, then, Illinois was under the jurisdiction of the customs, "our edicts, ordinances, and customs, and the usages of the Provostry and Vicounty of Paris."[50] The Coutume was technically a group of 362 legal titles treating all matters of inheritance, land tenure, property law, marriage, servitude, guardianship, and other civil concerns.[51] In addition, in 1724, the

Superior Council adopted a set of legal regulations concerning African slavery, the Code Noir. This legal code, originally developed in 1685 in the Antilles as part of Colbert's efforts to standardize the operation of the empire, contained sixty articles regulating the control, treatment, and legal status of slaves.[52]

These were the uniform imperial decrees that theoretically were meant to govern life in Illinois. But as Boisbriant had learned when he arrived in the colony in 1719, Illinois had its own idiosyncratic order dating back to its foundation outside the control of government authorities. As the colony expanded and grew in the 1730s, this local order in Illinois diverged in considerable ways from the strict order prescribed in the uniform law codes. In some cases of course this was simply because local officials were not well-enough informed to impose the Coutume de Paris or Code Noir exactly. Everywhere in colonial America "legal pluralism" developed because officials were untrained in the law, and Illinois certainly reflected this.[53] But there were also several ways in which the colonists purposefully defied the strict law codes. This was not because they were anarchic coureurs de bois or "wild Frenchmen." Instead, it was because their own pragmatic order worked well, and so they had little use for strict regulations imposed from outside. In several key areas, the inhabitants of Illinois made their own order and defied the official legal rules of the empire. Perhaps most conspicuous were intermarriage, slavery, and authority.

∾

For outside observers, the most conspicuous part of the Illinois's culture was intermarriage. It was definitely noticeable. As previously mentioned, 65 separate Frenchmen married Indian women before 1735, and these families had lots of children. From these marriages, it is likely that 72–100 mixed-race children were born in Illinois before 1730, a large percentage of the population.[54] Travelers always noted the large numbers of mixed-race people in Illinois. As one observed, it was one of the most striking things about the colony, since "the physical constitution of the settlers was affected" by "the closeness of the Indian nations" and "the admixture of their blood."[55]

But if travelers noted it, so did imperial authorities, and the interracial character of the colony continued to be a point of conflict with the empire. After first trying to prohibit the practice of intermarriage in the 1710s, Louisiana officials seemed to mostly ignore the issue through the 1720s. But as the colony became more robust in the 1730s, officials in Louisiana once again began to get serious about discouraging the practice in Illinois. As Louisiana *ordonnateur* Edmé Gatien de Salmon wrote about Illinois in 1732, intermarriage was making the colony quite *other*: "The habitants there are insolent, because there is nobody . . . who has not everyday made alliances with the Indians, and this by necessity. The *voyageurs* who have established themselves, not finding any young girls, have taken as wives the daughters of the savages. I understand that these sorts of marriages have been authorized by the missionaries, who say that there is not any difference at all between a Christian Indian woman and a white woman."[56]

By the 1730s French officials objected to intermarriage for two specific reasons: race and property. On the one hand, as we have seen, Louisiana officials became increasingly convinced that Indian and French "blood" should not be mixed. Meanwhile, however, they also had a compelling practical concern. The Coutume de Paris spelled out the inheritance laws of the French empire, and under its terms, Indian widows and mixed-race children stood to control lots of French colonial property when their husbands and fathers died. Assuming that some of these widows and children might not always be friendly to French colonial goals, this was a dangerous prospect to Louisiana officials.[57] In 1732, in a flurry of discussion, imperial officials once again decided to try to shut down intermarriage in Illinois.[58]

But meanwhile in Illinois itself, intermarriage continued to be an important part of the social life of the colony. And while the French empire tried to define intermarried families and mixed-race children as outsiders, the Illinois colonists seemed to define them very much as insiders. The Illinois colonists were not simply defying the French empire's desire for order and preferring anarchy. Instead, they were insisting that intermarriage in their colony had its own logic and order.

Although officials in Louisiana wanted to strictly segregate the races, interracial families in fact lived in Kaskaskia along with the French families. Socially and economically, Indian wives and their children were mostly assimilated into the French villages.[59] For one thing, they lived in agrarian households, and the mixed-race families on the 1726 census possessed collectively 343 arpents of cleared land, or an average of 38.1 per family.[60] But evidence suggests they were also assimilated in other ways. As we have seen, the initial community in Illinois was established by godparentage, as the fictive kinship of godparentage—especially godmotherhood—helped define insiders and outsiders in the multiracial borderlands. This only continued in the 1720s and 1730s as Frenchwomen arrived and the colony became more ethnically "French." Rather than segregating themselves into a new, all-French network, the newcomers integrated themselves into the existing community. Examining the network of godmotherhood in the 1720s and 1730s, it is clear that a large number of newly arrived Frenchwomen entered the network by serving as godmothers to Indian women's children or by inviting Indian women to stand as godmothers to their own children. Evidence suggests that the newly arrived French colonists accepted the mixed-race families as full members in the "French" cultural world in Illinois.

A Social Network Analysis of godparentage in Illinois during the 1720s and 1730s reveals how Frenchwomen incorporated themselves into the existing community in the Illinois, effectively co-opting the network. As French-women began arriving in Illinois in growing numbers, certain of them became prominent players of the godmother role. As French families began to arrive to the colony after 1717, there were 27 baptisms of children born to mixed-race parents in Illinois in five years. In 17 of these 27 baptisms (63 percent), a newly arrived Frenchwoman stood as godmother to the child. By 1730, dozens of Frenchwomen were incorporated into the network of 55 Indian women.

An important pattern emerges when we examine the identities of the Frenchwomen in this social network. The Frenchwomen who joined the godmother network most actively were from the most prominent and most powerful households in the emerging French agricultural community. They included women like Françoise La Brise, who between 1715 and 1730 served as godmother for Indian women six times and invited two Indian women to be godmother to her own children. Or Marie-Magdeleine Quesnel, who served as godmother five times and invited two Indian women to be god-mother to her offspring. And then there was Elisabeth Deshayes, who stood godmother for two different Indian women and invited three Indian women to be godmother for her children. Each of these women belonged to a prominent agrarian household in Illinois, according to the 1726 census.[61] The correlation could not be accidental. With just one exception, each of the twelve most active Frenchwomen in the godmotherhood network in Illinois was wife to one of the most well-established farmers in the colony.[62] By the bonds of godmotherhood, it seems, these women surely reinforced the Illinois women's membership in the emerging agrarian culture of Illinois and helped include them within the "French" local culture. Rather than segregating the mixed-race families, the French colonial society in Illinois did what it could to further "Frenchify" them through fictive kinship.

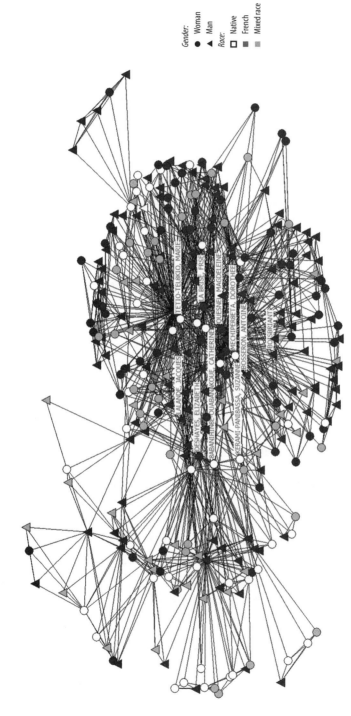

Figure 16. Godparent and marriage network in Kaskaskia, *1700–1735.* By 1735, the connections of kinship and fictive kinship united mixed-race and French families of Kaskaskia in a dense network in which members of the wealthiest agrarian families played the most central roles.

Data from *FB* and *KM.* Image created with and courtesy of Stephen P. Borgatti, *NetDraw Software for Network Visualization* (Lexington, Ky.: Analytic Technologies, 2002).

Gender:
● Woman
◀ Man
Race:
□ Native
■ French
▨ Mixed race

The same general trend holds true when we examine the role of god-fathers. Again, certain men were more highly connected than others through links of marriage and godparenthood. However, these men were not the most important fur traders of Illinois trying to gain an economic advantage. Rather, they fall into two main categories. Some of them, like Jacques Guille-mot-Lalande or Antoine Bosseron dit Leonard, were the most important and wealthy farmers in Illinois Country. Others, such as Pierre Dugué de Boisbri-ant, were the most important military officers, provincial authorities, and landlords. In short, the men with the highest connectivity were not renegade fur traders seeking instrumental trade relationships but rather the best repre-sentatives of an emerging French agrarian culture.

Meanwhile, the mixed-race families were not just connected to promi-nent agrarian households; they represented prominent agrarian households themselves. Even more so than in the founding generation, key Indian women were now particularly prominent in the network of mixed-race fami-lies, connected to an unusually large number of other individuals by the bonds of godmotherhood. Among the most well connected now were Suzanne Kerami-Peni8aasa, Catherine 8abanakic8e, Marie Tetio, and Doro-thee Mechipe8ata (also sometimes written as Michi8e8a). These women belonged to major agrarian households. For example, Suzanne Kerami-Peni8aasa was the wife of Antoine Bosseron dit Leonard, among the most successful farmers in the early mixed-race community. On the 1726 census, Antoine Bosseron dit Leonard possessed 100 arpents of cleared land, 7 black slaves, and 2 Indian slaves, as well as much other capital. When Kerami-Peni8aasa remarried upon the death of Bosseron, the inventory of their prop-erty demonstrated considerable agricultural wealth and the kind of material cultural that reflected their important position in the French world.[63] Likewise, Dorothee Mechipe8ata's husband, Louis Turpin, was a wealthy farmer, in possession of 30 arpents of land, 4 slaves, and 9 cattle in 1726. By 1732, he had cleared 100 arpents of land. Marie Tetio and her husband Jacques Guillemot-Lalande owned a farm of 50 acres along with 5 slaves in 1726; he was captain of the militia.[64] And finally, Catherine 8abanaki8e was the wife of Jean-Baptiste Guillemot-Lalande, the wealthiest farmer in Illinois in the founding generation.[65] All of these women's positions in influential farming and Christian families surely reinforced the "Frenchifying" effect of the kinship network in the Illinois, given their prominence and high connec-tivity in the network.

Other evidence suggests that the mixed-race families became full mem-bers in the "French" cultural world of Illinois. Although imperial officials in

Louisiana worried that intermarriages produced offspring who were "more libertine than the [Illinois] savages themselves," it is clear that the Illinois colonists thought differently, as many mixed-race children married into even the most prominent French families in Illinois.[66] For example, Jean Baptiste Barron, the son of the notary in Fort de Chartres and thus among the village elite, married Domitille Rolet, who was the daughter of the farmer Xavier Rolet and his Peoria wife, Domitille Apani8ois.[67] While it was by no means unique for a mixed-race child to marry into a French family, Barron's lofty position both in Illinois and within the provincial government reflect that the métis children raised in the French villages were considered full members of local French society. To take another example, Marianne Migneret-Milleret, daughter of Suzanne Kerami and Pierre Migneret-Milleret, married Jean Baptiste Texier dit Lavigne in the 1720s. By the 1750s, they were one of the wealthiest families in Kaskaskia.[68] Finally, the children of Marie Rouensa, whose two marriages with Frenchmen produced several daughters and sons, also married into prominent French families in Illinois. One of Rouensa's daughters married Étienne Hébert, a widower with considerable property and capital.[69] Another daughter would in 1737 marry René Roy, son of another important habitant.[70] The fate of these mixed-race children in Illinois suggests that the colonists regarded these families as "Frenchified."

When it came to concerns about inheritance, meanwhile, the Illinois colonists worked out an idiosyncratic practice for interracial families. As mentioned, the Coutume de Paris prescribed that property passed in equal parts to the spouse of a deceased person and to his children. But if this meant that Indian widows controlled the communal property of their marriages in the case of their husband's death, evidence suggests that local practice in Illinois mitigated against their ability to actually exercise this control. One reason was because when one Frenchman died, another was ready to occupy his place by marrying the widow, thereby gaining control of her property.[71] A good example is Marguerite 8assicani8e, who was widowed by Jacques Bourdon in 1723. Records show that 8assicani8e married Nicolas Franchomme dit Pelletier within the first year after Bourdon's death, a fairly typical phenomenon.[72] There is even some evidence that the men who married Indian widows were friends or associates of the deceased husband, suggesting that there was a planful succession in some cases.[73]

Frenchmen of the Illinois Country occasionally used what seems an even more explicit strategy to prevent the dilution of French property through the Coutume de Paris. Rather than allowing Indian widows to control their own property as they saw fit, the French of Illinois appointed guardians to "over-see" and "assist" Indian widows with the disposition of their property. For example, after habitant Louis Pessier was killed at the Natchez in 1721, local authorities in Illinois appointed a "caretaker of the estate" for his widow, Catherine 8a8anakikoy.[74] In 1728, Illinois colonists even petitioned the Louisiana Superior Council—the colony's highest authority—for a modification of the Coutume de Paris's inheritance laws. Petitioning together with Jesuit Jean-Baptiste Le Boullenger, the inhabitants asked for an idiosyncratic law that would stipulate "That Indian women . . . [who] shall become widows of Frenchmen, shall not have the disposal of any real property remaining after the death of their husbands; that they shall only be paid an annual pension of one-third of the revenue of the said property; and that the remaining two-thirds shall belong to the children and heirs, if any, and if none there be, the property shall be administered by a curator for vacant property."[75]

Finally, when it came to the children of mixed-race families, the agrarian community in Illinois sometimes simply ignored the official rules of the Coutume de Paris and disinherited children who threatened to take their inheritances outside the French villages. The best example in this connection is Marie Rouensa, who disinherited her son after he married an Indian woman and went to live in the Indian village. As Marie announced in her will, "He has persisted in his folly and never repented by remaining among the Savage Nations." For this decision, he lost his share of the family estate, which instead passed to his brothers and sisters, all of whom had sensibly married into the French community. He could have his property back, but only if he repented and came back to live among the French. His family would always be "waiting for his return and his repentance."[76]

In 1732, Louisiana officials once again renewed the call for a law to prevent intermarriages between Frenchmen and Indian women in Illinois. As Salmon wrote, intermarriages were ruining the colony, especially on account of the "mixed blood of the *Métis* who are . . . established [in Illinois]." These people, Salmon wrote, "have corrupted hearts [and are] more dangerous than the pure Illinois (*Illinois francs*), which is known already from experience in the past."[77] Moreover, rather than slowing, the pace of intermarriage was actually increasing in the colony, despite Louisiana officials' efforts. As the president of the Navy Board wrote regarding the matter:

Le Governeur and the Commandant Ordonnateur of Louisiana
have informed me that the marriages of Frenchmen and Indian

women are becoming more frequent in Illinois. It has been observed
that not only are such alliances dishonorable for the Nation; They
could have consequences very dangerous for the tranquility of the
colony. It has been represented that the missionaries make these
kinds of marriages too easily and that they even have contracted two
of them in a very short time, although the commandant of that post
had been informed and he had judged that the children that they
produce will be more libertine than the Savages themselves.[78]

By 1735, determined officials in Louisiana wrote finally to ban the practice.[79]
    But in Illinois, because of the measures they had taken to make intermar-
riage work as a tool for integration, colonists rejected these imperial decrees.
Composing a kind of manifesto to Louisiana officials in response to their
charges and the new restrictions, Jesuit Father René Tartarin mounted an
important defense of intermarriage in the colony. As he wrote in a six-page
letter, the Illinois colony had its own local order. In Illinois, he asserted,
mixed-race families were not corrupt, far from it. These families were "fixed
among the French." The offspring of the families were "able to marry into
French families and thus . . . completely lose the tendencies that their original
birth has given them." Indian wives had fully "left behind their [Indian]
families." Their children were raised as "true Creole Frenchmen and Frenchwomen [véritable creol françois et françoise]." And in general, these mixed-
race families were helping to produce a prosperous, stable community.[80]
    Here was an important moment in Illinois history. Unlike the imperial
officials, the Illinois inhabitants cared little about ideas of race or the technical rules of the Coutume de Paris. The Frenchmen and Illinois women had
come together pragmatically to create successful agrarian households. This
put them in tension with the empire, but it was a hallmark of the local
culture.

                                    ✌

The debate over intermarriage reflects how Illinois colonists worked out their
own ideas of racial boundaries and identity, distinct from the strict logic of
Louisiana and the workings of the Coutume de Paris. Meanwhile, slavery was
another area of colonial life that the empire tried to control through strict
regulation. To be sure, when it came to relationships between slaves and free
people, the racial hierarchy in Illinois was quite rigidly defined. But as in the
case of interracial marriages, the racial order of Illinois fell out of step with

the official imperial decree. The Illinois system was idiosyncratic and practical and did not closely follow the prescriptions set forth by the Louisiana government.

What were race relations like between slaves and free in Illinois? Stereotypes held that Illinois farmers lazily and brutally lived off the labor of their powerless slaves.[81] But the situation seems more complicated than this. Indeed, although the labor system was defined by a strict racial logic, both slaves and masters held power in Illinois.

Owing to a lack of records, it is hard to reconstruct the labor system in Illinois with any specificity. Indian slaves—especially women—might well have specialized as domestic laborers.[82] Meanwhile, black slaves were more likely to do field work on most farms and possibly were the exclusive agricultural labor on the big farms. But there is important circumstantial evidence to suggest that just about everybody in Illinois—slave and free, Indian and black and French—worked in the fields, side by side, to produce the impressive agricultural yields that defined Illinois farming in this period. This conclusion involves deductive logic and some basic calculations. Using eighteenth-century farming techniques like the ones employed by the Illinois farmers, ten arpents were the most that one person could manage to farm on his own. This is because when the wheat ripened, there was a window of ten days to get it off the stalks before it rotted.[83] Since one man could handle roughly one arpent per day, ten arpents was the maximum that any one man could reap during the harvest by himself. Since we know the number of acres under production on each farm in the Illinois Country in this period, we can make some guesses about how the farms were actually worked. The important point is this: by 1732, habitants and slaves in Illinois had put so much land under cultivation as to suggest that everybody in the colony—slave and free—was probably farming. Moreover, given the fact that most farmers employed a small number of slaves, it seems very likely that most farmers worked side by side with their slaves in the field. In contrast to the image of the lazy French farmer living off the back of his slaves, everybody in Illinois shared the labor burden and worked hard.

The basic fact of working together probably went far to define the nature of slavery and race relations in Illinois. Another important factor was the frontier location of the colony. As several scholars have argued, the frontier environment of Louisiana meant that slaves had many options for escape. Further, since the colony was so far from a supply of more African slaves, and since we know that the supply was much lower than demand, masters

Table 4. Labor in Illinois (burden per worker)

		Average number of laborers per farm	Average holdings per farm	Average number of arpents per laborer
1726	Not counting children	4.1		5.7
	Counting children	5	25.4	4.94
1732	Not counting children	4.1		11.5
	Counting children	6.2	41.9	7.5

had to take care of their valuable slave property. These facts mitigated against the brutal labor discipline that characterized other colonial zones.[84] Slaves exercised considerable power relative to their masters and could not be "dominated" as in other places, as one French observer noted.[85] Rather than dominating them, then, French colonists "integrated" slaves into village life in Illinois.[86] Slaves worshiped along with the French community at the Catholic churches. Almost all the slaves in Illinois were baptized, as records show.[87] Furthermore, since two-thirds of slaves lived and worked in the "small world" of their master's household, rather than on a big plantation, they may not have preserved any cohesive African identity among themselves as slaves did in other early American colonies.[88]

Meanwhile, slaves were also "integrated" into village life through the institution the family. Many slaves married in the church, and they had considerable families. As the census for 1732 shows, the thirty-three black female slaves in the colony collectively bore sixty-seven children, more than two children per mother; these numbers were almost on par with those of the Frenchwomen of the colony. Even slaves in households without many other slaves were not excluded from family life, since slaves belonging to different owners could and did marry. When slaves were baptized, their godparents often were the same people who were prominent in the godparentage network discussed earlier.[89] In addition, godparents to slaves were frequently not their owners, suggesting that slaves had social connections beyond their households.[90] Given the collaborative labor relationships between masters and slaves, together with the integration of slaves into French colonial life, it is easy to imagine that race relations were more harmonious in Illinois than in other slave societies.[91]

On the other hand, slavery in Illinois was certainly brutal in many cases. We get glimpses of this in court records showing slaves who were whipped, who tried to escape, and, in one poignant though mysterious case, who committed infanticide.[92] A convict called Perico was executed in 1725 after whipping "in order to intimidate those who might count upon a lengthy delay in punishment for any misdeeds."[93] In 1738, a Frenchman broke the arm of a slave he was leasing from the Jesuits.[94] In 1743, several runaway slaves were corporally punished according to the Code Noir, and another ran away and later died after being "mistreated."[95] Still, even as slaves' lives no doubt were defined by cruelty and violence, evidence suggests that bonds of affection often existed between some owners and their slaves. For instance, in his will of March 1728, Nicholas Pelletier de Franchomme, one of the wealthiest colonists in Kaskaskia, requested his heirs to "be kind to the slaves" and to show special kindness to one of the slaves in particular.[96] And while uncommon, it was not at all unheard of for owners to manumit their slaves in their wills, suggesting that freedom for blacks and Indian slaves was a possibility.[97] One habitant manumitted his slave "in recompense for the services which she has rendered me" and stipulated that "she can establish herself wherever she sees fit."[98] One dying man made sure to settle debts owed to his slave through his will, suggesting the slave exercised a level of economic autonomy and power.[99] Furthering this impression, labor contracts and other documents suggest that some blacks acquired their freedom and worked for their own wages in Kaskaskia.[100]

In short, it is hard to generalize about slavery as it evolved in Illinois, since much of the surviving record is ambiguous, and evidence is simply scarce.[101] But what is certain is that relations between slaves and masters in Illinois did not always follow the specific logic laid out by the Code Noir.[102] In Illinois, the code was definitely in effect, and we know that colonists knew about it. When thirteen slaves nearly escaped in 1743, Judge Delaloere Flaucour of the Provincial Council insisted that the Code Noir be read several times in public in Kaskaskia to remind residents of its terms.[103] Meanwhile, some colonists obviously knew about the Code Noir because they sometimes followed its stipulations to the letter. A good example is when Jean Bourbonnais and Elisabeth Deshayes petitioned to manumit their slave in 1746. In their petition, they specifically cited article 50 of the Code Noir, which stipulated that they needed permission from the council to make the manumission official.[104] Clearly habitants knew about and sometimes followed the Code Noir in their regulation of slavery.[105]

But not always. For instance, the Code Noir prescribed that the members of black slave families, particularly husbands and wives and their children, could not be sold separately. As Carl Brasseaux argues, this stipulation was rigidly enforced in Lower Louisiana.[106] In Illinois, however, it was routinely violated. To be sure, eighteen instances appear in the notarial records of slave families being sold together between 1720 and 1763.[107] But sales of individual slaves were much more common. Indeed, there were around 150 cases of slaves sold singly in Illinois during the French regime, and in at least 12 of these cases—and probably many more—families were dissolved.[108] In other words, this stipulation of the Code Noir was often ignored, and it is not hard to imagine why. Black slaves were important to the farming economy of Illinois, but not many people could afford to support or invest in a whole family of slaves.[109] Since most slave owners owned just a small number of slaves, and since many slaves belonged to families present in Illinois, the prohibition against breaking up families was a dead letter in Illinois. Frequently, the inheritance or sale of a slave in Illinois required violating the Code Noir. The colonists mostly ignored it because it did not fit their circumstances.

Other aspects of life in Illinois made it difficult to apply the Code Noir strictly. A dramatic and interesting example of Illinois colonists ignoring the code comes from the case of Jean Baxé. In 1730, a slave named Jean Baxé was convicted of striking a Frenchman named Bastien. In the trial, which established Baxé's guilt, the Code Noir was invoked.[110] In a case like this, as the Provincial Council ruled, and as the Code Noir stipulated, the slave Baxé deserved death.[111] But in a curious twist, he got off with a lighter sentence— whipping and a public apology. As documents show, the reason for the reduced punishment was because Mamantouensa, chief of the Kaskaskia, intervened in the court's proceedings and pleaded that mercy be shown to Baxé. And so the sentence was lightened. There's no telling why Mamantouensa stepped in or whether his action reflected a close relationship between himself and the slave or between Indians and black slaves more generally. But here's a case when local circumstances trumped imperial regulations; the multicultural community of Illinois resisted the neat and rigid logic of race relations encoded in the Code Noir.[112] And if the case of Baxé reflects a time when frontier conditions made it hard to apply the Code Noir strictly, it was not the only time when the colonists were lax in their enforcement of slave discipline. For instance, when a number of slaves escaped in 1743, colonists in Illinois were admonished for being too lenient. After tracking down the deserters, Judge Flaucour reminded the colonists to be strict in their treatment of their slaves and made the colonists promise to "conduct their slaves more carefully."[113]

The frontier conditions in Illinois created an idiosyncratic system of slavery, one that fit imperfectly with the strict logic of the Code Noir. As it did with the issue of intermarriage, the empire wanted to regulate the institution of slavery according to rigid and arbitrary rules. But the system of slavery and race relations in Illinois followed a different, locally determined logic, probably developed first and foremost in the context of the close relations between masters and slaves who worked side by side every day. Given the distinctive situation of the colony, the colonists were pragmatic and had little use for arbitrary rules on race relations.

❧

The pragmatism that Illinois habitants exhibited in their race relations also extended into their approach to political authority more generally. On the one hand, of course, the colonists welcomed empire and were enthusiastic users of imperial authority when it helped them. For instance, they petitioned the government regularly, sending well over a hundred petitions to the Provincial Council between 1720 and 1750. Some petitions sought government help in settling business disputes or debts.[114] Disputes over property damage also frequently prompted petitions to the council. One group of Kaskaskia residents petitioned the council to intervene when their land was damaged by other Kaskaskians driving carts to the saltworks.[115] Some even sought the government's intervention in gambling disputes, as a curious case from 1726 makes clear.[116] Most commonly, Kaskaskians petitioned the council to intervene on matters of succession or guardianship. Clearly Kaskaskians wanted the provincial government to assist in protecting the inheritance of minors more than anything else.[117] The colonial population in Illinois came to rely on the government to help them manage various areas of life, and they looked for the regularity of the Coutume de Paris to help them resolve questions in the trickiest matters of inheritance and property.[118]

Meanwhile, if they sought regularity in actual disagreements, they also increasingly used the legal institutions of the local provincial government to avoid disputes in the first place. The most important way in which Illinois colonists welcomed imperial authority and law was certainly by utilizing the office of the notary, or clerk of council.[119] Fifteen notaries served the Illinois Country throughout the French regime, and the colony was never without one after 1723. In fact, for the entire period between the founding of the

Table 5. Habitant Petitions to Provincial Council, 1720s–1750s

	1720s	1730s	1740s	1750s
Number of petitions to Provincial Council (not related to confirmation of land grants)	14	32	62	6

colony and the end of the French period, the colonists went to the notary to register approximately 5,200 documents and agreements.[120] Many of these documents reflect the colonists' desire to protect their assets and validate their economic ventures. Between 1735 and 1750, around 135 individual fur traders, voyageurs, and merchants appeared in over 200 official actions recorded by the Illinois notaries, mostly contracts and partnerships. Meanwhile, reflecting a similar opportunistic use of the notary as a means to secure property, habitants petitioned for land titles and official deeds.[121]

But even as they used the tools of the empire for their own purposes and to gain legitimacy, the colonists in Illinois did not fully accept imperial authority as absolute. For instance, while they registered their landholdings with the provincial government and sought legitimacy of their holdings, they actually set up a peculiar system of landholding that was significantly out of step with the prescriptions of the Coutume de Paris.[122] Although technically their situation required them to pay taxes and live according to traditional rules of manorial obligation and hierarchy, the colonists totally subverted, or simply ignored, these traditional expectations. Landlords who technically owned the concessions in Prairie du Rocher could not collect the taxes they were owed by habitants. As one would-be seigneur, Jacques-Gaspard Piot de L'Angloiserie, sieur de Ste. Thérèse, acknowledged in Illinois in 1737, nobody settled on his land actually paid any rent. "I exact nothing from the settlers on [my] prairie," he wrote. And since they paid no *cens et rentes* or any seigneurial obligations at all, Ste. Thérèse concluded, "They are all lords and masters."[123] In 1737, 1738, and 1740, the habitants of Prairie du Rocher were apparently delinquent on their tithes.[124] And evidence suggests that nobody ever paid the *taille*, the basic tax prescribed by the Coutume de Paris, in Illinois.[125]

This lack of seigneurial structure within the landholding system was no accident. Rather, it was the consequence of a conscious desire on the part of

Illinois inhabitants to maintain their independence. When they petitioned for and received their land grants, the habitants in Illinois sought to hold their land effectively in fee simple, freehold, or *en franc alleu*.[126] One dramatic example of this came in 1731 when the Seminarian priests at Cahokia began to disburse land from their concession to new settlers. Although the Coutume de Paris technically allowed the priests to treat the land as a seigneury and thus exact all the typical obligations from prospective settlers, the new settlers rejected this. As Father Mercier recalled, the habitants assertively demanded land on favorable terms from priests at Cahokia, refusing to pay *cens et rentes* or submit to any other obligatory arrangement. As Mercier concluded, the habitants, and not the Seminarian priests (the concessionaires) or the Louisiana government, were in charge of land: "The *habitants,* having absolutely demanded that their lands . . . [be granted] in the same manner as it was granted by all the concessioners or seigniors to all the *habitants* of the Illinois, we were not in a position to refuse them."[127] As he elaborated, "We could not refuse them, not only so that we would not live alone at this mission, which would not be expedient for us, but also not to give occasion of crying out against us, which would not have failed to happen."[128] It is interesting to note that the priest included here his hope that hierarchical arrangements would eventually be enforced: "As to the *cens et rentes*, no habitant pays it as yet in all this country; that, no doubt will be done later."[129] In fact, it never was. As another priest wrote, concessionaires were forced to give "tracts of land gratuitously to all."[130] This was, in short, an antifeudal land policy in Illinois, openly in violation of the Coutume de Paris.

The Illinois inhabitants thus took a pragmatic approach to their relationship with the government and ignored its authority in certain ways. In the 1730s, a frustrated official in Louisiana concluded that the situation had gone too far and lamented how the colonists in Illinois relished their position "out from under the eyes of the government."[131] As one Louisiana official complained: "They are [in Illinois] living in a sort of independence, not having at all a strong enough officer who can maintain the order and the police. . . . There is no kind of order there, and all the people are their own masters."[132]

This was an exaggeration. The colonists in fact were not living in independence and in many ways were inviting "the eyes of government" into their lives as businessmen and litigants. But at the same time, they were pragmatic and practical, asserting their own interests and ignoring some of

the imperial decrees that made little sense in the frontier environment. They
were insisting on collaboration.

❧

At the end of the colonial period, the traveler, mapmaker, and illustrator
Victor Collot visited Kaskaskia on a secret fact-finding mission for the French
Republic. Drawing an iconic Kaskaskia chief in traditional headdress
(although wearing a cloth cape) and creating a picture of a typical Illinois
habitant's house, Collot wrote that the French Creoles of the Illinois were
stubbornly traditional and backward. So stuck in their ways, these people
could not even see when their own interests conflicted with the "custom"
and tradition that they lazily upheld. As Collot wrote: "If they are advised to
change any practice which is evidently wrong, or if observations are made to
them respecting the amelioration of agriculture, or the augmentation of any
branch of commerce, the only answer they give is this: 'it is the custom; our
fathers did so: I have done well; my children will do the same.'"[133]

Here Collot articulated a stereotype of the French that would last in the
popular imagination into the nineteenth century. But this spirit of passivity
and traditionalism would not have been recognizable to the eighteenth-century
inhabitants of Illinois Country. In the colonies of Illinois, multicultural families
and slaves worked the maximum amount of land they could, ignoring inconvenient imperial decrees in order to maximize their profits and adapt flexibly to
frontier conditions. They lived nothing like their fathers but rather were Creoles whose lives were defined by hybridity and adaptation. Moreover, they
carried their creative and adaptive spirit into their relationship with government. In so many ways, they could not have been more different from the
"traditional" peasants that outsiders regarded them to be.[134]

Few French colonists of this era left documents to tell us what they
thought of their own identities or culture. But Mary Cerré, daughter to a
man who moved to Illinois in the 1730s, remembered her father as the opposite of Collot's passive traditionalist stereotype. Recalling what had brought
her father to Illinois, she explained that he was animated not by tradition but
by something modern, a "need to move, to change his situation, this desire
to see and feel new things."[135] The creole colonies of Illinois, defined by
diversity, exploitation, and flexibility, were shaped by this spirit of innovation
and adaptation, by a desire, or at least willingness, to "see and feel new
things." Far from an old world of peasants, the colonists of Illinois were
creole collaborators.

Drawe par Tardieu l'aîné.

French Habitation in the Country of the Illinois.

Figure 17. "French habitation in the country of the Illinois." Part of a late eighteenth-century American literary discourse that often represented the French as "traditionalists," Victor Collot made this depiction of a humble habitant's dwelling after his 1796 voyage to the Illinois Country. From Georges-Victor Collot, *A Journey in North America* (Paris: A Bertrand, 1826).

Grave par Tardieu l'aine

Indian of the Nation of the Kaskaskia

Figure 18. "Indian of the nation of the Kaskaskia." Victor Collot's depiction of a
Kaskaskia Indian emphasized the Indian as warrior and wearing a headdress. From
Georges-Victor Collot, *A Journey in North America* (Paris: A Bertrand, 1826).

Courtesy of the Illinois History and Lincoln Collections, University of Illinois Library.

Chapter 7

Strains on Collaboration in French Illinois

In the 1750s, the French government built a new Fort de Chartres, replacing the old, dilapidated one built in 1725. The new fort was a big improvement. Constructed of limestone from a quarry near the settlement of St. Philippe, it was upon its completion one of the largest stone forts in North America and the largest by far in the French empire between Mobile and Niagara.[1] It was fifty-two meters on a side, built on a "star" pattern with bastions at each corner. Inside were a spacious commandant's house, a chapel, two soldiers' barracks, a dungeon, a magazine, and other structures for military functions. As Philip Pittman, a member of an early British occupying force in Illinois in the 1760s, put it, "It is generally allowed that this is the most commodious and best built fort in North America."[2] Locating such an impressive monument in the remote middle of the continent was of course an effort by the French government to project imperial strength and power.[3] It was meant to communicate the French empire's control of the interior of the country.

But if the new fortress was meant as a straightforward projection of imperial power, the actual history of the building reveals a different dynamic—a complex collaboration between local communities and imperial authority. First of all, the operation and even construction of the fort followed a fraught process of cooperation and negotiation on the ground. Reliant on local laborers and soldiers to construct the fort, the engineers in charge of Fort de Chartres had to tolerate a slow schedule. The colonists charged high wages and badly delayed the fort's construction by profiteering. They helped French soldiers desert from the fort when military officials became arbitrary in their command. They treated the new fort opportunistically, as an occasion for local gain.

Figure 19. Fort de Chartres. This image of Fort de Chartres shows it in its reconstructed present state. British observer Philip Pittman called it the "finest" stone fort he had seen in North America in the 1770s.

Courtesy of the Illinois Historic Preservation Agency.

And even when things were operating smoothly from a logistical stand-point, the fort was more often the setting for negotiation than it was a base for the projection of imperial strength. Of course, the commandant of Illinois who oversaw the construction of the new fort, Jean Jacques de Macarty-Mactigue, tried hard to create a military command in the colony consistent with the powerful new structure. He began his administration with an ambition to create order and "dominate" Indian allies and French colonists. Questioning their loyalty, he refused local Indians when they sought protection inside the fort's walls. Ignoring previous lessons in Indian diplomacy, he tried to pressure the Illinois Indians to disregard their own longstanding politics in favor of French priorities. Meanwhile, he tried to press habitants into militia service in pursuit of imperial goals that they did not share. All of these were foolhardy attempts, however. Colonists and Indians rejected his authority and forced Macarty to follow and endorse their own priorities, insisting that the fort was there to serve their interests. By 1754, aware that the reality of French imperial power did not match the hopes expressed by the magnificent monument, the Louisiana government recalled Macarty and replaced him with a new commandant who recognized the necessity of collaboration.

As impressive as it was, the fort was not a symbol of simple power. It was a symbol of something more interesting: empire by collaboration. It was an imperial monument that actually was built by, and wound up serving the priorities of, the local population as well as the empire. And in this sense, the fort is a good symbol of the nature of imperial authority in Illinois in the 1740s and 1750s more generally. Indeed, the fort was created by a reluctant French government at the end of a period of considerable setbacks. After taking over the colony in 1731 from the failed Company of the Indies, the French government invested much and got little in return from its frontier colony. The French failed to project strength and lost credibility in the eyes of the local Indians. Threatened by English incursions and losing the allegiance of their longest-running allies, however, the French reinvested in Illinois, hoping to avoid losing their colonies in America altogether.

Like the fort itself, the French empire in Illinois was not a straightforward projection of power in the years leading up to the Seven Years' War. It was a product of failed imperial domination and its replacement with a different imperial approach, one that put French officials often at the direction of opportunistic French colonists and Indians. Together, colonists and officials rebuilt Fort de Chartres, and they rebuilt a strained collaboration in the final decades of the French regime.

೧

The period of the 1730s was a high point of collaboration between local and imperial agendas in Illinois Country as the colony grew and government became stable. Two commandants—Robert Groston de St. Ange, who held office from 1730 to 1733, and Pierre D'Artaguiette, who held office from 1733 to 1736—oversaw what historian Clarence Alvord calls the colony's romantic age, which is to say its most successful and prosperous period. These commandants established a solid relationship with the colonists.[4]

The process of establishing government in the colony had always been one of trial and error. St. Ange and D'Artaguiette were sent to Illinois in the 1730s to restore a good relationship after Boisbriant's early successes had taken a wrong turn. In 1726 a short-lived commandant called Sieur Pradel even temporarily lost control over the colony when he failed to collaborate with the inhabitants. Although details are scarce, it is clear that Pradel's main offense came when he arrested a colonist for "sedition" and, as a later investigation revealed, made several "imprudent orders" to the habitants. In response, the colonists revolted in defense of their "fellow citizens [*concitoyens*]."[5] As the report had it, "violence was exercised on many parts," as the colonists lost confidence in the provincial government in Illinois. Louisiana officials were forced to recall both the commandant and the garde magasin (who together made up half of the Provincial Council), sending new officers to "establish prudently the authority of the King and that of the Company, and cut off the insurrections of the habitants, and cause them to return to their duty." The colonists, badly aggrieved, needed to be reassured of the justice of the government. As the governor of Louisiana instructed the new provincial officials: "assure them of the protection of the Royal Council, which will return their pride and dignity."[6]

The new commandant was Pierre de Liette, and he was evidently popular.[7] But during two years in command at the Illinois, he replaced Pradel's too-strict regime with one that was too liberal. When the Louisiana colony became a royal possession in 1731, officials complained that the Illinois inhabitants lived "without a strong enough government."[8] The colony was full of "libertines who establish themselves in this place in order to be out from under the eyes of the government."[9] Louisiana officials viewed the Illinois inhabitants as "roguish" and "mutineers."[10] As one Louisiana official wrote, Illinois needed a government to "impose, both on the Indians and habitants alike who are roguish and turbulent and who cause altercations."[11]

St. Ange and D'Artaguiette were charged with increasing security, quelling the rebellions, and increasing safety. They succeeded, helping the colonists develop the prosperous economy and idiosyncratic systems of government that we explored in the last chapter.[12] The new government was in many ways self-directed. In Kaskaskia, the colonists petitioned for the right to elect a syndic in 1738, and Antoine Bienvenu became the first to hold this office of local authority.[13] They also elected a Marguillier, or church warden, who managed many local affairs.[14] They ignored imperial decrees that went counter to their pragmatic goals, but they created a colony that Louisiana officials nevertheless regarded as well ordered. As one wrote, the colony had tremendous potential; it just needed more settlers.[15] Illinois quickly became the third largest population center in French North America. Reflecting their confidence in the stability and order of the colony, Louisiana officials discussed reducing the number of troops at Fort de Chartres in 1734.[16] As an imperial project, it was working, not by force but by collaboration.

But while the government was successful in its relations with the French settlers, Indian relations deteriorated. The situation had changed. With the Fox Wars basically over after 1731, the Illinois Indians felt less tied to their alliance with the provincial government at Fort de Chartres. Their strategies broadened as they interacted with British-allied groups in the Southeast and on the Ohio River. In 1731, three Chickasaw emissaries pressured the Illinois, particularly the Cahokia, to unite with them against the French in the wake of the Natchez Revolt.[17] The Illinois handed these Chickasaw over to the Louisiana governor, who promised not to hurt them, but then he clumsily killed them. This made the Chickasaw hostile to the Illinois and in turn made the Illinois mistrustful of the French. According to Father Mercier, resident missionary priest among the Cahokia, the Indians now began to seek security by reorienting their old alliance system, formerly a bastion of French support, against the French. As he wrote: "The Indians are intriguing with the Osages and Kansas to aid them against the French; the chiefs are friendly, but they cannot control their youths." The traditionally strong alliance between the French and the Indians of the Illinois was under strain.[18]

The Illinois had plenty of reason for dissatisfaction. Visiting Paris in 1725, Illinois chiefs had asked the French government not to let the growing French colonies in Illinois crowd out their villages, but that's what was happening. Cattle wandered from French farms into Indian agricultural fields at Kaskaskia and Cahokia. Coureurs de bois traveled through the country with impunity, much to the Illinois Indians' dismay. Newly arrived habitants frequently bought land directly from Indians, a practice that caused tension as well.[19] And although Mamantouensa had secured a promise from the French king that the French would never again ask the Illinois to relocate their villages, the provincial government in Illinois proposed just that as the solution to the Illinois's problems. In 1733, D'Artaguiette suggested "distancing the Illinois villages from the French establishments, because by this means, many disputes will be avoided, of which this closeness is the cause, and which have truly been the principal source of the inquietude which the savages have demonstrated."[20] Confirming the plan, the Louisiana government suggested removing the Illinois villages a full two or three days' journey away from the French villages.[21] As Mamantouensa had said in 1725, even small relocations were inconvenient, let alone a move of this scale: "Such moves disrupt the prayer, upset my young people, and even the Black Robe wearies of endlessly building anew and is thus not quick to follow us. Our wives and children suffer from it."[22] By 1735, ignoring the Indians' requests, officials made a plan to once again relocate the Illinois Indians. They also issued a prohibition against Frenchmen "wintering" with the Indians.[23]

All of this added up to a rift between the French provincial regime and the Indians, which began to produce open conflict. The first disturbances took place at Cahokia in May 1732.[24] In the following fall, a Cahokia Indian killed a Frenchman.[25] For the next several years, the settlements at Cahokia were a tense environment; Indians regularly killed French cattle in 1734 and threatened an open revolt that year. As D'Artaguiette wrote to Louisiana officials, the habitants were "afraid of being massacred . . . which has obliged the missionaries and several habitants to leave."[26] In general, relations were so fraught that officials feared the Cahokia were about to "imitate" the Natchez's rebellion.[27]

Meanwhile, there was mistrust between the French officials and the Illinois more generally. The Illinois had professed to have "French hearts" and to be loyal to the French. But in the 1730s, observers wondered whether these promises had just been opportunistic. Writing to Louisiana officials in 1733, D'Artaguiette wondered if Illinois Indians had professed loyalty only "in the hope of presents." Now, suddenly, the Illinois were making all sorts of new demands: "They pretended that we owed them the payment for the lands that they had ceded to us and for the mines that they contained." Unhappy, the Indians threatened violence, and D'Artaguiette confessed his belief that a "storm . . . appears to be rumbling in that direction." As D'Artaguiette concluded, "God grant that my conjectures are false and my anxieties ill-founded. The revolt of this nation might be regarded as a mortal blow to the colony."[28] By rebuilding alliances in the West, as well as building new ones in the East, the Illinois reminded the French that they had other options and were not desperate.

These reminders pushed the French to demonstrate their loyalty to the Illinois, as well as their strength. As in previous years, the French used military power in defense of Illinois's interests. In 1733, D'Artaguiette sent a detachment under Pierre St. Ange and Louis Dutisné, both ambitious sons of previous Illinois commandants, to attack the remaining Foxes in Missouri as a show of strength and solidarity with the "domiciled Indians."[29] Meanwhile, another big threat to the Illinois came from the Chickasaw. In part to show the Illinois that the French were strong enough to dominate the Chickasaw, D'Artaguiette raised an expedition to attack the latter group in 1735–36. The expedition was a total disaster, only adding to French problems. D'Artaguiette was supposed to meet up with forces from the South under Bienville, but the rendezvous was unsuccessful. D'Artaguiette's army was routed.[30]

It was a devastating defeat, one of the crucial turning points in Illinois colonial history. D'Artaguiette's army included 130 French—regulars and militia. The rest were Illinois, Miami, Quapaw, and Iroquois Indians. When the ill-designed attack failed, the Illinois and Miami fled, leaving the French badly outnumbered. Reflecting the low ebb in the Illinois-French alliance, more than forty French soldiers and militiamen were captured and killed, including the commandant D'Artaguiette, as well as St. Ange and Dutisné.

The fiasco in the Chickasaw campaign undermined French credibility and revealed the strains on the alliance between the French and the "domiciled" Indians. The French spent the next three years planning another attack but never pulled it off. French officials finally made peace with the Chickasaw in 1739, but the latter group continued attacking the French convoy with impunity, a reminder of French vulnerability in the upper Mississippi Valley.[31]

ᐇ

If the Chickasaw campaigns revealed the vulnerability of the French empire in Illinois and its waning power in the region at the end of the 1730s, matters deteriorated further in the 1740s. A new governor, Pierre de Vaudreuil, took control of Louisiana in the 1740s, and a new commandant, Sieur de Bertet, took office in the Illinois Country between 1742 and 1749.[32] The correspondence between these two officials provides a great window into the nature of imperial power in Illinois in this period. It reveals a tense relationship between Illinois colonists and Illinois Indians on the one hand, and imperial authorities who were increasingly unenthusiastic about the colony on the other. The 1740s were a time of great strains in the relationship between people and government in Illinois.

In response to the losses in the Chickasaw campaign, the Louisiana government proposed strengthening the imperial presence in Illinois by committing thirty thousand livres for a renovation of Fort de Chartres. This would remind colonists and Indians of the power of the French. However, Illinois farmers, busy with their booming export economy, did not volunteer to help build the new military installation but rather treated it as an opportunity for gain.[33] As officials complained, "Labor is so expensive in Illinois and the workers so lazy that they love much better to sit around and rest than to work for a reasonable price."[34] Of course, the habitants were busy with farming and pursuing their self-interest, not lazing about. But they exploited the empire's investment in their colony for local benefit, demanding high wages and not working much. The result was a still-unfinished fort, and officials noted that "The fixed fund for this fort will be consumed before there is much labor actually done."[35] Bertet's new government began on a footing of weakness owing to the failure to enhance its military power in the colony.

But if the Louisiana government failed to increase its strength in the Illinois Country, Bertet's administration had a hard time even maintaining its baseline strength. The problem was desertion. French soldiers in Illinois recognized that there were opportunities for gain in the borderlands, especially as British traders expanded their operations in the West in the 1740s. Soldiers, some of whom were mercenaries, abandoned Fort de Chartres and began working together with British traders in Pennsylvania.[36] They also went west, as far as New Mexico, and became go-betweens for the trade between Indians, Spanish, and Frenchmen in that region. As in the past, the presence of competing empires gave them options, and Bertet's weak administration could not prevent soldiers from seeking their self-interest. As Vaudreuil wrote in 1743, it was a major frustration:

> I do not know to what to attribute the frequent desertions that
> occurred last year in that district. Mr. de Bertet writes me that ten
> soldiers had this summer undertaken to reach New Mexico by hav-
> ing themselves guided by Indians of the Missouri [country] from
> one nation to another. I doubt that they will arrive there without
> accidents. A short time before six others [deserted], all of German
> nationality although serving in our troops and I think Protestants,

having got it into their heads to go and join the English traders established among the Chickasaws.[37]

Bertet and Vaudreuil blamed the problems with desertion on the fact that soldiers and inhabitants in Illinois had close relationships. Since soldiers never rotated out of Illinois but stayed at the post permanently (a cost-saving measure enacted by Louisiana officials), civilians came to know and employ the soldiers in their dubious economic activities, especially trading. As Vaudreuil complained, "this is very wrong, for the Soldiers by this means form Connections with the Inhabitants, which in time renders them useless for the Service."[38] Bertet's regime had a difficult time projecting power among disloyal troops and scheming habitants.

Meanwhile, Bertet's administration had other headaches as well. There were many illegal fur traders in Illinois, and their activity was almost completely unregulated. As Vaudreuil complained, trade regulation in the Illinois Country was much too liberal: "Liberty . . . is allowed to all sorts of persons, even to the travellers from Canada to carry on a trade with . . . savages, from which arise many inconveniences, both to the good of the trade and contrary to good order."[39] These traders undercut one another's prices and made it hard for anybody to profit in the trade. Moreover, despite his considerable diplomatic skills, Bertet was powerless to stop these "disorders." As Vaudreuil wrote, "Vagrants from Canada as well as those from this place [commit] with impunity all kinds of disorders, which very often bring on troublesome quarrels which one day may occasion a good deal of difficulty to quash."[40] Vaudreuil also complained that the anarchy of the trade gave the colony an autonomous spirit. As he wrote, "vagabonds from this colony and those from Canada have made in a small time in this place [Illinois] a little republic."[41]

If these troubles reflected Bertet's impotence as a commandant, there were other circumstances, mostly out of Bertet's control, that prevented him from projecting much power. Many times in the 1740s, convoys between New Orleans and the Illinois were interrupted by attacks by the Chickasaw and other groups in the Southeast, preventing Bertet from receiving communications and supplies from the governor.[42] A blight in the wheat crop reduced wheat exports two years in a row starting in 1741, harming the colony's economy.[43] By 1744, Fort de Chartres was in utter disrepair, and Vaudreuil admitted that it was "rotting" in 1744 and "falling down" in 1746.[44] In 1747, in an ultimate sign of imperial weakness, Bertet moved the garrison from Fort de Chartres to Kaskaskia and abandoned the fort altogether. To top it all off, finances were a disaster. A reckoning of October 19, 1744, placed the total expense of the Illinois colony, including the purchase of provisions, munitions, and merchandise, at 713,055 livres, while the total revenue from the colony was just 192,610 livres.[45]

Meanwhile, Bertet's and Vaudreuil's response to weakness in the Illinois colony mostly involved new restrictions and laws. And while these measures made sense, they often alienated the colonists. In 1745, for instance, imperial officials discussed new trade rules to prevent deserters and vagabonds in the Illinois.[46] As the minister wrote to the Canadian governor Beauharnois, "nothing is more expedient than to take steps to restrain the Coureurs de bois whose number increases yearly in the Illinois country, and to stop the desertion of soldiers from that post."[47] The government proposed several measures, all of which clamped down on the liberty to trade in the colony by requiring traders to have licenses and passports.[48] Vaudreuil sent a detachment to establish a new fort on the Missouri to regulate illegal trade.[49] Bertet's top priority became to prevent desertions and shut down illegal trade.[50]

At the same time, reflecting their increasing doubts about the usefulness of the colony, officials tried to reduce expenses by encouraging colonists to become more productive. Both Vaudreuil and Bertet considered the colonists in Illinois to be lazy, despite the impressive economic output of the colony. In their view, colonists wasted too much time in the fur trade or searching for mines and needed to spend more time in agriculture.[51] Moreover, when it came to agriculture, Vaudreuil complained that the colonists in Illinois were too dependent on the labor of their slaves. Describing the inhabitants as "naturally lazy," Minister Maurepas complained that they "had depended upon the labor of these slaves, [and] had remained in a state of indolence very prejudicial to a new settlement."[52] Convinced by this logic, he felt that the only way to entice the colonists to do more work was to deny them any more slaves.[53] In 1746, authorities banned further imports of slaves to the Illinois Country.[54]

By denying the colonists the slaves they wanted and shutting down their free trade, Bertet and Vaudreuil alienated the habitants. Moreover, officials sent a signal that the interests of the colonists were not a priority of the larger Louisiana administration. Given the weakness of the Illinois government, colonists surely must have lost confidence. By the late 1740s, children of Illinois inhabitants were not taking up their parents' farms and were leaving the colony for New Orleans and Canada. As one official later noted, "The children don't replace their fathers as one sees from the abandoned farms."[55]

One observer complained that these children were "wayward" and that they lacked "filial tenderness."[56] But perhaps this ignored their real motives. Indeed, the top-down plans of the Bertet administration and its failure to collaborate probably pushed inhabitants away. And if this was true for the colonists, it was doubly true for the Illinois Indians.

ひ

If the French colonists had other options besides submitting to Bertet's top-down administration of the colony, this was also true of the Illinois Indians in the 1740s. With British traders coming up the Cherokee River and down the Ohio, the Illinois were once again in between empires.[57] And in the 1740s, when the Iroquois began sending belts around to the Algonquians of the West, western Indians like the Illinois had a new opportunity to play the two imperial powers against one another. By the end of the decade, Governor Hamilton in Philadelphia started sending presents to the Miami, and British trader George Croghan wrote to Hamilton to encourage the creation of a British fort on the Ohio.[58] These were dangerous prospects for the French.[59]

The French response to these threats was orchestrated by both Canada and Louisiana, since the main theater of intrigue here was the Ohio Valley, in the middle of the two governments. The French had been active in the region for some time, trying to secure French alliances and project strength in the Wabash River Valley.[60] Back in 1732, Louisiana had appointed Francois-Marie Bissot, Sieur de Vincennes, to establish an official post on the lower Wabash near the White River. After Vincennes died in the unsuccessful Chickasaw campaign in 1736, Louis Groston de St. Ange de Bellerive took control of the new post. St. Ange began a settlement, named for its founder, Vincennes, on land he acquired from Miami Indians. Further up the Wabash, the Canadian government made other small establishments, such as Fort Miami at the Miami settlement called Kekionga.[61] From these outposts, as Vaudreuil put it, the French and French-allied Indians could hope to "chase [the British traders] from Our Rivers, where they have had storehouses for a long time."[62] But French officials committed few resources to the fledgling outposts where British-allied Indians were most active.[63] For instance, plans for a new Wabash fort were halted in 1747.[64]

This proved a strategic mistake. In 1747, a group of Miami and Piankeshaw Indians organized themselves under the leadership of Memeskia, a Piankeshaw chief known to the French as La Demoiselle. This group attacked Fort Miami, or Kekionga, in 1747, out of resentment toward the French.

Now La Demoiselle established a town, Pickiwillany, where he allowed the British to set up a trading post. From Pickawillany, La Demoiselle built an anti-French movement that lasted through 1752. It was a direct challenge to French authority in the West.

From Pickawillany, La Demoiselle began organizing a new Algonquian alliance by exploiting kinship networks among different Algonquian groups. The movement tried especially hard to recruit the Illinois. The Piankeshaw were Miami-Illinois-speakers and had already allied with the Wea and some Miami. Within these groups, some individuals had relatives among the Illinois villages that the French considered their "domiciled Indians"—the Cahokia, Kaskaskia, and Metchigamea. In 1747, La Demoiselle sent an English flag to the Illinois Country in the hands of two Wea Indians who had relatives there. These emissaries further exploited kinship networks to spread La Demoiselle's anti-French message around first to the Cahokia, then to the Peoria, and finally to the Kaskaskia. Since the emissaries were family members of the Rouensas, the "first chiefs of the Illinois," their message spread even beyond the Illinois villages themselves and into extended networks in the West, including to the Missouri and the Osage.[65] As the commandant at Illinois wrote, the Illinois received La Demoiselle's invitation happily, and all but two Illinois villages allegedly accepted the message: "We have but two bands, which are very small, who do not assent to this affair."[66] The upshot was what the French considered a "universal conspiracy." As Vaudreuil wrote, "The Chevalier de Bertet then informed me that there was an almost universal conspiracy on the part of the Illinois tribes as well as those of the Wabash to destroy the posts of that region at the request of the English and by the intervention of the Huron and of the Iroquois of the Five Nations."[67]

To the extent that the French understood the Illinois behavior in this period, they viewed it as a consequence of weakness. The Illinois joined La Demoiselle out of desperation, French observers assumed, after Wea emissaries threatened them with violence.[68] But this was not quite right. A better way to understand the Illinois in this moment is not as desperate but once again opportunistic. For the Illinois, it was useful to have their relatives, particularly the Wea and Piankeshaw, allied to the British, as this gave the Illinois a good opportunity to play the imperial rivals against each other. Kinship, the connections between the emissaries and Rouensa, gave them bonds to the English "republic" at Pickiwillany. But kinship did not wholly determine their actions in any reductionist way. Indeed, the Illinois made La Demoiselle promise "that they shall have goods at a low price."[69] Meanwhile, they reminded the French that their longstanding declaration of "French hearts" was dependent on the French supplying them with cheap goods.[70] The truth was, as the Canadian governor realized, the Illinois were simply pragmatic: "I see it daily and am not surprised. . . . The French themselves devote themselves to those who treat them most favorably [and so do the Indians]. It is a maxim obeyed in all past ages, and it is moreover the universal law of all the world to be for him from whom one draws the greatest advantage."[71]

The hallmark of the Illinois strategy for the next several years was, as French officials said, to "hold themselves aloof."[72] The Illinois never actually joined La Demoiselle's movement, never moved to Pickawillany, and never joined the Piankeshaws in a military attack. They stalled when La Demoiselle pressured them to commit to the alliance.[73] So they were not clearly part of the "conspiracy." On the other hand, when the French tried to get them to participate in fights against the Chickasaw, they did not, causing the French to doubt their loyalty.[74] French officials admitted their confusion. Typical French letters in this period remarked on how the Illinois kept people guessing. Their "answer has not yet come" and "I do not know what they will decide" were not uncommon sentiments in French correspondence on the Illinois.[75] Moreover, the various familles of the Illinois each acted independently of one another, making it difficult for the French to predict their movements.

Given rumors of rebellion that circulated widely, and given the Illinois's now questionable loyalty, the Bertet regime was especially vulnerable. In late 1747, Bertet had to move the whole colony into the village of Kaskaskia and fortify it with palisades "in order to put himself in a state of defense."[76] While in this compact arrangement, the colony suffered two years of epidemics that killed "a good many of the inhabitants," including Bertet himself.[77] And now the imperial strength of the colony reached its nadir. The French government returned to the old debate about whether the colony should be under Canadian authority or the Louisiana administration.[78] Mindful of the pathetic financial state of the colony, officials discussed bizarre schemes to make the colony pay, including by producing buffalo wool and wax.[79] Chickasaw attacks resumed on the yearly convoy, interrupting the commerce and the communication between Illinois and New Orleans.[80] At one point, Illinois went fifteen months without any communication from New Orleans. When prices in the colony rose nearly 400 percent as a result of the shortage of merchandise, colonists nearly revolted.[81]

The colony was breaking down. Versailles instructed Quebec and Louisiana to minimize expenses in the West.[82] But meanwhile Vaudreuil came to a renewed realization of the Illinois colony's value to Louisiana, no matter the cost, arguing that Louisiana could not subsist without Illinois. In 1748, Vaudreuil made an impassioned plea to keep Illinois a part of Louisiana.[83] But as Vaudreuil saw it, what the colony needed was military power. Given the lack of military strength in the Illinois Country, Vaudreuil wrote, the colonists were "too headstrong, reckless, and independent to put themselves under any subordination."[84] The traders in Illinois—coureurs de bois and half-breeds—"cannot be disciplined." As Vaudreuil complained, "The major in Command there has infinite trouble in maintaining a little discipline, and he has succeeded in doing so only by showing himself severe."[85] To fix these problems, as well as to respond to English movements on the Ohio, Vaudreuil announced a plan to increase the military detachment at Illinois from two companies to six, or three hundred men.[86] He appointed Louisiana's engineer, François Saucier, to design a new stone fort for the colony.[87] And he tapped a new commandant, the French-born son of Irish Jacobin refugees, Macarty. Writing his instructions to Macarty in 1751, Vaudreuil impressed upon the officer the importance of establishing order, by domination and force if necessary, employing new and powerful symbols and tools of military authority.

❧

Many of Macarty's specific instructions for his new command were identical to those of previous administrations in Illinois. For example, Vaudreuil ordered Macarty to keep farms and settlements from being established too close to Indian villages.[88] Macarty was to restrain illegal traders. Moreover, he should "prevent the marriages which the French have hitherto contracted with Indian women." Echoing the racial language of early Louisiana pronouncements on intermarriage, Macarty's orders read that "Such alliances are shameful and of dangerous consequence for the familiarity they create between Indians and the French, and for the ill breed which they produce."[89] In general, Vaudreuil wrote, the priority was to "remedy as soon as he possibly can the abuses which may have intruded themselves whether with respect to religion, to the police, to the military discipline, or to the government of the Indians, which are the principal objects which should divide his attention."[90]

What was different about Macarty's orders was a strikingly imperious tone. Irreligion could be solved by "chastisements which he will inflict on those who hold to evil conduct and give rise to scandal." The colonists were too litigious, so Macarty should reestablish the Coutume de Paris strictly and reduce the "spirit of chicanery" in legal affairs.[91] As for the Indians, Vaudreuil insisted that Macarty be strict, especially in matters of diplomacy. According to Macarty's instructions, "most of these tribes receive presents from us which we can cut off, being today in a situation to lay down the law to them more than formerly." Macarty should "punish those of them who become obnoxious with respect to the French, as often happens among the Illinois tribes who kill cattle or injure the inhabitants in other ways which may have serious results." And in general, Vaudreuil wanted Macarty to constantly remind the Indians of French authority: "It is proper for M. de Macarty to make them feel that the presents we make them are only in consideration of the occasions when they so act as to do us service, and give us marks of their attachments instead of holding aloof as they so often do."[92]

To implement these imperious plans, Macarty needed power. Shortly after arriving, François Saucier and Macarty made a tour to decide on a site for the new fort.[93] As Vaudreuil and Michel's instructions to Saucier said, the point was "To accommodate and lodge the strong garrison. . . . [in order to] insure the possession of the country, to make an impression on the Indians, and to check and halt the progress of the English in our territory."[94] In addition to the fort, Macarty employed other tools of statecraft, and the beginning of his regime reflected his ambitions to create top-down order in the colony. He took a census, reflecting his desire to simplify the complex reality of Illinois into a simple grid of imperial knowledge.[95] Matching this ambition for rational planning, Macarty even contemplated refashioning the streets at Fort de Chartres into a more symmetrical grid, since he viewed the haphazard layout of the streets and property lines to be the height of disorder. As he wrote, although several houses would have to be taken down, "the evil is not yet irremediable."[96] He fantasized about turning the colony into a strictly ordered, symmetrical, legible territory.

But if Macarty sought to make the colony legible, some of the information he collected should have told him what a challenge he faced in dominating the population. The results of the census revealed a larger colony than what previous administrators dealt with.[97] In the twenty years after 1732, the overall population of the colony nearly doubled, so that it numbered around 1,300. The average farm in the colony was 25 arpents, reflecting the enterprise of the colonists. Despite the discouragement that Louisiana officials had always shown toward slavery in Illinois, there were now 476 black slaves in the colony, together with 176 Indian slaves. Even as officials worried that some children of Illinois inhabitants were not remaining in the colony, the Illinois settlements continued to grow; Illinois was no longer just a fledgling outpost.

∾

As Macarty got to work, his first priority was to get a handle on the relationship with the Illinois Indians. As Vaudreuil wrote, rumors of the alleged conspiracy of the Illinois Indians had only increased after Bertet's death and during the brief administration of the interim commandant, Jean Baptiste Benoist de St. Clair. According to Vaudreuil, "M. Benoist informs me that all the tribes of the Illinois dependence have formed a conspiracy against all the French of this country, whom they are to destroy at the instigation of the English."[98] To be sure, Vaudreuil wrote, these were just rumors. But one of the goals of the new regime was to take a more proactive and aggressive stance toward the Indians, to root out disloyalty and not tolerate the Illinois's "aloof" behavior. Vaudreuil urged, "however it may be, you will go to the bottom of the affair and take in this respect the proper measures so as to have nothing to fear from them, and so as to dominate them." It was a bold statement of an ambitious new Indian policy in Illinois.[99]

But these plans for domination soon came up against a messy reality. First, the Kaskaskia Illinois killed two black slaves soon after Macarty arrived in the colony.[100] Next, the Illinois started hostilities with the Potawatomis to the north, interfering with Canadian diplomacy at Fort St. Joseph.[101] Continuing their violence, the Illinois attacked some Shawnee in the Ohio Valley, who then turned around and threatened the French settlements, "saying that it was the Illinois who were the children of the French who had made the attack."[102] In short, the Illinois acted autonomously, in ways that went counter to French goals and Macarty's new desire for control.

But if all of these actions dismayed Macarty, the biggest strain in the relationship between the Indians and the commandant of course was the Illinois's continuing relationship with the rebellious Piankeshaw under La Demoiselle. As Macarty learned upon arriving in Illinois, a delegation of seven Illinois Indians, likely Kaskaskia, had spent the previous summer with La Demoiselle in his village. The following year, in December 1751, the Illinois at Chartres received a Piankeshaw party whose alleged purpose was to organize an attack on the French colonists one Sunday as they were leaving church. Although the alleged plot was revealed to Macarty by a loyal Cahokia

Indian, the commandant launched a full investigation. His instinct, following his instructions from Vaudreuil, was to dominate.[103]

Macarty took a heavy hand. Upon learning of the plot, Macarty arrested several chiefs of the Kaskaskia and Cahokia and jailed them, pressuring the Indians to surrender the traitors. His approach was strict. As he told Vaudreuil, "The two Illinois who are in prison are punished like French scoundrels, whom it is necessary to punish. . . . Were not these men caught with our enemies?"[104] Macarty held them in prison for months and demanded that they would be released only when they agreed to "a conduct that satisfies me." What Macarty stubbornly wanted from the Illinois was for them to demonstrate their commitment to the French alliance by attacking the Piankeshaw. As he said, "Whatever protestations our domiciled Indians may make to me, I shall always be suspicious of them until they have made some attacks on our enemies."[105]

But Macarty never really understood the complexity of the Illinois's position or the logic of their aloof behavior. In reply to Macarty's questioning, various Illinois chiefs explained their actions during the alleged conspiracy. As one chief related, the Illinois never joined with La Demoiselle's rebels and actually turned the plotters away (excusing themselves by saying they had no chief).[106] They remained neutral and instead revealed to the French all the blankets and diplomatic symbols that the conspirators carried to their villages. Sure, they had gone to Pickawilanny the previous summer, but that was "because it was said that goods were cheap there."[107] They always remained loyal.

They emphasized that it was kinship that kept them loyal to the French. As Macarty recounted in his letters detailing his meetings with Illinois leaders, the Illinois kept insisting on the loyalty that grew out of their kinship bonds. According to one Illinois chief, "They had always been attached to the French, who were their own blood, to whom they had given wives."[108] As another told Macarty, "they had French hearts and the French were their own blood."[109] Another reaffirmed his people's "attachment to the French—to whom they are allied by blood, since they have given them wives."[110] One Illinois chief professed that "he had his mother and children with the French," probably meaning that they lived at the mission.[111]

This was important. Kinship was an important marker of Illinois identity, and several of the Illinois chiefs, as well as countless other Illinois, were personally connected to the French. Several chiefs of the Illinois were mentioned in the investigation of the conspiracy, including Chareragoue,

Jassicoueta, Dacouarens, Papechingouya, Mantapnia, Apekonaninsa, Pichia-
gosenca, Rissachara, Neprera, Miceprata, Patissier, Thomas, La Puce,
Papechingouya, Ouycouetiata, Eskepakingonet, Ouabichagana, Abasoua-
chinga, and Achicoua.[112] Significantly, many of these individuals had daughters, sisters, or nieces who had married into French families. For instance,
chief Eskepakingonet was likely father or uncle to Catherine Ekepakin8a,
wife of the French colonist Jean Colon dit LaViolette. Cecile Moninapita,
wife to Pierre Circe-St. Michel, another habitant, was probably Chief
Mantapnia's daughter or niece. Jassicoueta was probably the father or uncle
of Marguerite 8assicani8e, who was married to Jacques Bourdon and later,
Nicholas Pelletier de Franchomme, one of the wealthiest colonists in
Kaskaskia. Chief Apekonaninsa was likely related to Marie Apecke8rata, wife
of Guillaume Poitiers-Dubuisson.[113] And Chief Miceprata was almost certainly the father or uncle of Dorothee Mechipe8ata, wife of Charles Dany
and Louis Turpin in turn. Together, these families had many descendants in
the Illinois villages. And of course the relatives of Marie Rouensa, a descendant herself of the "first chiefs of the Illinois," were probably the most
numerous family in the entire French community. The Illinois were bound
to the French by strong bonds of kinship, as they insisted to Macarty.

But just as they were bound as kinsmen and in-laws to the French, so
too were they bound by kinship to the Wea, Miami, and Piankeshaw among
La Demoiselle's movement. Le Loup, the Kaskaskia chief Macarty held in
prison, was probably a member of the Rouensa family, but he also had a
brother-in-law and father-in-law—Voitquoitigana and Chenguikataka—who
were leaders in the Piankeshaw rebellion.[114] Other Illinois chiefs had similar
connections through their in-laws among the Weas, as they told the
French.[115] Two Kaskaskia chiefs were brothers to La Mouche Noire, one of
the leaders at Pickawillany.[116] In short, the same kinds of kinship connections
that bound the French to the Illinois also bound the Illinois to the conspirators. Their kinship connections secured their place in between, which they
exploited strategically. As they promised, they were not going to attack the
French, their kin. But nor were they going to attack the Piankeshaw.

And this is what Macarty wanted them to do. His goal was to prevent
the Illinois from "holding aloof as they so often do." Macarty kept Le Loup
in jail, insisting that he atone by assisting the French in attacking the Piankeshaw. As he wrote, "I will speak to them more forcefully, if I can assemble
the chiefs this spring and form some war parties against our enemies."[117] But
this was a foolish demand. And even as Macarty was insisting on these terms

of alliance, Governor Vaudreuil saw the folly of his diplomacy. Writing at the beginning of 1752, Vaudreuil explained that the Illinois simply could not be forced into the kind of military action that Macarty envisioned: "Apparently he is not informed that there are few of these tribes who have not relatives by blood or marriage among these refugees. As a result they will with difficulty be induced to strike, especially today when they are more than ever persuaded that we are in no situation to undertake anything against them."[118]

Of course Macarty was informed of that fact; he was just ignoring it as he tried to carry out his new plan of "dominating" the Illinois. Now, Vaudreuil suggested, it was better to follow the logic of the Indians' own alliance system rather than try to impose simplistic French goals. Macarty was just repeating old mistakes. Worse, Vaudreuil wondered whether recruiting the Illinois to attack the Piankeshaw might not produce even more trouble: "Supposing on the contrary that they should act sincerely in their movements without paying attention to the bonds of blood and marriage which they have with the greater part of these rebels, what would come of it save differences among the tribes which will not quickly be ended?"[119] As Vaudreuil saw it, Macarty's policy did not make sense because it ignored the kinship networks of the Illinois.

Although Macarty was slow to realize this logic, he did recognize another problem with his policy, which was that he was powerless to actually carry it out. By early spring 1752, Macarty saw that he was only alienating allies and weakening the French position further. As he wrote, "With difficulty our domiciled Indians have settled themselves in their villages between fear and hope, making resolutions to abandon us."[120] Macarty now understood that he had to change course and follow the Illinois's own logic. He actually had no choice: "The necessity of our managing them tactfully made me take the method of gentleness since I was not strong enough to domineer over them, fearing they would be like a hive of bees which, spreading in all directions, would be more likely to make attacks on our Voyageurs."[121] As in the Fox Wars and the Missouri Valley, it was useless to try to resist the Indians' own alliances and priorities; French policy must follow the Indians' lead: "The tribes on that side are too much allied by blood even to our domiciles for it to be expected that they should attack each other."[122]

And so Macarty, together with Vaudreuil, arrived at the logic of collaboration. By the spring, Macarty released Le Loup from prison, admitting "there was no likelihood that [the Illinois] could be constrained to make war on the Piankashaw, many of whose women and children they have in this village, and among whom many of their men have married."[123] Addressing a delegation of the Kaskaskia, Cahokia, and Metchigamea, Macarty scaled back his demands and endorsed the Illinois's neutrality:

> Warrior, I do not ask you to make war against your wish. In no wise do I say to you, "Help me." But remember that the Frenchman has preserved you as long as you can remember, that he has saved your lives, that he has redeemed you from the house of your enemies, that he has held them back from you, that he has chastised the Foxes and Iroquois who were killing you. Once again I do not say to you, "Help me in your turn." . . . I only bid you keep our enemies off your lands, don't receive them in your village, don't go with them, lest I may have to strike my children along with them."[124]

It was a remarkably small demand, and a far cry from Vaudreuil's original purpose of "dominating" the Illinois. Like previous administrations in Illinois, Macarty recognized that he could not force the Indians to behave. He would have to respect their neutrality, and collaborate.

♻

If Macarty's efforts to "dominate" the Indians failed, he tried similar heavy-handed policies when it came to the French inhabitants. On the one hand, there were some ways in which he tried initially to accommodate, recognizing that successful colonization, as one Canadian official put it, "can be done only by the wisdom and gentleness of [the local] government."[125] Understanding the importance of Illinois agriculture, for instance, Macarty's new regime tried to get on good terms with the farmers. As Macarty arrived in Illinois in 1751, some French farmers were in a transition, their land exhausted by years of export farming. In a letter to Vaudreuil, Macarty noted that "The fields on this side are worn out; most of the inhabitants are taking up lands on the side of Ste. Genevieve [a new settlement across the river], there being no more lands to sow or to assign on this side."[126] Since these new farms needed lots of labor, officials realized that previous restrictions on slave imports to the Illinois were counterproductive and alienated the colonists.[127] And although Vaudreuil himself had created the prohibition to begin with, one observer noted that he "has since perceived that this prohibition was a great prejudice to the welfare of the good inhabitants of the Illinois who could no longer enlarge their farms."[128] As one Canadian official saw it, lifting the ban on slavery in Illinois was a kind of surrender: "there was no other means to induce the inhabitants of that country to cultivate their lands."[129] Macarty's administration started off with some accommodation to the habitants' interests.

But even as he reversed some of Bertet's and Vaudreuil's old restrictions on the colony, Macarty's priority still was to establish military force and military order. As he wrote to Vaudreuil, pleading for every last soldier that Vaudreuil could spare, the military strength of the colony could not be neglected. To make a useful colony, as well as useful colonists, he wrote, military control was the answer: "Forces and help are needed for what I cannot do."[130] And yet this was a challenge, if not a paradox. For if the military would be the means of establishing order among the colonists, the colonists themselves were supposed to supply the labor for constructing the new fort. As Macarty wrote, the fort was to be a kind of private-public partnership, and the engineer was to contract "each part of the work to private persons if that arrangement is most proper for the good of the service.[131] This kind of arrangement was a longstanding tradition in the Illinois, where the imperial government paid habitants for their help in the Chickasaw campaign in 1739, for the labor on repairs of the fort in the 1730s, and for other work they performed on behalf of the government.[132] As Vaudreuil put it, this arrangement was a win-win, since "the king, like private persons, may profit."[133] Macarty and the provincial government began in 1751 to make contracts with colonists, some of which survive in the notarial archives.[134] Tellingly, as they negotiated with Macarty, colonists insisted that their payment be made in the one thing that the colony needed most: slaves. According to Macarty, "Most of them would ask for negroes in payment as this country lacks labor for work in the fields."[135]

But the construction of the fort resulted right away in tensions. Some of this was inevitable: the colonists and officials had competing interests, as the officials tried to save money and construct the fort with "economy."[136] The engineer Saucier expressed pessimism about the plan to have inhabitants "contribute work or materials" and noted that they "pleaded their small resources and aptitudes" as an excuse.[137] Stubbornly, Macarty demanded that the colonists donate part of their labor for free and supply the fort with supplies amounting to a fourth of their produce. Macarty quickly became delinquent in paying wages, which is understandable given the scale of the work—the expense of the fort was over 450,000 livres, even though the budget was set at 270,000—as well as the difficulties in supplying merchandise

to the colony. When this happened, however, it created tension between the
workers and the military command.

Meanwhile, as this was unfolding, an old problem began to plague the
fort-in-progress: the desertion of soldiers. In the first years after Macarty
arrived, seventy-nine soldiers deserted.[138] When they did, Macarty turned to
the habitants for help tracking them down since, as one officer put it, "It is
only the inhabitants who in concert with the Indians can pursue the deserters
and prevent them from carrying out their ill designs."[139] To Macarty, pressing
the habitants into service was a natural response, since he felt militia duty
was a service that the colonists owed their government. As he wrote, "each
inhabitant is a soldier who costs the king nothing."[140] But inhabitants did
not share his view. Not only did the inhabitants feel unenthusiastic about
helping track down deserters, they purposefully aided the deserters as a way
to express their frustration with their delinquent wages. Rather than turn
them in, they aided deserters by giving them supplies. When Macarty
requested help in tracking them down, many refused.[141] Then, when Macarty
arrested a defiant habitant, the colonists "assembled . . . with their arms . . .
being afraid I would send the young man off to New Orleans in the night."[142]
In short, although they refused to track down deserters from Fort de Chartres, the militia did muster to defend one of their own against Macarty's
arbitrary command. Soon Macarty evidently had to organize his remaining
troops to quell the "insubordination" among the militia and the habitants.[143]
It was a total breakdown of authority.

Just as he did in the case of the Illinois Indians, Macarty had to adjust
his expectations of the colonists. As Macarty wrote, the inhabitants were
hostile to his plans, but he could do nothing about it. The colonists, after all,
were "volunteers." "They justly bear the name of volunteers which has made
me postpone punishing them as they deserve."[144] Moreover, they had a keen
sense of their self-interest and did not care much for the military authority
that Macarty was enforcing or for the fort that was the hallmark of his new
regime. As he noted, the colonists resented the "demands" that Macarty
made on them: "They are discontented at having to build the stockade at
their own costs, as well as the demands made on them for the proposed fort,
for a fourth of the pork for the king which I threatened to make them pay,
and for a detachment of militia and troops."[145] Writing apologetically to
Vaudreuil, Macarty explained to the governor how little power he actually
had. He would like to be more strict, but he could not. He was "afraid of
disaffecting the habitants . . . in the present situation."[146]

Vaudreuil chastised Macarty, obviously considering this episode the opposite of the kind of order that he expected Macarty to establish. As Vaudreuil wrote, the colonists should recognize that they are "subject to such tours of duty since the safety of their country depends on our being able to preserve our garrisons."[147] Of course, considering it from their perspective, it was clear why the colonists revolted: "I do not doubt that the weakness of that detachment contributed to make the inhabitants consider the risks which they had to run, which occasioned the ill will you found among them."[148] In the end, Vaudreuil realized that Macarty was right. There was nothing he could do, and his biggest priority should be "to avoid all insubordination on the part of the inhabitants and never . . . find yourself in such a situation with respect to them."[149] The answer, Vaudreuil said, was basically to collaborate: "You should exact nothing of them save after much thought, approaching them with gentleness, though always with firmness. You will do better so, than by harshness. The [Illinois colonist] is high-spirited, as you know; but he is brave and enterprising. All that is necessary is to take them on the side of honor and reason to bring them easily to your wishes."[150]

As in the case of his negotiations with the Indians, Macarty had to change his approach. The empire was dependent on the local colonists. Just as he could not "dominate" the Indians, he also could not dominate the colonists.

ℂ

Macarty's regime was moving toward collaboration, starting to follow the logic of the Native alliance system and the French colonists' priorities. But the commandant was moving too slowly. In 1752, a crisis in Indian affairs revealed how Macarty's expectations for his own authority remained far out of touch with those of local Indians and French colonists. An attack by the Foxes on the Cahokia demanded a leader who could adapt his priorities to local needs. Macarty, still hoping to project French power, failed the test.

In 1751, conflict between the Illinois and their enemies the Foxes renewed when a small war party of Foxes, Sauk, and Sioux attacked the Cahokia and killed a woman.[151] The Illinois immediately responded, chased down the attackers, and killed all seven of them. One of the Illinois's victims was Pemoussa, the son of the chief of the Foxes. As a result, the following summer, the Foxes organized a major expedition, bringing with them numbers of their traditional allies including Sioux, Sauk, Potawatomi, Winnebago, and Menominee. They numbered, according to one estimate, around four to five hundred strong. This formidable force inflicted an attack that was certainly the most significant military offensive ever suffered by one of the Illinois Indian villages in the vicinity of the French settlements and probably the worst one suffered by the Illinois since the Beaver Wars. The Foxes and their allies "killed or captured seventy people, men, women, and children, burned ten or twelve cabins, and scattered about the limbs of the dead."[152] As the French report had it, "They had thirty scalps, they had burned three or four persons, and were taking the prisoners with them."[153]

The attack left the Cahokia village, as well as the Illinois in general, in disarray. What was worse, rumors now circulated that the Foxes might try to "finish the destruction of the Illinois."[154] And so one hundred victims sought refuge with their longest-standing allies, the French, arriving at Fort de Chartres later in June. As Macarty described the scene,

> All the men, women, and children of the three Illinois villages
> reached here early in the morning, having walked all night in a
> continual rain, all on the assurances of the man called Roulier com-
> ing from Cahokia, who said he had seen, counted, and spoken with
> ninety-four men, and who repeated his story to me. The terror of
> the Illinois was so great that I could not send them to reconnoiter.
> . . . The Illinois remained there until the eleventh, not daring to go
> beyond the houses of the French, although they were assured that
> there were no enemies to fear.[155]

Despite their victimhood, Macarty treated this group of Illinois with indifference. He refused the Indians shelter at the fort because, as one observer remarked, "Corn was scarce, and it would have been an expense."[156] Moreover, he wanted to use the occasion as a means of forcing the Illinois to reveal their Piankeshaw traitors. When rumors circulated that a new attack by the Foxes was imminent, Macarty coldly reflected that the desperate Indians might finally be induced to reveal the conspiracy. As he wrote, "I could have wished that it was the Foxes; and sent M. de Portneuf and several other persons to try to find them in order that the chiefs might be induced to come and speak with me [regarding the conspiracy]."[157]

Macarty's tactics here alienated the Indians. His disregard for the Illinois victims gave rise to rumors that the French had colluded with the Foxes.[158] Losing faith in the French alliance, the Illinois sought renewed connections in the West, and some made overtures once again to La Demoiselle and the

Piankeshaws.[159] Predictably, Macarty's policy succeeded in pushing the Illinois away from the French. Macarty had to conclude that "I think few are left who are not attached to the French by necessity and habit.[160] As Alexandre Xavier De Guyenne, priest at Kaskaskia, wrote, the alliance was broken. Macarty had given the Illinois several reasons to abandon the French: "The lack of a fort to which they could retire in case of alarm, the flight of several cabins who have withdrawn from the two villages to the Peoria and to the Pankashaw, their needs and the little apparent inclination to supply them, are causing a ferment which as I think will end in driving away next winter the most discontented and the most fearful."[161]

But if Macarty hereby alienated the French colony's most important allies, he simultaneously lost the confidence of the creole inhabitants, too. For while Macarty coldly ignored the Illinois when they were attacked by the Foxes, the inhabitants did not. "The principal inhabitants," Father Guyenne noted, "touched by the misery of all these fugitives, spoke and interceded for them, and urged in vain that they be lodged somewhere and given food."[162] When Macarty refused, colonists objected, protesting that "we would . . . [not] see them [the Cahokia and Metchigamea] die and remain unmoved."[163] As the colonists knew well, these refugees were sure to join with hostile Indians against the colony if they were turned away. Seeing this as foolish policy, the habitants at Kaskaskia took the hundred Indian refugees into their own houses and into the unfinished church building. The habitants clearly rejected Macarty's Indian policy and followed their own ideas.

∾

Macarty's administration never recovered from its early failures. Desertion continued to plague the fort, and progress on the new symbol of military force was slow. Macarty never really established a good working relationship with the colonists. As he wrote to Vaudreuil in 1752, the colonists were too independent: "No one can be gentler with the inhabitants than I have been. Most of them want to direct things themselves. That does well enough so long as nothing is asked of them."[164]

Macarty was right: the colonists did want to direct things themselves or at least to collaborate and not be bossed around. In the fall of 1752, after only a short while under the command of Macarty, Father Guyenne wrote to Vaudreuil on behalf of the colony. Macarty had failed. As Guyenne wrote, previous Illinois commandants had learned to "[distribute] favors wisely."[165] But Macarty did not know how to be beneficent or accommodating. "[He] is dreaded," Guyenne said, "he has the king's interest so much at heart that he seems to recognize no others."[166] When it came to Indian affairs, he was stingy with presents. Even when the Illinois tried to demonstrate their loyalty, the priest noted, Macarty turned them away. Guyenne complained that "I could get nothing for them. Accordingly the chiefs here say we are no longer afraid of them."[167] He ignored the protocol of Indian diplomacy and had little patience for the kind of ceremony that was essential to creating a good relationship with the Indians. "These petty annoyances make me uneasy and fearful lest these people take some evil course."[168] The bottom line was this: Macarty had ruined the Illinois alliance. In 1754, Father Michel Baudouin, Superior of the Jesuits in Louisiana, wrote to French authorities to complain about Macarty: "For several years past [the Illinois] have been of no great help because [Macarty has] not known how to gain their confidence and to guide them with that just temperament which, without derogating in anything from the authority proper to a person of position, does not commit His Majesty's arms against them and would have prevented many distressing catastrophes which have befallen in the Illinois."[169]

And as he failed with the Indians, Macarty also failed with the inhabitants. It was true that the colonists were self-interested and jealous of their time and energy. Macarty's expectations about labor on the fort were all wrong, as were his assumptions about militia service. The plain fact, Baudouin wrote, was that "[the habitants] ordinarily do no more than they can absolutely avoid doing." This reality required finesse, not authoritarianism: "When they take that attitude, a commandant finds himself hard pressed, especially when his soldiers take to deserting to the enemy as happened last year." The commandant was dependent on the colonists and had to seek their cooperation. But cooperating was a difficult thing: "This the inhabitants avoid doing when they have for a commandant a man who despises them and from whom they receive only ill treatment when he has no need of them." Macarty had failed because he was too slow to realize that good order in the Illinois was a matter of collaboration.[170]

Baudouin recommended Pierre Joseph Neyon de Villiers as the new commandant to replace Macarty. As Baudouin explained, Villiers was well suited for the position because "He knows how to handle the inhabitants and the Indians." The job was not impossible: "A person gentle, tractable and tactful can do much with the Indians, especially if they see him at the proper time give evidences of his friendship." Villiers was the kind of leader who could also make himself beloved by the inhabitants and bring them willingly to his side. And thus, even in trying times, he could succeed: "When [a hypothetical] unfortunate incident occurred in his post, cherished as he is by the inhabitants and the Indians, he would soon find the means of remedying it. Nothing is impossible with these people when they love a commandant, and without partiality it can be said that M. de Neyon is of all the officers of the country the one fittest to command the Illinois with dignity and success."[171]

It was an impressive statement of the imperial situation in Illinois, and officials in France listened. Neyon de Villiers took over the colony in 1754.[172] By this time Vaudreuil was gone, having left to take control of Canada the previous year, replaced by Louis Belcourt, Chevalier de Kelerec. With the departure of Vaudreuil, we lose the main source of correspondence that is our window into the colony, so it is difficult to say how Villiers or his successors managed their new authority.[173] Did he make better relationships with the Illinois? Did he give gifts more liberally? Did he treat the colonists more gently?

If we lack the documents to answer these questions fully, what we do have from this period of Illinois history is the material reality of Fort de Chartres, which, by 1754, was well underway. Reconstructed and today managed as a state historic site, it is easy to interpret the imposing structure as a monument of power. It is impressive. Its stone walls are a foot and a half to two feet thick, impregnable, secure. They stand about twenty feet high, with loopholes at regular intervals for ready defense. Each bastion wall contains two cannons. The barracks are massive timber frame buildings, in their day able to house the three hundred soldiers that Vaudreuil envisioned for the fort.

As a primary source, the fort tempts us to imagine a powerful military operation in Illinois, as well as an imperial order informed by a strict command. But if that's the story that the monumental Fort de Chartres silently suggests, it is misleading. For one thing, it was not completed until 1760, just three years before the official end of the French regime. But in a bigger sense, the history of the fort and its surrounding colony in this period suggests that none of the fort's suggested strength was really ever achieved. For years, leaders like Macarty, Vaudreuil, and Bertet failed when they tried to project top-down authority in the colony. Colonists and Indians insisted instead that imperial agendas be subordinate in important ways to their own local priorities. And as the appointment of Villiers reflects, the colonists' insistence on collaboration informed the way the French empire operated in Illinois, even in the shadow of the imposing Fort de Chartres.

Chapter 8

Demanding Collaboration in British Illinois

In 1763, at the end of the Seven Years' War, the middle of North America witnessed an imperial shakeup of the highest order. The villages of the Illinois Country, along with all the land west of the Appalachian Mountains, passed officially to British control. Under a secret treaty with France, meanwhile, Spain had gained jurisdiction over the territory west of the Mississippi River in 1762. Illinois Country settlements and villages were now in the heart of an international borderland. To be sure, Illinois Country had been a borderland throughout its history, existing between Algonquian and Siouan worlds, prairie and woodlands ecosystems, Canadian and Louisianan policies. But this was a radical change. All of the major settlements, including Kaskaskia, Cahokia, St. Philippe, Prairie du Rocher, and Fort de Chartres, were now—technically and officially—British. The 1,400 people living in the Illinois colonies and hundreds of Indians were, as the treaty said, in British-claimed territory.[1]

The British were in no rush to take over their new territories in the West. Primarily this was because in 1763 the Indians of the West, united together loosely under the leadership of Ottawa chief Pontiac, rebelled and conducted a series of military actions to expel the British from the Appalachians, the Great Lakes, and the Mississippi Valley. In the face of this resistance, any attempt at settlement would be expensive at a time when the British government was already deeply in debt. In 1763 the British government issued a proclamation prohibiting settlement in the West and providing for no new colonial activity in any of the newly acquired territories. The British government had other things to worry about.[2]

But even if they had wanted to, the British could not ignore the Illinois Country settlements. First of all, the region around Fort de Chartres was the

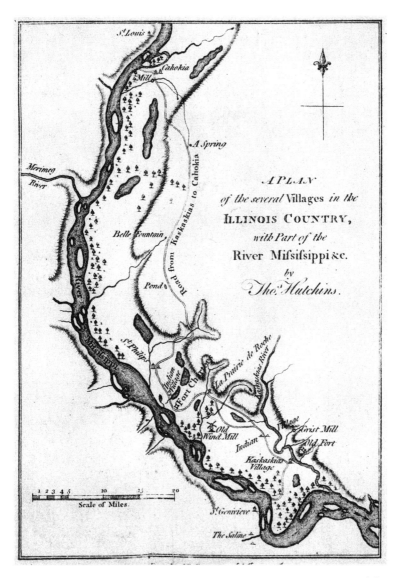

Figure 20. Map of "British" Illinois by Thomas Hutchins, circa 1770. From Philip Pittman, *The Present State of the European Settlements on the Mississippi; with a Geographical Description of That River* (London: Printed for J. Nourse, 1770).

Courtesy of the Rare Book and Manuscript Library of the University of Illinois at Urbana-Champaign.

center of Pontiac's resistance movement, and it was where Pontiac retreated in 1764 to regroup and plan more action. French traders in the region, who had supported Pontiac's original campaign, now continued to supply the Indians. Across the river from Fort de Chartres, French colonists began forming new settlements in what was now officially Spanish territory from which they provided Indians with trade goods and military support. When the Spanish made moves to set up a rudimentary government in Illinois, the French colonists in Illinois looked ready to establish a permanent colony hostile to British interests on the west side of the river.[3]

In the face of these developments, the British had to respond. Reluctantly, the government sent military forces to Fort de Chartres in 1765. Officials also sent a commissary to provide the Indians with gifts—an effort to win their loyalty. Inertia quickly took over. With the military occupation underway, British merchants arrived to supply the installation at Fort de Chartres. Speculators began planning a colony in the region and organizing to buy land from Indians.[4] By 1765, British planners were writing utopian prospectuses looking forward to a future western empire centered at the Illinois Country.[5] The British quickly had a fledgling—though from the standpoint of many imperial officials, unintentional—colonial project in the Illinois Country.[6]

For the French and Indians in Illinois, the occupation of their settlements by the British was of course on the one hand unwelcome. The British were their rivals, they were Protestant, and they looked down on the French and Indians. Many habitants and Indians left for Spanish territory in St. Louis, where a more friendly Bourbon government's flag now was flying. Hundreds of French inhabitants accompanied the French military officer Louis St. Ange de Bellerive after he surrendered Fort de Chartres and relocated in the new frontier city.

On the other hand, substantial numbers of Illinois French and Indians did not leave but rather viewed the new situation from a pragmatic angle. After all, the prospect of British investment in the region, combined with the prospect of a Spanish government to the west, brought new borderlands opportunities to the French and Indians. Once again, the French and the Indians of the Illinois Country would be between competing governments. They had been in this position before. Working both sides against each other, they could seek advantage and force the reluctant British government to accommodate to their needs. Quickly shedding old allegiances, they opportunistically professed new loyalties and made new partnerships with the British newcomers. As they had always been with the French government, they became pragmatic collaborators with the new British authorities.

But the British soon proved to be poor partners, especially to the French villagers. Given the lack of enthusiasm for western expansion in general and distractions in the East, the British government did little to put the colony on stable footing. Military commandants at Fort de Chartres were corrupt and arbitrary in their treatment of the French. The colonists suffered at the hands of despotic and overcontrolling British military regimes. But what was most distressing for the French colonists was that the empire did not follow through on its promise of a civil government for the region. The British outpost in Illinois languished as a simple military affair—troops and a commandant, without a real provincial government.

For the profit-minded, pragmatic inhabitants of Illinois, becoming "British" was actually not such a big deal—they did not care much about their imperial identity and had always been flexible about such matters.[7] They would have been happy to be British, Spanish, or whatever, as long as their needs were met. But disorder and imperial neglect were intolerable. When they did not get the government they wanted, the newly "British" subjects had to pull their new imperial bosses along. Beginning in the 1760s, the French inhabitants mounted a political campaign that was one of the most interesting episodes of political activism in Revolutionary-era North America. Although it is almost unknown, this was a surprisingly radical effort to insist on the Illinois inhabitants' long-established and distinctive political style: empire by collaboration. In hundreds of pages of petitions to the British authorities, as well as in on-the-ground protests and other actions, French colonists protested against the government in British Illinois.

Unlike the independence movement going on in British colonies to the east, however, the Illinois French did not protest empire itself. Just the opposite: what they protested was *neglect*. They argued for a collaborative government and for the ability to set their own Indian policy, as they always had. Most important, they called for a practical government that would facilitate economic activity and opportunity and support the development of their colonial project. Although the French colonists were surprisingly well versed in eighteenth-century political theory and the British constitution, their campaign was not an abstract argument about legal theory or principles. Rather, it was a practical campaign to force the English empire to make a government that worked for the "antient inhabitants."[8] The French colonists envisioned continuing their lives as they had always done—in cooperation with empire.

In doing so, they articulated a vision of republicanism that was distinctive and rooted in their long tradition of pragmatic politics and empire by collaboration.

ᆼᄼᄀ

The Seven Years' War was an important turning point in Illinois history. Having finally decided to commit major resources to eliminating French power in North America, the British empire began its unprecedented military action in the Ohio Valley by contesting (in 1755) and then conquering (in 1758) the French Fort Duquesne at modern Pittsburgh. From its location at the terminus of the contested Ohio Valley, the Illinois colony played a critical role in French efforts to preserve their empire. Once again under collaborative command in the person of Neyon de Villiers, the French colony supplied Fort Duquesne with needed support. French forces under Charles Philippe Aubry, who would later become the last French governor of Louisiana, set out from Fort de Chartres on expeditions up the Ohio Valley.[9] More important, Illinois farmers became a lifeline for Duquesne by redirecting their grain exports to the East. The commandant of Fort Duquesne requested huge quantities of grain and pork from the Illinois farmers, which they tried to supply. Opportunistic as ever, they benefited from the six hundred thousand livres in expenses that the French government paid at Fort de Chartres in 1758 alone. The French in Illinois could not prevent the British from assuming control of French North America, but they could—as usual—benefit from imperial contestation.

After the official peace between France and Britain, the war did not immediately end in Illinois. Supplied by traders from the French at Fort de Chartres, Pontiac's rebellion reached a climax in 1763, with the unsuccessful siege of Detroit.[10] But many of the rebellious groups retreated and regrouped in Illinois, near Fort de Chartres.[11] French traders supplied them using long-established trade routes through New Orleans, which was now officially Spanish but remained under acting governor Jean-Jacques Blaise d'Abbadie's authority. As the British commander John Stuart knew, "This is the Channel, by which Pondiac and his Party have been Enabled to Carry on the War."[12]

For the British, this was a problem. Since the Spanish had not yet occupied Louisiana, Frenchmen controlled Spanish Illinois and ran things as they wished. Indeed, the Spanish would leave Louisiana completely without government until 1766, when Antonio de Ulloa first arrived with ninety troops to command the territory. It would not be until 1767 that the Spanish would actually send a Spanish captain named Francisco Ríu to Illinois, and then only to maintain a nominal authority over what continued to be an exclusively Francophone population. In the meantime, the territory was effectively ruled by French traders. Governor d'Abbadie gave a trade monopoly to Maxent, Laclède and Company in 1764 to trade at the fledgling St. Louis colony with French-allied groups like the Illinois and Osage. Governor d'Abbadie also spread the word to French-allied Indians that the Spanish and French were one people. Under these circumstances, it would be difficult for the British to secure the West or even stop frontier attacks.[13]

Illinois commandant Villiers gives us a ground-level view of what was going on in Illinois in 1763–64. Villiers remained neutral after the war and in fact tried to persuade Pontiac to end his rebellion. He wrote to encourage Pontiac to end his attacks in October 1763, telling him to "Leave off spilling the blood of your brethren, the English; our hearts are now as one."[14] Villiers awaited British expeditions, beginning with Major Loftus, in 1763, to cede Fort de Chartres to the new authorities. When Loftus failed to arrive in Illinois owing to hostile Indian attacks, however, Pontiac's rebellion continued.[15] In 1764, Villiers wrote that Pontiac was organizing for a second attack against Detroit.

The Illinois themselves gave the British an opening. From Villiers, the British heard that the Illinois were willing to welcome the British and held themselves aloof from Pontiac's conspiracy. Villiers wrote in 1764 that "I had never looked upon the conspiracy as general; I excepted from it . . . the Ilinois nation which I had persuaded to receive you."[16] If Villiers was correct, then the Illinois's stance here was characteristically opportunistic. For many western Indian groups in 1763, the British had become the new hegemon and thus the enemy.[17] But to the Illinois, far on the frontier and adaptable as ever, the British were no more threatening than the French or the Spanish—they were simply another imperial power to exploit to their own ends. As General Gage would later write, Indians like the Illinois knew "their political interest extreamly well . . . to have a door open to treat with and trade with another power."[18] With the French still around and the Spanish regime coming, the British represented just another new "counterpoize" for the Illinois, as trader George Croghan observed.[19] Their loyalty was on a pivot. When Pontiac arrived in Illinois in the summer of 1764, he quickly persuaded the Illinois to join his movement. As d'Abbadie wrote in his journal in July 1764, "the savages living near the Illinois are as hostile as the others to the

English."[20] But as Gage wrote, the Illinois might change their tune: "The Savages of the Illinois . . . were well reconciled to our possessing their Country, till spirited up against us by the Delawares, and by Pondiac. . . . [T]here are therefore hopes . . . that Major Loftus may be enabled to obtain their consent, to his taking a quiet possession of the Country."[21]

Loftus never made it, and it was not until 1765 that Captain Thomas Sterling arrived with a detachment of the 42nd Regiment of Highland troops. In 1766, George Croghan came and held a general meeting for all the Indians at Fort de Chartres.[22] Croghan distributed presents, following the maxim that the new imperial powers were learning about this place.[23] The Illinois were "People who like to have lots of things given to them" and who "will sell their friendship for anything that is offered it."[24] For the British, here was the beginning of a halting experiment in empire. The Indians had forced the British, against their larger priorities, to set up a colony.

But of course it was not just the Indians that the British had to deal with. Hundreds of French Creoles, mixed-race Francophones, together with their slaves, were also in the region. The British had many negative stereotypes of these settlers. They were "Renegadoes" and fond of "extravagant Debaucheries."[25] According to British intelligence, *most* of the inhabitants of Illinois were "Convicts or people who have fled [to Illinois] for some Crimes." In the words of Lieutenant Alexander Fraser, member of the British party occupying Fort de Chartres in 1765, the majority of French colonists were alcoholic and lazy, "drunk every day while they can get Drink." To support themselves, they relied on "a good many Negroes, who are obliged to Labour very hard to Support their Masters."[26] When they weren't exploiting their slaves, they were living off the labor of Indians, without whom, it was thought, "they cannot Subsist."[27] Close relationships between the Indians and French were especially troubling. The Illinois habitants lived "In imitation of the Indians whose manners and Customs they have intirely adopted."[28] As one British administrator wrote, "by their Superior Address, and knowledge of the different Languages, they maintain their Influence [with the Indians]."[29] Yet while they were skilled at Indian affairs, in the view of the new imperial officers, the French in Illinois were hopeless when it came to maintaining social discipline. The Illinois inhabitants lived in ridiculously chaotic arrangements, "Dispersed through the country in Several Small villages." They had no discipline and virtually no government.[30] As one British commentator wrote, "The French Troops we relieved here might be called anything else but Soldiers; in Short I defy the best droll comick to represent them at Drury lane."[31] The British had hostile views of the French.

But the British were going to have to open their minds. For just like the Indians, the French in Illinois could not be ignored or dismissed. First of all, any British military installation in Illinois would need food and merchandise and would therefore rely on the cooperation of the farmers, hunters, and traders in the region for its support. Like the Indians, the French had the choice to abandon Kaskaskia and the other villages for the new Spanish settlements to the west, particularly after St. Ange de Bellerive, who had taken over upon Villiers's departure from Fort de Chartres in 1764, surrendered the fort and moved to St. Genevieve to establish an all-French regime under Spanish jurisdiction. As Lord Barrington wrote in 1766, the remaining French inhabitants in British Illinois could not be neglected: "if they should be left to themselves they may in time like the Acadians, assume a kind of independency."[32]

For all these reasons, the British had to accommodate both the French and the Indians. Sterling cursed his "disagreeable situation" as he contemplated what he could do to make these Indian and French settlements loyal to the English.[33] For the colonists and the Indians, it was a moment of opportunity.

ఴ

In 1765, immediately after occupying Fort de Chartres, Sterling received bad news. French traders from the west side of the river were enticing Indians and Frenchmen to leave the British settlements altogether. As Sterling reported to his commander: "the French Emmissarys have spared no pains to debauch the Indians & Inhabitants to leave us; And a report they have Spread that all the French Officers, are to be Continued by the Spaniards and the Government of the other side to be entirely French, has contributed not a little to it."[34] Antonio de Ulloa finally took possession of Louisiana in 1766 and began formulating his policy. Outgoing French governor d'Abbadie had urged him to "adopt French practices in the government of the Indians," and Ulloa took the advice to heart.[35] As Ulloa said, speaking like a seasoned veteran of Indian affairs in the Mississippi Valley, "We must make them believe that we go into their lands without any claim of right, but because they want us to go."[36] As Ulloa put it, Indians on the west side of the river would feel total continuity between the French and the Spanish regimes. The goal was for Indians to "understand that we want to do everything they have been accustomed to, and we do not wish to introduce any novelty among them."[37] From a newly planned Fort San Carlos on the Missouri River, as well as the small Spanish base at St. Louis, the Indians looked forward to supplies from the Spanish newcomers. Of course, the Spanish had little capacity in their new colony and certainly little direct power, since Francisco Ríu had only a few troops to enforce any laws or regulations. Through the 1760s, the Spanish province remained a fledgling operation, even after the appointment of a lieutenant governor, Don Pedro Piernas, who commanded a military force of only thirty-three troops.[38] But if the Spanish projected little direct power, their indirect influence through trade was considerable. By the late 1760s, most of the Indians of the region had been to the new Spanish commandant to receive gifts.[39]

These developments put considerable pressure on the British to run their own Indian policy generously. In other parts of North America, officials like Lord Jeffrey Amherst asserted that the key to a new Indian diplomacy was domination: "The Indians must be taught to fear us and they'll act like Fr[ie]nds."[40] But in Illinois this was sheer fantasy.[41] In fact, the new British regime could force almost nothing, especially as "enemy nations" in the northern Great Lakes continued to resist British occupation. In Illinois, the British accommodated to the Indians, bringing them benefits.

Shortly after the proclamation setting up the new administration for the Indian territory (the so-called Proclamation of 1763), the British devised a plan to send a commissary and gunsmith to each of the Indian posts, including Illinois.[42] Indian superintendent William Johnson sent Edward Cole to Illinois as the first Indian commissary. Cole arrived in Illinois in 1766. His account book from the fall of 1767—one of at least four extant—reveals how the Indians benefited from the new British regime. On a single month's ledger, commissioner Cole recorded valuable gifts to Peorias, Kaskaskias, Metchigameas, and Cahokias, as well as Missourias, Kickapoos, Musketons (Mascoutins), Osages, a party of the Vermillion Tribe, Wichitas, Arkansas, and other groups. In just this one month, Cole distributed over one thousand pounds' worth of goods.[43]

Cole's account books reveal how he had to pay for Indians' loyalty to their new British "Father." Each of approximately twenty entries features an Indian group receiving gifts like the ones the Peorias received: "Delivered to the Peorias with all their Chiefs who came to take leave of their Father, as they were going out to their Hunt and to assure him of their Strong Attachment to the English, praying He would take pitty on them and give them some assistance—they were to the number of 200."[44] Cole gave them ammunition, tools, clothing, blankets, wampum, and other items. The total amounted to ninety pounds.

The account book makes it clear how the Indians played on British fears and used the threat of anti-British activity in order to extort presents from Cole. Most typically they promised "to keep the path open and not listen to Bad Spirits." The Kickapoos received sixty-three pounds' worth of goods in exchange for a promise "that [the British] might send for them in case they should be wanted, as many as bad Reports was going about among the Northern Indians." Similarly, the Illinois Indians offered intelligence and promised to report any conspiracies to the British. Consider the case of Tamaroa, the Kaskaskia chief, who received seventy pounds' worth for "acquaint[ing] their fathers the English that there was Bad Belts going about among the Indians to the Northeast and to convince them of their firm Attachment and they shoud shut their Ears against all the bad Spirits."[45]

Although Cole gave gifts to several Indian groups, the Illinois-speakers were the greatest beneficiaries at Fort de Chartres. Aloof as always from the northern tribes, the Illinois made it their business to report conspiracies to the British, for which they were compensated handsomely. Four Fingers, a Metchigamea chief, "came from their Hunting Ground to acquaint their Fathers that they had heard the Indians towards the Lakes were badly disposed towards the English." For the second time in a month, Cole distributed payments to Tamaroa, the Kaskaskia chief, who promised that his people "would give him all the intelligence that should come to their knowledge" in case the chief heard any more "bad reports." And Black Collar, a Peoria chief, "Expressed the greatest friendship and a surety of the earliest intelligence if there was danger." When Baptist the Kaskaskia chief came to Cole "to inquire of their Father if he had received any further intelligence of the bad designs of the Indians to the Northward," Cole gave him 107 pounds' worth of merchandise. Finally, a Kaskaskia chief received 26 pounds' worth of goods when he "came to ask their Father if he had heard any faithful reports of the bad disposition of the Indians to the Northward [and promised] that he wou'd make the most diligent enquiry to know the truth, which he woul'd acquaint him with, that his heart was English, and he would continue faithfully to them."[46]

Of course it is impossible to know how real these threats were or whether these reports were mere rumor. Either way, what is clear is that the Illinois were taking advantage of the competition among different powers in the

region and making the British pay for their new "English hearts." Whatever
the reality of borderland threats, the Indians—and the Illinois in particular—
capitalized on the vulnerability of the British empire. What is especially significant about all this is the scale of the gift-giving. Cole spent so much in
1767 that Gage refused initially to pay his account and began an audit of
what he considered to be lavish spending.[47]

Meanwhile, the French gained as well from the new administration. In
1766, all of the British gifts to the Illinois Indians came from the French
merchants, since there were not any English merchants who could get supplies to the Illinois until 1767.[48] Thus French merchants like Daniel Blouin
saw great benefits with the arrival of the new British regime, as the British
bought from the French to give to the Indians, as well as provisions at the
fort.[49] What is more, the French charged very high prices, making the
British commandant at Illinois complain that "[t]his last 6 months are very
high; have had 4000 Indians and what adds greatly to it, is paying upwards
of 100 plus more for every article we get than in any other part of
america."[50]

In 1767, George Morgan arrived in Illinois as a representative of the
Philadelphia trading firm Baynton, Wharton and Morgan, which ended the
French traders' run as the suppliers of goods to commissary Cole. But even
as it closed them out of government contracts, Morgan's operation created
opportunity for the French traders in the fur trade. Morgan's business introduced a huge stream of goods—twenty-nine thousand pounds' worth—into
the Illinois economy in 1767.[51] He was a job creator as well, hiring French
hunters and laborers to assist him in his trading activities.[52]

For their part, the farmers of Kaskaskia also profited from the new British military economy. Most important, the new British regime came with
hundreds of soldiers, and the farmers now had a ready market for their produce at Fort de Chartres. They made contracts with the British commandant
for flour and livestock. They found in George Morgan an equally eager partner, who also brought a new and valuable commodity for the French farmers:
slaves.[53] Even as many farmers abandoned the Illinois for new farms on the
Spanish side, some farmers in Kaskaskia clearly prospered by serving the
needs of the newcomers. By 1767, General Gage wrote to complain about
the situation, calling the prices that the French charged "exorbitant": "The
Provision purchased at the Ilinois is excessive dear. . . . At the rate you
purchase it from the Inhabitants. I must beg of you to lower these exorbitant
prices as much as possible."[54]

The Indians and the inhabitants thus benefited from the new British regime. But if they made the new regime work to their advantage economically, they also forced the new regime to set up an accommodating political environment. The Proclamation of 1763, issued by the debt-ridden British empire at the end of the Seven Years' War, effectively created just two stripped-down governments for the West, one in Quebec and one in Florida. There was no provision for the establishment of provincial governments in places like Illinois. This left the colony to be placed under simple military command in 1765, when Thomas Sterling occupied Fort de Chartres. And while Gage fantasized about removing the colonists altogether and settling them under strict military government at Detroit, the reality was that the new British regime basically ordained the colonists' own way of doing things in the first couple of years.[55]

Almost everything about the new political order was accommodated to the inhabitants. The proclamation itself gave them certain basic rights. For instance, they were allowed to profess Catholicism.[56] General Gage added that the government would guarantee the security of property to all the current habitants who decided to stay in British territory and become British subjects.[57] The only requirement was that the new subjects swear a loyalty oath. As Gage wrote in 1765, "They are commanded by these presents to take the oath of fidelity and obedience to His Majesty, in presence of the Sieur Stirling, captain of the Highland regiment, the bearer hereof, and furnished with our full powers for this purpose. . . . We recommend forcibly to the inhabitants to conduct themselves like good and faithful subjects, avoiding, by a wise and prudent demeanor, all cause of complaint against them."[58]

And yet even when it came to the loyalty oath, which was the sole requirement that the British exacted of its new subjects, the British were not in a position to "recommend forcibly" to the colonists. Indeed, bristling at the idea of swearing a loyalty oath so quickly after the arrival of the new regime, the colonists petitioned in 1765 for more time to decide whether they would "become British" or not.[59] They wanted to wait and see. Gage, fearing that the colony would be "immediately depopulated" if he refused their request, granted the extension.[60] In 1766, the colonists again petitioned for a delay of nine months to remove their things if they decided to leave.[61]

Meanwhile, whether out of purposeful accommodation or sheer neglect, Sterling turned almost all local governmental matters over to the control of the inhabitants themselves. Sterling appointed an inhabitant, La Grange, to run a court, "according to the Laws and Customs of the Country," which is to say,

French law.[62] Sterling had his misgivings about this, since "Mr. La Grange['s] knowledge of the Law, is not Sufficient to fill that Employment as it Ought to be."[63] Moreover, it was strange that the new law court should not function according to British law, as was the precedent in Canada, for example. Still, the military commandant had little choice in the matter if he wanted the colonists to remain in their settlements. Two years later Gage still favored letting the colonists organize their own courts, "according to their own customs."[64]

At the beginning of the British regime, then, both Indians and French profited and felt no particular ill effects from the arrival of the British. Looking back years later, the French remembered this early period under British rule as characterized by "moderation, prudence, and justice." Indeed, as they wrote, "the new subjects of England in that colony . . . enjoyed a tranquility which began to console them for the change of dominion which had been made."[65] Furthermore, if the new regime seemed decent starting out, it looked even better moving forward. British agents like Philip Pittman had discussed the advantages of the British constitution with Illinois boatmen, contrasting it with Spanish oppression and promising the benefits of English liberty.[66] Colonists communicated with their family members and fellow Frenchmen in Canada and heard about the progress of British government there.[67] Most important, the colonists interacted with the new businessmen in the British regime, men like Morgan and Morgan's secretary, James Rumsey, who were associated with the land company lobbying for a civil government in the colony.[68] Evidence suggests that the French merchants felt a quick kinship with these entrepreneurs, and the two groups quickly shared a vision for a future commercial colony in Kaskaskia.

But the empire did not actually intend to send a government. In 1766, the Lords of Trade made it clear that they did not intend a civil government to be established piecemeal in just a "particular part" of the extensive Western territory. They instead wanted "one uniform plan" for the "whole of that interior Country."[69] In fact, British officials were looking to reduce, not increase, their investment in Illinois. This reality clashed with the hopes of the French and Illinois Indians who had pragmatically declared themselves "subjects of his British Majesty," with "English hearts." Of course they had done this based on the hope that the British regime could actually help, and not hurt, their interests.

☙

Things began to change in Illinois under the administration of a newly appointed lieutenant, John Reed, who arrived to take command of the colony in 1767. Most important, in 1767, after two years of liberal gift-giving to the Indians, Gage wrote that the expenses of the Illinois Indian policy needed to be reduced. As he wrote to Reed, "You must put the Ilinois on the Same Footing as other Places, by giving only what is absolutely necessary; and what is usual to Savages, and to deal out Presents with a sparing hand; And they must not be lavished any longer."[70] A month later, Gage signaled that Indian policy was entering a new phase: "At the taking possession of a new country, expenses of this kind may be allowed of, perhaps cannot be avoided, and every nation of Indians in the neighborhood expect some favors upon these occasions, and indeed they have been liberally dealt with . . . but this is now over."[71] The colony would henceforth operate by new rules: "I must observe to You that the Commissarys at the Posts are not Sent there, to lavish away Presents to every Strolling Indian that comes to a Fort; Presents are only to be given to the Heads of Nations, and then frugally on particular and necessary occasions."[72] British generosity, as well as the accommodating spirit of the early British regime in Illinois, had come to an end.

In addition to the new Indian policy, John Reed's regime was also charged with enforcing a stricter regulation of the French traders of the region. As Reed observed, "Traders are the worst of people, and speak the Language of most of the Nations, being continually marrying amongst Them."[73] Their most egregious crime was their refusal to obey British attempts to regulate the new international border between Spanish and British territory, which they violated with impunity. As George Morgan noted, French hunters, living in Spanish territory, constantly came into British territory to trade with Indians and to "procure meat for the Settlements on the West side of the Mississippi."[74] These subversives wore clever disguises, being "even so impudent as to wear English Colours" as they traded with neighbors who were now officially English. This was leading not only to losses and the depletion of valuable game but also to disorder, since "our good Friends [meaning the French traders] on the other side will always be ready to spirit [the Indians] up to mischief."[75] Gage instructed Reed to enforce the new border in Illinois more strictly.[76]

But if these were specific plans for reform in 1767, the most important change in the British administration was probably Reed's more domineering attitude toward the French inhabitants themselves. Arriving in the colony in

1767, the new commander complained that the Illinois Country was populated by "a sett of the greatest villans under the creation both on this and the
other side." He knew that the colony was "at very great expences both on
their account and the Indians," and he resented the colonists.[77] Other British
officials in Illinois felt the same way, complaining that the French were "cruel
and treacherous to each other & consequently so to Strangers, they are dis-
honest in every kind of Business, & lay themselves out to over reach
Strangers—which they often do, by a low cunning peculiar to themselves,
and their Artful flatteries, with extravagant Entertainments (in which they
affect the greatest hospitality) generally favor their schemes."[78]

These dismissive attitudes were soon reflected in the way Reed dealt with
the colonists in Illinois. Where Sterling had let the colonists run their own
affairs, Reed interfered and managed the colony as a military dictatorship,
and a punitive one at that. He imposed fines for issuing marriage licenses,
for instance, and even taxed colonists who wanted to pledge loyalty to the
British government. Taxing nearly every government function, Reed introduced what seems like a version of the hated Stamp Tax for provincial Illinois.[79] As the trader George Morgan observed:

> [Reed] has extorted their Money from them in the most Tyrannical
> Manner. If A French Man was seen to canter his Horse near or in
> the Town, or if his Horse started and got into a Gallop, he was made
> to pay 200 Livres & sometimes more. & that without being permit-
> ted to speak in his Defence. . . . He has also been so imprudent as
> to insist on 20 Lvres. for administ'ring the Oath of Allegiance. One
> who lately desired to be admitted as an English Subject, had the
> Spirit to refuse the Payment of this Fee—Saying he knew well that
> his Britannick Majesty would much Rather give Encouragement,
> than require Payment, for this admission. The Fees he has receiv'd
> from the French Traders for Permission to go up the Illinois &
> Wabash Rivers with Merchandize of French Manufacture has to my
> Knowledge been Great & Many.[80]

Reed's actions—interfering in trade, taxing the colonists arbitrarily,
throwing people in jail—convinced many to leave, and St. Louis welcomed
a number of new French inhabitants in the winter of 1767. However, even in
the face of a corrupt leader like Reed, many colonists held on. By 1767, many
of them had grown truly hopeful that the English government offered them

benefits they would not likely receive on the Spanish side of the river.[81] But what power did they have to change their situation, here on the edge of the empire?

Toward the end of the year, George Morgan brought the inhabitants together to plan a response to Reed's regime. In many ways, Morgan must have seemed an unlikely ally of the French. Here he was, a British merchant in a French colony, but he had not even bothered to learn to speak the French language. Moreover, his own business interests in many ways put him in competition with the French merchants. For their part, the French in 1767 were wary of Morgan and would only grow more suspicious of him over time. But if they regarded each other with coolness in some ways, Morgan and the French both shared an interest in good government for the colony.[82] They all were, above all, businessmen, with little time for petty prejudices or hang-ups about national identity. And so Morgan helped them plan the response, and they accepted his aid. What he gave them was a legal tool: petition.

Petitioning was one of the most important legal rights held by a subject of the British realm. The petition was considered "the indisputable right of even the meanest subject."[83] In early modern Britain, published petitions became a pillar of the public sphere in which subjects defined their rights and actively helped shape emerging democratic culture. Petitions echoed an established tradition in French law, under which subjects had four tools for addressing the French king: *mémoire*, *petition*, *requête*, and *remonstrance*.[84] The Illinois colonists were familiar with these. They had actively petitioned their governments, both the Provincial Council and Superior Council, from the 1720s through the end of the French regime, asserting their rights and expressing their communal identity within the empire.[85] Using petitions, the Illinois inhabitants had asked for security of land, for privileges in inheritance cases, for support of community policies. Their petitions both emphasized their subjecthood and usually asked for modifications of policy, requested local exceptions to imperial rules, or begged imperial action on their behalf. Petitions, in short, had been the Illinois colonists' essential tool for imperial collaboration.

After their meeting with Morgan in 1767, the French colonists of Illinois began a campaign of petitions that would last for the rest of the British regime. Their purpose was simple and straightforward. Military commanders were not enough for a colony as large as Illinois. They needed a civil administration. What they asked for, above all, was "the establishment of Civil Government in Illinois, according to the Laws of England."

Humbly Showeth:

That the supplicants having suffered great inconvenience, from the lack of a civil government established in the colony, according the constitution of England, and many among us having been witnesses of the advantages which our compatriots in Canada reap from the fair and moderate government which has been established there, we beg permission to lay before your lordships the inconveniences which result from our present situation and the great advantages which one would unfailingly reap if it was established in a country as fertile, and as attractive as that of Illinois.[86]

The petition was untroubled by questions of national identity. Never once did the French even mention Catholicism, the French language, or differences between French and British traditions. The Illinois colonists, most of whom were Creoles with flexible identities anyway, were much too pragmatic to quibble about such matters. What the inhabitants did want was more straightforward and practical: a fair government so that they could conduct business: "Trade cannot exist, or at any rate, it is restricted to very narrow bounds, through a lack of a civil government, because the great number of complicated difficulties which so often are born of the affairs of trade, are in such a manner out of the sphere of the knowledge of the military, that on the subjects so removed from their profession, it happens very frequently that they decide against the right."[87]

The colonists were confident that the Illinois colony had great potential and could be very valuable to the British empire, and so their petition explained the mutual benefits that civil government in Illinois would bring: "The population, and the increase of trade will soon make that colony a strong enough barrier to protect the others, with the advantages which are the result of good laws." Moreover, the petitioners said, civil government would serve to grow the colony, since "a great part of those who, in the fear of being abandoned by the two crowns, are establishing themselves on the Spanish side of the Mississippi, would return to share in the happiness which the English government would procure."[88]

It was an important moment. For one thing, the petition was a bold request. As the French must have known, British officials had never really wanted a colony in Illinois; the colony was simply an imperative of Indian affairs. Moreover, acknowledging that they primarily wanted a government to adjudicate trade disputes and economic matters, the French made it clear that what they were asking for would introduce exactly the kind of complexity and expense that the Proclamation—with its stripped-down military governments—had been designed to prevent. Confidently, the French of Illinois were now suggesting that the empire's reluctance was foolish. The colonists knew the potential of the "fertile" colony, and they insisted that whatever expense it required would be "amply compensated" in the long run by "the increase of trade." Moreover, the colonists insisted, the strategic value of the colony was greater than the British really understood. The colonists boldly gave the British authorities advice on how to run the empire, insisting on practical considerations that the British were overlooking.

But perhaps even more important here was the French colonists' suggestion that the current situation was actually a violation of their rights. As they pointed out, the Canadians had become British, and in return they had received a "fair and moderate" civil government. The Illinois habitants, on the other hand, had sworn allegiance just like the Canadians, but they suffered under despotic military command. This not only gave them great "inconvenience," it violated the implicit contract that they made when they swore allegiance. As they wrote, or even demanded, "Grant to those among us who were formerly subjects of his Most Christian Majesty the favor which we expected, when we took the oath of allegiance."[89]

The French did not merely send their petition to the Lords of Trade alone. Instead they circulated it widely. For instance, they enlisted James Rumsey, Morgan's secretary, to write to Governor Franklin of Pennsylvania to make him aware of their complaints. Since many speculators in Pennsylvania were planning for future colonies in the Illinois Country, the French wanted them to know about their ideas and their call for a civil government.[90]

And now it was time for the empire to respond. Acknowledging Reed's corruption, Gage soon recalled Reed and replaced him with a new commandant, Gordon Forbes.[91] The colonists' petition had done some good at least.[92] But, at the same time, Gage did not address the issue of a civil government or respond directly to the logic of the petition. It was not the response that the colonists were hoping for. Moreover, under Forbes, the colonists soon had even more reasons to complain about the arbitrariness of government in Illinois. Forbes arrived in Illinois just as the first Spanish forces arrived in St. Louis and as rumors of new anti-British conspiracy among the northern Indians circulated.[93] Thus Forbes's first action in Illinois was to organize a militia, for which he required the colonists to muster. Fearing that Forbes would try to involve the militia in British conflicts with the Indians, the colonists refused.[94] In response, Forbes threatened to confiscate their property and throw them in jail as "rebels."[95] So they once again quickly wrote a petition.

Addressing themselves to Forbes, the colonists focused on the injustice of military government.[96] "Military Government was not established here before the cession of the Colony to Great Britain; it is an evil which we daily expect to be delivered from," they wrote. Indeed, the Frenchmen worried, "Military Discipline might render us more wretched still than the wretched inhabitants of Morocco." What was more, there was no law, they insisted, that "obliges us to be embodied as soldiers, without our previous consent, and that before we have voluntarily submitted to Military Discipline." In all of their history, the French of Illinois never had submitted to military rule, and they never would. "[We are] fully informed of those Evils which we would be liable to under a Tyrannical and Revengeful and capricious Ruler, should we ever be so Stupid as to Subject ourselves to that Yoke." The Illinois colonists simply refused to obey a government on those terms. Such a regime would be "slavery," they wrote.[97]

In their petition, as well as in their discussions with Forbes, the Illinois French spelled out the specific ways in which they understood their membership in the British empire, as well as the limits of that membership. They were loyal subjects and were faithful to the king, they wrote. But their resistance to the idea of mustering in a militia in order to fight for British interests was rooted in their self-perception as essentially neutral agents. As Forbes wrote, the reason that the French refused military government in Illinois was because they knew the British would entangle them in British conflicts. But as Forbes acknowledged, "They represented to me that they were not obliged to obey such orders by the Oath of Allegiance they had taken to His Majesty [since] . . . it would give great umbrage to the Savages, who had no quarrel with them as they were Frenchmen."[98] In short, the Frenchmen asserted that "they were determined to remain neuter whatever Nations we might be at War with, either Civilized or Savage."[99] As Forbes concluded, "They were determined not to appear under arms nor fight under our Colours, which resolution they indeed stuck to on that occasion."[100]

In many ways, this position about Indian wars was based on long precedent; the Illinois colonies had often negotiated their own Indian policy distinct from official imperial priorities even under the French regime, and they sometimes resisted militia duty as well. They did not see why this could not continue, even as the British held the territory. But their biggest concern remained civil government. In their petition, the French inhabitants of Kaskaskia insisted that a civil government of Illinois be established "voluntarily." Forbes was a "tyrannical, capricious, and vindictive commandant." They had to resist his actions because they violated "what the Rights of Nature have most preserved."[101] But they were not disloyal or traitors. "In spite of the resolution that we have taken of not submitting to the slavery which would result from the plan projected against us, we are always faithful to His Majesty," they wrote. In conclusion, they asked Forbes for a government that worked for both parties. "Although yourself, Sir, be in the Military Order, we believe you too worthy a member of a free nation, to think that you will not co-operate with us."[102] They were calling for neutrality and collaboration.

By the beginning of 1768, the French of Illinois had begun a major campaign of negotiation with the imperial officials, sending numerous petitions to request a civil government and advance a pragmatic view of their own status as neutral subjects of the British empire. Gage never responded directly to any of these petitions, but he did recall Forbes as quickly as he had done Reed. Moreover, in 1768, he sent a new commander to Illinois, Lieutenant John Wilkins. Although Gage instructed Wilkins to accommodate with the inhabitants, tensions increased even further under his leadership.[103] Wilkins quickly became the most arbitrary commander yet in the British regime, and his abuses provoked a whole new phase of activism by the French colonists, who soon took their call for civil government directly to Gage in New York.

කට

High hopes surrounded the beginning of John Wilkins's new regime in Illinois in 1768. As Illinois Frenchmen would later remember, Wilkins arrived and quickly made promises to run the new regime cooperatively. According to one of the colonists, "The day of his arrival, he declared that he would initiate nothing without the consent of the habitants; that he would restore the goods unjustly confiscated." Wilkins promised to "establish a court of justice of which the habitants would choose the members," and he promised that this court would operate by the inhabitants' "ancient laws their privileges, and their customs." In the end, "he painted such an attractive picture of their future happiness that while one believed in general that he spoke in good faith, one felt with sadness that it would be impossible for him to carry out a project which, up to the present, has existed only in novels."[104]

Indeed, Wilkins quickly disappointed the habitants. Shortly after his arrival in Illinois, he posted three proclamations on the door of the church at Kaskaskia. Two of the three were extremely distressing. The first one was a plan to stop smuggling and contraband trade by the French traders, even going so far as to ban hunting without a license. The second one was a new ordinance outlawing "bons," the unofficial currency that traders used to manage debts in Illinois. Rather than bons, the colonists would henceforth be required to use official billets drawn on the British firm of Baynton, Wharton and Morgan. The third ordinance was actually great news: "It is our intention to propose in a little time a form of [civil] government which we hope will be agreeable and advantageous to all the world." Perhaps Wilkins intended to answer their petitions at last. Unfortunately, Wilkins spent much more time on the other two ordinances and ignored the issue of a civil government.

Wilkins quickly began to alienate the colonists by restricting their movements in an effort to control the trade. In his defense, the colony was losing lots of money. Three years into the new regime, border violations were epidemic in Illinois.[105] An estimated £5,000 worth of furs was shipped annually from British Illinois to New Orleans, in violation of British trade restrictions.[106] But Wilkins's answer to this problem, as ordered by General Gage, was harsh. As Gage wrote, "I have sent Directions to the Officer Commanding at Fort-Chartres, to Scour the aforesaid Rivers with armed Boats, and to make Prisoners of all People whom he shall find acting contrary to these Orders and to convey them to Fort-Pitt."[107] Even when French merchants tried to follow the ordinances, and paid for the licenses to trade, Wilkins did not give them their passports.[108] Even Morgan himself looked at the situation as very bad for the inhabitants, who faced increasingly strict regulations. As he wrote, enforcing the new border had placed drastic restrictions on the colonists: "Matters here are carried to ridiculous length on both sides just as if the Affairs of the two Nations depended on these despicable settlements. No Person whatever Officer, Merchant or Inhabitants can cross the river from either Side without a written Passport." Summing up the effect of Wilkins's actions, Morgan reflected, "I look upon the poor Inhabitants as in a state of Slavery."[109]

Meanwhile, Wilkins also enforced his new regulation regarding currency. As the colonists would later explain, the notes that Wilkins now banned—bons—were necessary for free trade in a colony without gold and silver.[110] Moreover, the new billets that Wilkins mandated would be drawn on Baynton,

Wharton and Morgan, which gave the powerful company more control over trade than it already had. To the colonists, it looked like Wilkins was favoring the English firm rather than supporting "the freedom of commerce."[111]

If it looked this way, that is because Wilkins was indeed favoring Morgan's firm. Before leaving Philadelphia for the Illinois, John Wilkins had made an arrangement with Baynton, Wharton and Morgan "to promote and advance the Interest of yourself and partners at the Illinois in preference to any Body else." According to their agreement, Wilkins would take five hundred pounds twice a year, as well as 6 percent of total revenue, as compensation for enforcing Morgan's monopoly on merchandizing in the Illinois. The new currency rule was part of this sweetheart agreement. Meanwhile, Wilkins looked the other way even though Morgan overcharged the government for supplies. Against Morgan and Wilkins's conspiracy, French merchants found themselves at a disadvantage.[112]

The Illinois habitants wrote their first petitions to Wilkins a few months after his administration started. They insisted that his new policies would "annihilate commerce" and drive all the colonists away.[113] Spelling out the harmful consequences of the new restrictions on their trade, they once again called for a real cooperative government: "The reiterated promises that you have made to us of giving us the joy of a Truly English Government, gives us the most reasonable promise that under your administration, we shall see at last the oppression passing from this unhappy Country. We are already beginning to persuade ourselves that, what we have understood told of English Liberty is not a fable."[114]

Wilkins's administration only became more oppressive, however. In November, he set up a Court of Inquiry.[115] Several things about the new court quickly alienated the French. First, it used British law, or "equity," on matters that the French felt should follow French customary law. Second, Wilkins made George Morgan president of the court. Colonists immediately perceived the whole institution as simply a means for Morgan to sue habitants to collect his debts, as indeed it was. The first case brought by the new court was the estate settlement of the merchant La Grange, the verdict of which resulted in Edward Cole and Morgan gaining property that later petitioners protested rightfully belonged to several of the Frenchmen.[116] The colonists were soon complaining to Wilkins that Morgan was using the court to seize people's houses.[117] Before long, there was open resentment of the court among the habitants, who allegedly were united in their hatred of "the Morganians."[118]

This prompted the most important petition writing so far during the British regime. In January, the colonists protested that the new court was unconstitutional, since Wilkins did not have the authority to "abrogate" the French laws of the colony—this was an imperial decision.[119] Moreover, they insisted that French law was far better suited for the colony anyway, as it did not open the door to so much litigation as British "equity" did. They also protested the makeup of the court, asserting that there were two judges "in whom no one has any confidence," referring most likely to Morgan and Cole. Since there was no mechanism to appeal the new court's verdicts, they concluded that the court was illegitimate. Suggesting an alternative, they called for jury trials according to "common law," since the current situation was guaranteed to disadvantage the French inhabitants.[120] They sent petitions to Wilkins, the president of the court (Morgan), and Cole.[121]

Daniel Blouin was the clear leader of these new petitions. Blouin, a merchant, had been active in trade in Illinois since the beginning of the British regime, and during Reed's administration he had opportunistically negotiated a contract with the captain for supplying merchandise to the fort. Wilkins's arrangements with Morgan negated this contract, and this made Blouin a natural enemy of Wilkins. But his resentment of Wilkins went beyond just the loss of his contract. For instance, immediately after Wilkins's arrival in Illinois in September, Blouin had paid two thousand livres for a passport for trade, which Wilkins never provided.[122] To make matters worse, Wilkins arrested Matthew Kennedy, Blouin's trading agent in Vincennes, on charges of selling alcohol to Indians, charges that Blouin found dubious. Most important, Blouin was one of the executors of the La Grange estate and felt personally cheated by the way that the Wilkins regime pursued the case.[123] In 1768 Blouin raised a charge against Wilkins's new court of inquiry accusing Cole, Morgan, and Wilkins of conspiring against the interests of the colony and its French inhabitants.[124]

Blouin's resentments were clear, but his knowledge of the law and of English was imperfect. In December 1768, Blouin recruited William Clajon, a bilingual French Protestant who was then living in St. Louis, to come to English Illinois to help the colonists press their case against the new court. Clajon is a curious but fascinating character in the history of Illinois. A native-born Frenchman, he had emigrated to the British colonies of North America for unknown reasons in approximately 1755. He spent at least half of the next fourteen years in New York.[125] He arrived in Illinois in 1767, hired by Forbes to be a translator for the British regime. At some point, he had moved to Spanish St. Louis.[126] Blouin recruited him to Kaskaskia and petitioned Wilkins for his safe passage as a translator.

But when Clajon arrived in Kaskaskia, the court immediately had both him and Blouin arrested. The charges were sedition. As Blouin and Clajon later asserted, Rumsey accused Clajon of being the mastermind of the petition campaign in Illinois:

> M Rumsey accused [Clajon] of being the author of many seditious documents, addressed by a large number of habitants to M. Lt. Colonel Wilkins, alleging that in these documents, [written] from the Spanish bank, he encouraged the spirit of rebellion on the English side in the Illinois; that these documents tended manifestly to render the habitants discontented; and to inspire them with contempt for those who governed them, for the court of judicature, and for His Excellency, Monsieur General Gage, and that he saw nothing more proper to reestablish the tranquility of the colony than to beg Monsieur the commandant to have him arrested as well as M. Blouin, one of the leaders of the faction which destroyed the peace of the Illinois.[127]

Echoing these charges in an official arrest warrant, Wilkins labeled Clajon "a public incendiary, for having spread misunderstanding and sedition among the people of the colony—and as an insolent scribbler of documents which evidently tended to inflame the spirit of the people against the government."[128]

∾

Wilkins threw Clajon and Blouin in jail. The two activists began to protest the court from their position in the dungeon of Fort de Chartres, as the French colonists quickly began to petition the court for the two leaders' release.[129] Soon a comprehensive protest movement spread throughout the colony.

The activists' long imprisonment turned what had begun as Blouin's personal quibbles over government policy, the proceedings of the court of judicature, and trade regulations—the kinds of things that might have annoyed a small class of merchants—into a dramatic example of the unfairness of the new regime, which affected everybody.[130] As the colonists could see, Clajon's treatment and Blouin's personal crusade for justice in the La

Grange case were both part of a larger story, one of arbitrary government going back to the militia, Reed's corruption, and other incidents. Not only that, Clajon's and Blouin's case united the French colonists on both sides of the river when the ethnically French commandant in Spanish Illinois, Philippe-François de Rastel de Rocheblave, sent a letter to Wilkins appealing on Clajon's behalf and eventually sending a bail for Clajon's release. Now backed up by Spanish authorities, who in their own weakness no doubt relished the opportunity to undermine British imperial order, the colonists appealed in even greater numbers for Clajon's exoneration. When the court went so far as to burn this and other appeals, there was no denying anymore that the Wilkins regime was corrupt, even tyrannical.[131] Wilkins went right on declaring new trade restrictions, seizing property, seizing slaves, and alienating the colonists with new regulations.

And matters only got worse, for meanwhile in the Indian villages of Illinois, momentous events were transpiring. In 1769, the Illinois Indians continued to seek advantage in between the new political regimes. They traded with the Spanish and sought presents from the English. Since Gage's audit of Indian expenses in 1768, times were lean for the Illinois, who continued to remain aloof from the European empires, as well as from the continuing entreaties of neighboring Indians hostile to the British regime. In 1769 Pontiac, who had mostly reconciled with the British, visited the Illinois at Cahokia. In an act that was probably a simple murder rather than a strategic act, a Peoria Indian killed Pontiac.[132] When rumors circulated that the murder was ordered by the British, Wilkins quickly called up a militia among the French at Kaskaskia and demanded that French colonists stand with the British.[133] Like Forbes, Wilkins insisted that the French follow a British Indian policy, despite their earlier claims of neutrality. The colonists once again refused to fight in a militia or join a fight "in which they had no part."[134]

Clajon meanwhile behaved with principle. Writing first from jail and then from Ste. Genevieve, he said that he did not want to be exonerated because Spanish officials or the habitants requested it; he wanted to be declared innocent because the British constitution required it.[135] Indeed, Clajon and Blouin ramped up the stakes of their case, turning their argument away from specific matters of law and into a more general argument about principles and precedents. If Clajon could not seek justice in British Illinois, they implied, then nobody could. Languishing in prison, he was a symbol not of an individual merchant's petty disputes against Morgan and Wilkins but of the arbitrary British regime and the powerlessness of the habitants in general. Clajon was now a political prisoner, deemed by Wilkins a felon and "enemy of the state."[136]

For their part, the habitants continued to protest with several more petitions, including to Gage himself. In 1770, they sent several new petitions, and the list of signatories grew as the movement gained traction and wider support.[137] But even as we recognize what the habitants did in their protests, it is important to note what the habitants did not do. Indeed, none of these events in Illinois Country was unfolding in a vacuum. Two years earlier, the habitants of New Orleans had expressed their discontent against a perceived arbitrary commandant, Antonio de Ulloa, by rebelling openly.[138] In the British colonies to the east, colonists violently attacked symbols of military command in Boston in the events that led up to the infamous Boston Massacre. In the face of an arbitrary regime in British Illinois, the habitants did no such thing. Even as they wrote petition after petition, they took no violent action. There is no evidence that they exercised their influence with Indians to oppose the British regime, as they might have. Instead, they continued their pragmatic call not for independence and the end of the British regime but rather for more government.

Meanwhile, Gage received word of disorder in the colony: "There has been a strange work at the Illinois, very bad Proceedings carried on.—indeed most shameful ones. A Quarrel amongst them has laid open scandalous Scenes—and able is Faction."[139] Up the chain of command, some British officials were starting to get the message. Lord Hillsborough by now felt that the lack of a civil government in Illinois was a mistake; if they had it to do over again, Illinois would have a government of its own.[140]

Wilkins finally released his prisoners but refused to exonerate them or bring their case before the court, which he suspended altogether in the spring of 1770. Now the French formulated a new plan. They would delegate Blouin and Clajon to take their petitions directly to General Gage himself. Ninety inhabitants of Illinois signed a commission in August authorizing the men "to intercede for us in front of his majesty in order to obtain the establishment of civil government in this colony."[141] In September 1770, Clajon and Blouin left Illinois and traveled down the Mississippi River, bound for New York City.

ℰℬ

Blouin and Clajon made it to New York and met with Thomas Gage on July
9, 1771. We know about the meeting itself only from Gage's brief descriptions. Clajon clearly made a strong impression as "a mere Republican" and
an "Adventurer, Artfull and intelligent." Gage considered him "the chief
mover, [who] puts all into the mouth of Blouin." Gage was dismissive of
the two activists, criticizing their "characters [and] the disturbance they had
occasioned in the Country." He had little time for "the extravagant Proposals
they brought," and he even doubted that they "were properly authorized
by the inhabitants to act for them." As a result, Gage ended the meeting
quickly.[142]

Clajon and Blouin had anticipated how easy it would be for Gage to
dismiss them, and they planned for it. Indeed, when they departed their brief
meeting with Gage, they left behind something truly extraordinary. Wrapped
in a binder with the title "Recueil" ("Anthology"), it was an archive of documents relating to the struggle for civil government in Illinois. Including every
major petition and letter that the inhabitants exchanged with their military
commanders and the British government, it was a history of their struggle for
civil government. Numbering 250 pages, in two parts, it is a window into, as
well as a symbol of, the community's struggle for empire by collaboration.[143]

The "Recueil" is a peculiar document reflecting the influence of its cre-
ators. Blouin was clearly a pragmatic businessman, and he had a tenacious
mind for detail. He also clearly saved every scrap of paper relating to the
controversy, which allowed the authors to compile them and present them as
one. The collection reflects how the editors saw these documents not as discrete controversies but rather as part of a comprehensive campaign, united
by the singular goal of a civil establishment. The collection contains more
than fifty-two documents, organized chronologically, with each document
printed verbatim, including signatures.

But that's not all. While Blouin was an amateur archivist, Clajon was a
cosmopolitan and a scholar. Where Blouin had a mind for evidence, Clajon
was a student of political philosophy who had read Machiavelli and had a
good understanding of the British constitution.[144] Thus in addition to com-
piling the documents, Clajon and Blouin teamed up to annotate their collection, providing "observations," including editorial explanations, context,
and, most important, analysis. Much of the analysis is fascinating, amplifying
and even qualifying the arguments of the petitions in long-winded footnotes.

But the real significance of the "Recueil" is its practical logic. People had
their passions, Blouin and Clajon wrote, but nobody could disagree with

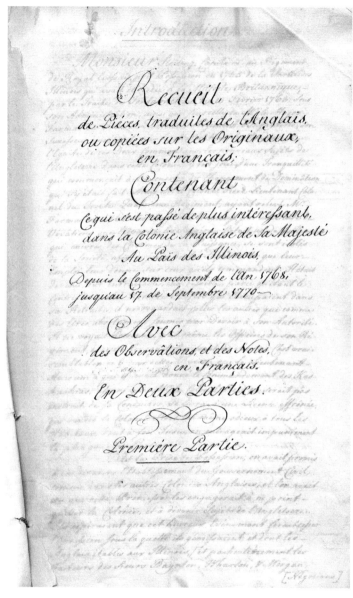

Figure 21. "Recueil de Piéces," anthology of French petitions. This two-part dossier was an extraordinary episode in political activism by the French inhabitants of Illinois, who used petitions to request an official civil government for their colony.

logic based on evidence. As they asserted, the point of the "Recueil" was to show Gage the evidence: "The *Recueil* will allow you to judge with certitude whether we are really oppressed or whether we are seditious." Without the evidence, Gage could not judge "the true motives of our refusal" to fight in the militia, for instance, and would accept Forbes's charge that they were "rebels." But with the "documents before him," Gage could not deny the truth of what they were arguing.

> This long recueil would certainly annoy people who would not read except for fun or to satisfy curiosity, because the prolixity of some of the documents and the dryness of them all would bore the readers of this class. But your patriotism, Monsieur, will make you find interesting everything that can help you discover the Truth. So that you can better feel it, I report the Acts of Authority which announced to us our Oppression, the repeated Representations which have been made by letters, or otherwise, and all the other Documents which constitute the Reality of a kind of Tyranny so extraordinary that, without evidence, it would not seem to be believable outside of our unfortunate Colony.[145]

The "Recueil" was a tour de force. But it was not the only document that Clajon and Blouin left with Gage at their brief meeting in 1771. In addition to the "Recueil," Blouin and Clajon presented Gage with a new petition, which later was filed in Gage's papers under the heading of "Memoire of Mr. Blouin." This "Memoire" was twenty-five pages long, a kind of super-petition.[146] Retelling the story of the colony's experience under British rule, the "Memoire" reiterated in eloquent terms the request for civil government. Here, Clajon and Blouin mustered their most powerful rhetoric, some of it reprised from earlier writings, and frequently referred to the "Recueil." The colonists were truly loyal British subjects: "The title of new subjects should . . . be regarded by Gage as the least equivocal, as should our fidelity and our attachment to the English government." The colonists preserved high hopes for all they had been told about British liberty, insisting that "our veneration for the constitution of Great Britain and our faith in the solemn promise that we have made to the name of the King are well known." But the colonists had been abused by "tyranny," and their history was one that would make the king "blush for the nation." Unfortunately, the English were at risk of appearing as hypocrites, "Free in their own homes . . . but charging the land with slaves." The colonists hoped for collaboration and to "taste the sweetness of a government veritably English." They had not lost hope but instead had brought their cause directly to Gage, the person possessing "the power to be able to stop a tyranny equally destructive and dishonorable."[147]

But they did not trust Gage himself. Instead, the purpose of the "Recueil" was to take their message up the chain of command to Dartmouth. Before ending their short meeting, Blouin made General Gage promise to send the documents on to the Lords of Trade.[148] As he later wrote, "The General then condescended to promise that he would do us all the Justice in his power, and send our complaints to his Majesty's Ministers."[149] Indeed, two years later, with the question of government in the Illinois still unsettled, Blouin met with Gage once again to ask him to bring a copy of their "Recueil" with him to London for Lord Dartmouth.

Taken together, this was a significant moment of political activism, the climax of years of petitioning and struggle. Treating the petitions as a single body of protest, the "Recueil" united the colonists' diverse concerns into a single history. What Blouin and Clajon called for in the "Recueil," as well as in their "Memoire," was simple: a fair civil government. What united their diverse protests over many years was the straightforward desire for laws to foster commerce and development in the colony. They were not calling for independence. Sending their petitions now to the highest authorities in the empire, they were calling for something else: collaboration.

❧

Since the beginning of the British regime in Illinois, the Illinois Indians and French colonists had forced the British officials to do things against their will. Exploiting the vulnerability of the British, and playing the Spanish and British regimes off against each other, colonists and Indians in Illinois had opportunistically cast themselves as members of the British regime and forced the British to an accommodating position. Through the 1760s, as the shortcomings of military government resulted in disorder and corruption in the colony, the colonists remained committed to their vision of a pragmatic collaboration between themselves and the British empire. In 1771, their petition campaign reached its climax in the meeting of Blouin, Clajon, and Gage. Although Gage mostly dismissed them, the two activists left him with an archive, which he promised to carry to the highest authorities in London. These extraordinary documents, the "Recueil" and "Memoire," stand as a monument to a distinctive political style on the early American frontier: empire by collaboration.

Conclusion

The End of Collaboration

The pamphlet titled Invitation sérieuse aux habitants de Illinois was published in Philadelphia in 1772, a few months after Daniel Blouin and William Clajon met with Thomas Gage and presented him with their extraordinary petitions for civil government. Of course, the *Invitation* was unsigned, and its author was identified merely as "un habitant de Kaskaskia," but it seems clear that the *Invitation* was written by Blouin and Clajon.[1] The *Invitation* made many points similar to ones in the petitions from Illinois in the 1760s and even contained phrases similar to those in documents in the "Recueil." Whether it really was the work of the two activists, the pamphlet belongs to the same historical moment. Like Blouin and Clajon's activism, the fifteen-page document expressed the Illinois habitants' pragmatic appeal for the improvement of the colony.[2]

The *Invitation* was unbelievably optimistic in its predictions for the Illinois Country. Although the inhabitants "suffer[ed] from great difficulties," they could expect a bright future if they worked hard enough: "If each one of us, according to his state and power, wishes to strive to improve our situation, and our country, we could, in a few years, render this colony the happiest of the continent."[3] But to achieve this progress, the colonists would have to be pragmatic and entrepreneurial. Moreover, they would have to adapt to changing times. As the author wrote, "It is often difficult to persuade ourselves to abandon a path marked out and frequented by our fathers and ourselves." People tended to be "prejudiced in favor of methods in which they have been raised," and this was to be expected. In Illinois, for instance, some complained about the arrival of English merchants, pretending that "their commerce is in some way injured" by newcomers. But this was foolishness, said the author. Most in

Illinois wisely had "a sincere desire to improve our situation and that of our posterity" and welcomed innovation. As for the others, "Let us not listen at all to what those people say, whose interest it is to hold us in ignorance upon which they wish to establish their advantage."[4] The Illinois inhabitants were *not* simple traditionalists.

Indeed, the *Invitation* argued, the habitants should welcome change and competition. The colonists knew that outsiders perceived them as "too ignorant and too indolent" to succeed. People chided them as "Creoles, a name which they apply to us in derision." But the inhabitants should not listen to such insults: "It is in fact but too true that up to the present, we have been held in great ignorance, but that does not prove that we should continue it." Indeed, "we are equal and in many cases superior to the Europeans. . . . Let us vie with them, by our industry and by our efforts to procure for ourselves the wealth and knowledge necessary for our welfare and that of our posterity and instead of passing our time smoking tobacco in vanity and indolence with which they reproach us, let us determine at once to regulate our conduct in quite a different manner."[5] Clearly this was a strong vision of an entrepreneurial, competitive society, open to the opportunities and changes of the day.

But to achieve all this potential, the habitants of Illinois needed one thing: government. As the colonists had said in their earliest petitions in 1768, only civil government could provide the security they needed for free trade and a commercial colony. Unfortunately, "It is true that up to the present, we have received little advantage from having become English subjects." Languishing in anarchy and confusion, the Illinois inhabitants had been neglected. They needed government, they needed laws, they needed imperial assistance. What they needed was collaboration: "We are true and zealous subjects of his Britannic majesty and we doubt not at all that in a short time . . . the administration of civil government will be established among us. We are able at present only to desire these happy results."[6]

Unlike other pamphlets in the Revolutionary ferment of 1770s Philadelphia, the *Invitation* was no declaration of rights, no philosophical treatise about abstract concepts of liberty. Indeed, the author began his tract by rejecting abstract theoretical debates, asserting that "knowledge is of little use when it is restricted to mere speculation." What the Kaskaskia colonists were interested in was practicality, the advantages that were created "when speculative truths are reduced to practical ones, when theories based upon experience are applied to the habits of life."[7] The message was simple. The inhabitants had lived under neglect and tyranny. They needed laws and government.

In so many ways, the *Invitation* declared the values that the Illinois colonists had embraced throughout their history: flexibility, pragmatism, opportunism. As the adaptable Illinois colonists asserted, they were not afraid of change. Although British observers would later stereotype the colonists as stuck in their ways, the colonists were in fact the opposite. Certainly there were some who, "for want of knowing better are prejudiced in favor of methods in which they have been raised, and as savages who do not wish to be instructed persist in their foolish ignorance." But the majority was ready to adapt, to change, and to partner with the British government, to "taste the blessings of that government." Here in many ways was a perfect expression of the ethos of this community, one that had always sought its own interests and then worked to pull governments alongside.[8]

And although it did not speak for them, the *Invitation* expresses some of the values of the Illinois Indians, too. They, too, had vied for opportunity. They were not stuck in their ways but highly adaptable. And, like the author of the *Invitation*, they had often called for closer alliance, for more assistance, for partnership with empire. As an expression of the philosophy of the inhabitants, and even the Indians, the *Invitation* captured the essence of their history in many ways.

☙

By highlighting the bright future of the Illinois colony and its need for government, the author of the *Invitation* was not alone. Others were making similar arguments throughout British America and in Britain itself. In the 1760s, an anonymous pamphlet circulated in London under the title "The Expediency of Securing our American Colonies by Settling the Country adjoining the River MISSISSPPI, and the Country upon the OHIO, CONSIDERED."[9] In 1770, Philip Pittman published an essay, originally written for the secretary of state, which included descriptions of the Illinois settlements and made an implicit argument in favor of building up British colonies in the Illinois.[10] It was called *The Present State of the European Settlements on the Mississippi*. Another book of anonymous "political essays" was published in London that, as Thomas Gage wrote, "talk[ed] of the great advantages to be obtained by establishing New Governments" in places like the Illinois.[11] Pennsylvania speculators, organized in a company under the leadership of Pennsylvania governor William Franklin, were putting together proposals that included models for a civil government in the region.[12] Many besides the author of the *Invitation* were convinced that Illinois needed a real imperial government in the 1770s.

But despite all of this, Gage was still not persuaded.[13] By 1772, Gage had grown even more hostile to government in the West, particularly in the Illinois.[14] As he wrote, "The Ilinois has been a gulph that has swallowed up everything and returned nothing back."[15] The colonists had only become notorious and aggravating to the officials. As Gage wrote, "Our New Subjects [in Illinois] deserve the same Treatment that the Accadians received and may possibly in time meet with it."[16] Gage was referring here, of course, to what Acadians called Le Grand Dérangement, when British authorities forcibly resettled the Acadians from their homelands in 1755 and deported them to such far-flung places as Louisiana, France, and New England.[17] In 1772, Gage renewed his plans to remove the Illinois colonists "into the Province of Quebec, that of West Florida, or any of the settled Colonies . . . as I think those People would be better placed anywhere else than where they are."[18] Hillsborough did not disagree.[19] Civil government for the Illinois, Hillsborough told Gage, would "only serve to fix what we both think it would be better to remove."[20] Gage was in no mood to collaborate.

But Gage could not do as he wished. Once again, the colonists and Indians of Illinois had their own power. Situated as they were in the borderlands, the multicultural population could always resist the British government and even rise against it.[21] Gage heard that the inhabitants were threatening to do just that in July 1772 when the British commander wrote to "accuse [them] in very strong terms . . . of being in League with the Enemy Savages, giving them Intelligence of our Motions, and Information of Opportunitys to fall upon our People."[22] Here was the familiar quandary that the British empire, like the French before it, faced in the Illinois Country. Given these rumored conspiracies, the British had to accommodate. Once again, Gage found himself dispatching a delegation to present the Indians with gifts for their loyalty.[23] As for the colonists, their needs also needed to be met.

And so, in spite of Gage's fantasies about treating the Illinois inhabitants like the Acadians, the British government began to acquiesce in the summer of 1772. In July, the new commandant at Fort de Chartres "conven'd the principal inhabitants of the three Villages and desired Mr. Deberniere to talk to them . . . about some scheme of Civil Government among them."[24] As Hamilton explained, the inhabitants made pretty strong demands for a republican form of government: "They were very high on the occasion and expected to appoint their Governor and all the Civil Magistrates."[25] Meanwhile, back in New York, Blouin echoed these demands when he offered Gage "a rough Sketch that corresponded with what Major Hamilton Mentions of the Expectations of the People to choose their Governor, Magistrates, &c., and appeared to have been drawn after some Republican Model, a good deal Similar to that of the Colony of Connecticut."[26] Connecticut's government was one of the most liberal in all the thirteen colonies, according to Gage.

Gage dismissed these plans as "extravagant proposals." As Gage said, "circumstanced and Situated as they were, they could not reasonably expect that a regular Constitutional Government could be formed, for the sake of a Small Settlement in a far distant Desert, of little worth or Benefit to the King or his Subjects."[27] According to Gage, it was especially ridiculous that the habitants should expect to choose all their own officials: "They were told, Propositions of that Nature would not be received; and that I would not confer with them on the Subject of a Government to be so constituted." Other officials in London agreed, concluding that the idea of "elected magistrates" in the colony was "very extravagant" and "inadmissible."[28] And yet, as closed-minded as they seemed, now the British were undoubtedly negotiating and acknowledging the inhabitants' desires. After all, Gage had asked Blouin directly "to know what kind of Government the People expected and would be satisfied with."[29] Moreover, the whole issue was being discussed at the highest levels of the government.[30] For the first time, the topic was "laid before the King."[31]

By March of the following year, Lord Dartmouth himself explained that the situation had changed. Writing to Gage, he said that providing a government to the Illinois was now a priority. Although officials would not endorse Blouin's plan, the colonists were right: they needed a government, and they deserved one: "It has always appeared and does still appear to one that if those inhabitants have (as I conceive they have) a Right under the Treaty of Paris to continue in their possessions, it is both dangerous and disgraceful to leave that district without such Regulations as may on the one hand insure to the inhabitants that protection in their Civil Rights which they are entitled to expect, or on the other hand secure their allegiance as subjects . . . I shall therefore think it my Duty to make this an object of my attention."[32]

Whether motivated by the colonists' petitions, their threats to leave for the Spanish colonies across the river, or their rumored collusions with the northern Indians, government officials had changed their position.[33] Soon

Gage himself was treating the proposal for civil government in Illinois as if it had been his own idea.[34] On June 17, 1773, at long last, Captain Hugh Lord, new commandant in the Illinois Country, proposed a model to the colonists, which seems to have been designed by Dartmouth himself. It featured an appointed governor and three magistrates, as well as "Five or Six persons from among the merchants or habitants of the country who will be named to a Grand Council with the Gov." As if taking its cues from the "Recueil," the new proposed government would operate according to French law: "[the] Ancient laws and Customs of Paris will be the base of all that will be ordered by the Gov. and Council." And perhaps more important to the colonists so recently burned by corrupt officials, officers of the new government would promise to "render faithful and disinterested justice."[35]

Boldly, the colonists quickly rejected this proposal for a government just as the authorities had previously rejected their scheme. Writing to the officials, one colonist insisted that "None of them [the colonists] had signed any Paper tending to solicit the Government therein described and Sketched out." Instead, the "said Inhabitants were, to the contrary, averse to the proposal made to them to that effect." Blouin now wrote directly to Lord Dartmouth to argue that this newly proposed government was still not sufficiently republican: "In that Sketch of Government, the whole Legislative Power is lodged in the hands of the Governor and his Council." At the same time, however, the government needed to be stronger. Under the proposed plan, Blouin wrote, "no offense, Murder only excepted, is to be punished with Death; and, the Governor is vested with the Power of remitting that, and every other Penalty!"[36] The inhabitants obviously had some contradictory expectations for what the government should look like, but they were sure of some things. As Blouin wrote, "The Inhabitants have unanimously rejected with abhorrence, a Plan of Government, so evidently contrary to that which they have applied for in their Memorial to His Majesty's Board of Trade, sent by me to their Lordships." Blouin concluded: "I join with the Inhabitants of the Illinois Country, in imploring Your Lordship's Intercession for the Establishment of a Civil Government amongst them, on British Principles."[37]

In November, Blouin again wrote to Dartmouth with a final appeal, reiterating an old and forceful argument. As he said, the whole matter of civil government in Illinois came down to mutual benefits. The British government would have to invest precious resources in order to give them a government, it was true. But it was through such investments that the British would finally defeat their rivals. Government would make the Illinois Country into the profitable colony that it could be. This was not just a matter of the colonists' interests but one of the empire's interests as well. It was a win-win: "My Lord, besides the Justice that there is in fulfilling the repeated Promises made to us, 'that we would enjoy that Blessing,' we know, how much France and Spain dread that Event; and therefore, we can easily conceive that the expense attending that Measure, would be most amply compensated, by advantages of the highest Nature, and of which narrow minds can have no idea."[38] Echoing one of the arguments—and indeed some of the words—in the *Invitation sérieuse*, here Blouin played the oldest card in the habitants' book: exploiting British fears of their rival empires in order to move the government to their side.

Whether Dartmouth was moved by this argument is unknown. One might expect him to have ignored it. After all, there were many other things on the mind of the secretary of state for the colonies in the winter of 1773, including the mounting rebellion in the eastern ports, where angry colonists were refusing to land British tea. And yet, in a surprising move, on December 1, just weeks before the tea went into Boston Harbor, Dartmouth responded to Blouin directly. He explained that he had seen Blouin's "Recueil" and had read the "Memoire."[39] And he promised that he had considered what Blouin—a lowly merchant from Kaskaskia—had to say. Dartmouth did not agree with everything the colonists proposed. But he was sympathetic to the larger point: "Some form of Government however seems essentially necessary. . . . [T]he Interests of his Majesty's new Subjects there will not be neglected, and they may rest assured of the King's Protection and the Enjoyment of every Privilege that their Situation can with propriety admit of."[40]

Here it was: *the Interests of his Majesty's new Subjects there will not be neglected.* The colonists had made their point.[41] To be sure, differences remained. But in 1774, under the terms of the new Quebec Act, Illinois finally received an official provincial government, to be established later that year. Preparations were made to send a new lieutenant governor to the region.[42] The fight for collaboration had finally borne fruit.

ೋ

As it happened, of course, the British empire was heading down a slippery slope to revolution in North America. The man appointed to head the new civil government for Illinois, Lieutenant Governor Matthew Johnson, never actually made it the colony, and the civil government never got off the ground.[43] Worse, in 1776, Hugh Lord, who had commanded successfully at

Fort de Chartres since 1773, was recalled, and British forces abandoned Fort de Chartres completely. Before leaving, Lord appointed Philippe-François de Rastel, chevalier de Rocheblave, lately living under Spanish rule in St. Louis, to take control of Fort de Chartres on behalf of the British government. As Governor Hamilton wrote from Detroit, Rocheblave was loyal to the British and a reliable character not likely to please malcontented French colonists. In Hamilton's snide words, "A more active and intelligent person is not to be found in this Country of ignorant Bigots, and busy rebels, and had he the means I doubt not of his curbing their insolence and disaffection."[44] Indeed, failing to bring an accommodating attitude to his new job, Rocheblave alienated colonists, issuing unpopular orders to the inhabitants and trying again to call up the militia to "test the loyalty of the British subjects" in Illinois.[45] With hopes for civil government in the colony fading, many French Creoles once again began to depart for the West and for New Orleans. Without the empire to collaborate with, they just moved on.[46] As for Blouin and Clajon, we don't know what happened to them next.[47]

But even though the Revolution prevented the fulfillment of the campaign to establish civil government, the campaign itself is no less significant. The Illinois colonists had indeed forced the British empire to move a long way. At the beginning, Gage and Hamilton had wanted to remove the Illinois inhabitants from their settlements altogether. The paltry military establishment at Fort de Chartres was neglectful and corrupt, reflecting the indifference that imperialists felt toward the colony. In response, Blouin had taken his case all the way to the top, to Dartmouth, to Hillsborough, persuading them to reverse the original plan to minimize investment in the West. Threatening the British empire with the rebellion of the French and enticing them with the loyalty of faithful subjects, he entreated his imperial audience. And, in many ways in spite of their original plans, officials responded. The year 1774 was a quintessential moment of empire by collaboration in the Illinois.

Of course it was nothing new, just the continuation of a long pattern and a distinctive form of colonialism at the edge of empire. Illinois colonists and Indians had always dragged imperial governments around to their own priorities. In the 1670s, illegal colonists, Jesuits, and Indians had forced the French empire to create a colony. Indian affairs and the importance of the powerful Illinois had forced the French empire to tolerate autonomous settlements. In 1717 French authorities finally sent a provincial government, not as part of some grand strategy but because, as they said, "we see no possibility of preventing it." Over the following years, this government condoned what autonomous colonists did, including an entrepreneurial export economy, an interracial social order, and a legal culture that did not fit the imperial model. For their part, the Illinois Indians forced the provincial government to take their side against larger imperial plans, especially in the Fox Wars and the western alliance system. When Fort de Chartres was constructed, it was less a symbol of top-down authority and more the reflection of a process of collaboration as the colonists and Indians persuaded the administration to satisfy their needs. The British and the new Illinois government under the Quebec Act were just the latest episode in this story.

And yet the Quebec Act was also, in some ways, the end of that story. When American forces arrived in Illinois under George Rogers Clark, the remaining colonists and Indians in Kaskaskia swore loyalty to Virginia and the new Congress. Establishing Illinois as a county of Virginia, Clark initially established a civil government. He set up a court, to which Frenchmen like Gabriel Cerré were appointed. Meanwhile, a Pennsylvanian called John Todd was appointed by Governor Patrick Henry to be the county lieutenant and head of the first Illinois civil government since the end of the French regime. But while this ostensibly was what the colonists had wanted all along, they were soon disappointed. Todd, trying to provision Clark's planned military expedition to attack the British at Detroit, forcefully requisitioned food from the French farmers. Todd was heavy-handed, and the colonists quickly rejected his plans. As an observer recounted: "[He said] that he would Call a counsel of the inhabitants and Compel them to furnish [food and supplies]. But when the[y] Met the[y] punkley [*sic*] denied him, he then told Them if the[y] did not Comply he would Give them up to the Miletery and Quit Them. The[y] answered him the[y] were well aGread to that & So parted."[48] True to his word, Todd abandoned Illinois, leaving various factions to fight for control in the languishing colony. As the American military continued to confiscate French goods and produce, the few remaining French settlers, including Cerré and many other notable inhabitants, abandoned in greater numbers.

But this was not the worst of it. In the 1780s, opportunistic American settlers, led by a man called John Dodge, had gained control of the colony. Unsympathetic to Frenchmen and Indians, and prejudiced against them, they did not collaborate but let the colony slide toward anarchy. If reports from French eyewitnesses are reliable, Kaskaskia now descended into chaos. As Father Gibault wrote to a friend in Canada, a Hobbesian nightmare had enveloped the colony since it had become part of Virginia. Complaining that "all is barbarous," in Illinois, he described extreme disorder and suffering in a colony where, as he put it, "injustice dominates." The colony was plagued by violence and poverty, drunkenness, "theft and rapine." As Gibault lamented, it was anarchy in Illinois: "Breaking of limbs, murder by means of a dagger, sabre or sword (for he who wills carries one) are common, and pistols and guns are but toys in these regions."[49]

As Gibault explained, the new American regime, what Jefferson celebrated as an "empire of Liberty," began in Illinois with chaos and disorder. The French now suffered with no government, "No commandant, no troops, no prison, no hangman . . . in a word absolute impunity for these and ill luck for the stranger." For the French, this truly was the beginning of what one historian calls the "American Leviathan."[50] Although the Illinois Country was organized under the new Ordinance of 1787 as a part of the Northwest Territory, it languished without a government for so long that most Frenchmen abandoned it. In 1790, Kaskaskia had just forty families.[51] More people remained in Cahokia, but the majority of French Illinois Country was gone. Only one consolation came from the new American government: in 1783, provisions were made to allow the French to keep their land.[52]

The Indians were not even that fortunate.[53] Beginning with the period of the Revolution, the Indians of Illinois experienced many hardships. First, during the Revolution, the Illinois experienced new attacks and the breakdown of their own alliance system. In the 1770s, they resumed war with the Foxes. As Arent DePeyster, British commandant at Michilimackinac, said, "the savages of La Baye and those of the Illinois Country are constantly at War with one another."[54] In these conflicts, the Illinois experienced a fast decline in numbers. By 1781, when British engineer Thomas Hutchins published his "Topographical Description" of the region, he counted just three hundred warriors among all of the Kaskaskia, Peoria, and Metchigamea combined.[55]

Of course, with the changing imperial situation, the Illinois tried to continue playing the governments off one another. When the Americans arrived under George Rogers Clark, the Illinois "immediately treated for peace."[56] In 1778, Clark made peace with dozens of Indian groups at Cahokia, including all the Illinois.[57] But secretly, Louis Ducoigne, a Kaskaskia chief and descendant of the Rouensa family, went to Ouiatenon and kept a back door open with the British.[58] According to Fernando de Leyba, now commanding in St. Louis, this strategy was less about opportunism and more about confusion: "The war with the English is causing a great number of

Indian tribes to go from one side to the other without knowing which side to take."[59] Still, the Kaskaskias continued to play Hamilton and Clark against each other for advantage.[60] Meanwhile, other Illinois-speakers made alliances with the Spanish at St. Louis.[61] But they continued to be vulnerable, and Mascoutens and Foxes attacked again in 1787.[62]

By 1796, the new governor of the Northwest Territory, Arthur St. Clair, wrote that constant warfare and disease had taken a mighty toll: "The Cahokia nation, reduced to four or five families, had abandoned the country entirely. The Peorias, amounting to about one hundred, had likewise abandoned it, and the Kaskaskia tribe, of about twenty families, laid claim to nothing but the site of an old village near Kaskaskia, and about four thousand acres of land, which was confirmed to them by an act of Congress."[63]

Ducoigne attended the Treaty of Greenville in 1795, trying to protect Illinois lands from the Americans.[64] Traveling through the Illinois in 1796, Moses Austin observed that most of the Illinois had moved permanently to the Spanish side of the river, following the majority of the French.[65] It is likely that some of the Illinois now amalgamated with other groups in the West for kinship and survival.[66] Meanwhile, Ducoigne and the Kaskaskia made a strategic decision to stay east of the Mississippi. For Ducoigne, this meant isolation from his Peoria kinsmen. As he wrote, "As I am an American . . . [they] threaten my life."[67]

But there was no more collaboration for Ducoigne or any of the Illinois east of the Mississippi. Declaring "I am an American" did not produce the benefits from the American government that the Illinois had received for their "French hearts" fifty years earlier. Jefferson himself reflected on the declining strength of the Illinois and wrote that U.S. policy was now aimed at finding a chief willing to sell land. The United States would "give him such terms as will make him easy for life, and take a conveyance from him."[68] Hardly a mutual collaboration, Jefferson noted that this would be "a small expense for us." Indeed, in 1803, St. Clair, governor of the Northwest Territory, purchased Kaskaskia land. Over the next generations, that group, once the most numerous of the Illinois, would amalgamate with the Peoria and move west to Kansas and then to Oklahoma.

✿

Given these outcomes in the 1790s and early 1800s, it seems that perhaps the Illinois Indians and French inhabitants had been naïve in their longstanding patterns of collaboration with imperial governments. Having repeatedly sought partnership with empires, the inhabitants of the region ironically got more than they bargained for in the 1790s—an imperial government that was finally strong enough to dominate them. Indeed, the end of empire by collaboration in Illinois seems like a familiar story in which colonial accommodations and Native autonomy were crushed under the new realities of American hegemony.[69] And if this is correct, the apparent demise of the colonial order in Illinois Country in the late eighteenth century suggests that empire by collaboration was just an insignificant phase, one that lasted only as long as empire was far off and weak.

But if collaboration ended in the settlements of the Illinois Country themselves, it was not just a forgettable phase of the American past. For one thing, the decline of collaboration in Illinois was not really a story of a too-powerful American juggernaut replacing formerly weak and impotent regimes and submitting the Illinois colonists and Indians to a new order. The Illinois world was not defined by an American hegemony during the 1780s and 1790s at all.[70] The villages of Kaskaskia and Cahokia, as well as surrounding Native villages, did surely and dramatically empty out in the American period, but this was mostly a result of chaos and confusion, not because of a heavy-handed and hegemonic authority that they could not handle. Departing for St. Louis, New Orleans, and points west, they abandoned Illinois to escape the frontier settlers whose anarchy and violence were incompatible with any kind of stable colony, let alone with the profit-minded and opportunistic priorities that they were used to pursuing.[71] The old world of French-Indian Illinois largely disappeared, but the people who created it were not wholly crushed or subdued by hegemony; rather, they moved on.

And when the pragmatic "antient inhabitants" mostly abandoned the actual settlements of Kaskaskia and Cahokia for points west in the 1780s, many aspects of their political traditions and political culture followed them. Indeed, the flexibility and adaptability that were at the center of the Illinois inhabitants' collaborative political culture for so long had an important legacy in the early West. To be sure, this legacy was very quickly covered up in nineteenth-century America and mostly forgotten. As more and more American settlers kept arriving in Illinois, the newcomers constructed influential and misleading stereotypes of the French and Indian people of this region. To the Yankee observers, French and Indians became a kind of quaint "picturesque," a foil of traditionalism, primitiveness, and backwardness against which to valorize Protestant, individualistic, and capitalistic American values. Authors constructed a vision of French "peasants" who were communitarian and wedded to tradition, unable to adapt to the coming American future. Submissive to authority and unable to think for themselves, they were time-less and unenterprising.[72] The Indians were even more stuck in their ways. Unable or unwilling to change, the Indians of Illinois were destined to disap-pear. When the American painter George Catlin made a portrait of a Kaskaskia woman named Wah-pe-seh-see in 1830, he imagined her, like many other Indians he painted, as part of a vanishing race, passively awaiting extinction in a changing, individualistic world.[73] In contrast to de Batz's depiction of Illinois Indians in the 1730s, which featured the Indians engaged in commerce, slavery, and enterprise, Catlin painted the woman alone, out of any context, with a vague look of defeat. Americans understood the Illinois as weak and dependent, defeated by American power.[74]

Ironically, when these stereotypes were created, the actual descendants of the colonial population of Illinois were acting in ways that were nearly opposite to those depicted or imagined in Catlin's work. Both French and Indians adapted in nineteenth-century America. Moving west, many descen-dants of French Illinois farmers became part of what one scholar calls a "bourgeois frontier," embracing opportunistic and pragmatic values to join the capitalistic activity of the early American West.[75] Once again situated between competing empires, merchants and farmers thrived in St. Louis and in the Missouri Valley, along the Santa Fé trail, and in other borderlands of the West. Illinois Indians, mostly excluded from this mercantile world in which their Osage neighbors now dominated, nevertheless adapted and amal-gamated into the Peoria tribe and moved west ahead of removal. Once there, Indians and mixed-race peoples often joined with the French and other new-comers in kinship networks that structured a complicated fur trade world.[76] Indeed, Catlin himself captured this spirit of adaptation in the portrait of a Kaskaskia chief, Kee-món-saw, whose genteel attire and fashionable pose betray his adaptability in the changing American West. None of the inhabi-tants of colonial Illinois Country failed to adapt to the nineteenth-century order.

The habits of adaptability, opportunism, and flexibility demonstrated by the French and Illinois in the early nineteenth-century West were the continuation of a longstanding political tradition. As this book has shown, in the seventeenth and eighteenth centuries, both French and Indians inhabi-tants of the region had made their world by pragmatically seeking opportu-nity and self-interest at the edge of empires. Hardly wedded to tradition or stuck in their ways, they were enterprising and innovative.

Figure 22. Wah-pe-seh-see, Mother of the Chief of the Kaskaskia, by George Catlin.
Painted in 1830.

Courtesy of the Smithsonian American Art Museum.

And if they were not static or timeless, they especially were not submissive and dependent. One of the most important themes in the history of the Illinois Country was the way that people sought self-interest by partnering with—not submitting to—the powerful forces that aimed to control the early Mississippi Valley. Far from passive, subservient, or dependent, the French and Indian inhabitants of Illinois acted in ways that clashed with government planning and were not aligned with imperial goals. And yet the people of Illinois convinced governments to work with them. As Dartmouth had in

Figure 23. Kee-món-saw, Little Chief, a Chief of the Kaskaskia, by George Catlin.
Painted in 1830.

Courtesy of the Smithsonian American Art Museum.

December 1773, governments had assured the renegade colony that "your interests will not be ignored."

Colonialism was never a simple matter, and the nature of empire was always a negotiation among many peoples. Very often this was a fraught process in early America, characterized by constant tension, conflict, cultural misunderstanding, domination, and resistance. And yet what is remarkable about the Illinois Country in the colonial period is the way people—colonists, Indians, governments, and even, in important ways, slaves—acted together to create an often intentional, purposeful collaboration. No one dominated in Illinois, and many people exercised power. This basic fact and the opportunism of people who saw collaborating as their best option among many helped create a distinctive culture and a fascinating kind of colonialism—with an important legacy—at the edge of empires.

AG	Archives de la Guerre, Centre Historique des Archives Nationales, Paris, France.
ANOM	Archives Nationales d'Outre Mer, Aix-en-Provence, France.
BWM	Papers of Baynton, Wharton, and Morgan. Library Company of Philadelphia, Philadelphia, Pa. Microfilm at Illinois Historical Survey, Urbana, Ill.
CISHL	Collections of the Illinois State Historical Library. 38 vols. Springfield: Illinois State Historical Library, 1903–70.
CO5	Colonial Office Papers, 5. North America and West Indies, Public Record Office, National Archives Center, Kew, England. Copies and photostats at Illinois Historical Survey, Urbana, Ill.
FB	Marthe Faribault-Beauregard. *La population des forts Français d'Amerique (XVIIIe siecle): Répertoire des baptêmes, mariages et sépultures* célébrés *dans les forts et les établissments Français en Amerique du nord au XVIIIe siècle.* 2 vols. Montreal: Editions Bergeron, 1982.
GP	Papers of General Thomas Gage. William L. Clements Library, University of Michigan, Ann Arbor.
JR	Reuben Gold Thwaites. *The Jesuit Relations and Allied Documents: Travels and Explorations of the Jesuit Missionaries in New France, 1610–1791.* 71 vols. Cleveland, Ohio: Burrows, 1896–1901.
KFD	Jacques Gravier. *Kaskaskia-to-French Dictionary,* ca. 1690. Manuscript held at Watkinson Library Special Collections, Trinity College, Hartford, Conn.
KM	Margaret Brown and Laurie C. Dean. *Kaskaskia Manuscripts, 1714–1816: A Calendar of Civil Documents in Colonial Illinois*

(microfilm, 14 reels). Original Notarial Documents held at Randolph County Museum, Chester, Ill.

Liette   Pierre-Charles de Liette. "Memorandum Concerning the Illinois Country, ca. 1693." In *The French Foundations, 1680–1693*, ed. Theodore Calvin Pease and Raymond C. Werner (Springfield, Ill.: Trustees of the Illinois State Historical Library, 1934). Collections of the Illinois State Historical Library 23. Original held in Ayer Collection, Newberry Library, Chicago, Ill.

Margry   Pierre Margry. *Découvertes et établissements des Français dans l'ouest et dans le sud de l'Amérique septentrionale (1614–1754)*. 6 vols. Paris: D. Jouast, 1879.

MPA   Dunbar Rowland, A. G. Sanders, and Patricia Kay Galloway, eds. *Mississippi Provincial Archives (French, English, Spanish Dominions)*. 6 vols. Louisiana, Nashville, New York, 1911–84.

NYCD   Edmund B. O'Callaghan. *Documents Relative to the Colonial History of the State of New York*. 9 vols. Albany, 1853.

"Recueil" "Recueil de Piéces, traduites de l'Anglais ou copiées sur les Originaux en Français; contenant cequi s'est passé de plus intéressant dans la colonie Anglaise de sa majesté au Païs des Illinois, Depuis le Commencement de l'an 1768, jusqu'au 17 de septembre 1770, Avec des Observâtions et des Notes, en Français. En Deux Parties." American Series, vol. 138, item 18. Thomas Gage Papers, William L. Clements Library, University of Michigan, Ann Arbor.

VP   Vaudreuil Papers. Subcollection of the Loudon Papers, Huntington Library, San Marino, Calif.

WHC   Collections of the State Historical Society of Wisconsin. 20 vols. Madison, Wis.: Madison State Printer, 1888–1931.

Introduction

1. Bernard Bailyn, *Pamphlets of the American Revolution, 1750–1776* (Cambridge: Belknap Press of Harvard University Press, 1965).

2. Daniel Blouin, William Clazon [*sic*], and Philippe Francois de Rastel Rocheblave, *Invitation se'rieuse aux habitants des Illinois*, ed. Clarence Edwin Carter and Clarence Walworth Alvord (Providence, R.I.: Club for Colonial Reprints, 1908). For a good translation, see Lydia Marie Brauer, trans., "Earnest Invitation to the Inhabitants of Illinois by an Inhabitant of Kaskaskia," in *Transactions of the Illinois State Historical Society for the Year 1909* (Springfield: Illinois State Historical Library, 1909), 261–68.

3. Despite its size, importance, and curiosity as a part of colonial America and the Atlantic world, Illinois Country still does not earn much attention from many historians. Nobody has done more to change this fact than Carl J. Ekberg, who has in several remarkable works provided valuable interpretations. See especially Carl J. Ekberg, *French Roots in the Illinois Country: The Mississippi Frontier in Colonial Times* (Urbana: University of Illinois Press, 2000). Other key modern works about Illinois include Sophie White, *Wild Frenchmen and Frenchified Indians: Material Culture and Race in Colonial Louisiana* (Philadelphia: University of Pennsylvania Press, 2012); Cécile Vidal, "Le pays des Illinois, six villages Français au coeur de l'Amérique du Nord, 1699–1765," in *De Québec à l'Amérique Française: Histoire et mémoire: Textes choisis du deuxième colloque de la commission Franco-Québécoise sur les lieux de mémoire communs*, ed. Thomas Wien et al. (Quebec City: Laval, 2007); and Cecile Vidal, "Les implantation Françaises au pays des Illinois au XVIIIe siecle (1699–1765)" (Ph.D. diss., Ecole des Hautes Etudes en Sciences Sociales, 1995). Some older works are still valuable. The first serious social history of the French villages in Illinois was Natalia Belting, *Kaskaskia Under the French Regime* (New Orleans: Polyanthos, 1975). Meanwhile, Raymond Hauser and Emily Blasingham wrote the first ethnohistories of the Illinois Indians. See Raymond E. Hauser, "An Ethnohistory of the Illinois Indian Tribe, 1673–1832" (Ph.D. diss., Northern Illinois University, 1973); and Emily Jane Blasingham, "The Illinois Indians, 1634–1800: A Study of Depopulation," *Ethnohistory* 3 (Summer/Fall 1956): 193–224, 361–412. Two useful ethnohistorical accounts are Joseph Zitomersky, *French Americans, Native Americans in Eighteenth-Century French Colonial*

Louisiana: The Population Geography of the Illinois Indians, 1670s–1760s (Lund, Sweden: Lund University Press, 1994); and Joseph Jablow, *Illinois, Kickapoo, and Potawatomi Indians*, American Indian Ethnohistory: North Central and Northeastern Indians (New York: Garland, 1974). Early work by Clarence Alvord, Clarence Carter, Marguerite Pease, and Theodore Calvin Pease and their colleagues at the Illinois Historical Survey made the first serious contributions to colonial Illinois history. See CISHL, vols. 1–26, and especially Clarence Walworth Alvord, *The Illinois Country, 1673–1818* (Chicago: Loyola University Press, 1920). The library they assembled—the Illinois History Survey—at the University of Illinois remains the most important collection of materials relating to the history of colonial Illinois.

4. Brauer, "Eamest Invitation," 267.

5. For an excellent interpretation of the "Revolt" in New Orleans, see Shannon Lee Dawdy, *Building the Devil's Empire: French Colonial New Orleans* (Chicago: University of Chicago Press, 2008), 219–46.

6. Brauer, "Earnest Invitation," 267.

7. This theme goes back to the works of nineteenth-century historian Francis Parkman, whose influence on later American historians' understanding of French colonization was enormous. Three outstanding and illuminating recent histories of French empire built around the theme of failure are Kenneth J. Banks, *Chasing Empire Across the Sea: Communications and the State in the French Atlantic, 1713–1763* (Montreal: McGill-Queen's University Press, 2002); James S. Pritchard, *In Search of Empire: The French in the Americas, 1670–1730* (Cambridge University Press, 2004); and Eric Hinderaker, *Elusive Empires: Constructing Colonialism in the Ohio Valley, 1673–1800* (New York: Cambridge University Press, 1997). For interesting commentary on this tradition, see Allan Greer, "Comparisons: New France," in *A Companion to Colonial America*, ed. Daniel Vickers (Malden, Mass.: Blackwell, 2005), 470.

8. For a summary of the historiography on French colonialism that addresses this question, see Christopher Hodson and Brett Rushforth, "Absolutely Atlantic: Colonialism and the Early Modern French State in Recent Historiography," *History Compass* 8, no. 1 (January 2010): 103. Especially important in this conversation about the nature of colonialism is Leslie Choquette, "Center and Periphery in French North America," in *Negotiated Empires: Centers and Peripheries in the Americas, 1500–1820*, ed. Christine Daniels and Michael V. Kennedy (New York: Routledge, 2002), 193–207. For a good review essay of French imperialism that shares the title of this book, see Philippe R. Girard, "Empire by Collaboration: The First French Colonial Empire's Rise and Demise," *French History* 19, no. 4 (December 2005): 482–90. See also Trevor Burnard, "Empire Matters? The Historiography of Imperialism in Early America, 1492–1830," *History of European Ideas* 33 (2007): 87–107. A useful theoretical point of departure that has shaped my thinking is Ann Laura Stoler, "On Degrees of Imperial Sovereignty," *Public Culture* 18, no. 1 (Winter 2006): 125–46. See also the excellent discussions in Dawdy, *Building the Devil's Empire*, 20–23; Jordan Kellman, "Beyond Center and Periphery: New Currents in French and Francophone Atlantic Studies," *Atlantic Studies* 10, no. 1 (2013): 1–11.

9. Literature that addresses this aspect of early modern colonialism is vast. For the most important example, see Richard White, *The Middle Ground: Indians, Empires, and Republics in the Great Lakes Region, 1650–1815* (New York: Cambridge University Press, 1991). For the influence of this book over a generation of scholarship, see the essays in "Forum: The Middle Ground Revisited," *William and Mary Quarterly* 63, no. 1 (2006): 3–96. An interesting alternative interpretation of the nature of empire and alliance is Gilles Havard, *Empire et métissages: Indiens et Français dans le pays d'en haut, 1660–1715* (Sillery, Quebec: Septentrion, 2003).

10. Shannon Dawdy calls this "rogue colonialism," in which imperialists and colonists constructed a version of imperialism through often illicit, if not illegal, activities. See Dawdy, *Building the Devil's Empire*. Legal scholars have come to understand "legal pluralism" as a fundamental component of early modern empires. See, especially, the recent essays in Lauren A. Benton and Richard J. Ross, eds., *Legal Pluralism and Empires, 1500–1850* (New York: New York University Press, 2013); see also Christopher L. Tomlins, *The Many Legalities of Early America* (Chapel Hill: University of North Carolina Press, 2001).

11. The most influential book on economic activity and the nature of French empire in America is Daniel Usner, *Indians, Settlers, and Slaves in a Frontier Exchange Economy* (Chapel Hill: University of North Carolina Press, 1992). See also Wim Klooster, "Inter-Imperial Smuggling in the Americas, 1600–1800," in *Soundings in Atlantic History: Latent Structures and Intellectual Currents, 1500–1830*, ed. Bernard Bailyn (Cambridge, Mass.: Harvard University Press, 2009); and Dawdy, *Building the Devil's Empire*. For a fascinating exploration of the contested nature of early North American French empire at both political and economic levels, see Alexandre Dubé, "Les biens publics: Culture politique de la Louisiane Française 1730–1770" (Ph.D. diss., McGill University, 2009).

12. As Greer argues, this clash of "overweening authorities" and swashbuckling freedom-loving colonists has characterized the historiography of French empire for generations. Greer, "Comparisons: New France," 470.

13. White, *The Middle Ground*, x. See also Richard White, "Creative Misunderstandings and New Understandings," *William and Mary Quarterly* 63, no. 1 (January 2006): 9–14.

14. Dawdy, *Building the Devil's Empire*.

15. A. J. B. Johnston, *Control and Order: In French Colonial Louisbourg, 1713–1758* (East Lansing: Michigan State University Press, 2001); Dawdy, *Building the Devil's Empire*, introduction; Sigmund Diamond, "An Experiment in 'Feudalism': French Canada in the Seventeenth Century," *William and Mary Quarterly* 18, no. 1 (January 1961): 4–34.

16. Much recent discussion of empire and imperialism is informed by the political theory of James C. Scott, who argues powerfully that imperialism is a dialectic between the officials who try to make landscapes and people "legible," and thus controllable, and the people and landscapes that resist this attempt. James C. Scott, *Seeing Like a State: How Certain Schemes to Improve the Human Condition Have Failed* (New Haven, Conn.: Yale University Press, 1998); James C. Scott, *The Art of Not Being Governed: An Anarchist History of Upland Southeast Asia* (New Haven, Conn.: Yale University Press, 2010); Dawdy, *Building the Devil's Empire*, 10.

17. Ronald Robinson, "Non-European Foundations of European Imperialism: Sketch for a Theory of Collaboration," in *Studies in the Theory of Imperialism*, ed. Roger Owen (London: Longman, 1972), 117–42.

18. See the debate among historians of early modern France regarding whether absolutism itself was an exercise in collaboration. See William Beik, "The Absolutism of Louis XIV as Social Collaboration," *Past & Present*, no. 188 (August 1, 2005): 195–224.

19. Nor do I wish to echo the myth that the French had a "génie coloniale," a natural sympathy with Indian peoples that their imperial rivals the British and Spanish did not share. Rather than generalizing about any French colonial "genius," this book explores the specific collaboration between the Illinois and the French and its specific motivations. In this sense, it is inspired by Gilles Havard and Cécile Vidal, *Histoire de l'Amérique Française* (Paris: Flammarion, 2003), 251–54.

20. Rich recent scholarship on borderlands has influenced this book's approach. For a useful overview of the concept, see Pekka Hämäläinen and Samuel Truett, "On Borderlands," *Journal of American History* 98, no. 2 (September 2011): 338–61. For a still powerful argument that inspired this study's central questions, see Jeremy Adelman and Stephen Aron, "From Borderlands to Borders: Empires, Nation-States, and the Peoples in Between in North American History," *American Historical Review* 104, no. 3 (1999): 814–41.

21. White, *The Middle Ground*, x, 52.

22. Ramezay and Bégon to French Minister, November 7, 1715, WHC, 16:332. Original document of Ramezay and Bégon, serie B1, vol. 8, p. 274, Archives Nationales de la Marine, Paris, France.

23. Duclos to Pontchartrain, December 25, 1715, *MPA*, 2:208; Guillaume Aubert, "'The Blood of France': Race and Purity of Blood in the French Atlantic World," *William and Mary Quarterly* 61, no. 3 (July 2004): 439–78.

24. A major goal of this study is to reconsider the Illinois Indians in the colonial period as a powerful and often dominant people. Much writing about the early Illinois has focused on decline, dependence, and weakness. This book takes cues from recent work in Indian history that emphasizes the power of Native peoples, particularly in borderlands regions like the Mississippi Valley. Two works that have especially inspired my approach are Pekka Hämäläinen, *The Comanche Empire* (New Haven, Conn.: Yale University Press, 2008); and Kathleen DuVal, *The Native Ground: Indians and Colonists in the Heart of the Continent* (Philadelphia: University of Pennsylvania Press, 2006). See also Elizabeth A. Fenn, *Encounters at the Heart of the World: A History of the Mandan People* (New York: Hill and Wang, 2014).

25. White, *The Middle Ground*, x; White, "Creative Misunderstandings and New Understandings"; Richard White, "Preface to the 20th Anniversary Edition," in *The Middle Ground: Indians, Empires, and Republics in the Great Lakes Region, 1650–1815* (New York: Cambridge University Press, 2011), xi–xxiv.

26. Many of the premises of this book have been inspired and informed by recent work on intercultural understanding, linguistic exchange, and the question of what happens when different people learn to communicate and understand each other. In addition

to works by Richard White, this book's approach is indebted to James Hart Merrell, *Into the American Woods: Negotiators on the Pennsylvania Frontier* (New York: Norton, 1999); and Jill Lepore, *The Name of War: King Philip's War and the Origins of American Identity* (New York: Knopf, 1998).

Chapter 1

1. Marquette's description of the calumet ceremony is in *JR*, 59:117–23.

2. Marquette notes in his account that he received several bison products from the Illinois in this meeting, including "Belts, garters, and other articles made of the hair of bears and [bison], dyed red, Yellow, and gray." As he put it, "As they are of no great Value, we did not burden ourselves with Them." *JR* 59:111, 123. A long tradition associates the hide robes at the Musée du Quai Branly with Marquette, and while there is no way to prove the association, it seems likely that he or some Frenchman involved in these early French-Illinois encounters collected these robes. For good reproductions, and some discussion, of the hide robes, see George P. Horse Capture, W. Richard West, and Anne Vitart, *Robes of Splendor: Native American Painted Buffalo Hides* (New York: New Press, 1993), 35–42, 48–54, 115–21. See especially Anne Vitart, "From Royal Cabinets to Museums: A Composite History," in that volume. See also Christian-F. Feest, *Premieres nations, collections royales: Les Indiens des forets et des prairies d'Amerique du Nord* (Paris: Quai Branly, 2007); Feest, *Native Arts of North America* (New York: Oxford University Press, 1980), 81; E.-T. Hamy, "Note Sur D'anciennes Peintures Sur Peaux Des Indiens Illinois," *Journal de la Société des Américanistes* 2, no. 1 (1898): 184–95.

3. This interpretation runs counter to most of the standard ethnohistorical work on the early Illinois Indians, much of which follows baffled French eyewitnesses to tell a story of declension, ignoring Illinois power. The standard works are Raymond E. Hauser, "The Illinois Tribe: From Autonomy and Self-Sufficiency to Dependency and Depopulation," *Journal of the Illinois State Historical Society* 69 (May 1976): 127–38; Margaret Kimball Brown, *Cultural Transformations Among the Illinois: An Application of a Systems Model* (East Lansing: Michigan State University, 1973); Emily Jane Blasingham, "The Illinois Indians, 1634–1800: A Study of Depopulation"; and Zitomersky, *French Americans, Native Americans.*

4. For the idea of "transitional culture," see Charles Callender, "Illinois," in *Handbook of North American Indians*, vol. 15, *Northeast*, ed. Bruce G. Trigger (Washington, D.C.: Smithsonian Institution Press, 1978), 673. See also Feest, *Premières nations, collections royales,* 44.

5. Many histories of colonial Illinois begin in 1673 and look forward to Illinois decline, ignoring what came before. Recent works have focused on the pre-contact era in Illinois, however. The best include Alan G. Shackelford, "The Illinois Indians in the Confluence Region: Adaptation in a Changing World," in *Enduring Nations: Native Americans in the Midwest*, ed. R. David Edmunds (Urbana: University of Illinois Press, 2008); Alan G. Shackelford, "The Frontier in Pre-Columbian Illinois," *Journal of the*

Illinois State Historical Society 100, no. 3 (2007): 182–206. Jacob F. Lee gives the most detailed and nuanced synthesis of pre-contact history in Illinois and, like the present chapter, characterizes the Illinois's occupation of the region as an "invasion." See "Rivers of Power: Indians and Colonists in the North American Midcontinent" (Ph.D. diss., University of California, Davis, 2014), chap. 1. Of course, archaeologists have also provided syntheses of the pre-contact period. The best are Robert Mazrim and Duane Esarey, "Rethinking the Dawn of History: The Schedule, Signature, and Agency of European Goods in Protohistoric Illinois," *Midcontinental Journal of Archaeology* 32, no. 2 (October 1, 2007): 145–200; James Brown and Robert F. Sasso, "Prelude to History on the Eastern Prairies," in *Societies in Eclipse: Archaeology of the Eastern Woodlands Indians, A.D. 1400–1700*, ed. David S Brose, C. Wesley Cowan, and Robert C. Mainfort (Washington, D.C.: Smithsonian Institution Press, 2001); Thomas E. Emerson and James Allison Brown, "The Late Prehistory and Protohistory of Illinois," in *Calumet and Fleur-de-Lys: Archaeology of French and Indian Contact in the Mid-Continent*, ed. John A. Walthall and Thomas Emerson (Washington, D.C.: Smithsonian Institution Press, 1978); and Kathleen L. Ehrhardt, "Problems and Progress in Protohistoric Period Archaeology in the Illinois Country Since Calumet and Fleur-de-Lys," *Illinois Archaeology* 22, no. 10 (2010): 256–87. Many historians now dismiss the distinction between prehistory and history; one argument of this chapter is that history is distorted and misunderstood by beginning our trajectories at the moment of "contact." See Daniel Lord Smail and Shryock Andrew, "History and the 'Pre,'" *American Historical Review* 118, no. 3 (June 1, 2013): 709–37.

6. For a recent synthesis of climate change and its effect on Natives in North America, see Daniel K. Richter, *Before the Revolution: America's Ancient Pasts* (Cambridge, Mass.: Harvard University Press, 2011).

7. Richard White characterized the Great Lakes Algonquians—including the Illinois—as a "world made of fragments" during the Beaver Wars. White saw much of the Illinois's behavior in the late seventeenth century as the defensive, if not desperate, actions of "refugees." But the Illinois were themselves aggressors who could have chosen to stay out of the violence but instead acted belligerently. See White, *The Middle Ground*, chap. 1.

8. Given their significance and scale, historians have paid surprisingly little attention to the natural and cultural divisions that characterized Illinois in the colonial period. See M. J. Morgan, *Land of Big Rivers: French and Indian Illinois, 1699–1778* (Carbondale: Southern Illinois University Press, 2010). In linking human history to environmental realities in borderlands, this chapter is inspired by Pekka Hämäläinen, "The Politics of Grass: European Expansion, Ecological Change, and Indigenous Power in the Southwest Borderlands," *William and Mary Quarterly* 67, no. 2 (April 1, 2010): 173–208; and James D. Rice, *Nature and History in the Potomac Country: From Hunter-Gatherers to the Age of Jefferson* (Baltimore: Johns Hopkins University Press, 2009).

9. Shackelford, "The Frontier in Pre-Columbian Illinois," 182–83.

10. Stephen Aron, *American Confluence: The Missouri Frontier from Borderland to Border State* (Bloomington: Indiana University Press, 2006), 4–8.

11. George R. Milner, "The Late Prehistoric Cahokia Cultural System of the Missis-sippi River Valley: Foundations, Florescence, and Fragmentation," *Journal of World Pre-history* 4, no. 1 (March 1, 1990): 1–43; Thomas E. Emerson and R. Barry Lewis, *Cahokia and the Hinterlands: Middle Mississippian Cultures of the Midwest* (Urbana: University of Illinois Press, 2000).

12. Timothy R. Pauketat, *Cahokia: Ancient America's Great City on the Mississippi* (New York: Penguin Books, 2010), 4; Larry V. Benson, Timothy R. Pauketat, and Edward R. Cook, "Cahokia's Boom and Bust in the Context of Climate Change," *American Antiquity* 74, no. 3 (July 2009): 467–83.

13. An especially good discussion of the cultural influence of Cahokia is Pauketat's discussion of Chunkey, the Mississippian ball game, which spread throughout much of Native North America in the prehistoric period. Pauketat, *Cahokia*, chap. 5. For more on Cahokia's long-distance trade, see Richter, *Before the Revolution*, 28–29. For doubts about the degree of centralization in Cahokia, see Milner, "The Late Prehistoric Cahokia Cul-tural System of the Mississippi River Valley."

14. For the best discussion of the rise of urban centers and their relationship to the hinterlands environments of the West and Midwest in the modern period, see William Cronon, *Nature's Metropolis: Chicago and the Great West* (New York: Norton, 1992); and William R. Iseminger, "Culture and Environment in the American Bottom: The Rise and Fall of Cahokia Mounds," in *Common Fields: An Environmental History of St. Louis*, ed. Andrew Hurley (St. Louis: Missouri Historical Society Press, 1997), 38–57.

15. The best natural history of tallgrass prairie is John Madson, *Where the Sky Began: Land of the Tallgrass Prairie* (Iowa City: University of Iowa Press, 2004). Edgar Transeau explained prairie formation as a consequence of "depth of evaporation," not soil, glacial history, fire, or other factors. Edgar Nelson Transeau, "The Prairie Peninsula," *Ecology* 16, no. 3 (July 1, 1935): 423–37. For an in-depth look at prairie formation from a scientific standpoint, see James E. King, "Late Quaternary Vegetational History of Illinois," *Ecologi-cal Monographs* 51, no. 1 (March 1981): 43–62. Recent research at Konza prairie has estab-lished the critical role of grazing and fire in prairie creation and maintenance, suggesting a new way of thinking about prairie history. For a good introduction, see Alan K. Knapp et al., "The Keystone Role of Bison in North American Tallgrass Prairie," *BioScience* 49, no. 1 (January 1, 1999): 39–50.

16. Morgan, *Land of Big Rivers*, chap. 1; see also "Native Americans:Historic:Illinois Country:Plants," http://www.museum.state.il.us/muslink/nat_amer/post/htmls/ic_plants .html (accessed June 2, 2012). For some of the best reports on early Illinois environments, see the work of John White on the ecologies of various river valley/watershed areas. These are published in a series by the Illinois Department of Natural Resources. See, for instance, John White, *Kankakee River Area Assessment: Early Accounts of the Ecology of the Kankakee Area*, vol. 5 (Springfield: Illinois Department of Natural Resources, 1998). See also Edgar Nelson Transeau, "The Prairie Peninsula"; Diane Greer et al., "Land Cover of Illinois in the Early 1800s" (Champaign: Illinois Natural History Survey, 1990).

17. David Rindos and Sissel Johannessen, "Human-Plant Interactions and Cultural Change in the American Bottom," *Cahokia and the Hinterlands: Middle Mississippian*

Cultures of the Midwest (Urbana: University of Illinois Press, 1991), 35–45; Milner, "The Late Prehistoric Cahokia Cultural System of the Mississippi River Valley," 5.

18. Benson, Pauketat, and Cook, "Cahokia's Boom and Bust in the Context of Climate Change," 475; Larry V. Benson et al., "Possible Impacts of Early-11th-, Middle-12th-, and Late-13th-Century Droughts on Western Native Americans and the Mississippian Cahokians," *Quaternary Science Reviews* 26, no. 3–4 (February 2007): 336–50.

19. Iseminger, "Culture and Environment in the American Bottom," 54.

20. Neal Lopinot and William Woods, "Wood Overexploitation and the Collapse of Cahokia," in *Foraging and Farming in the Eastern Woodlands*, ed. C. Margaret Scarry (Gainesville: University Press of Florida, 1993). For a more skeptical view of the role of environmental factors in the decline of Cahokia, see Timothy R. Pauketat, *Ancient Cahokia and the Mississippians* (New York: Cambridge University Press, 2004), 36–42.

21. Emerson and Brown, "The Late Prehistory and Protohistory of Illinois," 103, 111; Iseminger, "Culture and Environment in the American Bottom," 54; David A. Baerreis, Reid A. Bryson, and John E. Kutzbach, "Climate and Culture in the Western Great Lakes Region," *Midcontinental Journal of Archaeology* 1 (1976): 39; "Native Americans: Historic: Illinois Country: Climate," http://www.museum.state.il.us/muslink/nat_amer/post/htmls/ic_climate.html (accessed June 2, 2012).

22. Charles R. Cobb and Brian M. Butler, "The Vacant Quarter Revisited: Late Mississippian Abandonment of the Lower Ohio Valley," *American Antiquity* 67, no. 4 (October 1, 2002): 625–41. For the descendants of the Cahokians and Mississippians, see Charles M. Hudson and Robbie Ethridge, "From Prehistory Through Protohistory to Ethnohistory in and near the Northern Lower Mississippi Valley," in *The Transformation of the Southeastern Indians, 1540–1760* (Jackson: University Press of Mississippi, 2002).

23. Shackelford, "The Illinois Indians in the Confluence Region," 22; Brown and Sasso, "Prelude to History," 206; Transeau, "The Prairie Peninsula"; Ehrhardt, "Problems and Progress," 259.

24. For a good explanation of Oneota subsistence, see Brown and Sasso, "Prelude to History," 215.

25. Emerson and Brown, "The Late Prehistory and Protohistory of Illinois," 100–101; Brown and Sasso, "Prelude to History," 215.

26. For a good overview, see Emerson and Brown, "The Late Prehistory and Protohistory of Illinois," 100–103; Thomas E. Emerson, "The Langford Tradition and the Process of Tribalization on the Middle Mississippian Borders," *Midcontinental Journal of Archaeology* 24, no. 1 (April 1, 1999): 38; The most conspicuous example of warfare and violence in Oneota-era Illinois comes from George R. Milner, Eve Anderson, and Virginia G. Smith, "Warfare in Late Prehistoric West-Central Illinois," *American Antiquity* 56, no. 4 (October 1, 1991): 581–603.

27. For a good general overview, see Brian M. Fagan, *The Little Ice Age: How Climate Made History, 1300–1850* (New York: Basic Books, 2001).

28. See Raymond S. Bradley and Philip D. Jonest, "'Little Ice Age' Summer Temperature Variations: Their Nature and Relevance to Recent Global Warming Trends," *The Holocene* 3, no. 4 (December 1, 1993): 367–76.

29. If this is true, it would be a good example of what one historian calls an "ungulate irruption." See Elinor Melville, *A Plague of Sheep: Environmental Consequences of the Conquest of Mexico* (New York: Cambridge University Press, 1997), 7.

30. There is some disagreement about when the bison actually did arrive east of the Mississippi. Tankersley puts the date at 1650, while Griffin and Wray say 1600. Iseminger has the date earlier, during the 1500s, and Brown and Sasso say "after 1400." Shackelford has it in the 1500s. Brown and Sasso, "Prelude to History," 217; "Kenneth B. Tankersley, "Bison and Subsistence Change: The Protohistoric Ohio Valley and Illinois Valley Connection," in *Long-Term Subsistence Change in Prehistoric North America*, ed. Dale Croes, Rebecca Hawkins, and Barry Isaac, *Research in Economic Anthropology* 6 (1992): 103–30; John W. Griffin and Donald E. Wray, "Bison in Illinois Archaeology," *Transactions of the Illinois State Academy of Science* 38 (1945): 21–26; Iseminger, "Culture and Environment in the American Bottom," 55; Shackelford, "The Illinois Indians in the Confluence Region"; Emerson and Brown, "The Late Prehistory and Protohistory of Illinois," 86. For a good discussion of the established archaeology and likely earlier arrivals of bison into the region, see Terrance J. Martin and Alan Harn, "The Lonza-Caterpillar Site: Bison Bone Deposits from the Illinois River, Peoria County, Illinois," in *Records of Early Bison in Illinois*, ed. R. Bruce McMillan, Scientific Papers/Illinois State Museum, vol. 31 (Springfield: Illinois State Museum, 2006), 44–49, 60–61. The fact that no archaeological trash pits contain bison remains before the 1500s suggests that bison may have been present but not numerous before that period.

31. Tankersley, "Bison and Subsistence Change," 105; R. Bruce McMillan, ed., *Records of Early Bison in Illinois* (Springfield: Illinois State Museum, 2006).

32. The combination of glacial and wind-borne loess deposits, together with the constant decomposition of grasses over time, made the prairie soil of the Illinois extraordinarily deep and fertile. See Madson, *Where the Sky Began*, 109, 118.

33. James Allison Brown and Patricia J O'Brien, *At the Edge of Prehistory: Huber Phase Archaeology in the Chicago Area* (Kampsville, Ill.: Illinois Department of Transportation/Center for American Archeology, 1990), 275–76.

34. Brown and Sasso, "Prelude to History," 208.

35. Hämäläinen, "The Politics of Grass," 180.

36. Ibid.; Elliott West, *The Contested Plains: Indians, Goldseekers, & the Rush to Colorado* (Lawrence: University Press of Kansas, 2000), chaps. 2–3. For excellent descriptions of the "solar economy" of bison, see Dan Flores, "Bison Ecology and Bison Diplomacy: The Southern Plains from 1800 to 1850," *Journal of American History* 78, no. 2 (September 1991): 469. See also Andrew C. Isenberg, *The Destruction of the Bison: An Environmental History, 1750–1920* (New York: Cambridge University Press, 2000), 68.

37. Liette, 307–18; Robert Cavelier La Salle, *Relation of the Discoveries and Voyages of Cavelier De La Salle from 1679 to 1681, the Official Narrative*, trans. Melville Best Anderson (Chicago: The Caxton Club, 1901), 81; La Salle, *Official Narrative*, 81, 221; Hennepin, *A New Discovery*, 1: 146–52; Nicolas Perrot, "Memoir on the Manners, Customs, and Religion of the Savages of North America," in *The Indian Tribes of the Upper Mississippi Valley*

and Region of the Great Lakes, ed. Emma Helen Blair (Lincoln: University of Nebraska Press, 1996), 1:119–25.

38. Tankersley, "Bison and Subsistence Change," 105.

39. Shackelford, "The Illinois Indians in the Confluence Region," 22; Tankersley, "Bison and Subsistence Change," 105.

40. Dale Henning, "The Oneota Tradition," in *Archaeology on the Great Plains*, ed. W. Raymond Wood (Lawrence: University Press of Kansas, 1998). For this idea of transitional culture, see Callender, "Illinois"; Brown and Sasso, "Prelude to History," 215; and Shackelford, "The Illinois Indians in the Confluence Region," 22.

41. Paul W. Parmalee, "The Faunal Complex of the Fisher Site, Illinois," *American Midland Naturalist* 68, no. 2 (October 1, 1962): 399–408; Emerson and Brown, "The Late Prehistory and Protohistory of Illinois," 87; Henning, "The Oneota Tradition," 372; Brown and Sasso, "Prelude to History," 215.

42. Emerson and Brown, "The Late Prehistory and Protohistory of Illinois."

43. David S Brose, "Penumbral Protohistory on Lake Erie's Southern Shore," in *Societies in Eclipse: Archaeology of the Eastern Woodlands Indians, A.D. 1400–1700*, ed. C. Wesley Cowan, Robert C. Mainfort, and David S. Brose (Washington, D.C.: Smithsonian Institution Press, 2001), 55, 61.

44. The best explanation of the complex and competing theories for the origins and associations of Danner series pottery is Mazrim and Esarey, "Rethinking the Dawn of History," 158–63.

45. Brose, "Penumbral Protohistory on Lake Erie's Southern Shore"; Penelope B. Drooker, *The View from Madisonville: Protohistoric Western Fort Ancient Interaction Patterns* (Ann Arbor, Mich.: Museum of Anthropology, 1997), 47, 317–32; Tankersley, "Bison and Subsistence Change," 105; Shackelford, "The Illinois Indians in the Confluence Region," 24.

46. Shackelford, "The Frontier in Pre-Columbian Illinois," 200. For the adoption of the calumet among the Oneota in Illinois, see Brown and Sasso, "Prelude to History."

47. Tankersley, "Bison and Subsistence Change." For bison in the Ohio Valley, see John A. Jakle, "The American Bison and the Human Occupance of the Ohio Valley," *Proceedings of the American Philosophical Society* 112, no. 4 (August 1968): 299–305.

48. See Mazrim and Esarey, 158–64; Ehrhardt, Problems and Progress, 260–61.

49. Brown and Sasso, "Prelude to History," 215.

50. Shackelford, "The Illinois Indians in the Confluence Region," 25.

51. There is evidence that the Huber phase Oneota were the proto-Winnebago, and historical evidence makes clear that the Illinois and Winnebago were at war in the 1630s. This evidence is a retrospective relation, contained in Claude Charles Le Roy, Bacqueville de La Potherie, "History of the Savage Peoples Who Are Allies of New France," 2 vols., in *The Indian Tribes of the Upper Mississippi Valley and Region of the Great Lakes*, ed. Emma Helen Blair (Lincoln: University of Nebraska Press, 1996), 1:291–300.

52. Brown and Sasso, "Prelude to History," 206.

53. West, *The Contested Plains*, 63–93. For a similar story of Indian "conquests" of the grasslands in the eighteenth century, see Richard White, "The Winning of the West:

The Expansion of the Western Sioux in the Eighteenth and Nineteenth Centuries," *Journal of American History* 65, no. 2 (September 1, 1978): 319–43. It is important to understand Indian peoples before contact as conducting a series of invasions. See also Isenberg, *The Destruction of the Bison*, chap. 2; Flores, "Bison Ecology," 468.

54. Surprisingly few historians have paid attention to the radically different lifeway that distinguished the Illinois from other Great Lakes groups. I argue that the bison and the prairies made the Illinois almost completely distinct among Algonquians and that we need to consider the Illinois as a unique group, a "transitional culture," belonging both to Algonquian and Siouan cultural worlds. Callender, "Illinois," 672–80. For contrast, consider the Cheyenne and Arapahoe, Algonquians who moved wholly into the western plains, practically relinquishing their Great Lakes ties. See West, *The Contested Plains*, 63–93; Isenberg, *The Destruction of the Bison*, 39; Flores, "Bison Ecology and Bison Diplomacy," 474.

55. Brown and Sasso, "Prelude to History," 217.

56. Elizabeth Cardinal, "Faunal Remains from the Zimmerman Site—1970," in *The Zimmerman Site: Further Excavations at the Grand Village of Kaskaskia*, ed. Margaret Kimball Brown, Reports of Investigations, Illinois State Museum No. 32 (Springfield: Illinois State Museum, 1975), 74–75; Henning, "The Oneota Tradition," 372–33.

57. The descriptions of Illinois bison-hunting practices in the contact era are scattered in several French accounts which, taken together, provide a fairly complete picture. Important sources include Nicolas Perrot, "Memoir," 119–26; Antoine Denis Raudot, "Memoir Concerning the Different Indian Nations of North America," in *The Indians of the Western Great Lakes, 1615–1760*, ed. W. Vernon Kinietz (Ann Arbor: University of Michigan Press, 1940), 407–8; and Liette, esp. 307–23.

58. Liette, 311; White, *Kankakee River Area Assessment*, 5:9.

59. La Salle, *Official Narrative*, 81.

60. Liette, 309–10. See also Raudot, "Memoir," 407–8.

61. The original manuscript is held at Watkinson Library Special Collections, Trinity College Library, Hartford, Connecticut. For a well-edited edition, see Carl Masthay, *Kaskaskia Illinois-to-French Dictionary* (St. Louis: C. Masthay, 2002).

62. Hennepin, 1683, quoted in White, *Kankakee River Area Assessment*, 5:13.

63. Perrot, "Memoir," 120; Dablon, *JR*, 55:193.

64. Raudot, "Memoir," 407–8.

65. Perrot, "Memoir," 124. To be sure, many eyewitnesses noted that the Illinois divided the fruits of the hunts equally, but since men competed to provide the most meat to their own and others' households, this redistribution took place only after the hunting and processing were over.

66. Isenberg, *The Destruction of the Bison*, 95–100. For more of this argument, see Robert Michael Morrissey, "Bison Algonquians: Cycles of Violence and Exploitation in the Mississippi Valley Borderlands," *Early American Studies* 13 (April 2015), forthcoming.

67. Louis Hennepin, *A New Discovery of a Vast Country in America*, ed. Reuben Gold Thwaites, 2 vols. (Chicago: A. C. McClurg, 1903), 1:150–51.

68. Henri de Tonti, *An Account of Monsieur de La Salle's Last Expedition and Discoveries in North America* (London: Printed for J. Tonson at the Judge's Head, 1698), 260–61. See also Louis Hennepin, *A Description of Louisiana*, ed. John G. Shea (New York, 1880), 149. Jacques Marquette and Louis Jolliet, "The Mississippi Voyage of Jolliet and Marquette, 1673," in Louise Phelps Kellogg, ed., *Early Narratives of the Northwest, 1634–1699* (New York: Scribner's, 1917), 238. *JR*, 67: 167.

69. See White, *Kankakee River Area Assessment*, 5:13. See also La Salle, *Official Narrative*, 81–2; *JR*, 67:165–67.

70. Emerson and Brown, "The Late Prehistory and Protohistory of Illinois," 90; Cardinal, "Faunal Remains from the Zimmerman Site," 73–79.

71. *JR*, 54:185–89.

72. *JR*, 59:127; Liette, 339.

73. *JR*, 59:167.

74. *JR*, 59: 111.

75. David W. Benn, "Hawks, Serpents, and Bird-Men: Emergence of the Oneota Mode of Production," *Plains Anthropologist* 34, no. 125 (August 1, 1989): 233–60.

76. Ibid., 244.

77. See E.-T. Hamy, "Note sur d'anciennes peintures sur peaux des Indiens Illinois," 184–95.

78. Kathleen L. Ehrhardt, "Linking History and Prehistory in the Midcontinent: Archaeological Investigations at Marquette and Jolliet's Peouarea," in *Aboriginal Ritual and Economy in the Eastern Woodlands: Essays in Memory of Howard Dalton Winters* (Springfield: Illinois State Museum Press, 2004), 287–302.

79. Raymond J. DeMaillie, "Kinship: The Foundation for Native American Society," in *Studying Native America: Problems & Prospects*, ed. Russell Thornton (Madison: University of Wisconsin Press, 1998), 307.

80. For instance, we don't even know if clan identity was important to the Illinois-speakers. David J. Costa, "The Kinship Terminology of the Miami-Illinois Language," *Anthropological Linguistics* 41, no. 1 (April 1, 1999): 28–53; Brown, *Cultural Transformations Among the Illinois*; Charles Callender, "Great Lakes-Riverine Sociopolitical Organization," in *Handbook of North American Indians*, vol. 15, *Northeast*, ed. Bruce G. Trigger (Washington, D.C.: Smithsonian Press, 1978), 610–21.

81. Kathleen L. Ehrhardt, *European Metals in Native Hands: Rethinking Technological Change, 1640–1683* (Tuscaloosa: University Alabama Press, 2005), 84. The original La Salle account is in Margry, 2:93–102, esp. 96. See also La Salle, in CISHL 23: 5. Note that the Metchigameas in the 1680s lived so far to the southwest that La Salle did not even count them; their language supposedly had much in common with those of their Siouan-speaking neighbors.

82. Liette, 364.

83. *KFD*, 36, 307.

84. Zitomersky, *French Americans, Native Americans*, 78; Callender, "Illinois," 674.

85. *JR*, 41:247.

86. La Salle, 1680, CISHL, 23:5.

87. For a good summary of all the various theories regarding the villages that composed the Illinois, see Ehrhardt, *European Metals in Native Hands*, 83–88. The Marquette map of 1673 shows most of the Illinois villages located west of the Mississippi. The Jesuit Claude Dablon wrote in 1670 that "Now the Ilinois, of whom we are speaking, lie on the farther side of this great river." *JR*, 55:207.

88. Perrot, "Memoir," 120.

89. DuVal, *The Native Ground*, chap. 1.

90. Juliana Barr, *Peace Came in the Form of a Woman: Indians and Spaniards in the Texas Borderlands* (Chapel Hill: University of North Carolina Press, 2007), 86.

91. Brown and Sasso, "Prelude to History," 220.

92. Ibid., 219–20.

93. See Mazrim and Esarey, "Rethinking the Dawn of History"; Ehrhardt, *European Metals in Native Hands*; and Margaret Kimball Brown, *The Zimmerman Site: Further Excavations at the Grand Village of Kaskaskia*, Reports of Investigations, Illinois State Museum No. 32 (Springfield: Illinois State Museum, 1975).

94. Lucien Campeau, "La route commerciale de l'ouest au dix-septième siècle," *Les cahiers des dix* 49 (1994): 21–49. See also Mazrim and Esarey, "Rethinking the Dawn of History," 149–51.

95. Mazrim and Esarey, "Rethinking the Dawn of History," 149–51.

96. Ian W. Brown, "The Calumet Ceremony in the Southeast and Its Archaeological Manifestations," *American Antiquity* 54, no. 2 (April 1, 1989): 314. It is important to note that the northeastern traditions of diplomacy were different, reflected most importantly in the wampum exchange.

97. *JR*, 59:135.

98. Ibid.

99. One estimate puts the Illinois population at one hundred thousand in the early 1600s. For a good, concise discussion of population, see Brown, *Cultural Transformations Among the Illinois*, 228.

100. Historians disagree about the motives for Iroquois violence, but it seems clear that captives were probably the primary objective of the wars. See José António Brandão, *Your Fyre Shall Burn No More: Iroquois Policy Toward New France and Its Native Allies to 1701* (Lincoln: University of Nebraska Press, 1997), 78; and Daniel K. Richter, *The Ordeal of the Longhouse: The Peoples of the Iroquois League in the Era of European Colonization* (Chapel Hill: University of North Carolina Press, 1992), chap. 3.

101. Richter, *The Ordeal of the Longhouse*. In 1680, La Salle estimated that the Iroquois killed six hundred thousand in the course of the wars to that point. La Salle, *Official Narrative*, 189.

102. See Tom Holm, "American Indian Warfare: The Cycles of Conflict and the Militarization of Native North America," in *A Companion to American Indian History*, ed. Philip J. Deloria and Neal Salisbury (New York: Blackwell, 2007), 156. Daniel K. Richter describes these new Indian wars as characterized by a cycle—a "spiral" of mourning war, trade, and disease. Daniel K. Richter, "War and Culture: The Iroquois Experience," *William and Mary Quarterly*, 3rd ser., 40, no. 4 (October 1, 1983): 540. Another excellent

description is Richter, *The Ordeal of the Longhouse*, 74. See also Brandão, *Your Fyre Shall Burn No More*, 72.

103. Perrot, "Memoir," 154.

104. *JR*, 54:237.

105. Jacques Du Chesneau, "Memoir on the Western Indians, September 13, 1681," NYCD, 9:161–62.

106. *JR*, 54:237; La Potherie, "History of the Savage Peoples Who Are Allies of New France," 1:300.

107. Du Chesneau, "Memoir," 161–62.

108. Hauser, "Warfare and the Illinois Indian Tribe During the Seventeenth Century," *Old Northwest* 10, no. 4 (1984): 368.

109. Perrot, "Memoir," 162.

110. *JR*, 60:161.

111. La Potherie, "History of the Savage Peoples Who Are Allies of New France," 1:300.

112. Allouez, *JR*, 54:237.

113. DeMaillie, "Kinship," 306–56; Brett Rushforth, *Bonds of Alliance: Indigenous and Atlantic Slaveries in New France* (Chapel Hill: University of North Carolina Press, 2012), chap. 1.

114. Christina Snyder, *Slavery in Indian Country: The Changing Face of Captivity in Early America* (Cambridge, Mass.: Harvard University Press, 2012), chap. 4; Michael Witgen, "The Rituals of Possession: Native Identity and the Invention of Empire in Seventeenth-Century Western North America," *Ethnohistory* 54, no. 4 (Fall 2007): 649. This flexibility of identity is mirrored by several other practices in Illinois culture, for instance the berdache. As Liette noted, Illinois culture made room for biological males to "become" females in the case that they, as children, preferred farming to hunting. See Raymond E. Hauser, "The Berdache and the Illinois Indian Tribe During the Last Half of the Seventeenth Century," *Ethnohistory* 37, no. 1 (January 1, 1990): 46–47.

115. *JR*, 67:173.

116. Rushforth, *Bonds of Alliance*, 48, 387–91. For other kinship terms related to captive adoption in Illinois Country, see "nisakica8a": "adopté pour son fils mort, fais ressouvenir." *KFD*, 520.

117. See Snyder, *Slavery in Indian Country*, 22, 56–57.

118. Brett Rushforth, "Slavery, the Fox Wars, and the Limits of Alliance," *William and Mary Quarterly*, 3rd ser., 63, no. 1 (January 1, 2006): 53–80.

119. Heidi Bohaker, "Nindoodemag: The Significance of Algonquian Kinship Networks in the Eastern Great Lakes Region, 1600–1701," *William and Mary Quarterly*, 3rd ser., 63, no. 1 (January 2006): 23–52.

120. *KFD*, 36.

121. La Potherie, "History of the Savage Peoples Who Are Allies of New France," 1:300.

122. *JR*, 59:127.

123. *JR*, 51:47–51; Carl J. Ekberg, *Stealing Indian Women: Native Slavery in the Illinois Country* (Urbana: University of Illinois Press, 2007), 11.

124. Rushforth, *Bonds of Alliance*, chap. 1 and 388–90.

125. La Salle, in CISHL, 23:10. For evidence of enslaved women performing the bison processing labor in the Illinois's economy, see Morrissey, "Bison Algonquians."

126. One village had eight thousand in 1673. *JR*, 58:99. Like almost all Native groups in the contact period, the Illinois were suffering population losses overall as a result of disease and violence. Among the Illinois, the 1690s seem to be the start of major disease outbreaks, at least ones big enough to appear in the sources. See *JR*, 64:175. In any event, it is clear that slavery helped them compensate for population losses and their village populations actually grew.

127. *JR*, 54:165–67, 55:207–17, 58:19.

128. *JR*, 54:167, 59:175.

129. *JR*, 59:175.

130. Rushforth, *Bonds of Alliance*, 55; La Salle, CISHL, 23:10.

131. *JR*, 59:127.

132. *JR*, 54:185.

133. *JR*, 59:14.

134. *JR*, 55:213–25.

135. *JR*, 55:209.

136. *JR*, 58:265.

137. *JR*, 55:215.

138. *JR*, 58:19.

139. *JR*, 55:215.

140. *JR*, 59:103.

141. *JR*, 51:51.

142. *JR*, 58:265.

143. *JR*, 58:267.

144. *JR*, 58:265–67.

145. White, *The Middle Ground*, 26. For the best recent treatment of Illinois-Jesuit interactions, see Tracy Neal Leavelle, *The Catholic Calumet: Colonial Conversions in French and Indian North America* (Philadelphia: University of Pennsylvania Press, 2011). See also Christopher Bilodeau, "'They Honor Our Lord Among Themselves in Their Own Way': Colonial Christianity and the Illinois Indians," *American Indian Quarterly* 25, no. 3 (2001): 352–77.

146. *JR*, 51:47–51.

147. *JR*, 60:163.

148. *JR*, 55:213.

149. *JR*, 51:51.

150. *JR*, 51:51; *JR*, 55:213; *JR*, 51:51.

151. *JR*, 54:181.

Chapter 2

1. La Salle, *Official Narrative*, 237.
2. Ibid., 213; Margry, 1:506–20; C¹¹ᴬ, vol. 5, fol. 310, ANOM.
3. La Salle, *Official Narrative*, 253.
4. Du Chesneau, "Memoir on the Western Indians," 162.
5. La Salle, *Official Narrative*, 215. See also "A Summary of Iroquois Attacks, Relation of 1681," *JR*, 62:10.
6. *JR*, 51:106.
7. Du Chesneau, "Memorandum on the Western Indians," 162.
8. White, *The Middle Ground*, 30–31.
9. Ibid., 34–35.
10. Talon to Minister, November 2, 1761, C¹¹ᴬ, vol. 3, fols. 159–71, ANOM.
11. *JR*, 59:105.
12. Summary of Jolliet and Marquette expedition, 1673, Margry, 1:268.
13. "Memoire on the proposal of Sieur de La Salle, for the discovery of the Western Part of Middle America," 1677, Margry, 1:331.
14. Hennepin, *A New Discovery*, 1:185. Henri Joutel, another member of La Salle's second party in the 1680s, praised the Illinois Country likewise: "It may be truly affirm'd that the Country of the Illinois enjoys all that can make it accomplished, not only as to Ornament, but also for its plentiful Production of all Things requisite for the Support of human life." Henri Joutel, *Joutel's Journal of La Salle's Last Voyage*, ed. Melville Best Anderson (Chicago: The Caxton Club, 1896), 171.
15. Jolliet and Marquette expedition, 1673, Margry, 1:264.
16. Most important was their discovery of the calumet, with which the explorers traveled throughout the region, "because [the calumet] is a passport and a safeguard to go with assurance among all the nations without receiving a single offense." Jolliet, quoted in Margry, 1:264.
17. Henri de Tonty, *Relation of Henri de Tonty Concerning the Explorations of La Salle from 1678 to 1683*, ed. Melville Best Anderson (Chicago: The Caxton Club, 1898), 303.
18. *JR*, 55:209.
19. See Mary Louise Pratt, *Imperial Eyes: Travel Writing and Transculturation* (New York: Routledge, 1992); and Richard White, "Discovering Nature in North America," *Journal of American History* 79, no. 3 (1992): 874–91.
20. For Talon's efforts at reform, the best sources are his annual memoires to the king, in which he explains his tireless activities directed at rationalizing administration and conducting surveillance in the colony. For example, Talon to Minister, November 1671, C¹¹ᴬ vol. 3, fols. 159–71, ANOM. Diamond, "An Experiment in 'Feudalism,' " 5.
21. Denonville to Minister, August 10, 1688, C¹¹ᴬ, vol. 10, fols. 63–71v, ANOM. See also W. J. Eccles, *The Canadian Frontier, 1534–1760* (Albuquerque: University of New Mexico Press, 1983), 126–28.
22. Colbert to Talon, June 4, 1672, B, vol. 4, fol. 61, ANOM; W. J. Eccles, *Frontenac: The Courtier Governor* (Lincoln: University of Nebraska Press, 2003), 78.

23. White, *The Middle Ground*, 24.

24. Colbert to Talon, March 30, 1666, Margry, 1:78; original is C¹¹ᴬ, vol. 9, fol. 266, ANOM. Colbert elaborated a few years later: "The intention of his majesty is not that you make great voyages in mounting the St. Lawrence River, nor that in the future the *habitants* extend even as far West as they have in the past. To the contrary, [his Majesty] desires that you work always and incessantly while you are in that country to tighten, collect and compose all the villages and cities, to place them as much as possible in a state of defending themselves." Colbert to Frontenac, May 17, 1674, Margry, 1:256.

25. Jolliet's Narrative, in Margry, 1:261.

26. Ibid.

27. Jolliet, in Margry, 1:269.

28. See report of Jolliet's discoveries, in Margry, 1:260.

29. King's response to Jolliet, in Margry, 1:329.

30. Colbert to Talon, January 5, 1666, quoted in Saliha Belmessous, "Assimilation and Racialism in Seventeenth- and Eighteenth-Century French Colonial Policy," *American Historical Review* 110, no. 2 (2005): 328.

31. For an excellent study of Jesuit activity in the New World, see Dominique Deslandres, *Croire et faire croire: Les missions Françaises au XVIIe siècle, 1600–1650* ([Paris]: Fayard, 2003).

32. Ignatius Loyola's credo explicitly endorsed the idea that priests meet the indigenous people on their own terms. As he quoted from St. Paul, "Be all things to all men in order to win all to Jesus Christ." Quoted in Peter A. Dorsey, "Going to School with the Savages: Authorship and Authority Among the Jesuits of New France," *William and Mary Quarterly*, 3rd ser., 55, no. 3 (1998): 399. See Loyola's letter to Joao Nunes Barreto, in John Patrick Donnelly, ed., *Jesuit Writings of the Early Modern Period, 1540–1640* (Indianapolis: Hackett, 2006), 25. See also James Axtell, *The Invasion Within: The Contest of Cultures in Colonial North America* (New York: Oxford University Press, 1985), chap. 5, "When in Rome."

33. Brebeuf engraving, frontispiece in Carole Blackburn, *Harvest of Souls: The Jesuit Missions and Colonialism in North America* (Montreal: McGill-Queen's University Press, 2000).

34. *JR*, 23:207.

35. Pierre-François-Xavier de Charlevoix, 1741, quoted in Axtell, *Invasion Within*, 69.

36. Ironically, this peace was the result of the troops of the Regiment de Carignan-Salières, whom Colbert dispatched to accompany the new royal government in 1663. These troops quickly brought the Iroquois to terms in 1667. Peace with the Iroquois "opened the floodgates" for colonists, such as the Jesuits, to plan for distant colonial projects. Eccles, *The Canadian Frontier*, 105.

37. Joseph P. Donnelly, *Jacques Marquette, S.J., 1637–1675* (Chicago: Loyola University Press, 1968), 91, 104.

38. Colbert to Talon, April 5, 1666, C¹¹ᴬ, vol. 2, fol. 205, ANOM.

39. King's decree paraphrased in Frontenac, in Margry, 1:249.

40. Frontenac to Colbert, 1672, Margry, 1:248–50.

41. Donnelly, *Jacques Marquette*, 104–14.

42. For more of this argument, see Robert Michael Morrissey, "The Terms of Encounter: Language and Contested Visions of French Colonization in the Illinois Country, 1673–1702," in *French and Indians in the Heart of North America, 1630–1815*, ed. Robert Englebert and Guillaume Teasdale (East Lansing: Michigan State University Press, 2013), 43–75.

43. *JR*, 54:185.

44. *JR*, 51:51.

45. *JR*, 54:181.

46. Eccles, *Frontenac*, 81.

47. La Salle's *Procès Verbal*, the document confirming the possession of Louisiana, is published in CISHL, 1:106–13.

48. Duchesneau to Minister, November 13, 1680, C^{11A}, vol. 5, fol. 180, ANOM.

49. Duchesneau to Minister, November 13, 1681, C^{11A}, vol. 5, fol. 290, ANOM; King to Frontenac and Champigny, 1692, CISHL, 23:259.

50. Duchesneau to Minister, November 13, 1680, C^{11A}, vol. 5, fol. 180, ANOM.

51. Denonville to Seignelay, November 13, 1685, CISHL, 23:79, 80.

52. Tonty, *Relation of Henri De Tonty*, 86; La Salle memoir, in Margry, 2:69.

53. La Salle memoir, in Margry, 2:68–73.

54. Zenobé Membré, in *Historical Collections of Louisiana and Florida: Including Translations of Original Manuscripts Relating to Their Discovery and Settlement, with Numerous Historical and Biographical Notes*, ed. B. F. French (New York: A. Mason, 1875), 49.

55. Hennepin, *A New Discovery*, 1:171.

56. La Salle, *Official Narrative*, 233.

57. *JR*, 64:213.

58. See Hennepin, *A New Discovery*, 1:182.

59. Ibid., 1:289.

60. Ibid.

61. Ibid.

62. Ibid., 1:204.

63. Ibid.

64. De La Barre to the king, November 4, 1683, C^{11A}, vol. 5, fol. 137v, ANOM.

65. La Salle, *Official Narrative*, 209–15.

66. "The Irroquois [*sic*] . . . steadily advanced until they encountered a small Illinoët village [where] they killed the women and children therein, for the men fled toward their own people, who were not very far from that place." Perrot, "Memorandum," 154.

67. La Salle said this outright, calling the Illinois "incapable of resistance." *Official Narrative*, 111.

68. White, *The Middle Ground*, 30.

69. Denonville to Minister, C^{11A}, vol. 9, fol. 85, ANOM. A year later, Tonty and La Forest arrested Englishmen bound for Illinois, causing governors in New France to worry

that "[the English] are our most dangerous enemies which we have more to fear" than the Iroquois. Champigny to Minister, July 16, 1687, C[11A], vol. 9, ANOM.

70. King's instructions to Denonville, 1685, CISHL, 23:70.

71. "Memoir of Fr. Jean Cavalier [La Salle's Brother]," 1688, Margry, 3:593.

72. Memorial to the king, 1686, C[11A], vol. 8, fols. 42–43, ANOM.

73. "Extract of Memorial Concerning Canada," 1685, Margry, 5:11.

74. Minister to Denonville, 1686, CISHL, 23:104; Denonville to the king, 1686, C[11A], vol. 8, fol. 178, ANOM. See also C[11A], vol. 8, fols. 42–43, ANOM.

75. Instructions of the king to Denonville, March 10, 1685, B11, fols. 6–18, ANOM; see also CISHL, 23:69–70.

76. Duchesneau, quoted in White, *The Middle Ground*, 31.

77. Ibid.

78. For the account of Membré's adoption, see Membré in *Historical Collections*, ed. French, 149.

79. Liette, 328.

80. La Salle, *Official Narrative*, 193.

81. Ibid., 277.

82. La Salle, in Margry, 2:93–102.

83. Ibid.

84. La Salle, *Official Narrative*, 277.

85. For a similar case, see Richard White, "Although I Am Dead, I Am Not Entirely Dead, I Have Left a Second of Myself: Constructing Self and Persons on the Middle Ground of Early America," in *Through a Glass Darkly: Reflections on Personal Identity in Early America*, ed. Mechal Sobel, Ronald Hoffman, and Fredrika J. Teute (Chapel Hill: University of North Carolina Press, 1997).

86. White, *The Middle Ground*, 34–36.

87. La Salle "Memoire" from 1680, Margry, 2:6.

88. *JR*, 51:106.

89. Claude Allouez, "Relation of 1676," *JR*, 60:158. "One cannot well satisfy himself as to the number of people who Compose that village. They are housed in 351 cabins."

90. *JR*, 60:158.

91. La Salle Memorandum, 1680, CISHL, 23:6; see also Margry, 2:96.

92. La Salle, "Decente du Mississippi," Margry, 2:201. La Salle said that these villages had 460 cabins, four or five fires per cabin, and two families per fire. This was a huge population.

93. Michael Witgen, *An Infinity of Nations: How the Native New World Shaped Early North America* (Philadelphia: University of Pennsylvania Press, 2012), 19.

94. La Salle, "Decente du Mississippi," Margry, 2:163, 201.

95. DuVal, *The Native Ground*, 24.

96. La Salle, "Decente du Mississippi," in Margry, 2:201.

97. Ibid. The different groups, about thirty leagues away from the Grand Village, included Matchinkoa, Emissourites, Peanghichia, Kolatica, Megancockia, and Melomelinoia.

98. Hennepin, *A New Discovery*, 1:175. See also La Salle, *Official Narrative*, 137; Juliana Barr, "From Captives to Slaves: Commodifying Indian Women in the Borderlands," *Journal of American History* 92 (Summer 2005): 19–46; and Margry, 2:324–26. See also Ekberg, *Stealing Indian Women*, 12; and Henri de Tonty, "Memoir on La Salle's Discoveries, by Tonty, 1678–1690," in *Early Narratives of the Northwest*, ed. Louise Phelps Kellogg (New York: Charles Scribner's Sons, 1917), 303.

99. Rushforth, *Bonds of Alliance*, 55; La Salle, in CISHL, 23:10.

100. Tonti, "Memoir on La Salle's Discoveries," 303.

101. Hauser, "Warfare and the Illinois Indian Tribe," 379.

102. La Potherie, "History," 2:36.

103. Liette, 386; see also Hauser, "Warfare and the Illinois Indian Tribe," 376.

104. La Potherie, "History," 2:36.

105. Raudot, "Memoir," 403.

106. Barr, "From Captives to Slaves," 23–24.

107. Liette, 391.

108. Hauser, "Warfare and the Illinois Indian Tribe," 379; Raudot, "Memoir," 404.

109. For the opening of the bison hide trade in Illinois, see La Salle to his men, 1683, CISHL, 23:40.

110. Raudot, "Memoir," 404.

111. Liette, 376.

112. For the Illinois's patrilineal organization, see Callender, "Illinois," 673–80; Callender, "Great Lakes-Riverine Sociopolitical Organization"; and Brown, *Cultural Transformations Among the Illinois*.

113. Liette, 377.

114. See Snyder, *Slavery in Indian Country*, 94; and Rushforth, *Bonds of Alliance*, 46.

115. La Potherie, "History," 300.

116. *JR*, 59:127. In the early 1700s, Andre Pénicaut noted the continued preference for women and children as slaves among the Illinois. See Margry, 5:492–93.

117. Liette, 387, 381. As Sebastien Rasles wrote in this period, an Illinois warrior was "at the height of his glory when he takes prisoners and brings them home alive." Sebastien Rasles, in *JR*, 67:171–73.

118. La Salle, *Official Narrative*, 145.

119. Ibid.

120. Liette, 358, 381–82.

121. This made slavery among the Illinois very different from other forms of slavery in the Atlantic world, in which status followed the mother. For a great study of slavery and reproduction, see Jennifer L. Morgan, *Laboring Women: Reproduction and Gender in New World Slavery*, Early American Studies (Philadelphia: University of Pennsylvania Press, 2004).

122. For descriptions of this event, see La Salle, *Official Narrative*, 209–15, 237. See also "A Summary of Iroquois Attacks, Relation of 1681," JR, 62:10. La Salle, *Official Narrative*, 209–15.

123. Ibid., 255.

124. Liette, 311. For a similar description, see La Salle's official narrative, in which he describes Illinois hunters: "When they see a herd, they assemble in great numbers and set fire to the grass all round, with the exception of a few passages which they leave open, and at which they station themselves with their bows and arrows. In attempting to escape from the fire, the cattle are thus compelled to pass by these savages, who sometimes kill as many as two hundred in a single day." La Salle, *Official Narrative*, 81.

125. For Liette's hunt, which is the best detailed description of Illinois bison hunting from the Grand Village, see Liette, 307–18.

126. La Forest's request, 1688, Margry, 5:36–37.

127. Ibid.

128. Frontenac to the king, November 5, 1694, C^{11A}, vol. 13, fols. 4–27v, ANOM. Tonty's own report listed 334 Iroquois men, 111 women, killed or taken prisoner since 1687; Tonty's report, April 11, 1694, C^{13a}, vol. 1, fol. 27, ANOM. The tally became something of a preoccupation. Frontenac ordered Illinois proprietors to keep a detailed journal of Illinois-Iroquois engagements, with a running total of how many Iroquois killed. Frontenac and Champigny to Pontchartrain, 1695, C^{11A}, vol. 9, fol. 243, ANOM.

129. The French noted that the Illinois went to the Iroquois frequently: "[The Illinois] constantly [go to] the country of the Iroquois, whom, at my instigation, they continually harass. Not a year passes in which they do not take a number of prisoners and scalps." Tonty, *Relation of Henri De Tonty*, 303. For the most comprehensive accounting of the casualties taken by Illinois attacks on the Iroquois (and vice versa) in this period, see the charts compiled by Brandão, *Your Fyre Shall Burn No More*, appendix.

130. La Salle grant to Michel Disy, December 2, 1683, CISHL, 23:42.

131. Petition of La Forest, 1688, Margry, 5:36.

132. Minister to Denonville, 1686, CISHL, 23:122.

133. Denonville to Seignelay, November 13, 1685, CISHL, 23:79, 80.

134. Nicolas Perrot, "Memoir," 243.

135. Grant to Jacques Bourdon, Sieur D'Autray, CISHL 23:20–27. Note that this is not the same man who appears in Chapter 4, who was also called Bourdon.

136. La Barre to Minister, November 4, 1683, C^{11A}, vol. 5, fol. 137v, ANOM.

137. Denonville to Minister, August 25, 1687, CISHL, 23:89; see also Margry, 3:563.

138. Denonville to Seignelay, November 13, 1685, C^{11A}, vol. 7, fols. 88–89v, ANOM.

139. King to Denonville, Champigny, March 8, 1688, Margry, 3:576.

140. Grant to Tonty and La Forest, July 14, 1690, Margry, 5:51.

141. The description of this event comes from the concession, April 19, 1693, CISHL, 23:265.

142. La Salle's description of Hennepin's exploration, August 22, 1862, Margry, 2:245.

143. White, *The Middle Ground*, 30–31.

Chapter 3

1. Hennepin noted that Pimitéoui was translated as the "Place where there is an abundance of Fat beasts," reflecting the continued importance of bison to the Illinois lifeway. Hennepin, *A New Discovery*, 1:155.

2. Liette, 362.

3. For the concept of "creative misunderstandings" see White, *The Middle Ground*, x. White explains that many intercultural accommodations were made possible in early America because diverse people fundamentally did not understand each other. The point of this chapter is to suggest that Illinois in the 1690s was no longer characterized by this early condition. For a fuller argument, see Robert Michael Morrissey, "'I Speak It Well': Language, Cultural Understanding, and the End of a Missionary Middle Ground in Illinois Country, 1673–1712," *Early American Studies: An Interdisciplinary Journal* 9, no. 3 (2011): 617–48. See also White, "Creative Misunderstandings and New Understandings" and "Preface to the 20th Anniversary Edition," xi–xxiv.

4. For an example of this kind of critique of Jesuit sources, see Blackburn, *Harvest of Souls*.

5. For an extraordinary reflection on the dilemma of historians who rely on early American eyewitnesses to tell their histories but then find their sources faulty and naïve and clouded with misunderstanding, see White, "Creative Misunderstandings and New Understandings," 12–14.

6. A fine edition of Gravier's dictionary was edited by Carl Masthay, *Kaskaskia Illinois-to-French Dictionary*.

7. De Liette's manuscript is held at the Newberry Library. It was edited and published by Pease and Werner, CISHL, 23:302–96.

8. Leon Pouliot, "Claude Allouez," in *Dictionary of Canadian Biography*, ed. George Brown (Toronto: University of Toronto Press, 1966–2005).

9. A typical example of Allouez's encounters with the Illinois was his journey from Green Bay to the Mascouten village in August 1672, where he stayed for less than a full month.

10. These time spans are all estimated from sources in the *JR*. See also Michael McCafferty, "The Latest Miami-Illinois Dictionary and Its Author," in *Papers of the 36th Algonquian Conference*, ed. H. C. Wolfart (Winnipeg: University of Manitoba, 2005), 274. For Largillier, see *JR*, 71:148; Michael McCafferty, "Jacques Largillier: French Trader, Jesuit Brother, and Jesuit Scribe 'Par Excellence,'" *Journal of the Illinois State Historical Society* 104, no. 3 (October, 2011): 188–98. It is important to note that Largillier represents a "bridge" between the first and second generation Jesuits in Illinois. He accompanied the earliest Jesuits, and then remained in Illinois as a vital member of the Jesuit project with Gravier, Rasles and others who arrived after 1690,

11. Marquette to Jesuit Superior, 1670, *JR*, 54:187.

12. Allouez to Jesuit Superior, 1670, *JR*, 54:233.

13. The best overview of French Jesuit linguists is Victor Egon Hanzeli, *Missionary Linguistics in New France: A Study of Seventeenth- and Eighteenth-Century Descriptions of American Indian Languages* (The Hague: Mouton, 1969).

14. McCafferty, "Jacques Largillier," 189–92.

15. In addition to Gravier's dictionary, cited earlier, see also Le Boullenger's *Dictionary and Catechism*, which le Petit called the most extraordinary book of its kind in 1730. *JR*, 68:211. See Jean Baptiste Le Boullenger, *French and Miami-Illinois Dictionary*, Codex Ind 28, 2-SIZE, John Carter Brown Library, Providence, R.I.

16. For the best discussion of Jesuits and language learning, see Margaret J. Leahey, "'Comment peut un muet prescher l'evangile?' Jesuit Missionaries and the Native Languages of New France," *French Historical Studies* 19, no. 1 (1995): 105–31. See also Hanzeli, *Missionary Linguistics*, chap. 4. For Jesuits and language learning in a very different context, see Liam Matthew Brockey, *Journey to the East: The Jesuit Mission to China, 1579–1724* (Cambridge, Mass.: Belknap Press of Harvard University Press, 2007), especially chap. 7, "Learning the Language of Birds." See also Leavelle, *The Catholic Calumet,* chap. 5.

17. Liette, for example, noted how they "applied themselves to the language" every afternoon (362–63).

18. Binneteau to a Fellow Jesuit, 1699, *JR*, 65:69.

19. Binneteau to a Fellow Jesuit, 1699, *JR*, 66:67.

20. Sébastien Rasles to his Brother, October 12, 1723, *JR*, 67:143.

21. This was what Marest described as "reducing the language to rules." *JR*, 66:245.

22. Rasles to his Brother, October 12, 1723, *JR*, 67:133.

23. Rasles to his Brother, October 12, 1723, *JR*, 67:147.

24. Allouez, Relation of 1669–1670, *JR*, 54:237.

25. See Beschefer, 1683, *JR*, 62:205–13.

26. Marest to Germon, November 12, 1702, *JR*, 66:253.

27. Marest to a Jesuit, April 29, 1699, *JR*, 65:83.

28. Gravier to Lamberville, February 16, 1701, *JR*, 65:103.

29. Marest, to Lamberville, November 26, 1702, *JR*, 66:39.

30. Gravier, 1694, *JR*, 64:255.

31. Marest to Germon, November 12, 1702, *JR*, 66:255.

32. Rasles to his Brother, October 12, 1723, *JR*, 67:139.

33. See Loyola's letter to Joao Nunes Barreto, in *Jesuit Writings of the Early Modern Period*, ed. Donnelly, 25. See also Axtell, *Invasion Within*, chap. 5, "When in Rome."

34. Boullenger, *Dictionary*, "aider," 6. Boullenger's dictionary also includes suggestions of the language-learning process such as in the entry for "essayer," to try: "I try to pronounce it, I repeat my speech." Or, "He puts one word in front of the other."

35. *KFD*, 105. See Leavelle's similar emphasis on collaboration, *The Catholic Calumet,* 101–2.

36. Marquette, Relation of 1669–1670, *JR*, 54:55.

37. Rasles to his Brother, October 12, 1723, *JR*, 67:143.

38. Marest to Lamberville, 1707, *JR*, 66:117.

39. Ibid.

40. Liette, 362. In 1703, Pinet was singled out for having exceptional language skills in a letter from Bergier to Marest, June 15, 1703, in Garraghan, "New Light on Old Cahokia," *Illinois Catholic Historical Review* 11, no. 1 (1928): 126–27.

41. For a full analysis of Gravier's sober new understanding of Illinois spirituality, see Morrissey, "'I Speak It Well,'" 640–44.

42. *KFD*, 144.

43. *JR*, 64:187.

44. *KFD*, 307.

45. Liette, 364.

46. Ibid., 328.

47. *KFD*, 307.

48. Ibid., 210.

49. Liette, 328.

50. *KFD*, 509, 346, 335, 394, 37.

51. Ibid., 51.

52. Diron D'Artaguiette, "Journal of Diron D'Artaguiette," in *Travels in the American Colonies*, ed. Newton Dennison Mereness and National Society of the Colonial Dames of America (New York: Macmillan, 1916), 73.

53. Historians have argued that women were relatively empowered in Illinois culture. Richard White, for instance, writes that Illinois women were "masters" of their bodies. White, *The Middle Ground*, 72. Susan Sleeper-Smith suggests that Illinois households were matrifocal in *Indian Women and French Men: Rethinking Cultural Encounter in the Western Great Lakes* (Amherst: University of Massachusetts Press, 2001), chap. 2. However, evidence from the Grand Village suggests Illinois women and slaves were the "property" of their male relatives and had little power in the patrilineal society. Although there's no way to know about gender relations in the pre-contact era, it seems likely that the negative experiences of women in the contact era were a new phenomenon or worsening as a consequence of the increasing violence of the late 1600s, the bison economy, and especially the slave trade.

54. See Hauser, "The Berdache and the Illinois Indian Tribe," 128.

55. Binneteau, 1699, *JR*, 65:66.

56. Hennepin, *A New Discovery*, 2:480–81.

57. Liette, 353; see also Hauser, "The Berdache and the Illinois Indian Tribe," 129.

58. Liette, 369.

59. La Salle, *Official Narrative*, 295.

60. *KFD*, 13.

61. Jacques Marquette, quoted in Hennepin, *A New Discovery*, 2:652; La Salle, *Official Narrative*, 145.

62. Liette, 335. Another description from a later period among the Miami confirms that this was not an isolated incident. As Cadillac observed, "When [a wife] is convicted of unfaithfulness or adultery, her husband has her head shaved, cuts off her nose and ears,

and thrusts her out of his cabin. After that she goes whither she wills, and her kindred have nothing to say, for such is the law of the Nation." "Relation of Sieur de Lamothe Cadillac," 1718, in Margry, 2:75–132; see also WHC, 16:350.

63. When she refused the marriage he arranged for her, chief Rouensa stripped his daughter Marie and kicked her out of his house. Stripping was an act often associated with slaves, as Rushforth has shown. If Marie, the daughter of a chief, was not free from misogynistic abuse, it is likely that most women in this society felt similar constraints and even oppression. Rushforth, *Bonds of Alliance*, 44.

64. Liette, 361, 334.

65. Unidentified Frenchman quoted in Hauser, "The Berdache and the Illinois Indian Tribe," 129.

66. Rasles to his Brother, October 12, 1723, *JR* 67:167.

67. Many sources document women's role in hide processing and meat preservation. See Louis Hennepin, *A Description of Louisiana* (New York: John G. Shea, 1880), 144; Raudot, "Memoir," 407–8; Liette, "Memoir," 312.

68. Rasles to his Brother, October 12, 1723, *JR*, 67:165–67.

69. Gravier, 1694, *JR*, 66:231.

70. Marest to Germon, November 12, 1702, *JR*, 66:229.

71. Gravier, 1694, *JR*, 64:185.

72. Gravier, 1694, *JR*, 64:199.

73. Gravier, 1694, *JR*, 64:177.

74. Marest, April 29, 1699, *JR*, 65:79.

75. Gravier, 1694, *JR*, 64:165.

76. Gravier, 1694, *JR*, 64:167.

77. Gravier, 1694, *JR*, 64:177.

78. Gravier, 1694, *JR*, 64:229.

79. Gravier, 1694, *JR*, 64:227.

80. Ibid.

81. See Sleeper-Smith, *Indian Women and French Men*, 24–25; and Liette, 362.

82. *KFD*, 10.

83. Ibid., 51.

84. Ibid., 10, 53.

85. Marest to Germon, November 9, 1712, *JR*, 66:249, 251.

86. Gravier, 1694, *JR*, 64:191.

87. Gravier, 1694, *JR*, 64:167.

88. Gravier, 1694, *JR*, 64:211–13.

89. Gravier, 1694, *JR*, 64:165.

90. Binneteau, *JR* 65: 66.

91. Gravier, 1694, *JR*, 64:191.

92. Binneteau, *JR*, 65:67.

93. D'Artaguiette, "Journal," 73.

94. Liette, 361.

95. Gravier, 1694, *JR*, 64:175.

96. Gravier, 1694, *JR*, 64:227.

97. Gravier, 1694, *JR*, 64:163.

98. Binneteau, *JR*, 65:67.

99. Gravier, 1694, *JR*, 64:189.

100. Gravier, 1694, *JR*, 64:191.

101. Gravier, 1694, *JR*, 64:181.

102. Binneteau, *JR*, 65:65.

103. White, *The Middle Ground*, 59.

104. *KFD*, 288.

105. Liette, 361.

106. Binneteau, *JR*, 64:211.

107. Gravier's description of this event is in his 1694 Journal, *JR*, 64:193–215. See Sleeper-Smith, *Indian Women and French Men*, chap. 2; and Carl J. Ekberg and Anton J. Pregaldin, "Marie Rouensa-8cate8a and the Foundations of French Illinois," *Illinois Historical Journal* 84 (Fall 1991): 146–60.

108. Gravier, 1694, *JR*, 64:195.

109. Gravier, 1694, *JR*, 64:201–2.

110. Gravier, 1694, *JR*, 64:203.

111. Gravier, 1694, *JR*, 64:205.

112. Gravier, 1694, *JR*, 64:211.

113. Gravier, 1694, *JR*, 64:213.

114. Gravier, 1694, *JR*, 64:233.

115. Jean Francois Buisson de St. Cosme, 1700, quoted in Mary P. Palm, "The Jesuit Missions of the Illinois Country, 1673–1763" (Ph.D. diss., St. Louis University, 1931), 38.

116. Gravier, 1694, *JR*, 64:197.

117. Gravier to Tamburini, March 6, 1707, *JR*, 66:121.

118. Gravier, 1694, *JR*, 64:217.

119. Gravier, 1694, *JR*, 64:171.

120. Binneteau, *JR*, 65:67.

121. Binneteau, *JR*, 65:53.

122. Our only source on this question is La Salle, who as early as the 1680s noted that the bison had begun to decline near the population center. It is hard to imagine that the huge population center had not made a serious impact on the bison resource in the region. See Margry, 2:95.

Chapter 4

1. Ramezay and Bégon to French Minister, November 7, 1715, WHC, 16:332. Original document of Ramezay and Bégon, Archives Nationales de la Marine, serie B1, 8:274.

2. Ibid.

3. Vaudreuil and Bégon to Minister, November 15, 1713, C^{11A}, vol. 34, fol. 4, ANOM. Also WHC, 16:299.

4. Ramezay and Bégon to Minister, November 7, 1715, WHC, 16:332.

5. Lallement, "A copy of a letter from Lallement to the Directors of the Company of the Indies," April 5, 1721, , Service Hydrographique, 115–10, Archives Nationales, Paris.

6. Ramezay and Bégon to Minister, November 7, 1715, WHC, 16:332.

7. Denonville to Minister, August 25, 1687, in CISHL, 23:89. Also see Margry, 3:562–63.

8. "Bureau of the Marine concerning the commerce in beaver," 1695, C¹¹A vol. 13, fols. 400–401, ANOM; Alvord, *The Illinois Country*, 23.

9. Champigny to Minister, C¹¹A, vol. 15, fols. 120–138v, ANOM. See also Champigny to Minister, October 14, 1698, WHC, 16:175.

10. Minister to Denonville, March 8, 1688, C¹¹A, vol. 10, fols. 20–22, ANOM. Denonville to Minister, C¹¹A, vol. 9, fol. 85, ANOM.

11. Champigny to Minister, July 16, 1687, C¹¹A, vol. 9, fol. 36v, ANOM.

12. Frontenac and Champigny to Minister, November 3, 1693, C¹¹A, vol. 12, fols.207–22, ANOM.

13. Helen Hornbeck Tanner, "The Career of Joseph La France," in *The Fur Trade Revisited: Selected Papers of the Sixth North American Fur Trade Conference, Mackinac Island, Michigan, 1991*, ed. Jennifer S. H. Brown, W. J. Eccles, and Donald P. Heldman (East Lansing: Michigan State University Press, 1994), 182.

14. Henri de Tonty to Cabart de Vilhrmont, October 11, 1694, Margry, 4:4. Similar appeals came to the king from people like La Porte de Louvigny, captain of the troops of the Marine in Canada; Sieur d'Ailleboust de Mantet, a lieutenant; Sieur de Rémonville, friend of La Salle; and Sieur Argoud, all of whom urged the king to continue La Salle's original proposal and establish the Louisiana colony. See Alvord, *Illinois Country*, 125; and Margry, 4:v, 9.

15. *Dictionary of Canadian Biography Online*, s.v. "Juchereau de Saint-Denys, Charles," http://www.biographi.ca (accessed August 5, 2010). The best study of Juchereau's tannery, which was the center of a flourishing bison trade, is John Fortier and Donald Chaput, "A Historical Reexamination of Juchereau's Illinois Tannery," *Journal of the Illinois State Historical Society (1908–1984)* 62, no. 4 (December 1, 1969): 385–406.

16. "Memoir on the Establishment of Mobile and the Mississippi," 1702, Margry, 3:587–600. See Marcel Giraud, *A History of French Louisiana* (Baton Rouge: Louisiana State University Press, 1974), 86–88; and Alvord, *Illinois Country*, 130. Iberville laid out this plan in a 1702 memorial, June 20, 1702, Margry, 4:587, 596–607.

17. Callière and Champigny, October 18, 1700, C¹¹A, vol. 18, fols. 3–21, ANOM.

18. Callière and Champigny to Minister, October 5, 1701, Margry, 5:356–60.

19. As one petition to the king from New France officials argued: "It is [Canada's] loss, by the desertion of the best men and all the youths, who, under the hope of a great fortune, have begun to leave their relatives and go to the said establishment [Louisiana], above all the libertines and *coureurs de bois* who, bankrupting their creditors in Quebec and Montreal, have carried all their beaver and other pelts to M. de Iberville, who has begun to receive them well with their beavers and to the prejudice of the colony of

Canada." See "Petition that beavers not be carried to the Mississippi," Archives Nationales de la Marine, Louisiana volume, 1678–1706, Margry, 4:610.

20. See Stephen Aron, *American Confluence: The Missouri Frontier from Borderland to Border State* (Bloomington: Indiana University Press, 2006); Alan Gallay, *The Indian Slave Trade: The Rise of the English Empire in the American South, 1670–1717* (New Haven, Conn.: Yale University Press, 2002); Robert P. Wiegers, "A Proposal for Indian Slave Trading in the Mississippi Valley and Its Impact on the Osage," *Plains Anthropologist* 33, no. 120 (May 1, 1988): 191.

21. Mandeville's memorandum, 1709, C13a, vol. 2, fol. 471, ANOM.

22. Zitomersky, *French Americans, Native Americans*, 91.

23. John Francis McDermott, *Old Cahokia: A Narrative and Documents Illustrating the First Century of Its History* (St. Louis: St. Louis Historical Documents Foundation, 1949), 8.

24. Bergier from Cahokia, April 13, 1701, quoted in Palm, *Jesuit Missions*, 36.

25. Lallement, "A copy of a letter."

26. See Bergier's letter, April 13, 1701, in Palm, *Jesuit Missions,* 36.

27. Charlevoix, *Journal of a Voyage to North America*, ed. Louise Phelps Kellogg, 2 vols. (Chicago: Caxton Club, 1923), 2:171.

28. For a detailed study of this founding moment, as well as a conflict between the Jesuits and Seminarians that brought the Illinois Country to the attention of the French king for the first time, see Morrissey, "The Terms of Encounter."

29. Christopher Morris, "How to Prepare Buffalo, and Other Things the French Taught Indians About Nature," in *French Colonial Louisiana and the Atlantic World*, ed. Bradley G. Bond (Baton Rouge: Louisiana State University Press, 2005).

30. *MPA*, 3:24; Surrey, *The Commerce of Louisiana During the French Régime, 1699–1763* (New York: Columbia University Press, 1916), 338; Fortier and Chaput, "A Historical Reexamination of Juchereau's Illinois Tannery." The flourishing trade in bison hides helps us understand why the Illinois moved to this location in particular. Most likely, the location near the confluence allowed the Illinois not only access to slave markets but also to hunt in the two major bison-hunting grounds—the Illinois Valley and the Wabash—conveniently.

31. McDermott, *Old Cahokia*, 3.

32. Bienville to Minister, April 10, 1706, C^{13A}, vol. 1, fols.502–14, ANOM.

33. La Salle, Census of the Colony of Louisiana, August 12, 1708, C^{13A} vol. 2, fol. 225, ANOM.

34. See Pénicaut's Relation, in Margry, 5:427; Iberville to the Minister of the Marine, February 26, 1700, Margry, 4:364.

35. "Memoir on the Establishment of Mobile and the Mississippi," 1701(?), Margry, 4:591. This document alleged that these fur traders would "establish themselves" in the lower colony and "never return" to Illinois, but this seems like an unlikely expectation.

36. Callière and Champigny, October 5, 1701, Margry, 4:356–60.

37. Mermet to Cadillac, April 19, 1702, WHC, 16:211.

38. See Alvord, *Illinois Country*, 123.

39. Tanner, "Career of Joseph La France," 182.

40. Giraud, *A History of French Louisiana*, 81.

41. Mandeville Memoir, April 27, 1709, *MPA*, 2:49.

42. Vaudreuil and Bégon to Minister, November 15, 1713, C^{11A}, vol. 34, fol. 4, ANOM. Also WHC, 16:299, 303.

43. Ramezay to the Minister, September 18, 1714, C^{11A}, vol. 34, fols. 354–61, ANOM.

44. André Pénicaut, *Fleur de Lys and Calumet Being the Pénicaut Narrative of French Adventure in Louisiana*, ed. Richebourg Gaillard McWilliams (Baton Rouge: Louisiana State University Press, 1953), 122.

45. See "Ordinance on the trade in Illinois," October 1720, B, vol. 42 bis, fol. 391, ANOM. This ordinance makes specific reference to the practice of slave trading in Illinois in the 1720s, when it was widespread.

46. Ibid.

47. Proceedings in French Council of Marine, March 28, 1716, WHC, 16:339.

48. Pénicaut, "Narrative," in *Fleur de Lys and Calumet*, 136.

49. *JR*, 64:159.

50. Pénicaut, "Memorandum," in Margry, 5:488.

51. Mary Elizabeth Good, *Guebert Site: An 18th Century, Historic Kaskaskia Indian Village in Randolph County, Illinois* (Wood River, Ill.: Central States Archaeological Societies, 1972), 22.

52. Callière and Champigny to Seignelay, October 5, 1701, Bibliothèque Nationale, Manuscrits Français, 9292.

53. Pénicaut, "Narrative," in *Fleur de Lys and Calumet*, 138.

54. Ibid.

55. Ibid.

56. Ramezay and Bégon to French Minister, November 7, 1715, WHC, 16:332.

57. D'Artaguiette, "Journal," 67; Boisbriant, 1724, quoted in Ekberg, *French Roots in the Illinois Country*, 174; see also Charlevoix, *A Voyage to North America*, 2:206.

58. Louis XIV to De Muy, Memorandum, June 30, 1707, *MPA*, 3:56.

59. "Memoir on the Indians of Canada as far as the River Mississippi, with Remarks on their Manner of Trade," 1718, NYCD, 9:886.

60. Marest to Germon, November 12, 1712, *JR*, 66:293.

61. Ibid.

62. Marest to Germon, November 12, 1712, *JR*, 66:253.

63. Gravier, 1694, *JR*, 64:213.

64. Indeed, it is worth noting that these marriages could have happened *à la façon du pays*, which suggests that the Jesuits felt increasingly confident about them.

65. Marest to Germon, November 12, 1712, *JR*, 66:249.

66. Binneteau, 1699, *JR*, 65:67.

67. Lallement, "A copy of a letter."

68. For excellent studies of French colonial debates about intermarriage and race in the eighteenth century, see Jennifer M. Spear, *Race, Sex, and Social Order in Early New*

Orleans (Baltimore: Johns Hopkins University Press, 2009); and Aubert, "'The Blood of France.'"

69. Jean-Baptiste Colbert, 1699, quoted in Jennifer Michel Spear, "They Need Wives: Métissage and the Regulation of Sexuality in French Louisiana, 1699–1730," in *Sex, Love, Race: Crossing Boundaries in North American History*, ed. M. E. Hodes (New York: New York University Press, 1999), 41.

70. Spear, "They Need Wives," 41; memorandum on the conduct of the French in Louisiana, La Vente, 1713 or 1714, C¹³ᴬ, vol. 4, fols. 389–98, ANOM; La Mothe Cadillac on Louisiana, 1713, C¹³ᴬ, vol. 3 fol. 22, ANOM.

71. Bienville to Minister, August 20, 1709, C¹³ᴬ, vol. 2, fol. 413, ANOM.

72. Vaudreuil and Raudot to Minister, November 14, 1709, quoted in White, *The Middle Ground*, 70.

73. Vaudreuil in Aubert, "'The Blood of France,'" 457.

74. D'Artaguiette to Pontchartrain, February 12, 1710, *MPA*, 2:55–56.

75. Memorandum concerning the Illinois, 1732, F3, vol. 24, fol. 235, ANOM.

76. Spear, "They Need Wives," 44.

77. As D'Artaguiette wrote, "[sending French girls to Louisiana] is the only way I know to make the [French settlers in Louisiana] settle down." D'Artaguiette to Pontchartrain, February 12, 1710, *MPA*, 2:57–58.

78. D'Artaguiette to Pontchartrain, September 8, 1712, *MPA*, 2:72–73.

79. Cadillac wrote that among the greatest problems in the colony, the settlers gave themselves over to vice, "principally with the savage women, whom they prefer to Frenchwomen." Cadillac to minister, 1713, C¹³ᴬ, vol. 3, fol. 13, ANOM.

80. See Duclos quoted in Deliberation of the Navy Council, September 1, 1716, *MPA*, 2:218–19. Aubert, "'The Blood of France,'" 469.

81. Deliberation of the Navy Council, September 1, 1716, *MPA*, 2:218.

82. Duclos to Pontchartrain, December 25, 1715, *MPA*, 2:207.

83. Deliberation of the Navy Council, September 1, 1716, *MPA*, 2:219.

84. For this argument, see Aubert, "'The Blood of France.'" See also Belmessous, "Assimilation and Racialism."

85. Duclos to Pontchartrain, December 25, 1715, *MPA*, 2:208.

86. Deliberation of the Navy Council, September 1, 1716, *MPA*, 2:218.

87. It is important to note that although Duclos singled out Illinois women in his critique of intermarriage, his opinions were not informed by actual experience. Neither Duclos nor any of the major Louisiana officials involved in this debate had ever been to Illinois or met any of the Illinois-French families they discussed.

88. La Vente, quoted in Minutes of the Navy Council, 1716, C¹³ᴬ, vol. 4, fols. 255–57, ANOM, translation from *MPA*, 2:218–19.

89. Ibid.

90. Juchereau's tannery may indeed have created a circumstance similar to the full-scale adoption of bison hide trade among equestrian bison hunters described by Andrew Isenberg. In these cultures, the labor of hide production and meat processing for the market steadily eroded women's status and autonomy, something that might well have

happened as the Illinois produced unprecedented numbers of hides in 1703 for trade. See Isenberg, *The Destruction of the Bison*, 95–100.

91. Belmessous, "Assimilation and Racialism in Seventeenth- and Eighteenth-Century French Colonial Policy," 338.

92. For matrilineality among southeastern groups, descendants of the Mississippians, see Snyder, *Slavery in Indian Country*, 19–20, 106, 206.

93. Belmessous, "Assimilation and Racialism in Seventeenth- and Eighteenth-Century French Colonial Policy," 322–50.

94. Duclos to Pontchartrain, December 25, 1715, *MPA*, 2:207.

95. Almost all sources agree on this. Callender, "Illinois," 676; Brown, *Cultural Transformations Among the Illinois*, 237–39. This is the opposite of the kinship organization among groups where Frenchification had been such a failure previously, such as the Choctaw near Louisiana or the Iroquois and Huron near New France. All of these groups were matrilineal.

96. Callender, "Great Lakes-Riverine Sociopolitical Organization," 610.

97. Bohaker, "Nindoodemag"; Witgen, "The Rituals of Possession," 639–68. As Bohaker writes, "women generally married in from other families" into their husband's doodem. "In this cultural tradition, people inherited their nindoodemag identities from their fathers; they conceived of themselves as related to and having kin obligations toward those who shared the same other-than-human progenitor being" (25–26, 35).

98. Brown, *Cultural Transformations Among the Illinois*, 237; Callender, "Illinois," 675–76.

99. For a study that emphasizes this practice, see Sleeper-Smith, *Indian Women and French Men*.

100. For interesting studies of Godparentage in other contexts, see Raymond T. Smith, "Kinship Ideology and Practice in Latin America," in *Cleansing Original Sin: Godparenthood and the Baptism of Slaves in Eighteenth-Century Bahia*, ed. Stephen Schwartz Gudeman (Chapel Hill: University of North Carolina Press, 1984), 35–58; and Clodagh Tait, "Spiritual Bonds, Social Bonds: Baptism and Godparenthood in Ireland, 1530–1690," *Cultural & Social History* 2, no. 3 (2005): 301–27. Maria Elena Martínez has recently problematized the distinction between kinship and fictive kinship, an insight that is useful for thinking about Godparenthood in the context of Illinois. María Elena Martínez, *Genealogical Fictions: Limpieza de Sangre, Religion, and Gender in Colonial Mexico* (Stanford, Calif.: Stanford University Press, 2008).

101. Jesuits used a similar custom in the actual practice of marriage, requiring each couple to bring witnesses to endorse the marriage. Unfortunately many marriage records from this period of Kaskaskia are lost, but we have a surprisingly detailed run of baptism records that show a similar point about how marriages created relationships between individuals and to the larger community. See *FB* for the best set of marriage and baptism records available.

102. Many fine previous studies of intermarriage in the pays d'en haut have focused on individual families and family trees. See Sleeper-Smith, *Indian Women and French Men*; and Jacqueline Louise Peterson, "The People in Between: Indian-White Marriage

and the Genesis of a Métis Society and Culture in the Great Lakes Region, 1680–1830" (Ph.D. diss., University of Illinois at Chicago, 1981). The extensive baptismal records in Kaskaskia allow us to consider individual families in the context of an entire baptismal network.

103. For two good primers on the method of Social Network Analysis and its application to historical problems, see Bonnie H. Erickson, "Social Networks and History," *Historical Methods* 30, no. 3 (Summer 1997): 149–57; and David Easley and Jon Kleinberg, *Networks, Crowds, and Markets: Reasoning About a Highly Connected World* (Cambridge: Cambridge University Press, 2010). See also Claire Lemercier, Sandro Guzzi-Heeb, and Michael Bertrand, "Introduction à l'Analyse des réseaux et l'histoire: Outils, approches, problèmes," *Revista-Redes* 21 (December 2011), http://revista-redes.rediris.es/indicevol21.htm (accessed April 26, 2012). For more discussion, see Robert Michael Morrissey, "Kaskaskia Social Network: Kinship and Assimilation in the French-Illinois Borderlands, 1695–1735," *William and Mary Quarterly* 70, no. 1 (January 1, 2013): 103–46.

104. All data for this analysis and for Figure 11 are taken from *FB* baptism records and *KM*.

105. All Social Network Analysis performed with Stephen P. Borgatti, Martin G. Everett, and Lin Freeman, *Ucinet for Windows: Software for Social Network Analysis* (Cambridge, Mass.: Analytic Technologies, 2002). For visual clarity, the links on the figures produced in this chapter are simple, unweighted, directed links. This means that even though some nodes have more than one connection linking them (i.e., an individual served as godmother to another's child more than one time), the figure includes only a single line linking them together.

106. Among others, Susan Sleeper-Smith has argued influentially that godparentage often functioned instrumentally as a way for individuals—Frenchmen and Indian women alike—to increase their positions within fur trade economies throughout the pays d'en haut. See Sleeper-Smith, *Indian Women and French Men.*

107. Gravier, *JR*, 64:217.

108. Morrissey, "Kaskaskia Social Network," 127–28.

109. Marest, *JR*, 66:229.

110. Binneteau, 1699, *JR*, 65:67.

111. "Order to unite and incorporate the Country of the Savages of the Illinois under the government of Louisiana," September 27, 1717, B, vol. 39, fols. 459–459v, ANOM.

112. Ekberg, *French Roots in the Illinois Country*, 37.

113. Jay Higginbotham, *Old Mobile: Fort Louis de La Louisiane, 1702–1711* (Tuscaloosa: University of Alabama Press, 1991), 213.

114. Reglement pour l'établissement, April 15, 1721, B, vol. 43, fol.103, ANOM.

115. Etat des Officiers, December 19, 1722, B, vol. 43, fol. 272, ANOM. See also census of troops in Louisiana in 1716, which lists Illinois as receiving forty troops, C^{13a}, vol. 4 fol. 1022, ANOM.

116. Dutisné's commission, October 21, 1722, B, vol. 43, fol. 352, ANOM.

117. "Order to unite and incorporate the Country of the Savages of the Illinois under the government of Louisiana," September 27, 1717, B, vol. 39, fol. 459–459v, ANOM.

118. Vaudreuil to Minister, October, 11, 1723, *WHC*, 16:438.

119. Ekberg, *French Roots in the Illinois Country*, 40.

120. *KM*, 22:6:22:1, 22:5:10:7, 22:5:10:1–8. Note: numbers after *KM* citations represent *Year* (in 17—): *Month: Day: Document Number produced on that day.*

121. *KM*, 23:2:22:2.

122. *KM*, 22:5:10:7, 22:5:10:1–8, 22:6:22:1.

123. Ekberg, *French Roots in the Illinois Country*, 42–46.

124. Ekberg, *French Roots in the Illinois Country*, 36, 65.

125. For discussion of de Ville's proposal to move the Indians away from Frenchmen and prevent them from living "pesle mesle" together, see C¹³ᵃ, vol. 10, fols. 112–13, 115–16, ANOM. For evidence that there was little separation among French and Illinois social worlds before 1719, see, for instance, Anakapita and Massauga's appeal to Le Chat Blanc, where they describe an attack by Foxes in which a French family "and their Illinois relatives" were captured together, possibly in a shared home. *WHC*, 16:459.

126. "Extracts of Particular Letters Received from Louisiana During the Year 1721, No. 1, Letters Concerning the Illinois," AG A-2592, fols. 97–99.

127. Good, *Guebert Site*, 32.

128. Historians have credited Boisbriant with moving the Indians and French apart for the first time without acknowledging evidence that they were already moving apart by the time he arrived. As a document from 1732 has it: "The Kaskaskia, so-called by the French, drew their origin from an Indian village of the same Illinois name, who lived in this place formerly and who ceded lands to the Canadians nearly 20 to 22 years ago, and have retired a league and a half from the French, where they still are to the number of about 200 men." F3, vol. 24, fol. 235, ANOM.

129. Kaskaskia Marriages, September 20, 1724, *FB* 2: 89.

130. Kaskaskia Marriages, November 11, 1724, *FB*, 2: 101.

131. For Bourdon's "scandalous behavior," see Vaudreuil and Bégon to minister, November 15, 1713, *WHC*, 16:302–3.

132. Champigny to minister, October 14, 1698, C¹¹ᴬ, vol. 16, fols. 102–26, ANOM.

133. Vaudreuil and Bégon to Minister, November 15, 1713, C¹³ᵃ, vol. 34, fol. 4, ANOM.

134. "M. de Cadillac has been instructed to arrest the men Bourdon and Bourmont [sic] when they reach Mobile, for their scandalous conduct among the Illinois." B vol. 36, fol. 359, ANOM.

135. For arrest warrants, see Ponchartrain to Ramezay, July 13, 1715, excerpt in *Report on Canadian Archives* (Ottawa: Maclean Roger, and Company, 1899), 497.

136. An ironic postscript to Bourdon's story comes from an episode a few years later. In 1721, Diron D'Artaguiette, organizing the Illinois colonists for a campaign during the Fox Wars, called on Bourdon to round up his militia for action defending the village of Cahokia against the Foxes. Witnessing him in action, however, D'Artaguiette found Bourdon and his fellow Illinois habitants grossly underprepared for the roughness of frontier warfare. D'Artaguiette complained of "the bad Leadership of Bourdon who is not fit for

this sort of employment [fighting Indians] and is more skillful at goading oxen in plough-ing than in leading a good troop of warriors." The irony here, of course, is that Bourdon was likely more expert than anyone in the challenges of frontier warfare, having spent so much of his life as an independent and illegal operator in the slave trade and the Illinois Country. In 1721, within the empire of collaboration, Bourdon's previous identity had been buried. See D'Artaguiette, "Journal," 32. For a similar story, see Richard White's discussion of Bourgmont in "Creative Misunderstandings and New Understandings," 11–12.

137. Depositions in the Bourdon estate case, September 11, 1723, *KM*, 23:9:11:1.

138. He would leave four hundred livres to the Parish of Notre Dame at Kaskaskia and two hundred livres to the Indian mission. *KM*, 23:6:25:1.

139. See D'Artaguiette, "Journal," 76.

140. "Extracts of Particular Letters Received from Louisiana During the Year 1721, No. 1, Letters Concerning the Illinois," AG A-2592, fols. 97–99.

141. Lallement, "A copy of a letter."

142. D'Artaguiette, May 9, 1723, "Journal," 76.

143. Boisbriant, "memorandum," C13A, vol. 8, fols. 447–50, ANOM.

144. Ibid.

145. "Extracts of Particular Letters Received from Louisiana During the Year 1721, No. 1, Letters Concerning the Illinois," AG A-2592:97–99.

Chapter 5

1. Father le Petit, Missionary, to Father d'Avaugour, Procurator of the Missions in North America, at New Orleans, July 12, 1730, *JR*, 68:201–3.

2. Ibid., 203.

3. Ibid., 201–3.

4. Lallement, "A copy of a letter." Certain historians have agreed with Lallement's description, notably the ethnohistorian Joseph Jablow, who sees a transformation of the Illinois in this period to the role of "proletariat," "subordinate to the objectives of the dominant cultural influence." See Jablow, *Illinois, Kickapoo, and Potawatomi Indians*, 173.

5. From 1,500 warriors in 1710, the tribes around Kaskaskia and Cahokia were reduced by disease and the Fox Wars to approximately 700 warriors in 1722. An epidemic in Kaskaskia in the 1710s had killed many; another struck in 1723. Marest to Germon, November 12, 1712, *JR*, 66:239. By 1732, there were 200 warriors among the Kaskaskia; 100 warriors among the Metchigamea (a village closely related to the Kaskaskia and located near Fort Chartres); and 300 or 400 at Cahokia; D'Artaguiette, "Journal," 52. For good estimates, see Brown, *Cultural Transformations Among the Illinois*, 232. See also Zitomersky, *French Americans, Native Americans*.

6. Boisbriant, 1720, quoted in Joseph H. Schlarman, *From Quebec to New Orleans: The Story of the French in America* (Belleville, Ill.: Buechler, 1929), 196–98.

7. *JR*, 68:205.

8. While others "incorporated" Europeans and European empire into essentially Native political space, the Illinois partnered with empire in a more closely entangled history. For an illuminating contrasting case, see DuVal, *The Native Ground*. For a sharply different Native response to imperialism, see Hämäläinen, *The Comanche Empire*.

9. For an excellent overview of the Fox Wars, see R. David Edmunds and Joseph L. Peyser, *The Fox Wars: The Mesquakie Challenge to New France* (Norman: University of Oklahoma Press, 1993); Jablow, *Illinois, Kickapoo, and Potawatomi Indians*, chaps. 5–7.

10. White, *The Middle Ground*, 143.

11. Gilles Havard, *The Great Peace of Montreal of 1701: French-Native Diplomacy in the 17th Century* (Montreal: McGill-Queen's University Press, 2001), 186–88.

12. Vaudreuil, quoted in Rushforth, "Slavery, the Fox Wars, and the Limits of Alliance," 54.

13. Perrot, "Memoir," 260.

14. Havard, *The Great Peace of Montreal of 1701*, 175.

15. White, *The Middle Ground*, 147–48.

16. Perrot, "Memoir," 260.

17. As Brett Rushforth has written, "It was clear from the beginning that the French had a problem. New France's allies, including the Illinois, Ottawa, Ojibwa, Miami, and Huron, detested the Fox. Even as these peoples needed Fox cooperation during the Iroquois Wars, they expressed deep enmity toward their Fox neighbors, seeking their exclusion from French protection and trade." Rushforth, "Slavery, the Fox Wars, and the Limits of Alliance," 57.

18. Ibid., 58.

19. Edmunds and Peyser, *The Fox Wars*, 16.

20. Ibid., 23–24.

21. Perrot, "Memoir," 227.

22. Edmunds and Peyser, *The Fox Wars*, 24.

23. Ibid., 25.

24. The best sources for understanding this logic are in a series of correspondence between Canada officials and Illinois provincial authorities in the 1720s. See WHC, 16:200–400.

25. Although often hostile to one another, the Foxes and Sioux made alliances in 1695 and again in the 1710s. See Edmunds and Peyser, *The Fox Wars*, 77.

26. Bergier from Cahokia, April 13, 1701, in Palm, *Jesuit Missions,* 36.

27. Edmunds and Peyser, *The Fox Wars*, 62.

28. Rushforth, "Slavery, the Fox Wars, and the Limits of Alliance," 59.

29. Quoted in ibid., 61.

30. Edmunds and Peyser, *The Fox Wars*, 72.

31. Ibid., 75.

32. Dubuisson to Vaudreuil, June 14, 1712, WHC, 16:272.

33. Claude de Ramezay quoted in White, *The Middle Ground*, 160.

34. Vaudreuil and Bégon to the Minister, November 15, 1713, C11a, 34:4, ANOM, in WHC, 16:298.

35. The best account of these embarrassing setbacks to French policy is in Edmunds and Peyser, *The Fox Wars*, chap. 3. Vaudreuil to Council of Marine, October 14, 1716, C11a, 36:279, ANOM, and WHC, 16:341.

36. See Rushforth, "Slavery, the Fox Wars, and the Limits of Alliance," 62–65.

37. Vaudreuil to Council of the Marine, October 14, 1716, WHC, 16:343.

38. Vaudreuil to Council, October 28, 1719, C11a, vol. 10, 179, ANOM; WHC, 16:381.

39. Vaudreuil to French Minister, October 2, 1723, C11a, 45:136, ANOM; WHC, 16:428.

40. Vaudreuil to French Minister, October 2, 1723, C11a, 45:136, ANOM; WHC, 16:428.

41. Vaudreuil to French Minister, October 2, 1723, C11a, 45:136, ANOM; WHC, 16:428.

42. Boisbriant, 1719, quoted in Schlarman, *From Quebec to New Orleans*, 196–98.

43. Vaudreuil to Council, October 28, 1719, C11a, 40, 179, ANOM; WHC, 16:381.

44. Vaudreuil to Council, October 28, 1719, C11a, 40, 179, ANOM; WHC, 16:381.

45. Vaudreuil to Council, October 28, 1719, C11a, 40, 179, ANOM; WHC, 16:380–81.

46. Vaudreuil to Council, October 28, 1719, C11a, 40, 179, ANOM; WHC, 16:381.

47. See Vaudreuil to Minister, October 2, 1723, C11a, 45:136, ANOM; WHC, 16:429, 431.

48. For the best expression of this logic, see Le Boullenger and Kereben to Vaudreuil, January 10, 1725, C11a, 56:267, ANOM; WHC, 16:455.

49. Vaudreuil to Boisbriant, May 20, 1724, C11a, 56:255, ANOM; WHC, 16:441.

50. Vaudreuil to Boisbriant, August 17, 1724, C11a, 56:256, ANOM; WHC, 16:442.

51. De Lignery to Boisbriant, August 23, 1724, C11a, 56: 257, ANOM; WHC, 16:445.

52. Villedonné and Father Mesaiger wrote to Boisbriant on October 2, 4, and 15, 1724, letters to commandant at Kaskaskia, C11a, vol. 56, fols. 261, 262, 268, ANOM; WHC, 16:446–50.

53. Peyser and Edmunds, *The Fox Wars*, 99–102.

54. Dutisné, January 14, 1725, C11a, vol. 56, fols. 259, 268, ANOM; WHC, 16:450. See also Ekberg, *French Roots in the Illinois Country*, 48.

55. Anakapita and Massauga, and Jonachin recorded by Dutisné, January 14, 1725, C11a, vol. 56, fol. 268, ANOM; WHC, 16:458–63.

56. Dutisné to Vaudreuil, January 14, 1725, C11a, vol. 56, fol. 259, 268, ANOM; WHC, 16:451.

57. Anakapita and Massauga, and Jonachin recorded by Dutisné, January 14, 1725, C11a, vol. 56, fol. 268, ANOM; WHC, 16:457.

58. The Illinois did in fact have Fox slaves, and Illinois officials had even participated in burning several Fox slaves in 1724. Politics and rivalries between Canada and Illinois explain why the Illinois officials claimed innocence here. See Peyser and Edmunds, *The Fox Wars*, 101.

59. Le Boullenger and Kereben to Vaudreuil, January 10, 1725, C11a, 56:267, ANOM; WHC, 16:455.

60. Dutisné to Vaudreuil, January 14, 1725, C¹¹ᵃ, vol. 56, fol. 259, 268, ANOM; WHC, 16:451.

61. Ibid.

62. Ibid.

63. Ibid.

64. Le Boullenger and Kereben to Vaudreuil, January 10, 1725, C¹¹ᵃ, vol. 56, fol. 267, ANOM; WHC, 16:456.

65. Ibid.

66. Dutisné to Vaudreuil, January 14, 1725, C¹¹ᵃ, vol. 56, fol. 259, 268, ANOM; WHC, 16:451.

67. Anakapita and Massauga, and Jonachin recorded by Dutisné, January 14, 1725 C¹¹ᵃ, vol. 56, fol. 268, ANOM; WHC, 16:457.

68. Anakapita and Massauga, and Jonachin recorded by Dutisné, January 14, 1725, C¹¹ᵃ, vol. 56, fol. 268, ANOM; WHC, 16:458.

69. Anakapita and Massauga, and Jonachin recorded by Dutisné, January 14, 1725 C¹¹ᵃ, vol. 56, fol. 268, ANOM; WHC, 16:462.

70. Dutisné to Vaudreuil, January 14, 1725, C¹¹ᵃ, vol. 56, fol. 259, 268, ANOM; WHC, 16:451.

71. Of course, as Bienville wrote, collaboration was imperative, since the French were vulnerable. See Bienville to the Minister, April 22, 1734, C¹³ᵃ, vol. 18, fol. 142, ANOM.

72. "Extracts of Particular Letters Received from Louisiana During the Year 1721, No. 1, Letters Concerning the Illinois," AG 2592:97–99, 98ᵛ, ANOM.

73. For Louisiana's plans for the West, see Margry, vol. 6, chaps. 5–8, 11; on Bourgmont, see White, "Creative Misunderstandings and New Understandings," 9–14. See also Abraham Phineas Nasatir, *Before Lewis and Clark: Documents Illustrating the History of the Missouri, 1785–1804* (St. Louis: St. Louis Historical Documents Foundation, 1952), 12–20; and Barr, "From Captives to Slaves," 23–30.

74. "Extracts of Particular Letters Received from Louisiana During the Year 1721, No. 1, Letters Concerning the Illinois," AG 2592, fols. 97–99, 98ᵛ, ANOM.

75. Ramezay and Bégon to French Minister, November 7, 1715, Archives Nationales de la Marine, serie B1, vol. 8, 274; WHC, 16:332.

76. "The Company has learned . . . ," October 25, 1720, Margry, 6:316.

77. Decree of the Company, June 12, 1720, B 42:74–75, ANOM.

78. "Ordinance Regarding Prohibition of the Trade . . . without Permission of Boisbriant," October 25, 1720, B 42ᵇⁱˢ, 391, ANOM.

79. Ibid.; Wiegers, "A Proposal for Indian Slave Trading in the Mississippi Valley and Its Impact on the Osage," 191–92.

80. Investigation of Poudret, September 2, 1726, in Margaret F. Brown and Laurie C. Dean, *The Village of Chartres in Colonial Illinois, 1720–1765* (New Orleans: Published

for La Compagnie des Amis de Fort de Chartres by Polyanthos, 1977), doc K-411, pp. 891–94.

81. "Extracts of Particular Letters Received from Louisiana During the Year 1721, No. 1, Letters Concerning the Illinois," AG 2592, fols. 97–99, 98ᵛ.

82. Boisbriant to Minister, October 5, 1720, "Extracts of Particular Letters Received from Louisiana During the Year 1721, No. 1, Letters Concerning the Illinois," AG 2592, fols. 97–99, 98ᵛ.

83. Ibid.

84. Ekberg, *Stealing Indian Women*, 20. See also *KM*, 26:8:22:1, 26:10:15:1.

85. "Extracts of Particular Letters Received from Louisiana During the Year 1721, No. 1, Letters Concerning the Illinois," AG 2592, fols. 97–99, 98ᵛ.

86. Ibid.

87. This concern about alliance forming between the Foxes and Missouri Valley Indians was shared by Bourgmont by 1724. See Martha Royce Blaine, *The Ioway Indians* (Norman: University of Oklahoma Press, 1995), 31.

88. "Extracts of Particular Letters Received from Louisiana During the Year 1721, No. 1, Letters Concerning the Illinois," AG 2592, fols. 97–99.

89. "Extracts of Particular Letters Received from Louisiana During the Year 1721, No. 1, Letters Concerning the Illinois," AG 2592, fols. 97–99, 98ᵛ. See also Nasatir, *Before Lewis and Clark*, 17.

90. Ekberg, *Stealing Indian Women*, 20. To be sure, Bienville did note that "the slaves that the Missouri bring to us . . . serve very well. One doesn't even have to fear that they will desert [owing to] the great distance from their country." "Extracts of Particular Letters Received from Louisiana During the Year 1721, No. 1, Letters Concerning the Illinois," AG 2592, fols. 97–99, 98ᵛ.

91. Michael Dickey, *The People of the River's Mouth: In Search of the Missouria Indians* (Columbia: University of Missouri Press, 2011), 72. Eventually Bourgmont did make a temporary peace with the Comanche, but this did not last. See White, "Creative Misunderstandings and New Understandings," 12; and Henry Folmer, "Etienne Veniard de Bourgmond in the Missouri Country," *Michigan Historical Review* 36 (1942): 279–98.

92. "Extracts of Particular Letters Received from Louisiana During the Year 1721, No. 1, Letters Concerning the Illinois," AG 2592, fols. 97–99, 98ᵛ.

93. See Bourgmont's later participation (circa 1724) in the slave trade with the Illinois and Missouri, Margry, 6:406–7.

94. This trade continued through the 1720s, as demonstrated by an Apache chief who protested to Bourgmont in 1724, asking for the return of women captives sold to the French at Illinois. See the Apache chief quoted in Barr, "From Captives to Slaves," 25.

95. See discussion between Bienville and Boisbriant in 1720–21 regarding the separation. "Extracts of Particular Letters Received from Louisiana During the Year 1721, No. 1, Letters Concerning the Illinois," AG 2592, fol. 98.

96. Mercier and Courrier, 1735, "Plan de la Seigneurie et Establissement de la Mission Des Tamarois," in McDermott, *Old Cahokia*, 17.

97. Cécile Vidal, "From Incorporation to Exclusion: Indians, Europeans, and Americans in the Mississippi Valley from 1699 to 1830," in *Empires of the Imagination: Transatlantic Histories of the Louisiana Purchase*, ed. Peter J. Kastor and François Weil (Charlottesville: University of Virginia Press, 2009), 45.

98. David Lee Preston, *The Texture of Contact: European and Indian Settler Communities on the Frontiers of Iroquoia, 1667–1783* (Lincoln: University of Nebraska Press, 2009).

99. *JR*, 68, 201–3.

100. Like in other frontier zones, while domestic spaces were segregated, cultures in Illinois interacted "in the woods." See Merrell, *Into the American Woods*.

101. See, for example, the division of Jacques Bourdon's estate, *KM*, 23:11:8:1.

102. Bienville, 1726, *MPA*, 3:533.

103. "Louisiana Superior Council Records," *Louisiana Historical Quarterly*, 5 (1920), 378.

104. "Louisiana Superior Council Records," *Louisiana Historical Quarterly*, 5, (1920), 378; vol. 8 (1925), 275–76.

105. D'Artaguiette, "Journal," 73.

106. For guns, see *KM*, 37:1:21:1. Sophie White has made the most extensive study of material culture transformation among the Illinois in the eighteenth century in *Wild Frenchmen and Frenchified Indians*. For lists of trade goods to Illinois villages, as well as a catalog of material culture unearthed at the Guebert Site, see Good, *Guebert Site*, 8–9, 65–181.

107. D'Artaguiette, "Journal," 71.

108. Vidal, "From Incorporation to Exclusion," 76–82.

109. For this argument, see Morrissey, "I Speak it Well," 646–48.

110. Richard N. Ellis and Charlie R. Steen, "An Indian Delegation in France, 1725," *Journal of the Illinois State Historical Society* 67 (1974): 387.

111. Frank Norall, *Bourgmont: Explorer of the Missouri, 1698–1725* (Lincoln: University of Nebraska Press, 1988); the chapter "Indians in Paris" is a useful overview of the trip.

112. J. H. Elliott, *The Old World and the New, 1492–1650* (Cambridge: Cambridge University Press, 1970); John Alden and Dennis C. Landis, *European Americana: 1493–1750* (New York: Readex, 1980); Karen Ordahl Kupperman, *America in European Consciousness, 1493–1750* (Chapel Hill: University of North Carolina Press, 1995); Norall, *Bourgmont*; Gordon Sayre, *Les Sauvages Américains: Representations of Native Americans in French and English Colonial Literature* (Chapel Hill: University of North Carolina Press, 1997); Vanita Seth, *Europe's Indians: Producing Racial Difference, 1500–1900* (Durham, N.C.: Duke University Press, 2010); Alden T. Vaughan, *Transatlantic Encounters: American Indians in Britain, 1500–1776* (Cambridge: Cambridge University Press, 2006); Michael Wintroub, *A Savage Mirror: Power, Identity, and Knowledge in Early Modern France* (Stanford, Calif.: Stanford University Press, 2006).

113. Ellis and Steen dismiss these speeches in the *Mercure* as being full of simple cant. "They denigrated themselves in relation to members of the court, praised missionary efforts in Louisiana, and heaped outrageous flattery on the King. The speeches of the

Indians reveal little of their own lives and customs but do contain simple and dignified requests for assistance with the problems caused by the French presence in the Mississippi Valley." In fact, the speeches are an interesting transcript into the themes of empire by collaboration. Ellis and Steen, "An Indian Delegation in France," 387.

114. Ibid., 390.

115. Ibid., 405.

116. Ibid., 395. It is quite possible that some of these skins are the ones that wound up in the royal cabinet of objects from North America and that survive today in the collections of the Musée du Quai Branly. See Anne Vitart, "From Royal Cabinets to Museums: A Composite History," in *Robes of Splendor: Native American Painted Buffalo Hides*, by George P. Horse Capture, W. Richard West, and Anne Vitart (New York: New Press, 1993).

117. Ellis and Steen, "An Indian Delegation in France," 394.

118. Ibid., 405.

119. Ibid., 401.

120. Ibid., 399.

121. Ibid., 403.

122. Ibid., 400.

123. Ibid., 394.

124. Ibid., 400.

125. Ibid., 401.

126. Anakapita and Massauga, and Jonachin recorded by Dutisné, January 14, 1725, C^{11A}, vol. 56, fol. 268, WHC, 16:458–63.

127. Superior Council to Company Directors, March 8, 1725, C^{13A}, vol. 9, fol. 79. ANOM.

128. Ellis and Steen, "An Indian Delegation in France," 402.

129. During another point in their trip, the king also took the Illinois on a rabbit hunt, which may also have provided time for their diplomatic negotiations. Ibid.

130. Ibid.

131. Anakapita and Massauga, and Jonachin recorded by Dutisné, January 14, 1725, C^{11a}, vol. 56, fol. 268, ANOM; WHC, 16:463–66. For Bienville's new attitude about the Illinois diplomacy in 1725, see *MPA*, 3:533.

132. See "Narrative of De Boucherville," 1728, WHC, 17:48–55.

133. Joseph L. Peyser, "The 1730 Siege of the Foxes: Two Maps by Canadian Participants Provide Additional Information on the Fort and Its Location," *Illinois Historical Journal* 80, no. 3 (October 1, 1987): 147–54, doi:10.2307/40192141.

134. Edmunds and Peyser, *The Fox Wars*, 157.

135. *JR*, 68:203–5.

136. *JR*, 68:201.

137. For good examples of ethnohistory scholarship emphasizing Indians' preservation of traditional identity—their efforts to "preserve Indian identity" or "maintain their identity and independence"—see Edmunds and Peyser, *The Fox Wars*, xvii–xviii; and

Susan Sleeper-Smith, "Women, Kin, and Catholicism: New Perspectives on the Fur Trade," *Ethnohistory* 47, no. 2 (2000): 426.

138. It is important to note that Bourgmont brought a Comanche—or Padouke—slave with him to France in 1725, and she remained behind in Paris, raising a family. See Norall, *Bourgmont*.

Chapter 6

1. Edward Watts, *In This Remote Country: French Colonial Culture in the Anglo-American Imagination, 1780–1860* (Chapel Hill: University of North Carolina Press, 2006), 60–68.

2. Ibid., 63–64.

3. Gilbert Imlay, 1793, quoted in Watts, *In This Remote Country*, 67.

4. Timothy Flint, 1828, quoted in Watts, *In This Remote Country*, 71.

5. All the information in this paragraph comes from Jacques Bourdon's estate settlement. See *KM*, 23:7:1:1. For a recent and excellent study of the refined material culture of French Illinois, see White, *Wild Frenchmen and Frenchified Indians*.

6. For this Social Network Analysis, the sources are all contracts, estate settlements, and debts recorded in the Kaskaskia notarial Archives (*KM*) between 1717 and 1730. There are 190 records, yielding 2,482 connections. The graph is an "ego net" of Bourdon's connections, revealing the large number of people in his commercial network who were also commercially connected to one another.

7. Many previous works have emphasized continuities between European "peasantry" and the Illinois inhabitants. After Alvord essentially created this stereotype in his work, early social historians argued more seriously for continuing French peasant traditions in Illinois, especially Belting, *Kaskaskia Under the French Regime*. More recently, Carl Ekberg emphasizes continuity between the Old World and the New, pointing out similarities between French peasants and Illinois colonists. See Ekberg, *French Roots in the Illinois Country*, 241, 109, 123, 122, 112. For a good critique of this "gemeinschaft" emphasis in Canadian historiography, see Leslie Choquette, *Frenchmen into Peasants: Modernity and Tradition in the Peopling of French Canada* (Cambridge, Mass.: Harvard University Press, 1997), 280.

8. Choquette, *Frenchmen into Peasants*, introduction.

9. The concept of "creolization" is useful in understanding the creative adaptations and cultural and social innovations that Illinois inhabitants made in the eighteenth-century settlements. Like many scholars of "creolization," this chapter emphasizes creative innovations rather than continuities between Old World culture and colonial contexts. In Illinois, social and cultural exchange among diverse peoples, together with economic opportunism, produced an innovative, flexible culture. For influential works, see Shannon Lee Dawdy, "Understanding Cultural Change Through the Vernacular: Creolization in Louisiana," *Historical Archaeology* 34, no. 3 (June 2000): 107; Nicholas R. Spitzer, "Monde Creole: The Cultural World of French Louisiana Creoles and the Creolization of World

Cultures," *Journal of American Folklore* 116, no. 459 (2003): 57–72; Mechal Sobel, *The World They Made Together: Black and White Values in Eighteenth-Century Virginia* (Princeton, N.J.: Princeton University Press, 1987); T. H. Breen, "Creative Adaptations: Peoples and Cultures," in *Colonial British America?: Essays in the New History of the Early Modern Era*, ed. Jack P. Greene and J. R. Pole (Baltimore: Johns Hopkins University Press, 1984), 195–232; and John Smolenski, *Friends and Strangers: The Making of a Creole Culture in Colonial Pennsylvania* (Philadelphia: University of Pennsylvania Press, 2010). For the most important study that emphasizes continuities between French peasants and Illinois habitants, see Ekberg, *French Roots in the Illinois Country*.

10. Duclos to Minister, 1713, C¹³ᵃ, vol. 3, fol. 206, ANOM.

11. Company Advertisement, 1735, Nouvelles Acquisitions, 2552:161, Bibliothèque Nationale, France; see Carl J. Ekberg, "The Flour Trade in French Colonial Louisiana," *Louisiana History: The Journal of the Louisiana Historical Association* 37, no. 3 (July 1, 1996): 266.

12. Périer to Maurepas, March 25, 1731, , C¹³ᵃ, vol. 13, fol. 53, ANOM; Ekberg, "Flour Trade."

13. Salmon to Minister, May 15, 1732, C¹³ᵃ, vol. 15, fol. 133–34, ANOM.

14. Salmon to Minister, June 17, 1737, C¹³ᵃ, vol. 22, fol. 192–94, ANOM.

15. Bienville to Minister, April 26, 1738, C¹³ᵃ, vol. 23, fol. 52.

16. Le Page du Pratz, quoted in Ekberg, "Flour Trade," 273. For a still useful comprehensive study, see Surrey, *The Commerce of Louisiana During the French Régime*.

17. Minister to Salmon, September 2, 1732, Series B, vol. 57, fols. 817–18, ANOM.

18. Margaret Kimball Brown, *The Voyageur in the Illinois Country: The Fur Trade's Professional Boatman in Mid America* (Naperville, Ill.: Center for French Colonial Studies, 2002), 19.

19. D'Artaguiette, "Journal," 70.

20. Census records from throughout the first two generations of settlement are irregularly spaced (1723, 1726, 1732, 1737, 1752) but nevertheless give a fairly comprehensive view of the growth of the colony. Fortunately, three reliable and detailed censuses made on the ground by eyewitnesses in Illinois (1723, 1726, 1732) provide a fairly clear picture. These censuses are some of the most valuable sources for early Illinois history. The 1723–24 census is C¹³ᴬ, vol. 8, fols. 226–27, ANOM; the 1726 census is G1:464, ANOM. The census of 1732 is also found in G1:464, ANOM. The last two censuses include data on individual landholders and land use, in addition to many data concerning property ownership, household size, and other information. The quintessential study of the Illinois's agrarian patterns is Ekberg, *French Roots in the Illinois Country*.

21. Allan Greer, *The People of New France* (Toronto: University of Toronto Press, 1997), 28. See also Louise Dechêne, *Habitants and Merchants in Seventeenth-Century Montreal: Studies on the History of Quebec* (Montreal: McGill-Queens University Press, 1992), 152–56.

22. Boisbriant memorial, quoted in Ekberg, *French Roots in the Illinois Country*, 177. Boisbriant did not mean the tall-grass prairies, the roots of which were too dense to

plow up until the steel plows of the nineteenth century. Farming was restricted to the bottomlands.

23. D'Artaguiette, "Journal," 68.

24. I have constructed a comprehensive database of migrants to Illinois, including information on backgrounds, the rates of persistence, and other life outcomes. To build this database of Illinois migrants, I relied heavily on data in Renald Lessard, Jacques Mathieu, and Lina Gouger, "Peuplement colonisateur au pays des Illinois," *L'Ancêtre: Bulletin de la Société de généalogie de Québec* 14, nos. 6–7 (1988): 211–79. To their tables, I added all the available biographical and demographic information in the censuses from Illinois, as well as scattered information in sources such as the Kaskaskia Manuscripts and baptismal and marriage records in *FB*. In total, I identified 495 individual migrants between 1700 and 1750. Of this total, 87 are women, and 408 are men. This gives a pretty clear picture of the basic growth and "peopling" of the Illinois Country during the colonial period. For methods and ideas in the study of Atlantic world "peopling," see Choquette, *Frenchmen into Peasants*. See also Alison Games, "Migration," in *The British Atlantic World, 1500–1800*, ed. David Armitage and Michael J. Braddick (New York: Palgrave Macmillan, 2009).

25. These fifteen years witnessed by far the largest in-migration to the Illinois Country in the eighteenth century, with roughly 45 percent of known migrants arriving in this period.

26. There seem to be a small number of surviving permissions in the extant Canadian documents. See, for example, the permission granted to La Croix to settle with his wife and five children in Illinois, dated June 4, 1723, at Montreal. Canadian Archives, Call number MG8-C8, Registre des congés, 1721–26.

27. Of the 226 migrants, we know the origins of 87. Of these, 39 were from Montreal, while 17 were from Quebec, for a total of 56, or 64 percent. The origins of 28 of the migrants in this generation were in France itself. All of these French migrants arrived after 1720.

28. See Father Mercier, for example, who wrote to Seminarians in Canada to try to encourage them to send farmers. "If only twenty families would come down from Canada, that would start a parish. More than two hundred *habitants* could be wonderfully placed, and in a very short time they could live as comfortably as they do in Canada." M. Mercier, August 3, 1732, in McDermott, *Old Cahokia*, 15.

29. D'Artaguiette, "Journal," 70.

30. Liette commented on the reception of Madame Le Sueur by the curious Illinois Indians. See Liette, 338–39.

31. See Chassin to Father Bobe, July 1, 1722, *MPA*, 2:274–75. Here Chassin talks about the four or five hundred girls who have come to Louisiana, sent by the Company of the Indies. He also mentions the plan of sending Frenchwomen to Illinois from Canada.

32. White, *Wild Frenchmen and Frenchified Indians*.

33. Since we have little specific data on year-to-year births, calculating the birthrate in Illinois is impossible. But it was likely high; a continuous fragment of the Kaskaskia baptismal register survives from the period, showing a total of eighteen births between

August 1723 and April 1724. "Extract of the Register of Baptisms in the Parish of Notre Dame de Cas[kaskias], 1723–24," G1:412–412v, ANOM.

34. Quoted in Ekberg, *French Roots in the Illinois Country*, 177.

35. Ramezay and Bégon to French Minister, November 17, 1715, WHC, 16:331–32. See also notarial records and baptismal records, *FB*; See also See Margaret K. Brown and Lawrie Cena Dean, eds., *The Village of Chartres in Colonial Illinois 1720–1765*, (New Orleans: Polyanthos, 1977), D73.

36. See Chapter 5.

37. For a Fox slave held in Illinois, see *KM*, 46:3:5:1. For the best treatment of Indian slavery in Illinois, see part 1 of Ekberg, *Stealing Indian Women*. See also documents from the 1720s related to the Fox Wars and slavery in WHC, 16:445–62.

38. *KM*, 38:1:20:1.

39. See, for instance, *KM*, 48:7:15:1.

40. Barr, "From Captives to Slaves," 19–46.

41. Boisbriant memorial, quoted in Ekberg, *French Roots in the Illinois Country*, 177.

42. See Bourdon's will of 1723, which lists two black slaves, for example, *KM*, 23:6:25:1.

43. *KM*, 44:4:3:1; *KM* 37:7:2:2; *KM* 48:12:5:1; *KM* 39:3:13:1.

44. Winstanley Briggs, "Slavery in French Colonial Illinois," *Chicago History* 18 (1989): 75.

45. As one might expect, the biggest and most established holdings were in Kaskaskia, where the average holding was 59 arpents; For the concept of "movers" and "stayers," see Games, "Migration," 31–33.

46. Dechêne, *Habitants and Merchants*, 147–51.

47. Ibid., 31.

48. April 15, 1721, B vol. 43, fol. 103, ANOM.

49. Ibid.

50. Morris S. Arnold, *Unequal Laws unto a Savage Race: European Legal Traditions in Arkansas, 1686–1836* (Fayetteville: University of Arkansas Press, 1985), 11.

51. "Coutume de Paris," in G. Schmidt, "History of the Jurisprudence of Louisiana," *Louisiana Law Journal* 1 (1841–42): 9.

52. V. V. Palmer, "The Origins and Authors of the Code Noir," *Louisiana Law Review* 56 (1995): 363; Guillaume Aubert, "'To Establish One Law and Definite Rules': Race, Religion, and the Transatlantic Origins of the Louisiana Code Noir," in *Louisiana: Crossroads of the Atlantic World*, ed. Cécile Vidal (Philadelphia: University of Pennsylvania Press, 2013), 21–43.; Thomas Ingersoll, *Mammon and Manon in Early New Orleans: The First Slave Society in the Deep South, 1718–1819* (Knoxville: University of Tennessee Press, 1999), 39.

53. For a good primer on "legal pluralism," see Benton and Ross, *Legal Pluralism and Empires*. See also Tomlins, *The Many Legalities of Early America*.

54. There are actually seventy-two mixed-race babies in the baptismal records, but it is certain some were never recorded.

55. Marie-Anne Cerré, "Memoirs," in *La vie aux Illinois au XVIIIe siècle: Souvenirs inédits de Marie-Anne Cerré*, ed. Marthe Faribault-Beauregard (Montréal: Société de Recherche Historique, 1987), 8.

56. Salmon to Minister, July 17, 1732, C^{13A}, vol. 15, fol. 166, ANOM.

57. Spear, "They Need Wives," 44–45.

58. "Memorandum Concerning the Illinois Country," 1732, F3, vol 24, fol. 235, ANOM.

59. For a material culture–based argument about the assimilation of Indian women into the French agrarian society of Illinois, see White, *Wild Frenchmen and Frenchified Indians.*

60. G1:464, ANOM.

61. Elizabeth Deshayes was married to Jean Brunet Bourbonnais, the greatest property owner in the colony. Marie Quesnel's husband was Antoine Carriere, who owned eleven black slaves and eighty arpents of cleared land. Françoise La Brise was married to Jean-Bte Pottier, who also had eighty arpents and lots of livestock. For marriage and census data, see *FB*. See also *KM*.

62. These women included Deshayes, Marie Migneret, Pilet-Lasonde, Catherine Delamy, La Brise, Quesnel, and Helene Dany. With the exception of Dany, all of these women were in the top 10 percent of landowning families in Illinois, with each of their households possessing more than fifty arpents of cleared land and other capital besides. Both censuses from 1726 and 1732 are found in G1:464, ANOM.

63. See the transactions involving Kerami-Peni8aasa's estate, *KM*, 28:6:7:1, 28:6:8:1.

64. By 1732, Jacques had added another ten arpents of arable land to his estate.

65. Guillemot-Lalande had 150 arpents of property, 12 slaves, 16 cattle, and much else. See G1:464, ANOM.

66. "To the Abbé de Brizacier," October 4, 1735, B vol. 62, fol. 88.

67. *KM*, 48:8:18:1.

68. Illinois Census of 1752, LO 9, VP.

69. Hebert appears on the 1726 census as the husband of Marie Coignon, in possession of sixty arpents of land and many livestock, in addition to four black slaves. See G1:464, ANOM.

70. See *KM*, 37:7:6:1.

71. Ironically this practice resembled a similar custom practiced by the patrilineal Illinois themselves—albeit for different reasons. See Gravier's account, *JR*, 64:167.

72. *KM*, 23:9:11:1, 25:2:16:1; see also Bourdon's will, *KM*, 23:6:25:1.

73. Consider the case of Marie Chekoakia (Che8akokia). Her husband, François Cecire de Bontemps, died sometime around 1728. He was a business partner and probably close friend to a man named Jean-Baptiste Dupre, who had a son, Pierre. When François died in 1728, it was Pierre who stepped in to take the hand of the widow Marie Chekoakia, gaining control over the estate of Bontemps, his father's now deceased business partner. See *KM*, 23:9:10:4, 25:9:17:1, 26:1:29:1, 26:1:29:2; *FB*, 2:88.

74. *KM*, 21:9:13:1.

75. December 18, 1728, in *Report on Canadian Archives*, 135.

76. *KM*, 25:6:20:1. For more on this and other cases of Kaskaskia circumventing the inheritance laws of the Coutume, see Morrissey, "Kaskaskia Social Network," 143–45.

77. Memorandum Concerning the Illinois Country, 1732, F3 vol. 24, fol. 235, ANOM.

78. "To the Abbé de Brizacier," October 4, 1735, B vol. 62, fol. 88, ANOM; see also Bienville and Salmon to Minister, May 3, 1735, C¹³ᵃ, vol. 20, fols. 83–90, ANOM.

79. *Report on Canadian Archives*, 1904, 209.

80. René Tartarin's 1738 defense of intermarriage is in C¹³ᴬ, vol. 23, fols. 241–43, ANOM.

81. See, for instance, Vaudreuil to Minister, October 4, 1743, LO 26, VP.

82. Evidence for this is not extensive, although see La Vente's argument that Illinois women were "neater in the household work." The problem with the theory is that, anecdotally, several references to Indian slaves in the notarial record refer to both "laundry" and field work. See, for instance, *KM* 47:4:29:1.

83. Briggs, "Slavery in French Colonial Illinois," 74.

84. For a debate on the effect of frontier conditions on the nature of slavery in colonial Louisiana, see the contrasting interpretations of Gwendolyn Midlo Hall, *Africans in Colonial Louisiana: The Development of Afro-Creole Culture in the Eighteenth Century* (Baton Rouge: Louisiana State University Press, 1992); and Ingersoll, *Mammon and Manon in Early New Orleans*. For the Illinois Country context more specifically, the best work is Carl J. Ekberg, "Black Slaves in the Illinois Country, 1721–1765," *Western Illinois Regional Studies* 11 (1987): 265–77; Cécile Vidal, "Africains et Européens au pays des Illinois durant la période Francaise (1699–1765)," *French Colonial History* 3 (2003): 51–68, especially 64; and Briggs, "Slavery in French Colonial Illinois."

85. Memorial on Louisiana, 1722, AG, A-2592. This memorial referred specifically to the problem of mining in Illinois and recognized the near impossibility of *forcing* the Indians and blacks to mine. As the author concluded, it was necessary to get the Illinois Indians to *voluntarily* work the mines. This ethic, apparently, was the same one followed by the colonists with respect to the agricultural labor their slaves performed.

86. See Ekberg, *French Roots in the Illinois Country*, 148; Ekberg, *Stealing Indian Women*.

87. Ekberg, *French Roots in the Illinois Country*, 148.

88. Jean-Pierre Le Glaunec, "'Un Négre Nommè [sic] Lubin Ne Connaissant Pas Sa Nation': The Small World of Louisiana Slavery," in *Louisiana: Crossroads of the Atlantic World*, ed. Cécile Vidal (Philadelphia: University of Pennsylvania Press, 2013), 103–24.

89. Women like Elisabeth Philippe, Marie Françoise Lavigne-Rivard, for instance, were often godmothers to slaves in Kaskaskia. *FB*, 2:155–75.

90. *FB*, 2:155–75.

91. See Carl J. Ekberg, "Code Noir: An Introduction to Slaves and Slave Laws in French Colonial Mid America," in Carl J. Ekberg, Grady Kilman, and Pierre Lebeau, *Code Noir: The Colonial Slave Laws of French Mid-America* (Naperville, Ill.: CFCS Press, 2005), 7–8.

92. For a runaway, see *KM*, 41:3:3:1; for the infanticide, *KM*, 48:7:16:2.

93. See *KM*, 25:8:27:1. See also case against Perico, August 12–31, 1725, K-382, in Brown and Dean, eds., *The Village of Chartres in Colonial Illinois*, 853–63 (quote from 863); Ekberg, "Code Noir," 5,

94. *KM*, 38:8:20:1.

95. *KM*, 41:3:3:1, 43:5:7:2.

96. *KM*, 23:3:6:1.

97. For example, see Marie Rouensa's will, in which she manumitted her slave Bibianne. *KM, 25:6:13:1; KM*, 25:8:14:1. For other cases of emancipation, see *KM*, 26:7:26:1, 33:2:23:1; *KM*, 30:—:—:1.

98. *KM*, 33:2:23:1; Carl J. Ekberg, Grady Kilman, and Pierre Lebeau, *Code Noir: The Colonial Slave Laws of French Mid-America* (Naperville, Ill.: CFCS Press, 2005), 65.

99. *KM, 57:3:22:1.*

100. *KM*, 25:3:12:1; *KM*, 43:1:28:1; *KM*, 54:11:9:1.

101. There is very little evidence overall to glean the nature of slavery in Illinois. In the Kaskaskia Manuscripts between 1720 and 1763, roughly 182 documents pertain to African slaves. The vast majority of these are sales, wills, and transfers. Given the paucity of records, is almost impossible to write the history of individual slave lives in Illinois Country.

102. For the two authoritative treatments of the Code Noir in Illinois, See Ekberg, "Code Noir," 1–19; and Christopher Steinke, "The *Code Noir* in the Illinois Country: Slavery and the Law on a French-Indigenous Borderland," unpublished manuscript. Using all available evidence before 1750, Steinke argues that Illinois's borderland location led to a version of slavery that clashed strongly with the technical requirements of the code.

103. *KM*, 43:5:7:1.

104. *KM*, 46:10:8:1. Ekberg, Kilman, and Lebeau, *Code Noir,* 63.

105. The widespread baptism of black slaves in Illinois might in fact be considered evidence of that the Illinois population followed the terms of the code, since this was an important stipulation of article 2 of the code. C. A. Brasseaux, "The Administration of Slave Regulations in French Louisiana, 1724–1766," *Louisiana History* 21, no. 2 (1980): 148; Ekberg, "Code Noir," 9–10.

106. Brasseaux, "The Administration of Slave Regulations in French Louisiana, 1724–1766," 147–48.

107. For cases of entire slave families sold together, see, for instance, *KM* 37:12:20:1, 37:9:22:1, 41:3:24:1; 51:6:24:1. In total, there are 18 extant cases where it is certain or very probable that families were sold together.

108. Typical of these cases was that of Onesime de Fortunay, who in 1726 sold a four-year-old slave without his mother to Antoine Pelletier, dit La Plume. *KM*, 26:5:—:1. In 1757 (*KM* 57:3:14:1), the priest Joseph Gagnon willed to his godson a 10-year old boy, although his mother went to another heir. That same year (*KM* 57:11:10:1), a ten-year-old girl was given as a dowry. For other cases, see *KM* 31:2:1:1; *KM*, 37:11:2:2. 38:5:2:1; 39:1:27:2; 40:3:22:2; 40:3:29:1; 43:1:20:1; 47:3:12:1; 53:6:13:1.

109. In Illinois, evidence suggests that slave families were broken up especially frequently because of inheritance. See, for instance, *KM* 23:7:1:1.

110. *KM*, 30:12:22:2, 30:12:22:3.

111. *KM*, 30:12:22:3.

112. A similar case, not involving slaves, took place in Kaskaskia in 1723. In that year, Andre Perillaut, the garde-magasin and secretary of the colony, was convicted of murdering a drummer of the garrison. Although the crime merited death, thirty Kaskaskia Indians went to Boisbriant to beg for leniency. Perillaut's light sentence—he was back to work in 1724—reflects a similar flexibility in the application of law. "Summary of the speeches of the chiefs of two villages of savages arriving to the number of 30 to beg clemency for Sieur Perillaut," F3, vol. 24, fol. 454, ANOM; Schlarman, *From Quebec to New Orleans*, 225–31.

113. *KM*, 43:5:7:1.

114. *KM*, 39:1:12:2, 40:8:3:2.

115. *KM*, 37:5:15:1.

116. "Case Against Chetivau," April 29, 1726, K-399, in Brown and Dean, *The Village of Chartres in Colonial Illinois*, 880.

117. The nomination of guardians and transfer of estates is the most common purpose for the petitions made to the Provincial Council in the 1700s. See *KM*, 47:7:3:1 for just one typical example of this kind of case.

118. For an example of two habitants explicitly referring to the Coutume de Paris in an inheritance case, see February 16, 1727, K-420, in Brown and Dean, *The Village of Chartres in Colonial Illinois*, 907.

119. The first official notary, N. M. Chassin, was appointed by the provincial government in 1723. But by that time several men had already served unofficially as notary and created a wealth of official documents and transaction records. Technically, the clerk of council was supposed to be a different person from the notary—clerk and notary were not one and the same office. But usually in Illinois they were one and the same person, given the scarcity of persons capable of performing the job in the Illinois Country. See Margaret K. Brown and Lawrie C. Dean, "Introduction," in, *Kaskaskia Manuscripts: A Calendar of Civil Documents in Colonial Illinois*, ed. Brown and Dean (Chester, Ill.: Randolph County Archives, 1981), 6. By the 1750s, there was a distinct notary, Barrois, while the clerk was Joseph Buchet.

120. Dean and Brown calculate a total of 6,397 documents extant in the record either because they survived or because they were listed on a calendar or "notary list." Of those, 5,200 were made during the French regime. Dean and Brown, "Introduction," Table 6.

121. *KM*, 23:3:22:2. For two other petitions from Kaskaskia colonists for official titles, see *KM*, 24:2:7:1, 25:5:2:3. *KM*, 22:5:10:1, 22:5:10:2 (9 grants), 22:5:10:3, 22:5:10:4, 22:5:10:5, 22:5:10:6, 22:5:10:7, 22:5:10:8–9, 22:6:22:1, 23:6:14:1, 23:9:27:1, 24:2:7:1, 24:5:2:1, 24:5:2:2–4, 24:4:12:1–3, 24:5:20:4, 25:1:30:1.

122. Ekberg, *French Roots in the Illinois Country*, 40–41.

123. See Ekberg's great description of tenure and the "bastard manorialism" in Illinois, *French Roots in the Illinois Country*, 37–40.

124. *KM*, 37:5:7:1, 38:1:31:1, 40:7:3:1.

125. Ekberg, *French Roots in the Illinois Country*, 125.

126. Ibid., 40–41. Several of the early land concessions during the Boisbriant administration stipulate the terms of "freehold," or "fee simple," landholding. *KM*, 23:6:14:2, 24:5:12:1, 25:1:30:1; 24:5:20:4.

127. Mercier, quoted in Winstanley Briggs, "The Forgotten Colony: Le Pays Des Illinois" (Ph.D. diss., University of Chicago, 1986), 182.

128. Mercier, 1731, in McDermott, *Old Cahokia*, 17.

129. Briggs, "Forgotten Colony," 182.

130. Seminarian priests quoted in McDermott, *Old Cahokia*, 15.

131. Perier to Minister, March 25, 1731, C^{13A}, 13:47, ANOM.

132. Salmon to Minister, 1732, C^{13A}, 15:166, ANOM.

133. Collot made his journey in 1796, although his account was not published until 1826. Georges-Henri-Victor Collot, *A Journey in North America* (Paris: A. Betrand, 1826), 233.

134. Indeed, a special irony lies in how Collot critiqued the Illinois habitants' traditionalism even as he sketched the most famous colonial-era depiction of their distinctive architecture, itself a highly "creolized" cultural form. See Jay D. Edwards, "Upper Louisiana's French Vernacular Architecture in the Greater Atlantic World," *Atlantic Studies* 8, no. 4 (2011): 411–45.

135. Cerré, "Memoirs," 5.

Chapter 7

1. René Chartrand, The Forts of New France: The Great Lakes, the Plains and the Gulf Coast, 1600–1763 (Oxford: Osprey Publishing, 2010), 43.

2. Philip Pittman, *The Present State of the European Settlements on the Mississippi; with a Geographical Description of That River* (London: Printed for J. Nourse, 1770), 46.

3. Walter J. Saucier and Kathrine Wagner Seineke, "François Saucier, Engineer of Fort de Chartres, Illinois," in *Frenchmen and French Ways in the Mississippi Valley*, ed. John McDermott (Urbana: University of Illinois Press, 1969): 199–229.

4. Alvord, *The Illinois Country*, 174. A thorough study of the characters who occupied provincial posts in Illinois has not yet been undertaken. For an interesting recent prosopographical approach to imperial administrators in Louisiana and the Atlantic, see Alexandre Dubé, "Making a Career out of the Atlantic: Louisiana's Plume," in *Louisiana: Crossroads of the Atlantic World*, ed. Cécile Vidal (Philadelphia: University of Pennsylvania Press, 2013), 44–67. See also Carl J. Ekberg and Sharon Person, *St. Louis Rising: The French Regime of Louis St. Ange de Bellerive* (Urbana: University of Illinois Press, 2015).

5. November 9, 1725, C^{13A}, vol. 9, fol. 264, ANOM; see also Council of Louisiana to Directors of the Company of the Indies, November 1, 1725, *MPA*, 2:498–99.

6. November 9, 1725, C^{13A}, vol. 9, fol. 264, ANOM.

7. Note that it is not certain whether this Pierre de Liette is the same man as Pierre-Charles Liette who appears in earlier chapters. Perhaps he was, or perhaps he was Pierre-Charles's son or a more distant relative. See "Liette, Pierre-Charles de Liette," in *Dictonary of Canadian Biography*.

8. Salmon to Minister, July 17, 1732, C^{13a}, vol. 15, fol. 166, ANOM.

9. Perier to Minister, March 25, 1731, C^{13A}, vol. 13, fol. 47, ANOM.

10. For this reputation, see, for example, Loubey to Minister, May 20, 1733, C^{13A}, vol. 17, fol. 226, ANOM. See also Salmon to Minister, 1732, C^{13A}, vol. 15, fol. 166, ANOM.

11. Loubouey to Minister, May 20, 1733, C^{13a} vol. 17, fol. 226, ANOM.

12. Alvord, *The Illinois Country*, 174.

13. *KM*, 38:6:5:1.

14. Winstanley Briggs argues that Illinois politics were comparable to the town meeting politics that defined political life in New England. But since we really have no records of how parish meetings functioned, Briggs's work is highly speculative. Briggs, "The Forgotten Colony," chap. 4, and Winstanley Briggs, "Le Pays Des Illinois," *William and Mary Quarterly* 47 (1990): 30–56.

15. Perier to Minister, March 25, 1731, C13a, 13:47, ANOM.

16. Bienville to the Minister, August 27, 1734, C^{13a}, vol. 18, fol. 189, ANOM.

17. Alvord, *The Illinois Country*, 171.

18. Ibid.

19. For just one example, see *KM*, 43:9:19: 1. In 1730, records suggest that colonists were gaining land abutting the Indians' villages (see *KM*, 30:4:6:1). In the 1730s, they began buying lands in the Indians' village (*KM*, 34:5:23:1). And by the 1740s they were buying land *on the other side* of the Kaskaskia village, suggesting the extent to which they were crowding the Indians' space (*KM*, 41:2:14:2).

20. Minister to Bienville and Salmon, September 15, 1733, B vol. 59, fols. 586–87, ANOM.

21. *MPA*, 3:556.

22. Ellis and Steen, "An Indian Delegation in France," 400.

23. Minister to Bienville and Salmon, September 27, 1735, B vol. 63, fol. 601, ANOM. Another statement of this plan: Bienville and Salmon to Minister, April 11, 1734, C^{13a}, vol. 20, fol. 21, ANOM. For prohibition against wintering, see *KM*, 38:9:21:1.

24. Alvord, *The Illinois Country*, 171.

25. Minister to Bienville, October 14, 1732, ANC B vol. 57, fols. 859–62, ANOM.

26. Salmon to Minister, April 22, 1734, C^{13A}, vol. 19, fol. 45, ANOM.

27. "Analysis of Bienville's Correspondence," 1734, C^{13A}, vol. 18, fol. 225, ANOM.

28. *MPA*, 3:615.

29. Alvord, *The Illinois Country*, 175–77.

30. Ibid., 177.

31. See Vaudreuil to Minister, September 25, 1743, LO 9, VP.

32. For Vaudreuil's career, see Guy Frégault, *Le Grand Marquis: Pierre de Rigaud de Vaudreuil, et La Louisiane* (Montréal: Fides, 1966).

33. Bienville and Salmon to Minister, September 5, 1736, C¹³ᵃ, vol. 21, fol. 104, ANOM. See also Alvord, *Illinois Country*, 182.

34. Bienville and Salmon to Minister, September 5, 1736, C¹³ᵃ, vol. 21, fol. 104, ANOM.

35. Ibid.

36. "The Shawnee come and ask Bertet for a pardon for a French soldier/deserter who had been adopted among them." Vaudreuil Letterbook, November 20, 1746, LO 9, VP.

37. *MPA*, 5:776.

38. Vaudreuil Letterbook, July 22, 1743, LO 9, VP.

39. Vaudreuil Letterbook, October 4, 1743, LO 9, VP. See also Minister to Vaudreuil, October 8, 1744, ANC C¹³ᵃ, vol. 28, fol. 245, ANOM.

40. Vaudreuil Letterbook, August 4, 1743, LO 9, VP. See also Minister to Vaudreuil, October 8, 1744, C¹³ᵃ, vol. 28, fol. 245, ANOM.

41. Vaudreuil to Maurepas, October 30, 1744, LO 9, VP.

42. Vaudreuil to Maurepas, September 18, 1743, LO 9, VP.

43. Vaudreuil to Maurepas, September 22, 1743, LO 26, VP.

44. Vaudreuil to Maurepas, October 28, 1744, LO 9, VP. See also November 20, 1746, LO 9, VP.

45. Alvord, *The Illinois Country*, 201–2.

46. "Memoir on the desired borders between Canada and Louisiana," 1745, C13a, vol. 29, fol. 85, ANOM.

47. Minister to Beauharnois, April 28, 1745, WHC, 18:5–6.

48. Vaudreuil Letterbook, October 28, 1745, November 10, 1745, LO 9, VP; see also Maurepas to Vaudreuil and Le Normant, May 14, 1746, LO 73, VP.

49. Vaudreuil to Maurepas, March 15, 1747, CISHL, 29:9.

50. Vaudreuil Letterbook, March 18, 1747, LO 9, VP.

51. Bertet to Vaudreuil, October 6, 1744, C¹³ᴬ, vol. 28, fol. 248, ANOM; Minister to Bertet, January 1, 1744, B, vol. 78, fol. 8–8v, ANOM.

52. Vaudreuil Letterbook, August 4, 1743, LO 9, VP.

53. Maurepas to Vaudreuil, May 24, 1748, CISHL, 29:71.

54. Minister to Vaudreuil, October 9, 1747, CISHL 29:36; Maurepas to Vaudreuil, April 30, 1746, LO 66, VP.

55. Macarty to Vaudreuil, January 20, 1752, LO 328, VP. Here Macarty describes the trend, begun years earlier, for children to leave their parents' farms and seek opportunity elsewhere. See CISHL, 29:469.

56. Perrin collection, April 29, 1749, Illinois State Archives, Springfield.

57. Vaudreuil Letterbook, July 18, 1743, LO 26, VP.

58. Theodore Calvin Pease and Ernestine Jenison, *Illinois on the Eve of the Seven Years' War, 1747–1755* (Springfield, Ill.: Trustees of the State Historical Library, 1940), xxxv.

59. Ibid., xxi–xxii.

60. Bertet to Vaudreuil, October 8, 1744, C¹³ᵃ, vol. 28, fols. 245–50, ANOM; Vaudreuil Letterbook, November 20, 1746, LO 9, VP.

61. Vaudreuil to Maurepas, April 8, 1747, CISHL, 29:21.

62. Ibid.

63. For instance, Minister Maurepas suggested in 1746 that a new fort in the Wabash Valley was unnecessary seeing as the French were at peace with local Indians. Maurepas to Vaudreuil, October 10, 1746, LO 85, VP.

64. Maurepas to Vaudreuil, October 25, 1747, LO 108, VP.

65. Benoist to Raymond, February 11, 1750, CISHL, 29:165.

66. Ibid.

67. Vaudreuil to Maurepas, September 1, 1747, CISHL, 29:33; for Vaudreuil's further impressions about the conspiracy, see Vaudreuil Letterbooks, September 19, 1747, LO 9, VP; see also La Jonquiere to Rouille, October 15, 1750, CISHL, 29:241.

68. Pease and Jenison, *Illinois on the Eve*, xxii.

69. Benoist to Raymond, February 11, 1750, CISHL, 29:165.

70. Raymond to La Jonquiere, May 22, 1750, C^{11a}, vol. 95, fol. 394, ANOM; CISHL, 29:207–14.

71. Raymond to La Jonquiere, May 22, 1750, C^{11a}, vol. 95, fol. 394, ANOM, CISHL, 29:216. As Macarty himself later realized, "The Indians esteem people only in proportion as people give to them, or as they profit by them." Macarty to Rouille, February 1, 1752, C^{13a}, vol. 36, fols. 307, 480, ANOM; CISHL, 29:480.

72. Vaudreuil to Macarty, August 8, 1751, CISHL, 29:311.

73. Macarty to Vaudreuil, January 20, 1752, LO 328, VP; CISHL 29: 437.

74. Maurepas to Vaudreuil, April 25, 1746, LO 64, VP.

75. Michel to Rouille, January 22, 1750 CISHL, 29:165.

76. Vaudreuil to Maurepas, March 20, 1748, CISHL, 29:55.

77. Epidemic diseases in 1748–49: Vaudreuil to Rouille, September 26, 1749, CISHL, 29:103.

78. Maurepas to Vaudreuil, April 25, 1748, CISHL, 29:64; see also Maurepas to Vaudreuil, April 28, 1748, LO 127, VP.

79. Maurepas to Vaudreuil, April 1, 1748, CISHL, 29:58; Maurepas to Bertet, December 23, 1748, CISHL 29: 81–2; Maurepas to Vaudreuil, January 14, 1749, LO 163, VP. For the unrealistic buffalo wool craze in the Louisiana government, see Morris, "How to Prepare Buffalo."

80. Vaudreuil to Rouille, September 22, 1749, CISHL, 29:117.

81. Vaudreuil to Minister, report from Bertet, Vaudreuil Letterbooks, April 12, 1746, LO 9, VP.

82. Alvord, *The Illinois Country*, 228.

83. Vaudreuil to Maurepas, November 2, 1748, LO 26, VP.

84. Ibid.

85. Vaudreuil to Minister, November 2, 1748; WHC, 17:515.

86. Vaudreuil to Rouille, May 2, 1751, C^{13a}, vol. 35, fol. 90, ANOM.

87. Saucier and Seineke, "François Saucier."

88. Vaudreuil to Macarty, August 8, 1751, LO 325, CISHL, 29:295.

89. Ibid.

90. Ibid.

91. Ibid.

92. Ibid.

93. "Instructions to Saucier, the Engineer, on building Fort de Chartres," August 27, 1751, given by Vaudreuil and Michel; ANC, C¹³ᵃ, vol. 38, fol. 20, ANOM.

94. Ibid.

95. As James C. Scott has argued, this kind of information made the colony "legible" and more amenable to rational control. See Scott, *Seeing Like a State*.

96. Macarty and Buchet to Vaudreuil, January 15, 1752, CISHL, 29:556, 427.

97. The 1752 census of Illinois is in LO 52, VP.

98. Vaudreuil to Macarty, September 9, 1751, LO 309, VP; CISHL, 29:337.

99. Ibid.

100. Vaudreuil to Macarty, September 9, 1751, LO 309, VP; CISHL, 29:336.

101. La Jonquiere to Rouille, September 17, 1751, C¹¹ᵃ, vol. 97, fol. 69; CISHL, 29:354–55.

102. La Jonquiere to Rouille, September 25, 1751 C¹¹ᵃ, vol. 97, fol. 82; CISHL, 29:362.

103. For an interesting look into these events, see M. J. Morgan, "Indians on Trial: Crime and Punishment in French Louisiana on the Eve of the Seven Years' War," *Louisiana History: The Journal of the Louisiana Historical Association* 50, no. 3 (July 1, 2009): 293–319. See also Raymond Hauser, "The Fox Raid of 1752: Defensive Warfare and the Decline of the Illinois Indian Tribe," *Illinois Historical Journal* 86 (1993): 210–24.

104. Macarty to Vaudreuil, March 18, 1752, LO 338, VP; CISHL, 29:514.

105. Macarty to Rouille, June 1, 1752, 13 a, 36:309; CISHL, 29:642.

106. Macarty to Vaudreuil, January 20, 1752, LO 328; CISHL, 29:435–37.

107. Macarty to Vaudreuil, January 20, 1752, LO 328; CISHL, 29:449.

108. Macarty to Vaudreuil, January 20, 1752, LO 328; CISHL, 29:447.

109. Macarty to Vaudreuil, January 20, 1752, LO 328; CISHL, 29:449.

110. Macarty to Vaudreuil, March 18, 1752, LO 338; CISHL, 29:514.

111. Macarty to Vaudreuil, March 18, 1752, LO 338; CISHL, 29:521.

112. Others, such as Voitquoitigana and Chenguikataka, were Piankeshaw chiefs named in the proceedings. See LO 338–44, VP.

113. Or possibly Catherine Ai8insa.

114. Macarty to Vaudreuil, January 20, 1752, LO 328, VP; CISHL, 29:449; Benoist to Raymond, February 11, 1750; CISHL, 29:165.

115. See the example of Pedagogue, a Wea chief who had kin among the Illinois. CISHL 29: 164–65.

116. La Jonquiere to Rouille, September 25, 1751, C¹¹ᵃ, vol. 97, fol. 82; CISHL, 29:367.

117. Macarty to Vaudreuil, January 20, 1752, LO 328; CISHL, 29:463.

118. Vaudreuil to Rouille, April 8, 1752, C¹³ᵃ, vol. 36, fol. 66; CISHL, 29:578.

119. Vaudreuil to Celeron, April 25, 1752, LO 361, VP; CISHL, 29:607.

120. Macarty to Rouille, June 1, 1752, C¹³ᵃ, vol. 36, fol. 309; CISHL, 29:637.

121. Ibid.

122. Macarty to Vaudreuil, September 2, 1752, LO 376; CISHL, 29:687.

123. Guyenne to Vaudreuil, September 10, 1752; CISHL, 29:714.

124. Macarty to Vaudreuil, March 27, 1752, LO 339, VP; CISHL, 29:542.

125. Vaudreuil to Macarty, August 8, 1751, LO 325, VP; CISHL, 29: 295.

126. Macarty to Vaudreuil, September 2, 1752, LO 376, VP; CISHL, 29:693.

127. La Jonquiere to Vaudreuil, September 22, 1749, LO 184, VP.

128. La Jonquiere to Rouille, September 27, 1751, C¹¹ᵃ, vol. 97, fol. 90, ANOM; CISHL, 29:378.

129. Ibid.

130. Macarty to Vaudreuil, January 24, 1752, LO 330, VP; CISHL, 29:476.

131. "Instructions to Saucier, the Engineer, on building Fort de Chartres," August 27, 1751, given by Vaudreuil and Michel, C¹³ᵃ, vol. 38, fol. 20, ANOM; CISHL, 29:330.

132. *KM*, 39:3:1:1–3, 39:3:2:1–3, 39:3:4:1.

133. "Instructions to Saucier, the Engineer, on building Fort de Chartres," August 27, 1751, given by Vaudreuil and Michel, C¹³ᵃ, vol. 38, fol. 20, ANOM; CISHL, 29:330.

134. *KM*, 51:12:21:1, 51:12:27:1, 55:11:23:1.

135. Macarty and Buchet to Vaudreuil, January 15, 1752, LO 327, VP; CISHL, 29:425.

136. "The economy which we cannot too much recommend to him." See "Instructions to Saucier, the Engineer, on building Fort de Chartres," August 27, 1751, given by Vaudreuil and Michel, C¹³ᵃ, vol. 38, fol. 20, ANOM; CISHL, 29:330.

137. Saucier to Vaudreuil, January 20, 1752, LO 329, VP.

138. The desertions in 1752 alone amounted to twenty-eight soldiers. In the whole decade beginning in 1750, there were seventy-nine desertions, representing at least 27 percent of a now much larger military population in Illinois. Among the many documents detailing this problem: *KM*, 52:2:29:1, 52:5:17:1, 52:6:18:1, 52:6:30:1, 53:11:28:1; Vaudreuil to Rouille, April 8, 1752, C13a, 36:81, ANOM; Vaudreuil to Rouille, September 28, 1752, LO 395 ,VP; and especially "Criminal Proceedings against the Soldiers who deserted, March 6, 1752, Caskaskias," C¹³ᵃ, vol. 36, fols. 102–11, ANOM; C¹³ᵃ vol. 37, fol. 191, ANOM.

139. Baudouin to De L'Isle Dieu, June 28, 1754, CISHL, 29:873.

140. Macarty to Vaudreuil, January 20, 1752, LO 328, VP; CISHL, 29:469.

141. Macarty to Vaudreuil, March 18, 1752, LO 338, VP; CISHL, 29:525.

142. Macarty to Vaudreuil, March 18, 1752, LO 338, VP; CISHL, 29:526.

143. "I should not leave you ignorant of a report which is spread about here, that the insubordination of the inhabitants was carried to a point at which you had to put the troops under arms against them." Vaudreuil to Macarty, April 28, 1752, LO 365, VP; CISHL, 29:620.

144. Macarty to Vaudreuil, March 18, 1752, LO 338, VP; CISHL, 29:527.

145. Macarty to Vaudreuil, March 18, 1752, LO 338, VP; CISHL, 29:526.

146. Ibid.

147. Vaudreuil to Macarty, April 28, 1752, LO 365, VP; CISHL, 29:619.

148. Ibid.

149. Vaudreuil to Macarty, April 28, 1752, LO 365, VP; CISHL, 29:620.

150. Ibid.

151. La Jonquiere to Rouille, September 25, 1751, C^{11a}, vol. 97, fol. 82, CISHL, 29:361.

152. Macarty to Vaudreuil, September 2, 1752, LO 376, VP; CISHL, 29:654.

153. Macarty to Vaudreuil, September 2, 1752, LO 376, VP; CISHL, 29:655.

154. Macarty to Vaudreuil, September 2, 1752, LO 376, VP; CISHL, 29:658.

155. Ibid.

156. The description of this affair comes from Guyenne to Vaudreuil, September 10, 1752, CISHL, 29:712–22; and Hauser, "The Fox Raid of 1752."

157. Macarty to Vaudreuil, September 2, 1752, LO 376, VP; CISHL, 29:658.

158. Macarty to Vaudreuil, September 2, 1752, LO 376, VP; CISHL, 29:664, 672.

159. Macarty to Vaudreuil, September 2, 1752, LO 376, VP; CISHL, 29:680.

160. Macarty to Vaudreuil, September 2, 1752, LO 376, VP; CISHL 29:687.

161. De Guyenne to Vaudreuil, September 10, 1752, LO 312, VP; CISHL, 29:718.

162. De Guyenne to Vaudreuil, September 10, 1752, LO 312, VP; CISHL, 29:722.

163. De Guyenne to Vaudreuil, September 10, 1752, LO 312, VP; CISHL, 29:722.

164. Macarty to Vaudreuil, September 6, 1752, CISHL, 29:705.

165. De Guyenne to Vaudreuil, September 10, 1752, LO 312, VP; CISHL, 29:720.

166. Ibid.

167. De Guyenne to Vaudreuil, September 10, 1752, LO 312, VP; CISHL, 29:724.

168. De Guyenne to Vaudreuil, September 10, 1752, LO 312, VP; CISHL, 29:724.

169. Baudouin to De L'Isle Dieu, June 28, 1754, C^{11a}, vol. 99, fol. 476; CISHL, 29:872.

170. Baudouin to De L'Isle Dieu, June 28, 1754, C^{11a}, vol. 99, fol. 476; CISHL, 29:872–74.

171. Baudouin to De L'Isle Dieu, June 28, 1754, C^{11a}, vol. 99, fol. 476; CISHL, 29:873, 874.

172. Kelerec to minister, June 23, 1754, C^{13a}, vol. 38, fol. 79, ANOM; see also C^{13a}, vol. 38, fol. 134, ANOM.

173. After Vaudreuil left for Canada, the uniquely detailed correspondence relating to colonial Illinois ends, and we are left with the normal administrative correspondences to and from Louisiana and France, contained in the ANOM C13 and F series. Unfortunately these sources are particularly sparse for the remainder of the French regime.

Chapter 8

1. Colin G. Calloway, *The Scratch of a Pen: 1763 and the Transformation of North America* (New York: Oxford University Press, 2007).

2. The best treatment of Pontiac's rebellion is Gregory Evans Dowd, *War Under Heaven: Pontiac, the Indian Nations, & the British Empire* (Baltimore: Johns Hopkins University Press, 2002). For an excellent study of British imperial discussions related to the West, see Jack M. Sosin, *Whitehall and the Wilderness: The Middle West in British Colonial Policy, 1760–1775* (Lincoln: University of Nebraska Press, 1961). Still useful on

British views of the West is Clarence Walworth Alvord, *The Mississippi Valley in British Politics: A Study of the Trade, Land Speculation, and Experiments in Imperialism Culminating in the American Revolution* (Cleveland, Arthur Clark Company, 1917). See Lords of Trade to Johnson, July 11, 1766, CISHL, 11:336.

3. Sosin, *Whitehall and the Wilderness*, 101.

4. See "Articles of Agreement of the Illinois Company, March 29, 1766," CISHL, 11:203.

5. See Johnson to W. Franklin, May 3, 1766, CISHL, 11:224. See also "Reasons for Establishing a Colony in the Illinois," 1766, W. Franklin, CISHL, 11:248. Also see "The Expediency of Securing our American Colonies by Settling the Country adjoining the River MISSISSPPI, and the Country upon the OHIO, CONSIDERED," CISHL, 10:140–41.

6. For the best discussion of imperial officials' reluctance to establish colonies in the West, and their reasons, see Sosin, *Whitehall and the Wilderness*, chap. 1, chap. 4.

7. A study dedicated to the changing identities of colonists and communities in the borderlands of the Mississippi Valley in the Age of Revolutions would be a welcome contribution. For influential works about "flexible" identities between governments in other times and places, see Andrés Reséndez, *Changing National Identities at the Frontier: Texas and New Mexico, 1800–1850* (New York: Cambridge University Press, 2004); Lisbeth Haas, *Conquests and Historical Identities in California, 1769–1936* (Berkeley: University of California Press, 1995); and Peter Sahlins, *Boundaries: The Making of France and Spain in the Pyrenees* (Berkeley: University of California Press, 1989). See also Robert Michael Morrissey, *Bottomlands and Borderlands: Empires and Identities in the Illinois Country, 1673–1785* (Ph.D. diss., Yale University, 2006), chap. 8.

8. See "Instructions to John Hay to explore Illinois Country," New York, May 2, 1774, Haldimand Papers, Document 213, Chicago History Museum.

9. Alvord, *The Illinois Country*, 239.

10. Ibid., 262.

11. Calloway, *The Scratch of a Pen*, 72–76.

12. Dowd, *War Under Heaven*, 169.

13. "Should the French succeed in establishing a colony there (which they probably will, as it is in so fine a Country) and we have not another to Balance it, in that Part of the World, the Consequences may be very prejudicial to the British Interest." "Reasons for Settling a Colony in the Illinois," 1766, CISHL, 11:251.

14. Calloway, *The Scratch of a Pen*, 75.

15. Extract of a letter of M. Desmazellieres to d'Abbadie, March 14, 1764, CISHL, 10:235–36.

16. Neyon de Villiers to Loftus, April 20, 1764, CISHL, 10:244. For his influence among the Indians of Illinois, see Neyon de Villiers to d'Abbadie, December 1, 1763, CISHL, 10:54.

17. Croghan to Lords of Trade, June 8, 1764, CISHL, 10:257.

18. Dowd, *War Under Heaven*, 170.

19. Croghan to Lords of Trade, June 8, 1764, CISHL, 10:257.

20. D'Abbadie's Journal, July 1764, CISHL, 10:186.

21. Gage to Halifax, July 13, 1764, CISHL, 10:283.

22. Clarence Edwin Carter, *Great Britain and the Illinois Country, 1763–1774* (Washington, D.C.: American Historical Association, 1910), 59–60.

23. Jablow, *Illinois, Kickapoo, and Potawatomi Indians*, 237–50.

24. Ulloa quoted in Aron, *American Confluence*, 60. See also Sir William Johnson's thoughts about weaning the Illinois from the French interest in this period. "If these Indians are properly Treated I have good hopes they will be weaned from their Dependence upon and Friendship for the French Inhabitants of that Illinos Country." Jablow, *Illinois, Kickapoo, and Potawatomi Indians*, 247.

25. Fraser to Haldimand, May 4, 1766, CISHL, 11:230.

26. Ibid.

27. George Croghan, "Journal," August 1, 1765, CISHL, 11:37.

28. Ibid., 11:36.

29. William Johnson to Lords of Trade, November 16, 1765, CISHL, 11:118–19.

30. Sterling wrote that upon his arrival in Illinois, he "found no judges or police." Sterling to Gage, October 18, 1765, CISHL, 11:109.

31. Eddingstone to Anonymous, October 17, 1765, CISHL, 11:106.

32. "Lord Barrington's Plan for the West," May 10, 1766, CISHL, 11:239.

33. Sterling to Gage, October 17, 1765, CISHL, 11:109.

34. Sterling to Gage, December 15, 1765, CISHL, 11:127.

35. D'Abbadie to minister, September 30, 1764, CISHL, 10:316.

36. Ulloa quoted in Aron, *American Confluence*, 59.

37. Ibid., 60.

38. Aron, *American Confluence*, 64–65.

39. Jablow, *Illinois, Kickapoo, and Potawatomi Indians*, 266. See also Louis Houck, *Spanish Regime in Missouri*, 2 vols. (Chicago: R. R. Donnelly, 1909), 1:74.

40. Jeffrey Amherst, quoted in Aron, *American Confluence*, 55.

41. Sosin, *Whitehall and the Wilderness*, 101, 113.

42. Carter, "Great Britain and the Illinois Country," 56–60.

43. Several of Cole's account books survive in BWM. The one quoted here is dated September 26, 1767.

44. Cole's Account Book for Indians, September 26, 1767, BWM.

45. Ibid.

46. Ibid.

47. Reed to Gage, October 28, 1767, GP.

48. Carter, "Great Britain and the Illinois Country," 52.

49. Reed to Gage, July 21, 1767, GP.

50. Reed to Gage, October 5, 1767, GP.

51. See Morgan's account books, BWM, which detail his spending in the colony.

52. See wages for J. Baptiste LaCroix and others, George Morgan's Account Book, July 19, 1770, BWM.

53. See Morgan's Slave Account Book, 1767–1768, BWM.

54. Gage to Reed, July 15, 1767, GP.

55. Aron, *American Confluence*, 57–58.

56. Carter, "Great Britain and the Illinois Country," 47.

57. "Proclamation of Gage to the Inhabitants of the Illinois," 1765, CISHL, 10:396.

58. Ibid.

59. Sterling to Gage, October 18, 1765, CO5, 122.

60. Carter, "Great Britain and the Illinois Country," 48–49.

61. Memorial of the Illinois French to General Gage, January 16, 1766, CO5, 84.

62. Sterling to Gage, December 15, 1765, CISHL, 11:124.

63. Sterling to Gage, December 15, 1765, CO5, 84.

64. Gage to Reed, July 22, 1767, GP.

65. "Recueil," American Series, vol. 138, item 18. Despite its importance, no scholar has written about the "Recueil." It forms the main archive for the discussion that follows.

66. "Pittman addresses the Illinois Traders," August 12, 1764, CISHL, 10:299.

67. Although the Illinois colonists cited the situation in Canada approvingly in their writings, this is ironic. Newly British subjects in Quebec had mixed success under new British laws. See Michel Morin, "Les revendications des nouveaux sujets, francophones et catholiques, de la Province de Québec, 1764–1774," in Essays in the History of Canadian Law: Quebec and the Canadas, ed. Blaine Baker and Donald Fyson (Toronto: Osgoode Society, 2013), 131–86.

68. As merchants, and as members of the Illinois Company, which was lobbying for a land grant in the Illinois, Baynton, Wharton and Morgan also supported the creation of a civil government; see CISHL, 11:207. See Baynton to Rumsey, March 1, 1768, CISHL, 16:181.

69. Lords of Trade to George III, September 3, 1766, CISHL, 11:371.

70. Gage to Reed at Fort de Chartres, March 8, 1767, GP.

71. Gage to Reed, April 14, 1767, GP.

72. Ibid.

73. Reed to Gage, October 28, 1767, GP.

74. George Morgan, December 20, 1767, George Morgan Letterbook, BWM.

75. Reed to Gage, October 28, 1767, GP.

76. Gage to Haldimand, April 26, 1768, GP.

77. Reed to Gage, October 5, 1767, GP.

78. Fraser to Haldimand, May 4, 1766, CISHL, 11:228.

79. Carter, "Great Britain and the Illinois Country," 60–61; Morgan to Baynton and Wharton, December 10, 1767, Morgan Letterbook, BWM.

80. Morgan to Baynton and Wharton, December 10, 1767, Morgan Letterbook, BWM.

81. For difficulties emerging within Spanish Illinois, where "The French inhabitants appear to be so much disgusted," see Gage to Hillsborough, October 4, 1768, CO5.

82. See Illinois Company Correspondence from 1766, CISHL 10: 248–57; see also Morgan to Baynton and Wharton, February 1768, CISHL, 16:163.

83. David Zaret, *Origins of Democratic Culture: Printing, Petitions, and the Public Sphere in Early-Modern England* (Princeton, N.J.: Princeton University Press, 2000), 86.

84. For a brilliant treatment of how French colonists used their own traditions of petition to interact with the new British administration and monarch in Quebec after the Seven Years' War, see Hannah Weiss Muller, "From *Requête* to Petition: Monarchical Culture between the French and British Empires," paper presented at the symposium "Law and the French Atlantic," Newberry Library, Chicago, October 2012, 2–3.

85. See *KM*, 23:3:22:2, 38:6:4:1, 39:7:30:1. Most petitions in the Kaskaskia Manuscripts pertained to local administrative matters. But they nevertheless reflect the colonists' familiarity with this tool and the way in which colonists had grown used to making requests of government and collaborating with government power.

86. Petition of the Inhabitants of Illinois to Mr. Gage, 1767, "Recueil," 1:1–5.

87. Ibid.

88. Ibid.

89. Ibid. After writing this petition with Morgan's help, the habitants later protested that the final draft was altered by Morgan against their will. Nevertheless, from this beginning, their petition campaign grew. See "Recueil," 1:3–4.

90. Rumsey to Governor Franklin, January 30, 1768, BWM. Also, Morgan to Baynton and Wharton, February 1768, CISHL, 16:163. "They have appointed Mr. Rumsey and myself to forward this petition to Governor Franklin to inclose and recommend it to the Board of Trade." Morgan Letterbook, BWM. A copy of the petition wound up in the company papers of Baynton, Wharton, and Morgan. See BWM, reel 6.

91. Forbes to Gage, April 15, 1768, GP.

92. See especially Gage's reaction to Reed's actions. Gage to Reed, August 10, 1767., GP.

93. Gage to Reed, July 15, 1767, GP.

94. Forbes to Gage, April 16, 1768, GP.

95. Forbes was resentful of the habitants: "They have indeed given many proofs of their insolent and mutinous disposition, even when the French were masters of this Country." Forbes to Gage, April 15, 1768, GP.

96. Mémoire of French inhabitants of Kaskaskia to Forbes and Gage, April 15, 1768, GP.

97. Petition of Illinois inhabitants to Gordon Forbes, 1768, "Recueil," 1:6. An irony here is that the provincial government in Illinois under the French regime had in fact been led in part by military officers. In denying the previous establishment of "military discipline" under the French regime, then, the habitants were implying a history of autonomy, which was technically false.

98. Forbes to Gage, April 15, 1768, GP.

99. Petition of Illinois inhabitants to Gordon Forbes, 1768, "Recueil," 1:8.

100. Ibid.

101. Ibid.

102. Ibid.

103. Indeed, Gage's instructions to Wilkins encouraged the new commander to treat the Illinois French "with kindness and Moderation and on no account to suffer them to be ill treated or in any shape injured in their persons or properties by those under your command." Gage to Commanding officer at Fort Chartres, April 2, 1768, GP.

104. "Article V: Observation," "Recueil," 1:16.

105. Gage to Wilkins, May 25, 1768, GP.

106. Max Savelle, *George Morgan: Colony Builder* (New York: Columbia University Press, 1932), 45.

107. Gage to Shelburne, April 24, 1768, CISHL, 16:247–48.

108. After paying one thousand livres to trade, one Illinois trader was ignored. See "Recueil," 1: 31–32.

109. Morgan to Williamson, January 20, 1768, Morgan Letterbook, BWM.

110. "Recueil," 1:21.

111. "Recueil," 1:21–22.

112. Savelle, *George Morgan*, 47, 65–68.

113. "Recueil," 1:22.

114. Petition of Illinois inhabitants to John Wilkins, October 5, 1768, "Recueil," 1: 26–28.

115. See the court record in CISHL, 16:455–74.

116. Petition of the inhabitants, December 6, 1768, Article XVI, "Recueil," 1: 39–50.

117. Petition to General Gage, Article XXVII, "Recueil," 1:77–85.

118. Butricke to Barnsley, February 12, 1769, quoted in Carter, "Great Britain and the Illinois Country," 68.

119. Petition to General Gage, Article XXVII, "Recueil," 1:77–82. It is fascinating that the colonists themselves were here affirming the power of imperial authorities to create a uniform law, even as they defended French customary "legalities" in the colony. For "legalities" versus "law," see Christopher L. Tomlins, "The Many Legalities of Colonization: A Manifesto of Destiny for Early American Legal History," in *The Many Legalities of Early America*, ed. Bruce H. Mann and Christopher L. Tomlins (Chapel Hill: University of North Carolina Press, 2001), 3.

120. Petition of the inhabitants to Wilkins, December 6, 1768, "Recueil," 1:41–43.

121. See "Recueil," 1:50–77.

122. "Recueil," 1:23–24.

123. For Blouin's protests against the technical operations of the court, see Article 25–7, "Recueil," 1:50–88.

124. In fact, Blouin had one more serious run-in with the British administration. One of his trading vessels was seized by Spanish officials, and since Blouin was an English subject, he hoped for English help in seeking its return. See his petition, Daniel Blouin, Louis Viviat, "A summary account of what is contained in sundry papers relative to the Seizure of a Boat under an English Pass seized on the 20th May 1769 at English Manchac, by Order of Monsieur Aubry, Governor of Louisiana for His Most Christian Majesty, with Observations" (New York and Kaskaskia, June 1771), GP.

125. At least some of Clajon's time in New York was spent teaching French. See E. M. Rodrigue, "French Educators in the Northern States During the Eighteenth Century," *French Review* 14, no. 2 (December 1940): 95–97.

126. The first mention of Clajon in the documents is in 1768, when Captain Forbes wrote that he was "a most insolent and insignificant little fellow . . . who does everything in his power to sow sedition among the subjects on our side of the river." Forbes to Gage, April 15, 1768, GP. For more details about him, see Clajon's own comments, Clajon to Gage, February 11, 1769, "Recueil," 2:124–34.

127. "Order of Arrest of Messieurs Blouin and Clajon," January 3, 1769, "Recueil," 1:85–86.

128. Order of Arrest, January 3, 1769, Article 32, "Recueil," 1:92–93.

129. They also wrote to the Spanish authorities on the west side of the river to seek their intercession on Clajon's behalf. See Blouin et al. to M. de St. Ange, January 16, 1769, "Recueil," 1:102.

130. See "Request of some Residents at the Court of Judicature on the Imprisonment of Blouin and Clajon," February 1769, "Recueil," 1:121–22.

131. See Article 21, Recueil 2:184–85.

132. The best account of these affairs is in Dowd, *War Under Heaven*, 260–61.

133. Wilkins order for the militia, July 19, 1769, "Recueil," 2:157–59.

134. Habitants to Wilkins on the subject of the militia, April 27, 1770, "Recueil," 2:165–69.

135. Clajon to Wilkins, January 26, 1769, "Recueil," 1:103–4; Clajon to Gage, August 20, 1770, "Recueil," 2:179–81.

136. "Representation of Several Habitants to the Court of Judicature in Favor of Mr. Clajon," March 4, 1769, Recueil 2:143–44.

137. See "Recueil," part 2, for the escalating conflict and numerous petitions.

138. Wilbur E. Meneray, *The Rebellion of 1768: Documents from the Favrot Family Papers and the Rosamonde E. and Emile Kuntz Collection* (New Orleans: Howard-Tilton Memorial Library, 1995); Dawdy, *Building the Devil's Empire*, chap. 6.

139. Gage to Haldimand, New York, September 13, 1771, Haldimand Papers, Illinois History Survey. The understanding of the Illinois as rebellious was widespread. See CISHL, 16:497–98.

140. Hillsborough to Gage, December 9, 1769, CISHL, 16:638.

141. Habitants' petition to Gage, August 24, 1770, "Recueil," 2:191–93.

142. Gage to Hillsborough, September 2, 1772, CO5, 90; Gage to Haldimand, January 5, 1774, Haldimand Papers, Illinois History Survey.

143. No historian has ever written about the "Recueil," and little is known about it. It seems clear that Blouin and Clajon had worked on this document for months in 1769–70 and might have sent earlier copies to New Orleans, but those never made it to Gage in New York, necessitating that they bring the document themselves.

144. For some of Clajon's discussion of "Machiavellianism," and the British constitution, see Clajon to Gage, February 11, 1769, "Recueil," 2:128–33.

145. Blouin to Gage, February 12, 1769, "Recueil," 2:134–38.

146. "Memoire du Sieur Blouin," July 9, 1771, GP.

147. See ibid.

148. Daniel Blouin to Dartmouth, October 6, 1773, CO5, 74.

149. Ibid.

Conclusion

1. See Clarence Alvord's special introduction in Blouin, Clazon [*sic*], and de Rastel Rocheblave, *Invitation sérieuse*. For speculation about the actual publication of the pamphlet, see Alvord's bibliographical essay, 49–53.

2. Blouin, Clazon [*sic*], and de Rastel Rocheblave, *Invitation sérieuse*. For a good translation, see Brauer, trans., "Eamest Invitation," 261–68.

3. Brauer, trans., "Earnest Invitation," 262.

4. Ibid., 263.

5. Ibid., 266.

6. Ibid., 267.

7. Ibid., 262.

8. Ibid., 263, 266.

9. Printed in CISHL, 10:146.

10. Pittman, *The Present State of the European Settlements*, 42–43.

11. Gage to Haldimand, New York, May 18, 1772, Haldimand Papers, 21665:46, Illinois Historical Survey.

12. Alvord, *The Illinois Country*, 289.

13. Gage to Haldimand, New York, May 18, 1772, Haldimand Papers, 21665:46, Illinois Historical Survey. For a good discussion, see Sosin, *Whitehall and the Wilderness*, 221.

14. Gage to Hillsborough, July 1, 1772, CO5, 90.

15. Gage to commandant [Wilkins?], April 2, 1768, GP.

16. Gage to Wilkins, August 24, 1769, GP. This was not the only time that the British command compared their newly adopted Illinois subjects to the defiant Acadians. In 1766, Lord Barrington wrote to express his fear that the middle Mississippi Valley could become a hostile French-Indian republic. As Barrington wrote, "The most obvious Reasons for keeping a Garrison at Fort Chartres are, that there is a French Settlement in the Country of the Illinois, & the Inhabitants may possibly irritate the Indians of those parts against the English if not restrained by some force; Or if they should be left to themselves they may in time like the Acadians, assume a kind of independency." See "Barrington's Plan for the West, May 10, 1766," CISHL, 11:239.

17. John Mack Faragher, *A Great and Noble Scheme: The Tragic Story of the Expulsion of the French Acadians from Their American Homeland* (New York: Norton, 2005). See also Christopher Hodson, *The Acadian Diaspora: An Eighteenth-Century History* (New York: Oxford University Press, 2012).

18. Gage to Hillsborough, May 6, 1772, CO5, 90.

19. Hillsborough to Gage, April 18, 1772, CO5, 90.

20. Hillsborough to Gage, July 4, 1772, CO5, 90.

21. For Illinois actions against the British at Fort de Chartres in this period, see Jablow, *Illinois, Kickapoo, and Potawatomi Indians*, 275–77.

22. Gage to Hillsborough, July 1, 1772, CO5, 90.

23. Ibid.

24. Hamilton to Gage, August 8, 1772, CO5, 90.

25. Ibid.

26. Gage to Dartmouth, January 6, 1773, CO5, 90.

27. Ibid.

28. Dartmouth to Gage, November 4, 1772, CO5, 90.

29. Gage to Dartmouth, January 6, 1773, CO5, 90.

30. Gage to Hillsborough, September 2, 1772, CO5, 90.

31. Pownall to Gage, October 7, 1772, CO5, 90.

32. Dartmouth to Gage, March 1773, Haldimand Papers, Illinois Historical Survey.

33. Another thing that pressured the British government to act was the court case that made it legal to buy land from Indians, which made it clear that new settlements would soon begin in the Illinois Country. Haldimand to Gage, May 4, 1774, Haldimand Papers, Illinois Historical Survey.

34. "A Civil establishment at the Illinois has been very long an object of consideration; and as I have comprehended the Matter, the only obstacle towards the Completion of it, has been the Difficulty of forming a Government of small Expence, and suitable to their Situation and Circumstances. It was in consequences of Orders on this head transmitted to the Officer Commanding, that the Inhabitants of the Illinois, made the Propositions your Lordship mentions, and I do not recollect that it was a measure first suggested by themselves." Gage to Dartmouth, May 5, 1773, CO5, 90.

35. "A Sketch of a Government Proposed to the Inhabitants of the British Post of the Illinois Country," June 17, 1773, Dartmouth Papers, Illinois Historical Survey.

36. Daniel Blouin to Dartmouth, October 6, 1773, CO5, 74.

37. Ibid.

38. Daniel Blouin to Lord Dartmouth, November 4, 1773, CO5, 74.

39. Evidently Gage had in fact brought the documents with him, as requested. Unbelievably, Dartmouth called these extremely long and detailed reports "very general in their charges."

40. Dartmouth to Blouin, December 1, 1773, CO5, 74.

41. It is also possible that Dartmouth and others in the administration were reacting partly to the 1773 circulation in the colonies of news of the Pratt-Yorke decision, which many interpreted as nullifying the Proclamation of 1763's ban on purchasing land from Indians. In response to this, British speculators began insisting that their land claims in the West were valid, and William Murray became notable for buying land in Illinois. See Alvord, *The Illinois Country*, 301–5.

42. Sosin, *Whitehall and the Wilderness*, 242.

43. Alvord, *The Illinois Country*, 312.

44. Ibid., 319.

45. Ibid., 326.

46. Perhaps the breakdown in order in Illinois in this period helps explain the motives of Marianne, an Indian slave in Ste. Genevieve, whose decision to run away in 1773 prompted a fascinating investigation. See Ekberg, *Stealing Indian Women*, part 2.

47. See Alvord, *Illinois Country*, 318, for the best summary of this period.

48. John Montgomery quoted in Alvord, *The Illinois Country*, 346.

49. Gibault to Bishop, June 6, 1786, in Clarence Walworth Alvord, ed., *Kaskaskia Records, 1778–1790* (Illinois State Historical Library, 1909), 542.

50. Patrick Griffin, *American Leviathan: Empire, Nation, and Revolutionary Frontier* (New York: Hill and Wang, 2007).

51. Alvord, *Illinois Country*, 372.

52. As they did in the case of Blouin and Clajon in the 1770s, the remaining Illinois habitants deputized an emissary—Bartolemi Tardiveau—to lobby for land titles from the new U.S. government in the 1780s. See David Paton Dewar, "George Morgan's American Life, 1743–1810" (Ph.D. diss., University of Kansas, 2005), 225–31.

53. For a good overview of the "exclusion" of Illinois from coming American society, see Vidal, "From Incorporation to Exclusion," 82–83.

54. Jablow, *Illinois, Kickapoo, and Potawatomi Indians*, 282; *Michigan Pioneer and Historical Collections*, 10:273.

55. Jablow, *Illinois, Kickapoo, and Potawatomi Indians*, 286.

56. Ibid., 289.

57. Alvord, *Illinois Country*, 331.

58. Jablow, *Illinois, Kickapoo, and Potawatomi Indians*, 290.

59. Ibid. See Lawrence Kinnaird, *Spain in the Mississippi Valley, 1765–1794* (Washington, D.C.: GPO, 1946), 2:298.

60. Jablow, *Illinois, Kickapoo, and Potawatomi Indians*, 293.

61. Kinnaird, *Spain in the Mississippi Valley*, 3:49–54.

62. Jablow, *Illinois, Kickapoo, and Potawatomi Indians*, 299.

63. Arthur St. Clair, *The St. Clair Papers: The Life and Public Services of Arthur St. Clair, Soldier of the Revolutionary War, President of the Continental Congress and Governor of the North-Western Territory, with His Correspondence and Other Papers, Arranged and Annotated* (R. Clarke, 1882), 400–401.

64. Jablow, *Illinois, Kickapoo, and Potawatomi Indians*, 333.

65. Moses Austin, "Journal of Moses Austin," *American Historical Review* 5, no. 3 (1900): 539. It seems clear that the Kaskaskias had already relocated among the Quapaws and Spanish well before the American regime, part of their efforts to increase their options by connecting to imperial powers. See Robert Owens, "Jean Baptiste Ducoigne, the Kaskaskias, and the Limits of Thomas Jefferson's Friendship," *Journal of Illinois History* 5 (2002): 112–13.

66. Austin, "Journal," 535.

67. Jablow, *Illinois, Kickapoo, and Potawatomi Indians*, 337. For more on Ducoigne, see Owens, "Jean Baptiste Ducoigne," 109–36.

68. Jefferson to Harrison, February 27, 1803, in *Territorial Papers of the United States*, ed. Clarence Edwin Carter and John Porter Bloom, 26 vols. (Washington, D.C.: GPO, 1939), 7:88–92.

69. The most skillful examples of this narrative include White, *The Middle Ground* and DuVal, *The Native Ground*, especially chapter 8.

70. The essence of the trans-Appalachian West before 1812 was shifting imperial power, not hegemony. For the best treatment, see François Furstenberg, "The Significance of the Trans-Appalachian Frontier in Atlantic History," *American Historical Review* 113, no. 3 (June 2008): 647–77.

71. Most people in Illinois in the 1770s and 1780s sought stability and order. Consider the example of the Kaskaskias, who moved west to settle with the Quapaws in 1774, only to return to the east of the Mississippi a few years later. They declared their loyalty to "the Americans" only after years of experimenting with other partnerships. Their goal was neither total resistance to empire nor total dependence; they sought collaboration with whatever powerful agent would protect their world and their interests from the now open violence of settler colonialism. See Owens, "Jean Baptiste Ducoigne," 112–13.

72. For an excellent discussion of these stereotypes and images, see Watts, *In This Remote Country*. See also Robert Michael Morrissey, "Inventing a Creole Past: Midwestern Writers and the Memory of the French Illinois Country, 1890–1905," in *Auguste Chouteau's Journal: Memory, Mythmaking & History in the Heritage of New France*, ed. Gregory Ames (St. Louis: St. Louis Mercantile Library, University of Missouri–St. Louis, 2011), 17–24. For a different take emphasizing the blatant erasure of Indians from the early Midwest, see James Joseph Buss, *Winning the West with Words: Language and Conquest in the Lower Great Lakes* (Norman: University of Oklahoma Press, 2011).

73. Catlin also painted two Peoria men with a similar, albeit more prosperous, aspect.

74. Catlin's painting of the Kaskaskia Indian woman Wah-pe-seh-see was completed in 1830 at Fort Leavenworth, Kansas, after the Kaskaskia had relocated there. It is held by the Smithsonian, 1985.66.247. For stereotypes of Indians, see Brian W. Dippie, *The Vanishing American: White Attitudes and U.S. Indian Policy* (Middletown, Conn.: Wesleyan University Press, 1982).

75. Jay Gitlin, *The Bourgeois Frontier: French Towns, French Traders, and American Expansion* (New Haven, Conn.: Yale University Press, 2011).

76. Anne Farrar Hyde, *Empires, Nations, and Families: A History of the North American West, 1800–1860* (Lincoln: University of Nebraska Press, 2011).

Index

Page numbers in italics refer to illustrations

Acknowledgments

Given the theme of this book—collaboration—I am mindful of the many people who played important and generous roles in helping me with this project over many years. There is no way I could have created this book by myself, although any faults that remain in the final product are my own responsibility.

First thanks go to the people who helped me at the beginning. At Yale University, John Mack Faragher first encouraged me to write about the colonial history of the Mississippi Valley and Great Lakes, and he was a great mentor and friend. John Demos's *New York Times* manifesto about writing history was taped to the wall of my dorm room in college, and any merit in the prose and narrative of this book is owing to his inspiration and advice over many years. John has also been a great friend (and running companion), and I'm truly grateful for all his help. Jay Gitlin has had the most influence on me and this project since I started it, and his help on this book is just one of the countless reasons I feel fortunate to have him as a friend. Jay taught me the importance of the French in North American history, and he has read and critiqued parts of this book many times. He has also kept me enthusiastic and confident about this work over the long haul. I was also lucky to have help at early stages of this project from Jon Butler, Steven Stoll, George Miles, and Jennifer Baszile.

The research for this book was made possible by many people and institutions. From the beginning, the Newberry Library has been a home base for me, and I'm especially grateful for fellowship support from the Newberry, for opportunities to share work at the Newberry Early America Seminar, and for the particular assistance of Jim Grossman, Danny Greene, Diane Dillon, John Aubry, Scott Stevens, and Hjordis Halvorson. At the Sterling Memorial and Beinecke libraries at Yale, George Miles, Kevin Pacelli, and Nancy Godleski helped with many research problems. At the William L. Clements

Library at the University of Michigan, Brian Dunnigan was helpful and energizing about Great Lakes history. Thanks also to the Huntington Library, the Historic New Orleans Collection, and the Missouri History Museum, to Mark Wetherington and the Filson Historical Society, and the Chicago History Museum. Finally, I am most grateful to the Illinois History and Lincoln Collections at the University of Illinois, the most important single collection of materials on colonial Illinois. Without valuable help from that collection's curator John Hoffmann and his former assistants James Cornelius and Ryan Ross, the research for this book would have been much more difficult to conduct.

The research would have been downright impossible to conduct without generous financial support and fellowships. I am grateful to the Center for French Colonial Studies, the Illinois State Historical Library, the Newberry Library, the Huntington Library, the William L. Clements Library, the Beinecke Library, a Faculty Development Award from the University of Tennessee, and a Newberry Center for Renaissance Studies Consortium Fellowship through the University of Illinois. Other crucial support for the researching and writing of this book came from the Mrs. Giles Whiting Fellowship, the Yale Agrarian Studies Program, and the Howard Lamar Center for the Study of Frontiers and Borders at Yale. The Andrew W. Mellon Foundation also supported me early on in this project.

I have been lucky to have good colleagues who helped me as I worked on this book at three different institutions. At the University of Tennessee, Lorri Glover was both a mentor and a true friend—she's one of the best people I've met in the history business, and I value all the advice she gave me. Ernie Freeberg was also a generous friend and model for how to do this job, and I'm grateful for our many chats about writing. I am also grateful to Tennessee colleagues and friends Jeff Norrell, Robert Stolz, Chad Black, Jerry McIntosh, Denise Phillips, Todd Diacon, Lynn Sacco, Dan Magilow, Steve Ash, Bruce Wheeler, Dan Feller, and Jay Rubenstein. At Lake Forest College, I was also assisted by great colleagues. I am especially grateful to Anna Trumbore Jones, as well as to Carol Gayle, Steve Rosswurm, Dan LeMahieu, Michael Ebner, Dave Park, and Bill Moskoff. I have been incredibly fortunate to wind up among excellent colleagues in the history department at the University of Illinois. I thank especially the members of the History Workshop, the Early Modern Studies Reading Group, and the Environmental History Reading Group, all of whom have read parts of this book and provided me with help and encouragement. Individuals who deserve special thanks for their mentorship, collaboration, and direct assistance on this book are Craig Koslofsky, Antoinette Burton, Diane Koenker, Rod Wilson, Tariq Ali, David Lehman, Clare Crowston, and especially Fred Hoxie. Fred has provided generous coaching and feedback throughout the last stages of this project. His advice has greatly improved the work.

I am also grateful to others who have read or helped me with parts of this book. Special thanks to Carl Ekberg, Michael McCafferty, David Costa, Carl Masthay, John "Jack" White, Clayborne Skinner, Susan Sleeper-Smith, Brett Rushforth, Margaret K. Brown, Tom Emerson, and Sarah Pearsall, all of whom provided direct assistance. Over many years, this work has also been shaped in conversations with early American historians and frontier historians in many different seminars, colloquia, and conferences. For their feedback in those settings, I thank Nicole St. Onge, Steve Hindle, Tracy Leavelle, Jennifer Spear, Ken Loiselle, Sophie White, Jacob Lee, Andrew Sturtevant, Chris Parsons, Coll Thrush, Robbie Etheridge, Robert Englebert, Guillaume Teasdale, Gilles Havard, Lucy Murphy, Shannon Lee Dawdy, Joyce Chaplin, Chris Steinke, Allan Greer, Peter Wood, José Brandão, Michael Nassaney, Dan Usner, and Catherine Desbarats.

I have been very fortunate to have the help of Robert Lockhart at the University of Pennsylvania Press. Bob has been a model editor and sounding board over several years and has shepherded this project through a process that has greatly improved my work. I am grateful for his insights and help. Daniel Richter also read the work with special care, and his feedback helped me clarify and rethink key aspects of my story. I am especially grateful to Dan, as well as to anonymous readers for Penn Press whose comments helped me revise and saved me from errors.

Many friends have supported and helped me with this book over the years. A fellow traveler in French colonial and Great Lakes Indian history, Karen Marrero has assisted me and encouraged me in countless conversations along the way. Other old friends have helped me intellectually and otherwise. Thanks especially to Jake Lundberg, Rebecca McKenna, Gerry Cadava, Kathleen Belew, Blake Gilpin, Dan Gilbert, Amanda Ciafone, Wendy Warren, Sam Schaffer, Aaron Sachs, Andrew Weil, and Madeleine Klein. Jimmy Babst was a great friend in New Orleans, showing me around and exchanging stories.

Members of my family were the most important in helping me through and supporting this project. Thanks to Mike and Cathy, my siblings, as well as Katrina, Tom, Charlotte, and Cormac. Thanks to my cousin Jim Parenti and my uncle Tom Trucco for keeping me going during some rough patches. I met my wife, Haley, when this project was, as I told her, nearing completion. It turned out that there was still much more work to do, and I am grateful to her for her love and support in seeing me through it. It is much better thanks to her insights, her proofreading, and her belief in me.

The final thanks are to my parents, Mike and Flavia. They taught to be curious, to love books, and to love ideas from an early age. They have supported me through a long process and some setbacks. I am so grateful for their love and generosity, and I dedicate the book to them.